EVOLUTIONARY COMPUTATION

THEORY AND APPLICATIONS

EVOLUTIONARY COMPUTATION

THEORY AND APPLICATIONS

Editor

Xin Yao

University of Birmingham, UK

Published by

World Scientific Publishing Co. Pte. Ltd.

P O Box 128, Farrer Road, Singapore 912805

USA office: Suite 1B, 1060 Main Street, River Edge, NJ 07661

UK office: 57 Shelton Street, Covent Garden, London WC2H 9HE

British Library Cataloguing-in-Publication Data
A catalogue record for this book is available from the British Library.

EVOLUTIONARY COMPUTATION: THEORY AND APPLICATIONS

ISBN 981-02-2306-4

Printed in Singapore.

Preface

Evolutionary computation is the study of computational systems which use ideas and get inspiration from natural evolution and adaptation. It includes a wide range of topics. This book covers some of the most interesting research areas in evolutionary computation. It deals with both theories and applications. It is a self-contained volume which covers both introductory material and selected advanced topics.

Chapter 1 introduces the field of evolutionary computation. It reviews briefly the history and different branches of evolutionary computation. It also gives an overview of various applications of evolutionary computation techniques. Colombetti and Dorigo report their work on using ALECSYS to develop behavioral modules for mobile robots and discuss the potential advantages of using the evolutionary approach in behavioral engineering in Chapter 2. Schmidhuber describes a theoretical foundation for multi-agent learning and incremental self-improvement in an unrestricted environment in Chapter 3. Wah and Ieumwananonthachai introduce TEACHER, a genetics-based system for learning and generalising heuristics under resource constraints, in Chapter 4. Koza and Andre describe the automatic discovery of protein motifs using genetic programming in Chapter 5. Tsoi and Shaw present many results on emerging complex behaviors from multiple insect simulation in Chapter 6. Fukuda *et al.* introduce a new virus-evolutionary genetic algorithm and present the experimental results of its application to the traveling salesman problem in Chapter 7. Kim and Myung describe a hybrid evolutionary optimisation algorithm for constrained numerical optimisation problems in Chapter 8. de Garis discusses his dream machine, i.e., CAM-BRAIN, in Chapter 9. Finally, Yao and Darwen present some experiments on evolving strategies for N-person iterated prisoner's dilemma games (where $2 \leq N \leq 8$) in Chapter 10.

This book does not require previous background or experience in the field of evolutionary computation since introductory material is included in the book. It may be used as a textbook at the graduate or senior undergraduate level, or as a reference book for people interested in evolutionary computation.

Acknowledgements

This book was originally planned for publication in late 1995. However, it was delayed several times due to personal reasons. I would like to apologise to anyone, especially the authors, who has been affected by this delay. I am grateful to the editors from the World Scientific Publ. Co. and authors of individual chapters for their patience and understanding while I was putting the book together.

List of Contributors

Marco Colombetti
Artificial Intelligence and Robotics Project
Dipartimento di Elettronica e Informazione
Politecnico di Milano
Piazza Leonardo da Vinci, 32
20133 Milano, Italy
Email: colombet@elet.polimi.it
URL: http://www.elet.polimi.it/people/colombet/

Marco Dorigo
Chercheur Qualifie' du FNRS
IRIDIA CP 194/6
Universite' Libre de Bruxelles
Avenue Franklin Roosevelt 50
1050 Bruxelles, Belgium
Email: mdorigo@ulb.ac.be
URL: http://iridia.ulb.ac.be/dorigo/dorigo.html

Jürgen Schmidhuber
IDSIA, Corso Elvezia 36
CH-6900-Lugano, Switzerland
Email: juergen@idsia.ch
URL: http://www.idsia.ch/~juergen

Benjamin W. Wah
Department of Electrical and Computer Engineering
and the Coordinated Science Laboratory
University of Illinois at Urbana-Champaign
1308 West Main Street, Urbana, IL61801, USA
Email: wah@manip.crhc.uiuc.edu
URL: http://manip.crhc.uiuc.edu

Arthur Ieumwananonthachai
Department of Electrical and Computer Engineering
and the Coordinated Science Laboratory
University of Illinois at Rubana-Champaign
1308 West Main Street, Urbana, IL61801, USA
Email: arthuri@manip.crhc.uiuc.edu
URL: http://manip.crhc.uiuc.edu

John Koza
Department of Computer Science
Standford University
Stanford, CA 94305, USA
Email: koza@cs.stanford.edu
URL: http://www-cs-faculty.cs.stanford.edu/~koza

David Andre
Computer Science Division
Room 387, Soda Hall, #1776
University of California at Berkeley
Berkeley, CA 94720-1776, USA
Email: dandre@cs.berkeley.edu
URL: http://http.cs.berkeley.edu/~dandre

Ah Chung Tsoi
Faculty of Informatics
University of Wollongong
NSW, Australia
Email: act@uow.edu.au
URL: http://www.uow.edu.au/informatics/facultystaff.html

Jeff Shaw
Department of Electrical and Computer Engineering
University of Queensland
St Lucia, Queensland 4072, Australia

Toshio Fukuda
Department of Micro System Engineering
Nagoya University
Furo-cho, Chikusa-ku, Nagoya, 464-01, Japan
Email: fukuda@mein.nagoya-u.ac.jp
URL: http://www.mein.nagoya-u.ac.jp/staff/fukuda-e.html

N. Kubota
Department of Micro System Engineering
Nagoya University
Furo-cho, Chikusa-ku, Nagoya, 464-01, Japan

K. Shimojima
Department of Micro System Engineering
Nagoya University
Furo-cho, Chikusa-ku, Nagoya, 464-01, Japan

Jong-Hwan Kim
Department of Electrical Engineering
Korea Advanced Institute of Science and Technology
373-1, Kusung-dong, Yusung-gu, Taejon-shi
305-701, Republic of Korea
Email: johkim@vivaldi.kaist.ac.kr
URL: http://www-ee.kaist.ac.kr/department/professors/jhkim.html

H. Myung
Department of Electrical Engineering
Korea Advanced Institute of Science and Technology
373-1, Kusung-dong, Yusung-gu, Taejon-shi
305-701, Republic of Korea
Email: myung@vivaldi.kaist.ac.kr

Hugo de Garis
Evolutionary Systems Department
ATR Human Information Processing Laboratories
2-2 Kikari-dai, Seika-cho, Soraku-gun
Kansai Science City, Kyoto-fu, 619-02, Japan
Email: degaris@hip.atr.co.jp
URL: http://www.hip.atr.co.jp/~degaris

Paul Darwen
Department of Computer Science and Electrical Engineering
The University of Quensland
Brisbane, QLD 4072. Australia
Email: darwen@csee.uq.edu.au
URL: http://www.csee.uq.edu.au/~darwen

Contents

Chapter 1

Introduction

X. Yao

1.1 What Is Evolutionary Computation

Evolutionary computation is the study of computational systems which use ideas and get inspiration from natural evolution and adaptation. It aims at understanding such computational systems and developing more robust and efficient ones for solving complex real-world problems. The problems dealt with by such computational systems are usually highly nonlinear and contain inaccurate and noisy data.

Traditional computational systems are good at accurate and exact computation but brittle. They are not designed for processing inaccurate, noisy and complex data although they might excel at dealing with complicated data. For example, the classical simplex method is an invaluable mathematical programming technique which has been applied to numerous practical problems successfully. However, it requires a problem to be formulated in exact and accurate mathematical forms. It does not work well for problems where the objective function cannot be expressed mathematically, is noisy, and changes with time. Evolutionary computation is a field where such problems will be studied in depth. It complements the study of traditional computational systems.

Many evolutionary computation techniques get their ideas and inspirations from molecular evolution, population genetics, immunology, etc.

Some of the terminologies used in evolutionary computation have been borrowed from these fields to reflect their connections, such as *genetic* algorithms, *genotypes*, *phenotypes*, *species*, etc. Although the research in evolutionary computation could help us understand some biological phenomena better, its primary aim is not to build biologically plausible models. There is no requirement in evolutionary computation that a technique developed must be biologically plausible. The primary aim is to study and develop robust and efficient computational systems for solving complex real-world problems.

Evolutionary computation is an emerging field which has grown rapidly in recent years. There are at least two international journals which are dedicated to this field: *IEEE Transactions on Evolutionary Computation* and *Evolutionary Computation* (MIT Press). Other journals which have a large evolutionary computation component include *IEEE Transactions on Systems, Man, and Cybernetics* and *BioSystems* (Elsevier). There are also many international conferences on evolutionary computation held each year, such as the annual *IEEE International Conference on Evolutionary Computation*, *Evolutionary Programming Conference* and *Genetic Programming Conference*, and bi-annual *International Conference on Genetic Algorithms*, *International Conference on Parallel Problem Solving from Nature*, and *Asia-Pacific Conference on Simulated Evolution and Learning*.

1.1.1 A Brief History

Evolutionary computation encompasses several major branches, i.e., evolution strategies, evolutionary programming, genetic algorithms and genetic programming, due largely to historical reasons. At the philosophical level, they differ mainly in the level at which they simulate evolution. At the algorithmic level, they differ mainly in their representations of potential solutions and their operators used to modify the solutions. From a computational point of view, representation and search are two key issues. This book will look at their differences more at the algorithmic level than at the philosophical level.

Evolution strategies were first proposed by Rechenberg and Schwefel in 1965 as a numerical optimisation technique. The original evolution strategy did not use populations. A population was introduced into evolution strategies later [1, 2].

Evolutionary programming was first proposed by Fogel *et al.* in mid 1960's as one way to achieve artificial intelligence [3]. Several examples of evolving finite state machines were demonstrated [3]. Since late 1980's, evolutionary programming was also applied to various combinatorial and numerical optimisation problems.

The current framework of genetic algorithms was first proposed by Holland [4] and his students [5] in 1975 although some of the ideas appeared as early as 1957 in the context of simulating genetic systems [6]. Genetic algorithms were first proposed as adaptive search algorithms, although they have mostly been used as a global optimisation algorithm for either combinatorial or numerical problems. They are probably the most well-known branch of evolutionary computation.

A special sub-branch of genetic algorithms is genetic programming. Genetic programming can be regarded as an application of genetic algorithms to evolve tree-structured chromosomes. Historically, those trees represent LISP programs. The term of genetic programming was first used by Koza in the above sense [7, 8]. de Garis used the term of genetic programming to mean a quite different thing. He regarded genetic programming as the genetic evolution of artificial neural networks [9]. This book will follow Koza's explanation of genetic programming since de Garis is no longer using the term.

In recent years, a general term of evolutionary algorithms has been used by more and more researchers to include all three major algorithms, i.e., evolution strategies, evolutionary programming and genetic algorithms, since they use almost the same computational framework. This is the view taken by this book.

1.1.2 A General Framework of Evolutionary Algorithms

All evolutionary algorithms have two prominent features which distinguish themselves from other search algorithms. First, they are all population-based. Second, there is communications and information exchange among individuals in a population. Such communications and information exchange are the result of selection and/or recombination in evolutionary algorithms. A general framework of evolutionary algorithms can be summarised by Figure 1.1, where the search operators are also called genetic operators for genetic algorithms. They are used to generate offspring (new individuals) from parents (existing individuals).

1. Set $i = 0$;
2. Generate the initial **population** $P(i)$ at random;
3. REPEAT
   (a) Evaluate the fitness of each individual in $P(i)$;
   (b) Select parents from $P(i)$ based on their fitness;
   (c) Apply **search operators** to the parents and produce generation $P(i+1)$;
4. UNTIL the population converges or the maximum time is reached

Figure 1.1: A General Framework of Evolutionary Algorithms.

Obviously Figure 1.1 specifies a whole class of algorithms, not any particular ones. Different representations of individuals and different schemes for implementing fitness evaluation, selection and search operators define different algorithms.

1.1.3 Evolution Strategies

For evolution strategies [2, 10], the representation of individuals is often very close to a problem's natural representation. It does not emphasise the genetic representation of individuals. For example, an individual is represented as a vector of real numbers rather than a binary string for numerical optimisation problems. Evolution strategies usually use a deterministic selection scheme, Gaussian mutation, and discrete or intermediate recombination. The term crossover is seldom used in the context of evolution strategies because evolution strategies do not simulate evolution at the genetic level.

There are two major deterministic selection schemes in evolution strategies [1, 2], i.e., $(\lambda + \mu)$ and (λ, μ) where μ is the population size (which is the same as the number of parents) and λ the number of offspring generated from all μ parents. In $(\lambda + \mu)$ evolution strategies, λ offspring will be generated from μ parents. The μ fittest individuals from $\lambda + \mu$ candidates will be selected to form the next generation. In (λ, μ) evolution strategies, the μ fittest individuals from λ offspring only will be selected to form the next generation. As a result, $\lambda \geq \mu$ is required.

Mutation in evolution strategies is often implemented by adding a Gaussian random number to a parent. Assume $\mathbf{x} = (x_1, x_2, \ldots, x_n)$ is a parent (individual), then an offspring will be generated by mutation as follows:

$$x_i' = x_i + N_i(0, \sigma_i) \tag{1.1}$$

where $N_i(0, \sigma_i)$ is a normally distributed random number with mean 0 and standard deviation σ_i. The n random numbers are generated independently.

One important parameter in the Gaussian mutation is the standard deviation, σ_i. Its selection is quite important in determining the performance of evolution strategies. Unfortunately, its optimal value is problem dependent as well as dimension dependent. Schwefel [1] proposed to include σ_i's as part of an individual so that it can be evolved automatically. This is often called *self-adaptation* in evolution strategies. It is one of the major differences between evolution strategies and genetic algorithms. In many implementations, σ_i's will be mutated first, and then x_i is mutated using the new σ_i'.

Mutating different components of an vector independently may not be appropriate for some problems because those components may not be independent at all. To address this issue, co-variance has been introduced as another additional part of an individual. It is unclear at this stage whether such self-adaptation is beneficial for most problem as the search space will be increased exponentially as we triple (at least) the individual size. Further work will be necessary in this area.

Recombination in evolution strategies takes two major forms, i.e., discrete and intermediate recombinations. Discrete recombination mixes components of two parent vectors. For example, given two parents $\mathbf{x} = (x_1, x_2, \ldots, x_n)$ and $\mathbf{y} = (y_1, y_2, \ldots, y_n)$. The offspring $\mathbf{x}' =$

$(x'_1, x'_2, \ldots, x'_n)$ and $\mathbf{y}' = (y'_1, y'_2, \ldots, y'_n)$ can be generated as follows:

$$x'_i = \begin{cases} x_i & \text{with probability } p_{recombination} \\ y_i & \text{otherwise} \end{cases}$$

$\mathbf{y}'$ will be the complement of $\mathbf{x}'$.

Intermediate recombination is usually based on some kind of averaging. For example, given two parents $\mathbf{x} = (x_1, x_2, \ldots, x_n)$ and $\mathbf{y} = (y_1, y_2, \ldots, y_n)$. The offspring $\mathbf{x}' = (x'_1, x'_2, \ldots, x'_n)$ and $\mathbf{y}' = (y'_1, y'_2, \ldots, y'_n)$ can be generated as follows:

$$x'_i = x_i + \alpha(y_i - x_i)$$

where α is a weighting parameter in $(0, 1)$. It is traditionally set to 0.5. It can also be generated at random. $\mathbf{y}'$ can be generated similarly.

According to the description by Bäck and Schwefel [11], a (μ, λ) evolution strategy can be implemented as follows:

1. Generate the initial population of μ individuals, and set $k = 1$. Each individual is taken as a pair of real-valued vectors, $(\mathbf{x}_i, \eta_i)$, $\forall i \in \{1, \cdots, \mu\}$, where η plays the role of σ (i.e., the standard deviation).

2. Evaluate the fitness value for each individual $(\mathbf{x}_i, \eta_i)$, $\forall i \in \{1, \cdots, \mu\}$, of the population.

3. Each parent $(\mathbf{x}_i, \eta_i)$, $i = 1, \cdots, \mu$, creates λ/μ offspring on average, so that a total of λ offspring are generated: for $i = 1, \cdots, \mu$, $j = 1, \cdots, n$, and $k = 1, \cdots, \lambda$,

$$\eta_k{}'(j) = \eta_i(j) \exp(\tau' N(0, 1) + \tau N_j(0, 1)) \quad (1.2)$$

$$\mathbf{x}_k{}'(j) = \mathbf{x}_i(j) + \eta_i{}'(j) N_j(0, 1) \quad (1.3)$$

where $\mathbf{x}_i(j)$, $\mathbf{x}_k{}'(j)$, $\eta_i(j)$ and $\eta_k{}'(j)$ denote the j-th component of the vectors $\mathbf{x}_i$, $\mathbf{x}_k{}'$, η_i and $\eta_k{}'$, respectively. $N(0, 1)$ denotes a normally distributed one-dimensional random number with mean zero and standard deviation one. $N_j(0, 1)$ indicates that the random number is generated anew for each value of j. The factors τ and τ' are usually set to $\left(\sqrt{2\sqrt{n}}\right)^{-1}$ and $\left(\sqrt{2n}\right)^{-1}$ [11].

4. Evaluate the fitness of each offspring $(\mathbf{x}_i', \eta_i')$, $\forall i \in \{1, \cdots, \lambda\}$.

5. Sort offspring $(\mathbf{x}_i', \eta_i')$, $\forall i \in \{1, \cdots, \lambda\}$ into a non-descending order according to their fitness values, and select the μ best offspring out of λ to be parents of the next generation.

6. Stop if the stopping criterion is satisfied; otherwise, $k = k+1$ and go to Step 3.

1.1.4 Evolutionary Programming

When used for numerical optimisation, evolutionary programming [3, 12, 13] is very similar to evolution strategies in terms of algorithm. It uses vectors of real numbers as individuals, Gaussian mutation and self-adaptation as described above. The most noticeable differences between evolutionary programming and evolution strategies are recombination and selection. Evolutionary programming does not use any recombination or crossover, but uses a probabilistic competition (i.e., a kind of tournament selection) as the selection mechanism. Of course, there is no reason why evolutionary programming cannot have recombination and why evolution strategies cannot have a probabilistic selection scheme from the algorithmic point of view.

The origins of evolutionary programming and evolution strategies are quite different. Evolutionary programming was first proposed to simulate intelligence by evolving finite state machines, while evolution strategies were proposed to optimise numerical parameters. It was unclear how recombination could be usefully applied to finite state machines.

According to the description by Bäck and Schwefel [11], evolutionary programming can be implemented as follows:

1. Generate the initial population of μ individuals, and set $k = 1$. Each individual is taken as a pair of real-valued vectors, $(\mathbf{x}_i, \eta_i)$, $\forall i \in \{1, \cdots, \mu\}$, where $\mathbf{x}_i$'s are objective variables and η_i's are standard deviations for Gaussian mutations.

2. Evaluate the fitness score for each individual $(\mathbf{x}_i, \eta_i)$, $\forall i \in \{1, \cdots, \mu\}$, of the population.

3. Each parent $(\mathbf{x}_i, \eta_i)$, $i = 1, \cdots, \mu$, creates a single offspring $(\mathbf{x}_i', \eta_i')$ by: for $j = 1, \cdots, n$,

$$\begin{aligned} \eta_i'(j) &= \eta_i(j) \exp(\tau' N(0,1) + \tau N_j(0,1)) & (1.4) \\ x_i'(j) &= x_i(j) + \eta_i'(j) N_j(0,1), & (1.5) \end{aligned}$$

   where $x_i(j)$, $x_i'(j)$, $\eta_i(j)$ and $\eta_i'(j)$ denote the j-th component of the vectors $\mathbf{x}_i$, $\mathbf{x}_i'$, η_i and η_i', respectively. $N(0,1)$ denotes a normally distributed one-dimensional random number with mean 0 and standard deviation 1. $N_j(0,1)$ indicates that the random number is generated anew for each value of j. The factors τ and τ' have commonly set to $\left(\sqrt{2\sqrt{n}}\right)^{-1}$ and $\left(\sqrt{2n}\right)^{-1}$ [11, 14].

4. Calculate the fitness of each offspring $(\mathbf{x}_i', \eta_i')$, $\forall i \in \{1, \cdots, \mu\}$.

5. Conduct pairwise comparison over the union of parents $(\mathbf{x}_i, \eta_i)$ and offspring $(\mathbf{x}_i', \eta_i')$, $\forall i \in \{1, \cdots, \mu\}$. For each individual, q opponents are chosen uniformly at random from all the parents and offspring. For each comparison, if the individual's fitness is no smaller than the opponent's, it receives a "win."

6. Select the μ individuals out of $(\mathbf{x}_i, \eta_i)$ and $(\mathbf{x}_i', \eta_i')$, $\forall i \in \{1, \cdots, \mu\}$, that have the most wins to be parents of the next generation.

7. Stop if the halting criterion is satisfied; otherwise, $k = k + 1$ and go to Step 3.

1.1.5 Genetic Algorithms

Genetic algorithms [4, 15, 16] are quite different from evolution strategies and evolutionary programming in terms of individual representation and search operators. Genetic algorithms emphasise genetic encoding of potential solutions into chromosomes and apply genetic operators to these chromosomes. This is equivalent to transforming the original problem from one space to another space. It is obvious that the genetic representation will be crucial to the success of genetic algorithms. A good representation will make a problem easier to solve. A poor representation will do the opposite. The issues faced by genetic algorithms in general are the same as those which have haunted many artificial intelligence problems for years, i.e., representation and search. In other words, a crucial issue in applying genetic algorithms to a problem is how to find a representation which can be searched efficiently.

A canonical genetic algorithm (also called simple genetic algorithm sometimes) [15] is the one which uses binary representation, one point crossover and bit-flipping mutation. Binary representation means that each individual will be represented by a number of binary bits, 0 or 1. One point crossover is carried out as follows: Given two binary strings, x and y, of length n. Generate a crossover point between 1 and $n-1$ (inclusively) uniformly at random, say r. Then the first offspring consists of the first r bits of x and the last $n-r$ bits of y. The second offspring consists of the first r bits of y and the last $n-r$ bits of x. Mutation is carried out bit-wise. That is, every bit of an individual has certain probability of being flipped from 0 to 1 or from 1 to 0. A canonical genetic algorithm can be implemented as follows:

1. Generate the initial population $P(0)$ at random and set $i=0$;
2. REPEAT
   (a) Evaluate the fitness of each individual in $P(i)$.
   (b) Select parents from $P(i)$ based on their fitness as follows: Given the fitness of n individuals as $f_1, f_2, \ldots, f_n$. Then select individual i with probability
   $$p_i = \frac{f_i}{\sum_{j=1}^{n} f_j}.$$
   This is often called roulette wheel selection of fitness proportional selection.
   (c) Apply crossover to selected parents;
   (d) Apply mutation to crossed-over new individuals;
   (e) Replace parents by the offspring to produce generation $P(i+1)$;
3. UNTIL the halting criterion is satisfied

1.1.6 Other Topics in Evolutionary Computation

There are numerous variants of classical evolution strategies, evolutionary programming and genetic algorithms described above. Some of the evolutionary algorithms can hardly be classified into any of these three categories. Evolutionary computation includes much more than just three kinds of algorithms. It also covers topics such as artificial immune systems, artificial ecological systems, co-evolutionary systems, evolvable hardware, self-adaptive systems, etc.

1.2 A Brief Overview of Evolutionary Computation

The current research and development in evolutionary computation can be classified into three major areas, i.e., evolutionary computation theory, evolutionary optimisation and evolutionary learning. There are, of course, overlaps among these areas.

1.2.1 Evolutionary Computation Theory

The theoretical work in evolutionary computation has concentrated on three main topics. The first one is the theoretical analysis of convergence and convergence rate of evolutionary algorithms. There has been some work on the convergence and convergence rate of evolution strategies [1, 2, 17], evolutionary programming [18, 13] and genetic algorithms [19, 20, 21, 22, 23, 24, 25]. They are very general results which describe the asymptotic behaviour of certain class of evolutionary algorithms under different conditions. However, few of them studied the relationship between the convergence rate and the problem size.

The second main topic in evolutionary computation theory is the study of problem hardness with respect to evolutionary algorithms. That is, the aim is to investigate what kind of problems is hard for evolutionary algorithms and what is easy for them. If we knew the characteristics of a problem which make evolutionary algorithms hard or easy to solve, we would be able to better understand how and when evolutionary algorithms would work. This will be of enormous practical value in addition to of theoretical interest. Centered around this topic, there was some work on genetic algorithm deceptive problems [15, 26, 27]. Such work tried to characterise problems that are hard for genetic algorithms to solve as deceptive. It has been pointed out that this approach is rather problematic [28]. There have been other approaches to the understanding of what make a problem hard for genetic algorithms, such as building block and schema analysis [4, 15, 29], Walsh analysi based on Walsh functions [30], fitness landscape analysis [31, 32] and fitness distance correlation [33], etc. All these approaches have made certain progress towards a better understanding of how genetic algorithms work, but there is still a long way to go to gain a full understanding of how and when a genetic algorithm would work.

The third main topic in evolutionary computation theory is computational complexity of evolutionary algorithms. This is one of the most important research topics where little progress has been made. Evolutionary algorithms have been used extensively in both combinatorial and numerical optimisation in spite of the original emphasis on search and adaptation [3, 4, 34, 35]. There are established algorithms and their complexity results for many of these optimisation problems. However, it is unclear whether evolutionary algorithms can perform any better than other approximate or heuristic algorithms in terms of worst or average time complexity. There has not been any concrete result on the computational complexity of an evolutionary algorithm on a nontrivial problem, especially a combinatorial problem, although the complexity theory is well established for combinatorial decision and optimisation problems [36].

1.2.2 Evolutionary Optimisation

Evolutionary optimisation is probably the most active and productive area in evolutionary computation measured by the number of papers published and the number of successful applications reported. Although neither evolutionary programming nor genetic algorithms were first proposed as optimisation algorithms, people had quickly realised they could adapt these algorithms to carry out combinatorial and function optimisation. Hence a flood of variants of classical algorithms were proposed and applied to different optimisation problems.

So far most of the evolutionary optimisation work belongs to numerical optimisation. Both constrained [37, 38] and unconstrained [39, 40] numerical optimisation has been studied. There has also been research on multiobjective optimisation by evolutionary algorithms [41, 42, 43].

When genetic algorithms are applied to numerical function optimisation, vectors of real numbers are usually encoded into binary bit strings. Different binary encoding methods have been proposed, such as Gray coding [15] and delta coding [44]. Delta coding actually changes the representation during search. In spite of all these efforts in finding the best encoding method for real numbers, it is still unclear whether it is necessary to transform real numbers into binery strings.

Evolution strategies and evolutionary programming use vectors of real numbers directly as individuals and thus avoid the burden of finding a suitable encoding method for individuals. There have been some comparative studies between the binary representation used by genetic algorithms and the real representation used by evolutionary programming [45, 46]. However, more extensive comparisons need to be carried out to test the performance of different algorithms and find out why an algorithm performs well (or poorly) for certain problems.

In addition to numerical optimisation, evolutionary algorithms have also been used to tackle various combinatorial optimisation problems, such as the travelling salesman problem [47, 48, 49], transportation problem [50, 51], switchbox routing in integrated circuits [52], cutting stock problem [53, 54], lecture room assignment problem [55], etc. Some of these results are quite competitive in comparison with more traditional approaches. In particular, hybrid algorithms which combine evolutionary algorithms with others (such as simulated annealing [56] and local search methods [57]) have shown a lot of promises in dealing with hard combinatorial optimisation problems.

1.2.3 Evolutionary Learning

Evolutionary learning includes many topics, such as learning classifier systems, evolutionary artificial neural networks, co-evolutionary learning, self-adaptive systems, etc. The primary goal of evolutionary learning is the same as that of machine learning in general. Evolutionary learning can be regarded as the evolutionary approach to machine learning. It has been used in the framework of supervised learning, reinforcement learning and unsupervised learning, although it appears to be most promising as a reinforcement learning method.

Learning Classifier Systems

Learning classifier systems [58, 59], also known as classifier systems, are probably the oldest and best known evolutionary learning systems, although they did not work very well in their classical form [60]. Some of the recent systems have improved this situation [61, 62]. Due to its historical importance, a brief introduction to the classical learning classifier system [58, 59] will be presented here.

Learning classifier systems are a particular class of message-passing, rule-based systems [59]. They can also be regarded as a type of adaptive expert system that uses a knowledge base of production rules in a low-level syntax that can be manipulated by a genetic algorithm [63]. In a classifier system, each low-level rule is called a *classifier*. A classifier system proposed by Holland can be described by Figure 1.2 [59].

The general operational cycle for the classifier system is as follows:

1. Allow the detectors (input interface) to code the current environment status and place the resulting messages on the message list.

2. Determine the set of classifiers that are matched by the current messages.

3. Resolve conflicts caused by limited message list size or contradictory actions.

4. Remove those messages which match the conditions of firing classifiers from the message list.

5. Add the messages suggested by firing messages to the list.

6. Allow the effectors (output interface) that are matched by the current message list to take actions in the environment.

7. If a payoff signal is received from the environment, assign credit to classifiers.

8. Goto Step 1.

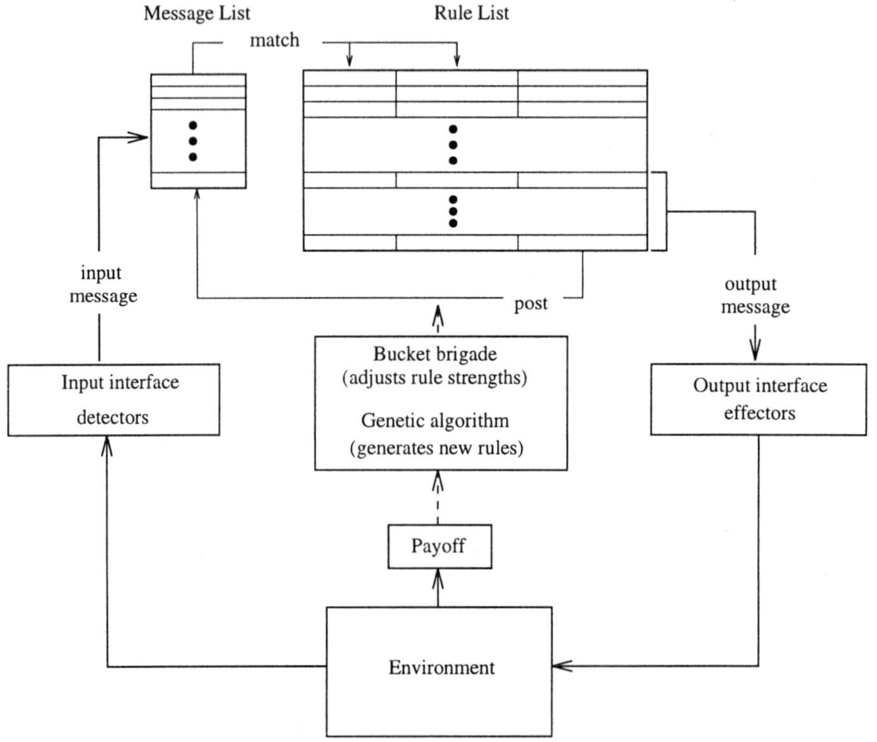

Figure 1.2: An overview of a classifier system [59].

Each rule is a simple message processor: Conditions look for certain kinds of messages and, when the conditions are satisfied, the action specifies a message to be sent. Messages are normally coded by symbolic strings. The alphabet of the symbols is $\{0, 1, \#\}$, where # is a "don't care" symbol which matches either 1 or 0. For example, 1### matches any length 4 messages starting with 1. An example of classifier can be described as:

condition-1,	condition-2 / action (message)	[strength]
111#####	10010010 / 00101101	[56]

One message is more *specific* than another if its condition is more specific than another's. One condition is more specific than another if the set of messages that satisfy the one is smaller than the set of messages that satisfy the other.

The usefulness of a classifier is determined by its *strength* and updated by the credit assignment scheme, which is based on its average usefulness in the contexts in which it has been tried previously.

All classifiers whose conditions are satisfied have to compete for the right to post their messages. Competition provides a simple, situation-dependent means of resolving conflicts between classifiers. The actual competition is based on a bidding process. The bid can be treated as some proportion of the classifier's strength. The bid ratio is determined by the number of specific bits divided by the total number of bits in a message. That is, the competition favours more specific classifiers.

An important feature of classifier systems is the possible adaptive formation of *default hierarchies*, i.e., layered sets of default and exception rules. A classifier system organises default hierarchies by favouring exception rules over defaults in its conflict resolution and credit assignment schemes. The simplest example of a classifier hierarchy consists of only two classifiers:

1. The first ("default") one has a relatively unspecific condition and provides action that is correct in most cases and incorrect sometimes.

2. The second ("exception") one is satisfied only by a subset of the messages satisfying the first classifier and its action generally corrects errors committed by the first classifier.

The specific classifier both provides the correct action and saves the general classifier from a mistake when it prevents the general classifier from winning. The exception classifier may in turn make mistakes that can be corrected by even more specific classifiers, and so on. Such default hierarchies can be learned by the classifier system.

Credit assignment is a very difficult task because credit must be assigned to early-acting classifiers that set the stage for a sequence of actions leading to a favourable situation. The most famous credit assignment algorithm is *bucket brigade algorithm* which uses metaphors from economics [59].

For a classifier called *middleman*, its *suppliers* are those classifiers that have sent messages satisfying its conditions, and its *consumers* are those classifiers that both have conditions satisfied by its message *and* have won their competition in turn. When a classifier wins in competition, its bid is actually apportioned to its suppliers, increasing their strengths by the amounts apportioned to them. At the same time, because the bid is treated as a payment for the right to post a message, the strength of the winning classifier is reduced by the amount of its bid. Should the classifier bid but not win, its strength remains unchanged and its suppliers receive no payment. Winning classifiers can recoup their payments from either wining consumers or the environment payoff.

A genetic algorithm is used in classifier systems to discover new classifiers by crossover and mutation. The strength of a classifier is used as its fitness. The genetic algorithm is only applied to the classifiers after certain number of operational cycles in order to approximate strengths better. There are two approaches to classifier systems; *the Michigan approach* and *the Pitts approach*. For the Michigan approach, each individual in a population is a classifier. The whole population represents a complete classifier system. For the Pitts approach, each individual in a population represents a complete classifier system. The whole population includes a number of competing classifier systems.

Evolutionary Artificial Neural Networks

Evolutionary artificial neural networks can be considered as a combination of artificial neural networks and evolutionary algorithms [64, 65, 66]. Evolutionary algorithms have been introduced into artificial neural networks at three different levels: the evolution of connection weights, architectures, and learning rules [65, 66]. At present, most work on evolutionary artificial neural networks concentrates on the evolution of architectures, i.e., connectivities of ANNs [67, 68, 69, 70]. Very good results have been achieved for some artificial and real-world benchmark problems.

One of the most important benefits of evolutionary artificial neural networks is that a near optimal (in terms of generalisation) artificial neural network with both structure and weights can be evolve automatically without going through a tedious trial-and-error manual design process. The results obtained so far have demonstrated that very compact artificial neural networks with good generalisation can be evolved [69].

Co-evolutionary Learning

"Coevolution refers to the simultaneous evolution of two or more species with coupled fitness." [71] Co-evolutionary learning has two different forms. In the first form, two or more populations are evolved at the same time [72]. The fitness of an individual in one population depends on the individuals in another population. There is no crossover or other information exchange between two populations. This can be regarded as co-evolution at the population level.

The second form of co-evolution is at the individual level. There is only one population involved. The fitness of an individual in the population depends on other individuals in the same population [73, 74, 75, 76, 77]. For example, the same strategy for playing an iterated prisoner's dilemma game may get quite different fitness values depending on what other strategies are in the same population. Both forms of co-evolution have a dynamic environment and a dynamic fitness function. This is an active area of research.

1.3 Evolutionary Algorithm and Generate-and-Test Search Algorithm

Although evolutionary algorithms are often introduced from the point of view of *survival of the fittest* and from the analogy to natural evolution, they can also be understood through the framework of **generate-and-test** search. The advantage of introducing evolutionary algorithms as a type of generate-and-test search algorithms is that the relationships between evolutionary algorithms and other search algorithms, such as simulated annealing [78, 79, 80, 81], tabu search [82, 83], etc., can be made clearer and thus easier to explore. Under the framework of generate-and-test search, different search algorithms investigated in artificial intelligence, operations research, computer science, and evolutionary computation can be unified together. Such interdisciplinary studies are expected to generate more insights into search algorithms in general. A general framework of generate-and-test search can be described by Figure 1.3.

1. Generate the initial solution at random and denote it as the current solution;
2. **Generate** the next solution from the current one by *perturbation*;
3. **Test** whether the newly generated solution is *acceptable*;
   (a) Accepted it as the current solution if yes;
   (b) Keep the current solution unchanged otherwise.
4. Goto Step 2 if the current solution is not satisfactory, stop otherwise.

Figure 1.3: A General Framework of Generate-and-Test.

It is quite clear that various hill-climbing algorithms can be described by Figure 1.3 with different strategies for perturbation. They all require the new solution to be no worse than the current one to be acceptable. simulated annealing does not have such a requirement. It regards a worse solution to be acceptable with certain probability. The difference among classical simulated annealing [78], fast simulated annealing [79], very fast simulated annealing [84], and a new simulated annealing [81] lies in the difference in their perturbations, i.e., methods of generating the next solution.

Evolutionary algorithms can be regarded as a population-based version of generate-and-test search. They use search operators like crossover and mutation to *generate* new solutions, and use selection to *test* which solutions are fitter than others. From this point of view, it is clear that we do not have to limit ourselves to crossover and mutation in an evolutionary algorithm. In principle, we can use any search operators to generate new solutions (i.e., offspring). A good search operator should always increase the probability of finding a global optimum. This is also true for selection.

1.4 Search Operators

There are many search operators that have been used in various evolutionary algorithms. Some of them are specialised in solving a particular class of problems. This section describes some search operators and selection schemes[1] commonly used. They do not represent a complete set of all search operators.

1.4.1 Recombination Operators

The essence of any recombination (crossover) operator is the inheritance of information (genes) from two or more parents by offspring. Although most recombination operator uses two parents, multiple parents may be useful in some cases. Two offspring are often produced by a recombination operator, but, again, other numbers might be appropriate for some problems.

Recombination for Real-Valued Vectors

These operators are mostly proposed for evolution strategies. They are used to process vectors of real numbers. In evolution strategies,

[1]Usually selection is not regarded as a search operator. It is included in this section for ease of discussions.

recombination is done independently for objective variables and strategy parameters (i.e., variance, etc.). It can be different for objective variables and strategy parameters.

Discrete Recombination In this case, an offspring vector will have components coming from two or more parent vectors. There is no change to any component itself. For example, given two parents $\mathbf{x} = (x_1, x_2, \ldots, x_n)$ and $\mathbf{y} = (y_1, y_2, \ldots, y_n)$. The offspring $\mathbf{x}' = (x'_1, x'_2, \ldots, x'_n)$ and $\mathbf{y}' = (y'_1, y'_2, \ldots, y'_n)$ can be generated as follows:

$$x'_i = \begin{cases} x_i & \text{with probability } p_{recombination} \\ y_i & \text{otherwise} \end{cases}$$

$\mathbf{y}'$ will be the complement of $\mathbf{x}'$. A global version of this recombination is that y_i will be taken from a randomly generated $\mathbf{y}$ for each i value. That is, for each i value, a $\mathbf{y}$ is generated uniformly at random in the whole population. Then its ith component will be used for recombination. Basically the number of parents is the same as the population size.

Intermediate Recombination In this case, a component of an offspring vector is a linear combination (average) of parent's corresponding components. For example, given two parents $\mathbf{x} = (x_1, x_2, \ldots, x_n)$ and $\mathbf{y} = (y_1, y_2, \ldots, y_n)$. The offspring $\mathbf{x}' = (x'_1, x'_2, \ldots, x'_n)$ and $\mathbf{y}' = (y'_1, y'_2, \ldots, y'_n)$ can be generated as follows:

$$x'_i = x_i + \alpha(y_i - x_i)$$

where α is a weighting parameter in $(0, 1)$. It is traditionally set to 0.5. It can also be generated at random. $\mathbf{y}'$ can be generated similarly. A global version of this recombination is that y_i will be taken from a randomly generated $\mathbf{y}$ for each i value. α can also be different for each i.

Recombination for Binary Strings

Common recombination operators for binary strings include k-point crossover ($k > 1$) and uniform crossover, although there are many other variants.

k-point crossover This crossover can actually be applied to strings of any alphabet. Given two parents of length n. k random numbers, $r_1, r_2, \ldots, r_k$, between 1 and $n-1$ will be generated uniformly (without repetition). Then an offspring is produced by taking segments (separated by $r_1, r_2, \ldots, r_k$) of parent strings alternately, i.e., the first segment from the first parent, the second from the second parent, the third from the first parent, and so on. For example, a 3-point crossover at $1, 4, 6$ of two parents 00000000 and 11111111 will produce two offspring 01110011 and 10001100.

uniform crossover This crossover is also applicable to strings of any alphabet. An offspring is generated by taking its each bit or character from the corresponding bit or character in one of the two parents. The parent that the bit or character is to be taken from is chosen uniformly at random.

Other crossover operators include segmented crossover and shuffle crossover [85]. They are not widely used in genetic algorithm applications.

Specialised Recombination

There are numerous recombination operators which have been proposed for different problems, especially combinatorial optimisation problems, such as matrix-based crossover [51, 55], permutation-based crossover [86, 49], tree-based crossover [87, 88], etc.

1.4.2 Mutation Operators

Mutation operators used for vectors of real values are usually based on certain probability distributions, such as uniform, lognormal, Gauss (normal) and Cauchy distributions. Mutation for binary strings is a lot simpler. It is usually a bit-fliping operation.

Mutation for Real-Valued Vectors

Gaussian Mutation In this case, an offspring is produced by adding a Gaussian random number with mean 0 and standard deviation

σ to the parent. For example, given $\mathbf{x} = (x_1, x_2, \ldots, x_n)$ as the parent, an offspring is produced as follows:

$$x'_i = x_i + N_i(0, \sigma_i)$$

where $N_i(0, \sigma_i)$ is a normally distributed random number with mean 0 and standard deviation σ_i. The n random numbers are generated independently for each dimension (thus the subscription i in $N_i(0, \sigma_i)$. For self-adaptive evolutionary algorithms, such as evolution strategies and evolutionary programming, σ_i's are usually mutated independently using a lognormal distribution. More details are given by Eqs. 1.2 and 1.3 in Section 1.1.3.

Cauchy Mutation Cauchy mutation differs from Gaussian mutation in the probability distribution used to generate the random number. The use of Cauchy mutation in evolutionary algorithms was inspired by fast simulated annealing [79, 81] and proposed indepedently by several researchers [39, 89]. A detailed study of Cauchy mutation will be presented later in this chapter.

Other Mutations Mutations based on other probability distributions, such as the t-distribution, may be introduced into evolutionary algorithms. An important question to ask when introducing a new operator is when the new operator will be most efficient for what kind of problems.

Mutation for Binary Strings

Bit-Fliping Bit-flipping mutation simply flips a bit from 0 to 1 or from 1 to 0 with certain probability. This probability is often called the mutation probability or mutation rate. Bit-flipping mutation can be generalised to mutate strings of any alphabet. The generalised mutation works as follows: for each character (allele) in a string, replace it with another randomly chosen character (not the same as the one to be replaced) in the alphabet with certain mutation probability.

Random Bit This mutation does not flip a bit. It replaces a bit by 0 or 1 with equal probability (i.e., 0.5 respectively). The generalised version of this mutation works as follows: for each character (allele) in a string, replace it with a randomly chosen character (could be the same as the one to be replaced) in the alphabet with certain mutation probability.

Specialised Mutations Similar to the situation for crossover, there are many other specialised mutation operators designed for various combinatorial problems, such as the operators for mutate finite state machines [3], artificial neural networks [69] and cutting stock problems [54].

1.4.3 Selection

A selection scheme determines the probability of an individual being selected for producing offspring by recombination and/or mutation. In order to search for increasingly better individuals, fitter individuals should have higher probabilities of being selected while unfit individuals should be selected only with small probabilities. Different selection schemes have different methods of calculating selection probability. The selection pressure has sometimes been used to indicate how large the selection probability should be for a fit individual in comparison with that for an unfit individual. The larger the probability, the stronger the selection pressure.

There are three major types of selection schemes, roulette wheel selection (also known as the fitness proportional selection), rank-based selection and tournament selection.

Roulette Wheel Selection

Let $f_1, f_2, \ldots, f_n$ be fitness values of individuals $1, 2, \cdots, n$. Then the selection probability for individual i is

$$p_i = \frac{f_i}{\sum_{j=1}^{n} f_j}.$$

Roulette wheel selection calculates the selection probability directly from individual's fitness values.

This method may cause problems in some cases. For example, if an initial population contains one or two very fit but not the best individuals and the rest of the population are not good, then these fit individuals will quickly dominate the whole population (due to their very large selection probabilities) and prevent the population from exploring other potentially better individuals. On the other hand, if individuals in a population have very similar fitness values, it will be very difficult for the population to move towards a better one since selection probabilities for fit and unfit individuals are very similar. To get around these two problems, various fitness scaling methods have been proposed [15]. These fitness scaling methods are used to scale fitness values before they are used in calculating selection probabilities.

Rank-Based Selection

Rank-based selection does not calculate selection probabilities from fitness values directly. It sorts all individuals according to their fitness values first and then computes selection probabilities according to their ranks rather than their fitness values. Hence rank-based selection can maintain a constant selection pressure in the evolutionary search and avoid some of the problems encountered by roulette wheel selection.

There are many different rank-based selection schemes. Two are introduced here. Assume the best individual in a population ranks the first. The probability of selecting individual i can be calculated linearly as follows [90]:

$$p_i = \frac{1}{n}\left(\eta_{max} - (\eta_{max} - \eta_{min})\frac{i-1}{n-1}\right)$$

where n is the population size, η_{max} and η_{min} are two parameters.

$$\begin{aligned} \eta_{max} \geq \eta_{min} &\geq 0 \\ \eta_{max} + \eta_{min} &= 2 \end{aligned}$$

The recommended value for η_{max} is 1.1.

A rank-based selection scheme with a stronger selection pressure is the following nonlinear ranking scheme [49]:

$$P_i = \frac{i}{\sum_{j=1}^{n} j}.$$

Tournament Selection

Both roulette wheel selection and rank-based selection are based on the global information in the whole population. This increases communications overheads if we want to parallelise an evolutionary algorithms on a parallel machine. Tournament selection only needs part of the whole population to calculate an individual's selection probability. Different individuals can also calculate their selection probabilities in parallel.

One of the often used tournament selection schemes is that used in evolutionary programming, which was described in Section 1.1.4. Another one is Boltzmann tournament selection [91], described as follows:

1. For tournament size 3, first select an individual i_1 at random. Then select i_2 also at random but must differ from i_1 by a fitness amount of Θ. Randomly selected i_3 must also differ from i_1, and half the time differ from i_2 as well, all by Θ.

2. i_2 competes with i_3 first. Then the winner competes with i_1. The winner is identified by the Boltzmann acceptance probability. The probability of individual x wining over y is:

$$P(x,y) = \frac{1}{1 + \exp((f_y - f_x)/T)}$$

   where T is the temperature. (Note that we are maximising fitness.)

Elitist Selection

Elitist selection is also known as elitism and elitist strategy. It always copy the best individual to the next generation without any modification. More than one individual may be copied, i.e., the best, second best, etc., may be copied to the next generation without any modification. Elitism is usually used in addition to other selection schemes.

1.5 Summary

This chapter introduces the basic concept and major areas of evolutionary computation. It presents a brief history of three major types of evolutionary algorithms, i.e., evolution strategies, evolutionary programming and genetic algorithms, and points out similarities and differences among them. It is also pointed out that the field of evolutionary computation is much more than just three types of algorithms. The field includes many other topics.

The chapter gives a quick overview of evolutionary computation without diving into too much detail. Three main areas of the field have been discussed: evolutionary computation theory, evolutionary optimisation and evolutionary learning. It is argued that much work on the computational complexity of evolutionary algorithms is needed among other things in order to better understand the computational power of these algorithms.

Bibliography

[1] H.-P. Schwefel, *Numerical Optimization of Computer Models.* Chichester: John Wiley & Sons, 1981.

[2] H.-P. Schwefel, *Evolution and Optimum Seeking.* New York: John Wiley & Sons, 1995.

[3] L. J. Fogel, A. J. Owens, and M. J. Walsh, *Artificial Intelligence Through Simulated Evolution.* New York, NY: John Wiley & Sons, 1966.

[4] J. H. Holland, *Adaptation in Natural and Artificial Systems.* Ann Arbor, MI: The University of Michigan Press, 1975.

[5] K. A. D. Jong, *An analysis of the behavior of a class of genetic adaptive systems.* PhD thesis, University of Michigan, Ann Arbor, 1975.

[6] A. S. Fraser, "Simulation of genetic systems by automatic digital computers. I. Introduction," *Australian Journal of Biological Sciences*, vol. 10, pp. 484–491, 1957.

[7] J. R. Koza, "Evolving programs using symbolic expressions," in *Proc. of the 11th Int'l Joint Conf. on Artificial Intelligence* (N. S. Sridharan, ed.), (San Mateo, CA), pp. 768–774, Morgan Kaufmann, 1989.

[8] J. R. Koza, "Genetic programming: a paradigm for genetically breeding populations of computer programs to solve problems," Tech. Rep. STAN-CS-90-1314, Department of Computer Science, Stanford University, June 1990.

[9] H. de Garis, "Genetic programming: modular evolution for Darwin machines," in *Proc. of Int'l Joint Conf. on Neural Networks,*

Vol. I, (Washington, DC), pp. 194–197, Lawrence Erlbaum Associates, Hillsdale, NJ, 1990.

[10] T. Bäck, *Evolutionary Algorithms in Theory and Practice.* New York: Oxford University Press, 1996.

[11] T. Bäck and H.-P. Schwefel, "An overview of evolutionary algorithms for parameter optimization," *Evolutionary Computation*, vol. 1, no. 1, pp. 1–23, 1993.

[12] D. B. Fogel, *System Identification Through Simulated Evolution: A Machine Learning Approach to Modeling.* Needham Heights, MA 02194: Ginn Press, 1991.

[13] D. B. Fogel, *Evolutionary Computation: Towards a New Philosophy of Machine Intelligence.* New York, NY: IEEE Press, 1995.

[14] D. B. Fogel, "An introduction to simulated evolutionary optimisation," *IEEE Trans. on Neural Networks*, vol. 5, no. 1, pp. 3–14, 1994.

[15] D. E. Goldberg, *Genetic Algorithms in Search, Optimization, and Machine Learning.* Reading, MA: Addison-Wesley, 1989.

[16] Z. Michalewicz, *Genetic Algorithms + Data Structures = Evolution Programs (3rd edition).* Berlin, Germany: Springer-Verlag, 1996.

[17] H.-G. Beyer, "Towards a theory of evolution strategies: the (μ, λ) theory," *Evolutionary Computation*, vol. 2, no. 4, pp. 381–407, 1994.

[18] D. B. Fogel, *Evolving Artificial Intelligence.* PhD thesis, University of California, San Diego, CA, 1992.

[19] A. E. Eiben, E. H. L. Aarts, and K. M. van Hee, "Global convergence of genetic algorithms: a markov chain analysis," in *Parallel Problem Solving from Nature* (H.-P. Schwefel and R. Männer, eds.), pp. 4–12, Springer-Verlag, Heidelberg, 1991.

[20] G. Rudolph, "Convergence properties of canonical genetic algorithms," *IEEE Trans. on Neural Networks*, vol. 5, no. 1, pp. 96–101, 1994.

[21] G. Rudolph, "Convergence analysis of evolutionary algorithms in general search spaces," in *Proc. of the 1996 IEEE Int'l Conf. on Evolutionary Computation (ICEC'96)*, (New York, NY), pp. 50–54, IEEE Press, 1996.

[22] D. Reynolds and J. Gomatam, "Stochastic modelling of genetic algorithms," *Artificial Intelligence*, vol. 82, no. 1-2, pp. 303–330, 1996.

[23] J. Suzuki, "A markov chain analysis on a genetic algorithm," in *Proc. of the Fifth Int'l Conf. on Genetic Algorithms* (S. Forrest, ed.), pp. 146–153, Morgan Kaufmann, San Mateo, CA, 1993.

[24] J. Suzuki, "A markov chain analysis on a simple genetic algorithm," *IEEE Trans. on Systems, Man, and Cybernetics*, vol. 25, pp. 655–659, 1995.

[25] G. Rudolph, "Convergence of non-elitist strategies," in *Proc. of the 1994 IEEE Int'l Conf. on Evolutionary Computation (ICEC'94)* (Z. M. et al., ed.), pp. 63–66, IEEE Press, New York, NY 10017-2394, 1994.

[26] G. E. Liepins and M. D. Vose, "Deceptiveness and genetic algorithm dynamics," in *Foundations of Genetic Algorithms* (G. J. E. Rawlins, ed.), vol. 1, (San Mateo, CA), pp. 36–50, Morgan Kaufmann, 1991.

[27] K. Deb and D. E. Goldberg, "Analyzing deception in trap functions," in *Foundations of Genetic Algorithms 2* (L. D. Whitley, ed.), (San Mateo, CA), pp. 93–108, Morgan Kaufmann, 1993.

[28] J. J. Grefenstette, "Deception considered harmful," in *Foundations of Genetic Algorithms 2* (L. D. Whitley, ed.), (San Mateo, CA), pp. 75–91, Morgan Kaufmann, 1993.

[29] Y. Davidor, "Epistasis variance: a viewpoint on GA-hardness," in *Foundations of Genetic Algorithms* (G. J. E. Rawlins, ed.), pp. 23–35, Morgan Kaufmann, San Mateo, CA, 1991.

[30] R. B. Heckendorn and D. Whitley, "A Walsh analysis of NK-landscapes," in *Proc. of the 7th Int'l Conf. on Genetic Algorithms* (T. Bäck, ed.), (San Francisco, CA), pp. 41–48, Morgan Kaufmann, 1997.

[31] B. Manderick, M. de Weger, and P. Spiessens, "The genetic algorithm and the structure of the fitness landscape," in *Proc. of the Fourth Int'l Conf. on Genetic Algorithms* (R. K. Belew and L. B. Booker, eds.), pp. 143–150, Morgan Kaufmann, San Mateo, CA, 1991.

[32] W. Hordijk, "A measure of landscapes," *Evolutionary Computation*, vol. 4, no. 4, pp. 335–360, 1996.

[33] T. Jones, *Evolutionary Algorithms, Fitness Landscapes and Search.* PhD thesis, The University of New Mexico, Albuquerque, New Mexico, May 1995.

[34] J. H. Holland, *Adaptation in Natural and Artificial Systems (1st MIT Press Edn).* Cambridge, MA: The MIT Press, 1992.

[35] K. A. DeJong, "Genetic algorithms are NOT function optimizers," in *Foundations of Genetic Algorithms 2* (L. D. Whitley, ed.), (San Mateo, CA), pp. 5–17, Morgan Kaufmann, 1993.

[36] M. R. Garey and D. S. Johnson, *Computers and Intractability: A Guide to the Theory of NP-Completeness.* San Francisco: W. H. Freeman Co., 1979.

[37] Z. Michalewicz and M. Schoenauer, "Evolutionary algorithms for constrained parameter optimization problems," *Evolutionary Computation*, vol. 4, no. 1, pp. 1–32, 1996.

[38] J.-H. Kim and H. Myung, "Evolutionary programming techniques for constrained optimization problems," *IEEE Transactions on Evolutionary Computation*, vol. 1, no. 2, pp. 129–140, 1997.

[39] X. Yao and Y. Liu, "Fast evolutionary programming," in *Evolutionary Programming V: Proc. of the Fifth Annual Conference on Evolutionary Programming* (L. J. Fogel, P. J. Angeline, and T. Bäck, eds.), (Cambridge, MA), pp. 451–460, The MIT Press, 1996.

[40] X. Yao and Y. Liu, "Fast evolution strategies," *Control and Cybernetics*, vol. 26, no. 3, pp. 467–496, 1997.

[41] C. M. Fonseca and P. J. Fleming, "An overview of evolutionary algorithms in multiobjective optimization," *Evolutionary Computation*, vol. 3, no. 1, pp. 1–16, 1995.

[42] C. M. Fonseca and P. J. Fleming, "Multiobjective optimization and multiple constraint handling with evolutionary algorithms — part i: A unified formulation," *IEEE Trans. on Systems, Man, and Cybernetics, Part A: Systems and Humans*, vol. 28, no. 1, pp. 26–37, 1998.

[43] C. M. Fonseca and P. J. Fleming, "Multiobjective optimization and multiple constraint handling with evolutionary algorithms — part ii: Application example," *IEEE Trans. on Systems, Man, and Cybernetics, Part A: Systems and Humans*, vol. 28, no. 1, pp. 38–47, 1998.

[44] K. E. Mathias and D. Whitley, "Changing representations during search: A comparative study of delta coding," *Evolutionary Computation*, vol. 2, no. 3, pp. 249–278, 1994.

[45] D. B. Fogel and J. W. Atmar, "Comparing genetic operators with Gaussian mutations in simulated evolutionary process using linear systems," *Biological Cybernetics*, vol. 63, no. 2, pp. 111–114, 1990.

[46] D. B. Fogel, "A comparison of evolutionary programming and genetic algorithms on selected constrained optimization problems," *Simulation*, vol. 64, no. 6, pp. 399–406, 1995.

[47] J. J. Grefenstette, R. Gopal, B. J. Rosmaita, and D. van Gucht, "Genetic algorithms for the traveling salesman problem," in *Proc. of the First Int'l Conf. on Genetic Algorithms and Their Applications* (J. J. Grefenstette, ed.), pp. 160–168, Carnegie-Mellon University, 1985.

[48] D. B. Fogel, "An evolutionary approach to the traveling salesman problem," *Biological Cybernetics*, vol. 60, pp. 139–144, 1988.

[49] X. Yao, "An empirical study of genetic operators in genetic algorithms," *Microprocessing and Microprogramming*, vol. 38, pp. 707–714, 1993.

[50] Z. Michalewicz, *Genetic Algorithms + Data Structures = Evolution Programs*.

Berlin, Germany: Springer-Verlag, 1992.

[51] G. A. Vignaux and Z. Michalewicz, "A genetic algorithm for the linear transportation problem," *IEEE Trans. on Systems, Man, and Cybernetics*, vol. 21, no. 2, pp. 445–452, 1991.

[52] J. Lienig and K. Thulasiraman, "GASBOR: A genetic algorithm for switchbox routing in integrated circuits," in *Progress in Evolutionary Computation, Lecture Notes in Artificial Intelligence, Vol. 956* (X. Yao, ed.), (Heidelberg, Germany), pp. 187–200, Springer-Verlag, 1995.

[53] R. Hinterding and L. Khan, "Genetic algorithms for cutting stock problems: with and without contiguity," in *Progress in Evolutionary Computation, Lecture Notes in Artificial Intelligence, Vol. 956* (X. Yao, ed.), (Heidelberg, Germany), pp. 166–186, Springer-Verlag, 1995.

[54] K.-H. Liang, X. Yao, C. Newton, and D. Hoffman, "Solving cutting stock problems by evolutionary programming," in *Evolutionary Programming VII: Proc. of the 7th Annual Conference on Evolutionary Programming* (V. W. Porto, N. Saravanan, D. Waagen, and A. E. Eiben, eds.), vol. 1447 of *Lecture Notes in Computer Science*, (Berlin), pp. 291–300, Springer-Verlag, 1998.

[55] F. Luan and X. Yao, "Solving real-world lecture room assignment problems by genetic algorithms," in *Complex Systems — From Local Interactions to Global Phenomena*, pp. 148–160, IOS Press, Amsterdam, 1994.

[56] X. Yao, "Optimization by genetic annealing," in *Proc. of Second Australian Conf. on Neural Networks* (M. Jabri, ed.), (Sydney, Australia), pp. 94–97, 1991.

[57] T. Kido, K. Takagi, and M. Nakanishi, "Analysis and comparisons of genetic algorithm, simulated annealing, tabu search, and evolutionary combination algorithm," *Informatica*, vol. 18, pp. 399–410, 1994.

[58] J. H. Holland, K. J. Holyoak, R. E. Nisbett, and P. R. Thagard, *Induction: Processes of Inference, Learning, and Discovery.* Cambridge, MA: The MIT Press, 1986.

[59] J. H. Holland, "Using classifier systems to study adaptive nonlinear networks," in *Lectures in the Sciences of Complexity* (D. L. Stein, ed.), pp. 463–499, Redwood City, CA: Addison-Wesley, 1988.

[60] T. H. Westerdale, "Classifier systems — no wonder they don't work," in *Proc. of the 2nd Annual Conf. on Genetic Programming* (J. R. Koza, K. Deb, M. Dorigo, D. B. Fogel, M. Garzon, H. Iba, and R. L. Riolo, eds.), (San Francisco, CA), pp. 529–537, Morgan Kaufmann, 1997.

[61] S. W. Wilson, "Classifier fitness based on accuracy," *Evolutionary Computation*, vol. 3, no. 2, pp. 149–175, 1995.

[62] M. Colombetti and M. Dorigo, "Evolutionary computation in behavior engineering," in *this volume*, World Scientific Publ. Co.

[63] R. E. Smith and D. E. Goldberg, "Reinforcement learning with classifier systems: adaptive default hierarchy formation," *Applied Artificial Intelligence*, vol. 6, pp. 79–102, 1992.

[64] X. Yao, "Evolution of connectionist networks," in *Preprints of the Int'l Symp. on AI, Reasoning & Creativity* (T. Dartnall, ed.), (Queensland, Australia), pp. 49–52, Griffith University, 1991.

[65] X. Yao, "A review of evolutionary artificial neural networks," *International Journal of Intelligent Systems*, vol. 8, no. 4, pp. 539–567, 1993.

[66] X. Yao, "Evolutionary artificial neural networks," in *Encyclopedia of Computer Science and Technology* (A. Kent and J. G. Williams, eds.), vol. 33, pp. 137–170, New York, NY 10016: Marcel Dekker Inc., 1995.

[67] X. Yao and Y. Shi, "A preliminary study on designing artificial neural networks using co-evolution," in *Proc. of the IEEE Singapore Intl Conf on Intelligent Control and Instrumentation*, (Singapore), pp. 149–154, IEEE Singapore Section, June 1995.

[68] Y. Liu and X. Yao, "A population-based learning algorithm which learns both architectures and weights of neural networks," *Chinese Journal of Advanced Software Research (Allerton Press, Inc., New York, NY 10011)*, vol. 3, no. 1, pp. 54–65, 1996.

[69] X. Yao and Y. Liu, "A new evolutionary system for evolving artificial neural networks," *IEEE Transactions on Neural Networks*, vol. 8, no. 3, pp. 694–713, 1997.

[70] X. Yao and Y. Liu, "Making use of population information in evolutionary artificial neural networks," *IEEE Trans. on Systems, Man, and Cybernetics, Part B: Cybernetics*, vol. 28, no. 3, pp. 417–425, 1998.

[71] C. D. Rosin and R. K. Belew, "New methods for competitive coevolution," *Evolutionary Computation*, vol. 5, no. 1, pp. 1–29, 1997.

[72] W. D. Hillis, "Co-evolving parasites improve simulated evolution as an optimization procedure," in *Santa Fe Institute Studies in the Sciences of Complexity, Volume 10*, pp. 313–323, Addison-Wesley, 1991.

[73] R. Axelrod, "The evolution of strategies in the iterated prisoner's dilemma," in *Genetic Algorithms and Simulated Annealing* (L. Davis, ed.), ch. 3, pp. 32–41, San Mateo, CA: Morgan Kaufmann, 1987.

[74] X. Yao and P. Darwen, "An experimental study of N-person iterated prisoner's dilemma games," *Informatica*, vol. 18, pp. 435–450, 1994.

[75] P. J. Darwen and X. Yao, "On evolving robust strategies for iterated prisoner's dilemma," in *Progress in Evolutionary Computation, Lecture Notes in Artificial Intelligence, Vol. 956* (X. Yao, ed.), (Heidelberg, Germany), pp. 276–292, Springer-Verlag, 1995.

[76] P. Darwen and X. Yao, "Automatic modularization by speciation," in *Proc. of the 1996 IEEE Int'l Conf. on Evolutionary Computation (ICEC'96), Nagoya, Japan*, pp. 88–93, IEEE Press, New York, NY 10017-2394, 1996.

[77] P. J. Darwen and X. Yao, "Speciation as automatic categorical modularization," *IEEE Transactions on Evolutionary Computation*, vol. 1, no. 2, pp. 101–108, 1997.

[78] S. Kirkpatrick, C. D. Gelatt, and M. P. Vecchi, "Optimization by simulated annealing," *Science*, vol. 220, pp. 671–680, 1983.

[79] H. H. Szu and R. L. Hartley, "Fast simulated annealing," *Physics Letters A*, vol. 122, pp. 157–162, 1987.

[80] X. Yao, "Simulated annealing with extended neighbourhood," *Int. J. of Computer Math.*, vol. 40, pp. 169–189, 1991.

[81] X. Yao, "A new simulated annealing algorithm," *Int. J. of Computer Math.*, vol. 56, pp. 161–168, 1995.

[82] F. Glover, "Tabu search — part I," *ORSA J. on Computing*, vol. 1, pp. 190–206, 1989.

[83] F. Glover, "Tabu search — part II," *ORSA J. on Computing*, vol. 2, pp. 4–32, 1990.

[84] L. Ingber, "Very fast simulated re-annealing," *Mathl. Comput. Modelling*, vol. 12, no. 8, pp. 967–973, 1989.

[85] L. Eshelman, R. Caruana, and J. D. Schaffer, "Biases in the crossover landscape," in *Proc. of the Third Int'l Conf. on Genetic Algorithms and Their Applications* (J. D. Schaffer, ed.), pp. 10–19, Morgan Kaufmann, San Mateo, CA, 1989.

[86] D. Whitley, T. Starkweather, and D. Shaner, "The traveling salesman and sequence scheduling: quality solutions using genetic edge recombination," in *Handbook of Genetic Algorithms* (L. Davis, ed.), ch. 22, pp. 350–372, New York, NY: Van Nostrand Reinhold, 1991.

[87] J. R. Koza, *Genetic Programming.* Cambridge, Mass.: The MIT Press, 1992.

[88] J. Koza and D. Andre, "Automatic discovery of protein motifs using genetic programming," in *this volume*, World Scientific Publ. Co.

[89] C. Kappler, "Are evolutionary algorithms improved by large mutations?," in *Parallel Problem Solving from Nature (PPSN) IV* (H.-M. Voigt, W. Ebeling, I. Rechenberg, and H.-P. Schwefel, eds.), vol. 1141 of *Lecture Notes in Computer Science*, (Berlin), pp. 346–355, Springer-Verlag, 1996.

[90] J. E. Baker, "Adaptive selection methods for genetic algorithms," in *Proc. of an Int'l Conf. on Genetic Algorithms and Their Applications* (J. J. Grefenstette, ed.), pp. 101–111, 1985.

[91] D. E. Goldberg, "A note on Bltzmann tournament selection for genetic algorithms and population-oriented simulated annealing," *Complex Systems*, vol. 4, pp. 445–460, 1990.

Chapter 2

Evolutionary Computation in Behavior Engineering

Marco Colombetti and Marco Dorigo

In the last few years we have used ALECSYS, a parallel learning classifier system based on the genetic algorithm, to develop behavioral modules for mobile robots, both simulated and real. In this paper we briefly report on our experience, and then reflect on various concepts stemming from the application of evolutionary computation to agent building. We propose a definition of agent, analyze the relationships holding between an agent and its external environment, and discuss some important similarities and differences between natural and artificial systems; in particular, we compare the concept of fitness of an organism with that of quality of an artifact. We then concentrate on adaptation, regarded as a basic process for the development of both biological organisms and artificial agents. We carry on our analysis trying to understand where and how Behavior Engineering (i.e., the discipline concerned with the development of artificial agents) might profit from the use of evolutionary strategies. We argue that an evolutionary approach might allow us to search the space of nonrational design, thus opening a whole new world of possibilities for the implementation of artificial systems.

2.1 Introduction

In the late fifties, computer scientists started to work on the project — known as Artificial Intelligence (AI) — of building intelligent computational systems. The basic assumption underlying most work in AI is that intelligence, either natural or artificial, intrinsically *is* a computational phenomenon, and therefore can be studied in disembodied systems, that is, in systems that have a "mind" but no "body" (with the exception of their computing "brain").

Forty years later, it is widely believed that — in spite of impressive local successes — AI will find it very difficult to reach its ultimate goal. Feeling unable to implement disembodied minds, several AI scientists turned to an apparently harder task, namely, to build intelligent robots endowed with a body and acting in the physical world. Such systems we shall simply call *agents*. In fact, the very term "intelligent", which has been adopted copiously not only in AI, but in various areas of Computer Science, will be used very sparingly in this paper. Later on we shall discuss other laudatory terms, like *autonomous* and *adaptive*, that seem to be more suitable, in that they are both easier to define rigorously and relevant to the analysis of agency.

The main motivation for turning one's interest to embodied agents is that intelligence — whatever it is — is a natural phenomenon, which appeared in animals in the course of biological evolution. Darwinian considerations suggest that intelligence must have adaptive value, that is, it must be relevant to the reproductive success of animals in the terrestrial environment. Therefore, directing one's attention to agents (i.e., to autonomous systems interacting with their environments) appears to be a sensible approach to understanding intelligence.

There is no need to stress that any important breakthrough in understanding agency would be relevant to many practical applications. Robotics is the most obvious example of a discipline that would profit from a better comprehension of how artificial agents behave in the physical world. But probably, the notion of agent is more general than the one of robot; for example, an industrial plant of high complexity can also be viewed as an agent of some sort. There is however much work to be done at the foundational level, before artificial agents can become an interesting industrial product.

Nature has populated the world with an astonishing variety of natural agents: animals, and in particular higher level ones, like mammals and especially primates. Even simple insects, like ants or bees, show a capacity of effective interaction with their environments which is by far superior to the most sophisticated robot realized up to now. As far as we know, natural agents have not been designed by a rational being, but result from a process of biological evolution and natural selection. It is therefore tempting to emulate Nature, and try to develop artificial agents through a process of artificial evolution and selection. An inquiry in the viability of this program, starting from a number of simple experiments we have performed in the last few years, is the subject of the present article.

There are reasons to believe that an artificial agent, to be understood, requires insights from both engineering and biology: more precisely, from at least such technological disciplines as Computer Science and Control Theory (on the engineering side) and from Ethology and Animal Psychology (on the side of biology). In spite of a wide-spread appreciation for interdisciplinary research, however, the worlds of biology and of engineering are still far apart. This frequently results into terminological misuse, or at least possible sources of misunderstanding, that we shall do our best to avoid. In fact, we believe that the attempt to establish a clear and rich terminology is of the greatest importance for a research area that still lacks universally accepted foundations — an area that we propose to call *Behavior Engineering* (BE), given that producing behavior is the characteristic feature of agents (see also Colombetti, Dorigo & Borghi, 1996).

The plan of the article is the following. First, in Section 2.2, we shortly describe our past experience in developing agents through evolutionary methods. We briefly sketch ALECSYS, a parallel implementation of a learning classifier system exploiting a version of the genetic algorithm, and report on the results of a number of experiments involving physical agents.

Then, in Section 2.3, we start reflecting on the concept of agent. We discuss whether it is possible to provide a complete and unambiguous definition of such terms as *agent*, *environment*, and *behavior*. We then consider the possible import on BE of basic biological concepts, like *function* and *fitness*. We shall not forget that BE, like any other engineering field, must look at its object — behavior — as a product, and shall therefore try to establish a notion of *behavior quality*.

In Section 2.4 we discuss adaptation as a basic process of agent development, considering both ontogenetic and philogenetic adaptation.

In Section 2.5 we take up the idea of building complex agents through artificial evolution. We analyze the notion of modularity as a basic component of rational design, and discuss the feasibility of using evolutionary computation as a means to search the space of nonrational design.

Our concluding remarks are given in Section 2.6.

2.2 The ALECSYS Experience

In the last few years, we have been experimenting on the application of evolutionary strategies to the development of agents, both in simulation and in the real environment. In our experiments, evolution is limited to behavioral components: both hardware and software architectures are designed, and do not evolve. In the following we describe the types of agents, environments and behaviors we have considered, the development tool we have used, and the experiments we have run.

2.2.1 AutonoMice and other robots

In our experiments, we have been inspired by Wilson's animat problem (Wilson, 1987), that is, the problem of having an artificial agent survive in the real world. Therefore, our robot are somewhat zoomorphic, and inhabit environments containing preys, predators, nests, etc. Although we have run a fair number of experiments in simulated environments, in this paper we shall briefly describe only the experimentation carried out with real robots. The interested reader is referred to (Dorigo & Schnepf, 1993; Dorigo & Colombetti, 1994a; Dorigo, 1995; Colombetti, Dorigo & Borghi, 1996) for more details.

We have used four different robots, that we call AutonoMouse II, AutonoMouse V, HAMSTER and CRAB. They all perform their activity in rooms and corridors, containing various kinds of obstacles, preys (light sources or colored objects), areas designated as nests, etc.

The AutonoMice are small mobile robots built for experimental purposes at our research Lab. AutonoMouse II (Figure 2.2.1) has four directional eyes and two motors. Each directional eye can sense a light source within a cone of about 60 degrees. Each motor can stay still or move the connected wheel one or two steps forwards, or one step backwards. The robot is connected to a transputer board on a PC via a 9600-baud RS-232 link. Only a small amount of processing is done on-board (i.e., the collection of data from sensors and to actuators and the management of communications with the PC); learning algorithms run on the transputer board.

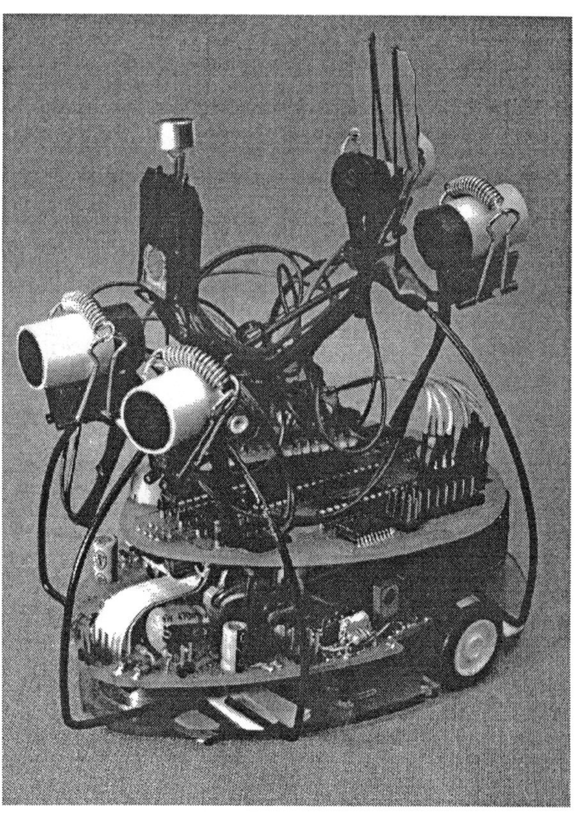

Figure 2.2.1 *AutonoMouse II.*

AutonoMouse V (Figure 2.2.2) has two directional eyes, a front sonar, front and side whiskers, a "change of direction" sensor (which we call a tail), and tracks moved by two motors. Each directional eye can sense a light source within a cone of about 180 degrees. The two eyes together cover a 270 degrees zone, with an overlapping of 90 degrees in front of the robot. The sonar is highly directional and can sense an object as far as 10 meters. Each motor can stay still or move the connected track one or two steps forwards, or one step backwards. AutonoMouse V is linked to a transputer board on a PC via a 4800-baud infra-red link.

Figure 2.2.2 *AutonoMouse V.*

HAMSTER (Figure 2.2.3) is a mobile robot based on Robuter, a commercial platform produced by RoboSoft. It is 102 cm long, 68 cm wide and 44 cm high. The configuration we used has a belt of 24 Polaroid sonars, surrounding the whole platform. Motion is produced by two motors acting on two independent wheels. HAMSTER uses a frontal color camera to identify the position of certain colored objects in the environment (food pieces and the nest). Moreover, it exploits an odometer (that is, a sensor that estimates the robot's position and heading), to approximately identify the position of the nest when this is not visible. A PC hosting a transputer board is carried on board.

Figure 2.2.3 *HAMSTER.*

CRAB (Figure 2.2.4) is a robotic arm based on a two-link industrial manipulator, an IBM 7547 with a SCARA geometry. The first link can rotate 200 degrees around the shoulder joint, and the second link can rotate 160 degrees, with respect to the first link, around the elbow joint. As a result the end effector, attached to the wrist, can cover the gray area shown in Figure 2.2.5. The actuators are two motors, acting on the shoulder and the elbow joints, that respectively rotate the first link (with respect to the fixed base) and the second link (with respect to the first link).

More details on the robots and their environments will be given in Section 2.2.3.

Figure 2.2.4 *CRAB.*

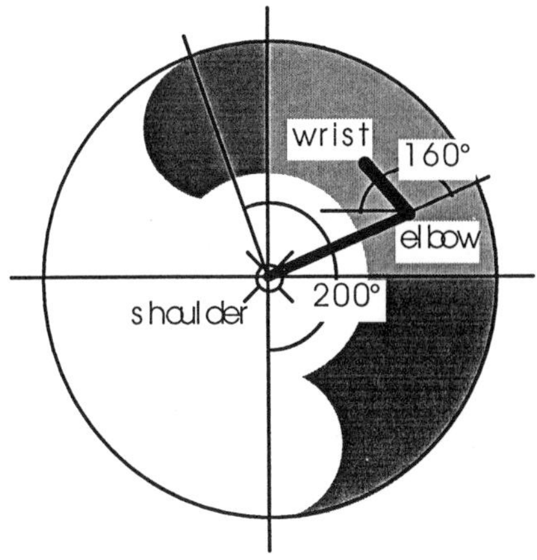

Figure 2.2.5 *A schematic drawing of CRAB.*

2.2.2 ALECSYS as a tool for agent development

ALECSYS is a distributed learning classifier system (LCS) that we have used to implement the learning control systems of our AutonoMice. The basic component of ALECSYS is a LCS, as depicted in Figure 2.2.6. A LCS is composed of three interacting systems: the performance system, a kind a production rule system which is in charge of directing the behavior of the controlled agent; the apportionment of credit system, which is in charge, by means of an algorithm called Bucket Brigade (Holland, 1980), of evaluating the usefulness of rules used by the performance system; and the genetic algorithm, whose duty is to discover new useful rules to be added to the knowledge base used by the performance system[1]. In our approach to the development of control systems by LCSs, which we call *robot shaping* (Dorigo & Colombetti, 1994a), the interaction between the agent controlled by the LCS and its environment is observed by a trainer which provides step-by-step (i.e., immediate) reinforcements: rewards when the agent does something correct, punishments when the agent does something wrong.

---

[1] A complete description of our version of the LCS, called *improved classifier system* (ICS), can be found in Dorigo, 1993.

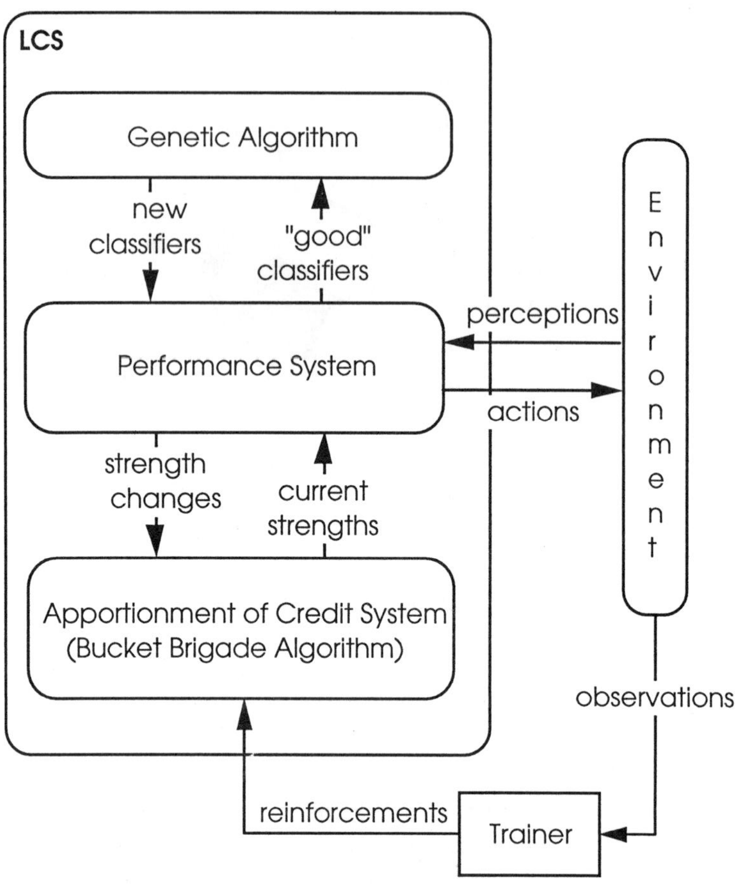

Figure 2.2.6 *The learning classifier system, the external environment, and the trainer.*

In ALECSYS a single LCS can be parallelized on a transputer network.[2] This allows one to increase the complexity of behaviors which can be learned by a single LCS. Moreover, ALECSYS allows for the distribution of a set of LCSs on a transputer network, so that we can have more LCSs cooperating to learn to solve a complex task. In fact, the basic idea underlying the ALECSYS system is that complex learning problems can be

---

2 The way we parallelized the LCS is described in details in (Dorigo, 1992; 1995).

attacked by decomposition into simpler problems: each simpler problem is then given as a learning task to a, possibly parallelized, LCS. Though this *divide et impera* approach is not a new idea in software design, we were among the first (Dorigo & Sirtori, 1991; Mahadevan & Connell, 1992; Dorigo & Schnepf, 1993; Lin, 1993) to combine the behavioral decomposition approach (Brooks, 1991) with reinforcement learning techniques. We will discuss in the following Section 2.5 some of the limits of this approach and will suggest that evolutionary techniques could be better exploited to develop "nonrational" solutions to the problem of designing the control architecture of an autonomous agent.

As we said, by using ALECSYS we can define a certain number of communicating LCSs: each LCS can implement either a basic behavioral module, or a coordination behavioral module. For example, in a *FollowPrey + AvoidObstacles* task, we can use three LCSs: one for the basic *FollowPrey* behavior, one for the basic *AvoidObstacles* behavior, and one for the behavior in charge of coordination between the two basic behaviors.

Given that by using ALECSYS the control system of an agent can be implemented by a network of different LCSs, it is interesting to study the issue of architecture, that is the problem of designing the network that best fits some predefined class of behaviors. We have experimented with different types of architectures, that can be broadly organized in two classes:

- *monolithic architectures*, built by one LCS directly connected to the agent's sensors and effectors;
- *distributed architectures*, built by many LCSs; in this case we distinguish between two subclasses:
  - *flat architectures*, built by more than one LCS, in which all LCSs are at "level 1", that is, directly connected to the agent's sensors and effectors;
  - *hierarchical architectures*, built by a hierarchy of levels.

In the following, we discuss a number of possible choices.

2.2.2.1 Monolithic architectures

The simplest choice is the *monolithic architecture*, with only one LCS in charge of controlling the whole behavior (Figure 2.2.7). If the target behavior is made up of several basic responses, there is a further choice to be made: the state of all sensors can be wrapped up in a single message (Figure 2.2.7a), or distributed into a set of independent messages (Figure 2.2.7b). We call the latter case *monolithic architecture with distributed input*. The idea is that inputs relevant to different responses can go into distinct messages; in such a way, input messages are shorter, and the overall learning effort can be reduced.

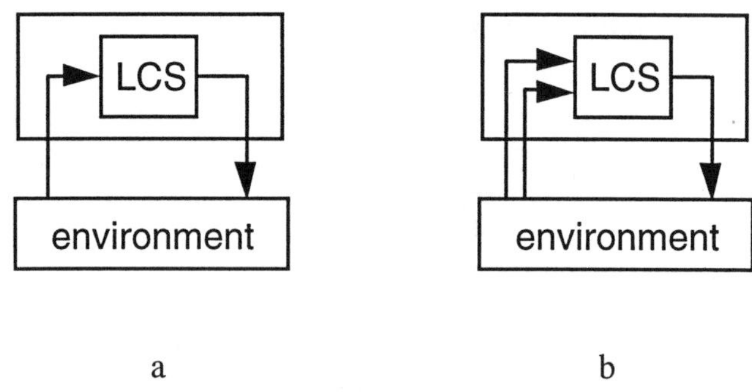

Figure 2.2.7 *Monolithic architectures.*

2.2.2.2 Flat architectures

A distributed architectures is made up of more than one LCS. If all LCSs are directly connected to the agent's sensors, then we use the term *flat architecture* (Figure 2.2.8). The idea is that distinct LCSs implement the different basic responses that make up a complex behavior pattern. There is a further issue, here, regarding the way in which the agent's response is built up from the moves proposed by the distinct LCSs. If such moves are independent, they can be realized by different effectors at the same time (Figure 2.2.8a); those moves that are not independent, however, have to be integrated into a single response before they are realized (Figure 2.2.8b).

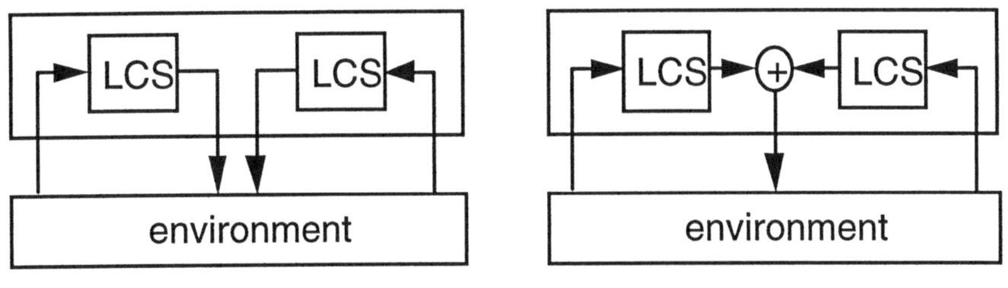

Figure 2.2.8 *Flat architectures.*

2.2.2.3 *Hierarchical architectures*

In a flat architecture, all LCSs receive input only from the sensors. In a *hierarchical architecture*, the set of all LCSs can be partitioned into a number of *levels*. A LCS belongs to level *N* if it receives input from systems of level *N*–1 at most, where level 0 is defined as the level of sensors. An *N*-level hierarchical architecture is a hierarchy of LCSs having level *N* as the highest one. Figure 2.2.9 shows two different two-level hierarchical architectures. First level LCSs implement basic behaviors, higher level LCSs implement coordination behaviors.

With a LCS in a hierarchical architecture we have two problems: first, how to receive input from a lower-level LCS; second, what to do with the output. Receiving input from a lower-level LCS is easy: given that all messages are bit strings of some fixed length, an output message produced by system LCS_1 can be treated as an input message by a different system LCS_2. Lower-level LCSs are viewed by higher-level ones as virtual sensors.

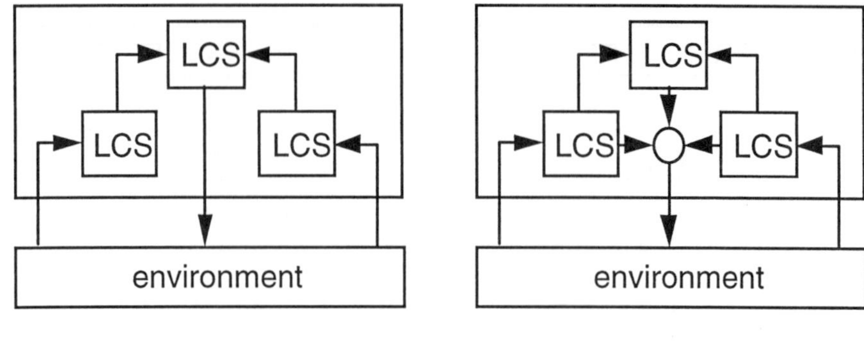

Figure 2.2.9 *Two-level hierarchical architectures.*

The problem of deciding what to do with the output of LCSs is more complex. In general, the output messages from the lower levels go to higher-level LCSs, while the output messages from the higher levels can go directly to the effectors to produce the response (see Figure 2.2.9a), or be used to control the composition of responses proposed by lower LCSs (see Figure 2.2.9b). How to compose responses of basic and coordination behaviors is an important aspect to be considered when using hierarchical architectures: different coordination mechanisms can give raise to different overall system behaviors. In our experiments we have studied the following composition mechanisms.

- *Independent sum*: two or more independent responses are produced at the same time; for example, an agent may emit a signal while escaping from a predator. The independent sum of behavior α and behavior β is written as:

  $\alpha \mid \beta.$

- *Combination*: two or more homogeneous responses are combined into a resulting behavior; for example, an agent could escape from a predator and at the same time avoid obstacles. The combination of α and β is written as:

  $\alpha + \beta.$

- *Suppression*: a response suppresses a competing one; for example, the agent may give up chasing a prey in order to escape from a predator. If α suppresses β, we write:

  $$\frac{\alpha}{\beta}.$$

- *Sequence*: a behavioral pattern is built as a sequence of simpler responses; for example, fetching an object involves reaching the object, grasping it, and coming back. The sequence of α and β is written:

  $$\alpha \cdot \beta;$$

  moreover, if a sequence σ is repeated forever, we write:

  $$\sigma^*.$$

Most of the experiments presented in this article were carried out using the suppression composition rule: we call the resulting hierarchical systems *switch architectures.* In Figure 2.2.10 we show an example of a three-level switch architecture. In this example the coordinator of level 2 ($COORD_1$) should learn to coordinate basic behaviors LCS_1 and LCS_2, while the coordinator of level 3 ($COORD_2$) should learn to coordinate $COORD_1$ and the basic behavior LCS_3.

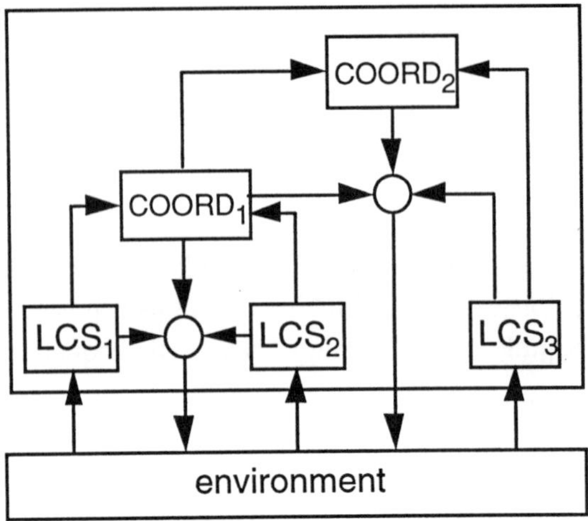

Figure 2.2.10 *An example of three-level hierarchical architecture composed of three basic behaviors and two coordinators.*

Another important aspect in the use of a distributed system, either flat or hierarchical, is the problem of selecting a *shaping policy*, that is, the order in which the various tasks are to be learned. We identified two extreme choices: holistic shaping and modular shaping.

- *Holistic shaping.* In holistic shaping the whole learning system is considered as a black box. The actual behavior of a single learning classifier system is not used to evaluate how to distribute reinforcements; when the system receives a reinforcement, it is given to all of the LCSs comprising the architecture. This can make the learning task difficult because there can be ambiguous situations in which the trainer cannot give the correct reinforcement to the component LCSs. A first example of ambiguous situation is when a correct action is the result of two wrong messages. Another example is when a LCS gets a punishment because of a mistake another LCS made.
- *Modular shaping.* In modular shaping each LCS is trained with a different reinforcement program, which takes into account the characteristics of the task that the considered LCS has to learn. We have found that a good way to implement modular shaping is to first

train the basic LCSs, and then, after they have reached a good performance level, to freeze them (i.e., basic LCSs are no longer learning, but only performing) and to start training upper level LCSs. Training of basic LCSs is usually done in a separate session (in which training of basic LCSs can be run in parallel).

2.2.3 Experiments

Here we shall only sketch the experiments we have carried out with our robots. The interested reader will be referred to more specific papers for details.

2.2.3.1 The AutonoMice

We trained AutonoMouse II to approach a light source. After a few successful experiments carried out under "normal conditions", we designed and carried out a number of experiments to assess the robot's behavior in degraded situations (Dorigo & Colombetti, 1994b; Dorigo, 1995), namely: robot with inverted eyes; robot with inverted motors; robot with one blind eye; robot with one badly regulated motor. The interesting results are that:

- Behavior does not suffer from inverting either eyes or motors. This is due to the fact that stimulus-response connections derive only from the learning activity, and no model of the robot's architecture is prewired into the controller. "Right" and "left" do not have any meaning other than the one which is directly assigned through the robot's own experience.
- With one blind eye, AutonoMouse II was still able to learn to approach the light, even if its performance was lower than that obtained under normal conditions. This shows that the agent is able to adapt to abnormal operating conditions.
- Analogously, the robot was still able to learn to approach the light when one of its motors was badly regulated (for example, made unable to move backwards). Again, this shows the capacity of the learning system to adapt the agent's behavior to abnormal conditions.

AutonoMouse V was mainly employed in experiments on tasks requiring the integration of different sensors, which was tested in an experiment on finding a hidden light source (see Figure 2.2.11) (Dorigo & Colombetti, 1994a; Colombetti, Dorigo & Borghi, 1996). The environment consisted of a large room containing an opaque wall, about 50 x 50 cm, and an ordinary lamp (50 W). The wall was realized as a pleated surface, in order to reflect back the sonar's beam coming from a wide range of directions. The input from the sonar was defined in such a way that a front obstacle was detected within about 1.5 m from the robot.

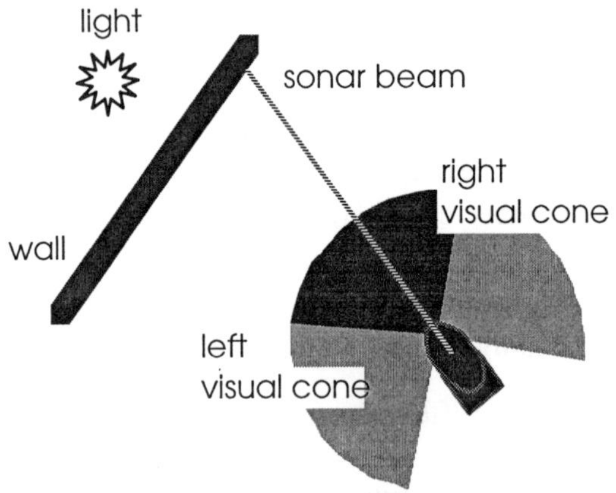

Figure 2.2.11 *Finding a hidden light source.*

AutonoMouse V was trained to carry out its task according to different strategies. The most successful included using the sonar to approach the wall until the whiskers could sense it, then using whiskers to follow it and turn around one of its edges until the eyes could sense the light. This experiment showed that a fairly complex behavior can be achieved by directly training a real robot, without resorting to simulation.

2.2.3.2 HAMSTER

HAMSTER's task was to hoard "food" bringing it to its "nest"[3] (Colombetti, Dorigo & Borghi, 1996), Its chief features are that it combines innate (i.e., prewired) and learned behaviors, and that training was carried out in a simulated environment and then transferred to the physical robot. The environment was a room of size 14 ∞ 13.3 m, with various obstacles (see Figure 2.2.12). Each piece of food was a cylinder (diameter 30 cm, height 70 cm) free to slide on the floor when pushed by HAMSTER, and the nest was located in a corner of the room. The food cylinders were wrapped into violet paper, and the nest's position was marked by another cylinder (diameter 30 cm, height 130 cm) wrapped in pink paper. HAMSTER used a frontal color camera to identify the position of food cylinders and of the nest, which are distinguished on the basis of color. Moreover, the nest sensor exploited an odometer (i.e., a sensor that estimates the robot's position and heading), to approximately identify the position of the nest when this was not visible.

Using the notation introduced in Section 2.2.2.3, the target behavior can be decomposed as follows:

$$HoardFood = (LeaveNest \cdot GetFood \cdot ReachNest)^{*} + AvoidObstacles.$$

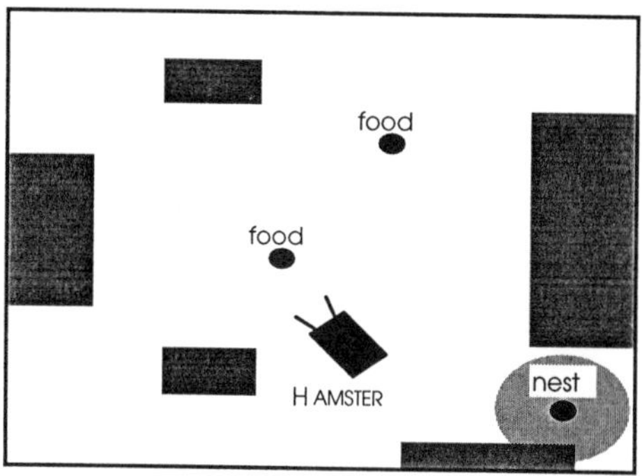

Figure 2.2.12 *Map of HAMSTER's environment.*

---

[3] This robot's name is mainly justified by its target behavior. It is also an acronym, namely Highly Autonomous Mobile System TrainEd by Reinforcements.

A main concern of the HAMSTER project was to combine learned and innate behavior modules. We chose to program *AvoidObstacles* directly, implementing a potential-based avoidance mechanism exploiting Robuter's sonars (see for example Latombe, 1991). The remaining part of the hoarding behavior was learned in an obstacle-free simulated environment, and then transferred to the physical robot.

We adopted a hierarchical controller architecture, with four behavioral modules at level 1, and a coordinator module at level 2. Each level-1 module proposes a direction for the robot's movement. The coordinator chooses one of the moves proposed by *LeaveNest*, *GetFood*, and *ReachNest* on the basis of the current situation, which is then combined with the move proposed by *AvoidObstacles* (see Figure 2.2.13). In general, this combination amounts to some kind of vector sum of the moves proposed by *AvoidObstacles* and by the rest of the system. There is, however, a more complex case. When HAMSTER is nearing a piece of food, the front part of the *AvoidObstacle* behavior has to be inhibited, otherwise the food could never be captured. Inhibiting obstacle avoidance in such cases is part of the coordinator's task.

HAMSTER was trained through a modular shaping policy: that is, each learned level-1 module was trained separately, and then frozen. The Coordinator was then trained to achieve the target behavior. We then transferred the controller onto the real robot, and ran some successful experiments in the real environment (with obstacles). The HAMSTER project shows that it is feasible to implement a robot's controller starting from both innate and learned behavioral modules.

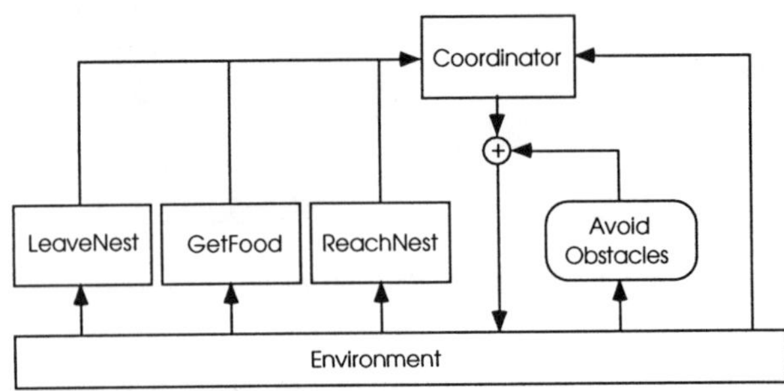

Figure 2.2.13 *Controller architecture for HAMSTER.*

2.2.3.3 *CRAB*

The experiment we have carried out with CRAB was intended to establish whether the light following task successfully learnt by AutonoMouse II could also be learned by a robot with a completely different geometry (Patel, Colombetti & Dorigo, 1995). In fact, reaching for an object by a mobile robot or by a manipulator are two different behaviors, because they require the two agents to perform different actions to achieve similar results. Consider for example the two configurations, *a* and *b*, shown in Figure 2.2.14. To move the end effector *P* forward in configuration *a*, the agent has to rotate link 1 right, and link 2 left; in configuration *b*, link 1 has to be rotated left, and link 2 right. This problem is typical of the polar geometry of a manipulator, and does not arise with mobile robots like the AutonoMice.

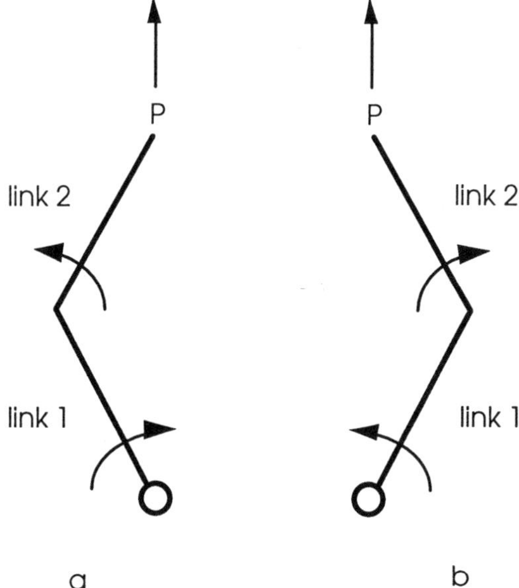

Figure 2.2.14 *Moving forward the end effector of a two-link manipulator.*

CRAB'S task was to reach a still infrared emitter by its end effector. The emitter was placed in a subarea of the manipulator's workspace (the light gray area in Figure 2.2.5), and was randomly displaced each time CRAB reached it.

The first problem we had to solve was in which position to place infrared sensors on the robot's arm. Using simulations, we found that such a choice was indeed critical for the agent to learn the task. A number of experiments allowed us to choose the following sensor configuration:

- an infrared light sensor placed on the end effector, able to detect in which of eight equal sectors the infrared emitter was placed;
- a proprioceptive sensor on the elbow, able to detect whether the second link formed, with respect to the first link, an angle between 0 and 80 degrees, or between 81 and 160 degrees.

With such a sensor equipment, CRAB was able to learn the light approaching behavior. To cut down learning time, we trained the real robot starting from an LCS initialized with the result of a learning session carried out in simulation. In fact, CRAB proved able to exploit such an initial state, and did improve its performance as a result of additional learning in the real environment.

2.2.3.4 Conclusions

As a whole, we believe we have proved that our evolutionary-based learning system, ALECSYS, is able to support learning of interesting behaviors by artificial agents acting in the real environment. The use of distributed, and in particular hierarchic, architectures allowed us to achieve fairly complex behaviors, that would have been hard to learn in a monolithic system.

However, we feel that our agents are very "rigid", in particular if compared with even the simplest natural organisms. In fact, in ALECSYS architecture has to be designed, and cannot be altered as an effect of evolution. Moreover, to achieve efficient learning the interaction among behavioral modules must be kept very simple, and this limits the variety and complexity of the behaviors that our agents can display.

Of course, it would be possible to implement a more powerful version of ALECSYS, in order to experiment with more complex behaviors; but we feel that such a work would not enrich our knowledge in important ways. As we shall argue in the following sections, major improvements in the complexity of agents probably call for a major change in the whole approach to agent development: less responsibility should be placed on the agent designer, and more on the process of spontaneous adaptation to the environment. We shall return to this important point in Section 2.5.

2.3 Agents and their Qualities

In this section, we first propose a general definition of agent. Then, we try to characterize the objects contained in the agent's environment in functional terms, analyzing the types of interaction between the agent and such objects.

2.3.1 Agents defined

Intuitively, an *agent*, *Ag*, is a dynamic system connected through a feedback loop with another dynamic system, called the *external environment*, *EE* (Fig. 2.3.1). It doesn't take much to realize that this definition is insufficient, because almost any dynamic system becomes an agent under such a characterization. Clearly, the definition must be refined.

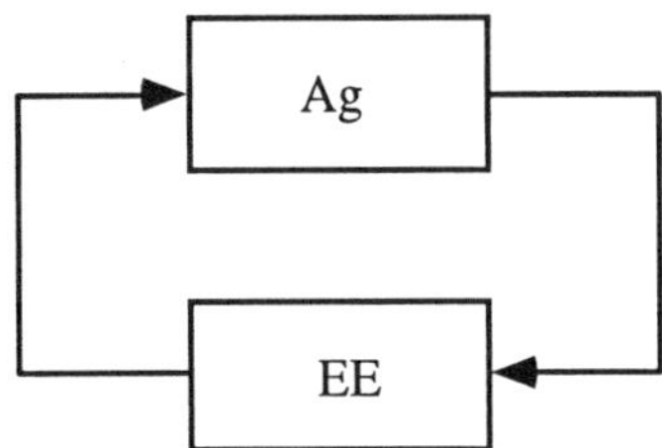

Figure 2.3.1 *Agent and external environment.*

We first notice that the relationship between the agent and its environment is not symmetrical. While all the agent's input comes from the external environment, and all the agent's output goes to the external environment, we cannot assume the reverse. In fact, there are outputs from *EE* that are not input to *Ag*, and inputs to *EE* that do not come from *Ag*. This is reflected in the scheme of Figure 2.3.2. We therefore rephrase our definition: an agent is a dynamic system connected through a feedback loop with another dynamic system, called the external environment, which for the agent is both partially uncontrollable and partially unobservable.

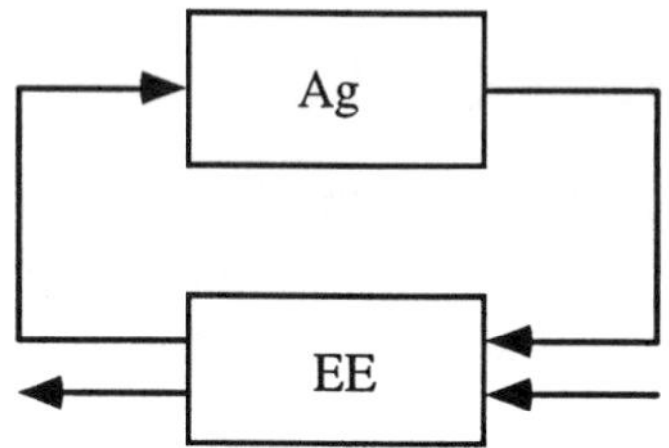

Figure 2.3.2 *The asymmetry between the agent and the external environment.*

This definition suggests that the agent can be regarded as a system controlling its external environment. However, this view is still too rough. An agent is made up of a "body", that we shall call the agent's *shell*, *Sh*, and by a "mind", the agent's *controller*, *C*. The controller collects information through *sensors*, *S*, and sends out information to the agent's *actuators*, *A*, which in turn produce behavior.

It is important to note that in general sensory information is not relative to the external environment alone, but to the interaction between the agent's shell and the external environment. For example, the light intensity sensors of AutonoMouse are not directly sensitive to the intensity of the light source, but rather to a complex function of the light source intensity, of the distance between the source and the sensors, and of the medium between the light source and the sensors. Analogously, the actuators do not directly change the external environment, but rather cause an interaction between the shell and the external environment: motors do not immediately displace the agent, but cause wheels to turn, and the agent moves as a result of the interaction between the wheels and the floor. We conclude that the controller controls the interaction between the agent's shell and the external environment (Fig. 2.3.3); such interaction is what we call the agent's *behavior*.

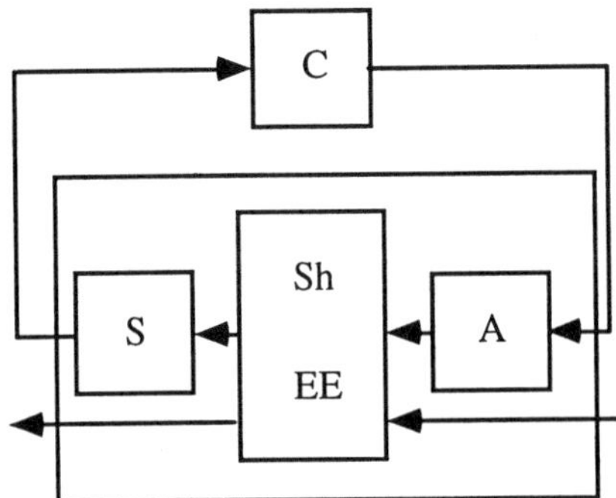

Figure 2.3.3 *The agent's controller controls the interaction between the shell and the external environment.*

Sensors collect information which is both *incomplete* and *noisy*: incomplete, because not all aspects of behavior are accessible to the controller through the agent's sensors; noisy, because real sensors are inaccurate. Moreover, the interaction between the shell and the external environment cannot be completely controlled, because of two reasons: (i) actuators are noisy; and (ii) the external environment is subject to its own dynamics, independently of the agent's actions (for instance, in the AutonoMouse experiments the light was at times moved by the experimenter).

2.3.2 The functional characterization of environmental objects

Our agents are *animat*-like robots (see Wilson, 1987) that carry out their activity in environments containing nests, obstacles, preys, hurting objects, etc. In most cases, the behavioral patterns exhibited by our agents are instances of *tactic behavior*, that is, they are directed at approaching, reaching, avoiding or fleeing from objects (*taxis*). Even if the class of tactic behavior is rather limited, it provides interesting problems for agent development, especially if we consider possible interactions between the agent and the objects when the agent comes to contact with them.

Terms like "nest" or "prey" obviously convey a zoomorphic metaphor. However, they can be defined at an abstract level in terms of the agent's behavior. Tactic objects (i.e., environmental objects involved in an agent's tactic behavior) can be classified according to a number of dimensions:

- The *appetitive* dimension: tactic objects can be *attractors* or *repellors*, with obvious meaning.
- The *locality* dimension: a tactic object is *local* if its attraction (repulsion) on the agent's behavior depends on the distance between the agent and the object, and it is *global* otherwise.
- The *geometrical* dimension: a tactic object is *point-shaped* if its center of attraction or repulsion is a geometrical point, and is *extended* otherwise.
- The *cinematic* dimension: a tactic object can be *still* or *moving*.

In our experiments, what we metaphorically call a prey is a moving, point-shaped global attractor; a predator is a moving, typically global point-shaped repellor; an obstacle is a typically still, extended local repellor, and so on.

In fact, the tactic aspect of an object does not completely characterize the agent's behavior with respect to it. Compare for example a food patch and the agent's nest. From the tactic point of view, both objects can be regarded as still, extended global attractors. The difference between the two is functional: nests are used to find shelter, and food is either eaten on the spot or hoarded.

In general, artificial agents interact with objects in a much simpler way than complex animals. Typically, a robot will grasp, drop or push certain types of objects (like preys or food pieces), and will enter or leave other types of objects (like nests). We therefore classify objects functionally according to two more dimensions:

- The *manipulation* dimension: some objects can be *grasped* and *dropped*, other objects can be *pushed*.
- The *topological* dimension: some objects can be *entered* and *left*.

A physical object need not maintain its features unaltered in time. For example, a predator is a repellor only if the agent is not in its nest; moreover, the presence of a predator typically turns the nest into an attractor. The functional characterization of objects is therefore dependent on the current *motivational state* of the agent. So far, we have considered motivations as just a type of agent's state (see Colombetti & Dorigo, 1994; Dorigo & Colombetti, 1994a). As our agents become more complex, however, we expect that the motivational aspects of behavior will be increasingly important and will deserve special treatment (see Section 2.5).

The previous analysis shows that the interdependence between the agent and its environment is indeed very tight: properties and capacities are not intrinsic, but relational. For example: no object is an obstacle *per se*: being an obstacle for an agent means being avoided by that agent; and the ability to manipulate is not just a property of the agent, but a property of the coupling between the agent and certain types of objects. Behavior Engineering, therefore, is not really concerned with the development of *agents*, but rather with the development of complex systems, of which agents are just a component.

2.3.3 The Natural and the Artificial

We must now ask the following question: *why* does an agent produce behavior? A common answer would be: to pursue its goals. However, the very concept of goal is highly ambiguous. What are the goals of animals? Is a robot acting to pursue its own goals or the goals of its designer? In fact, we believe that goals should be attributed only to those agents that can literally be said to have them. Human beings certainly have goals, and (at least sometimes) act according to plans produced in order to achieve them. Most probably, higher level animals, like primates and other mammals, do have mental states like beliefs and goals (Griffin, 1984; Prato Previde *et al.*, 1992). However, it is likely that lower level animals do not have mental states properly so called, and this is certainly the case for current artificial systems (for a philosophical argument, see Searle, 1992).

Darwin has taught us how to avoid teleological arguments in the analysis of living systems: organisms that undergo natural selection show features that tend to maximize their *fitness*, that is, their capacity to spread their own genetic makeup. As far as it is genetically determined, an aspect of animal behavior should therefore be explained in terms of its *adaptive value*, defined as its contribution to the overall fitness of the organism. As shown by contemporary ethology (see for example McFarland, 1981), this approach to the explanation of behavior is extremely powerful and productive.[4]

Clearly, we cannot apply the same line of thought to the analysis of artificial agents: robots are the result of explicit design, not of natural selection. Even when the agent controller is developed through evolutionary methods, we shall argue in the next section, strict Darwinian explanations do not apply. In fact, we cannot forget that a robot is designed to carry out a predefined task, that we shall call its *target behavior*. Typically, the target behavior is part of the initial requirements that a robot designer has to fulfill (see Colombetti, Dorigo & Borghi, 1996). So, it seems that we cannot immediately exploit the biological notion of fitness to formulate basic laws governing artificial agents.

Not only scientists have been intrigued by the problems connected with the basic laws of artificial behavior. In his celebrated collection of short stories, *I, Robot*, Isaac Asimov (1950) puts forward the Three Laws of Robotics,[5] claiming to quote them from the *Handbook of Robotics*, 56th edition, 2058 A.D.:

1. A robot may not injure a human being, or, through inaction, allow a human being to come to harm.
2. A robot must obey the orders given by human beings, except where such orders would conflict with the First Law.

---

4 So powerful and productive that it has become part of popular culture, unfortunately with a couple of misunderstanding: first, adaptive value is generally referred to survival, not to maximization of offspring; and second, it is believed that Nature cares after the survival of species, not of individuals. The first misunderstanding is almost harmless, given that, *ceteris paribus*, better survival means more offspring. The second misunderstanding is a plain logical error, given that the survival of a species can be defined either as the survival of its individuals (and in this case it is only a derivative phenomenon), or as the stability of individual features across generations (and this contradicts the very idea of adaptation: see Section 4).

5 Although it is not standard practice to cite science fiction in a scientific paper, it is interesting to note that a variant of the above mentioned "Three Laws of Robotics" were chosen as over-arching guidelines for the "Specification and Rules" document for the 1st Robot Exhibition and Competition held at the AAAI92 in San Jose, CA.

3. A robot must protect its own existence as long as such protection does not conflict with the First or Second Law.

Does all this have anything to do with real robotics in 1995? The first part of the First Law is certainly a wise design criterion, as far as injures to human beings and other accidents can be practically avoided through concern for safety (so far, nobody can cope with the second part). The Second Law assumes that robots can understand human orders; a weaker but more realistic version could be:

2'. A robot must carry out its target behavior, provided the given safety conditions are met.

Also the Third Law has concrete interest, in that an agent can carry out its task only as far as it survives.[6] We can therefore propose our version of this law:

3'. A robot must survive and work properly at least until it has accomplished its task.

We can now compare robots and living organisms. Animals do not have any predefined "task"; rather, they strive to spread their genetic makeup. However, to do so animals must survive. To enforce a parallel between robots and animals, we can compare a robot's target behavior with the biological function of maximizing one's offspring. While these two concepts are different, they both involve survival as a necessary condition: Survival then appears to be an important common feature of artificial and natural agents. We believe that this argument allows us to clarify the concept of an autonomous agent: an artificial agent can be said to be *autonomous* if it is able to survive in its environment while carrying out its target behavior.

We can know ask ourselves whether it is suitable to apply the notion of fitness to artificial agents. A first option is to redefine fitness as the ability to survive: in this case it would certainly apply to robots. However, we feel that the concept of fitness retains all its explicatory power only in the

---

[6] This is true also of systems whose task implies self-destruction: for example, a missile must survive until it hits its target.

context of an evolutionary process; therefore, we postpone its discussion to the next two sections.

There is certainly a metaphoric way of interpreting the fitness of an artifact in terms of its ability to "maximize its offspring". Commercial robots as Robosoft's Robuter (Robosoft SA, 1991) and Lausanne Polytechnic's Khepera (Mondada, Franzi & Ienne, 1994) show high fitness, in that they are spreading through robotics labs. In a less metaphoric way, we would probably interpret this as a consequence of the overall *quality* of such robots. Talking of artifacts, and in particular of industrial products, quality is probably the correct counterpart of biological fitness. How are we going to define, and hopefully measure, the quality of an artificial agent?

2.3.4 The quality of an artificial agent

In general, the quality of a product is made up of different components. As far as agents are concerned, the most obvious of such components is *performance*, that is, a measure of how efficiently the agent performs a predefined target behavior.

Another important component is *robustness*, understood as the capacity to perform acceptably well even if the operating conditions are different from the ones assumed during design and training. Robustness includes both graceful degradation of behavior in case of hardware and software faults, and insensitivity to limited changes in the structure and dynamics of the environment. Robustness of behavior does not presuppose any change in the agent's controller. For example, the AutonoMice trained to approach a steady light were still able to approach it if it started moving (see Dorigo, 1995). This is a consequence of the insensitivity of the controller to the motion state of the light.

Related to robustness is the concept of *adaptiveness*, which is understood as the robot's ability to modify itself in order to adapt to changes in the structure or the dynamics of the environment. This concept is very important for understanding agents, and so we have devoted Section 2.4 to its discussion. At the present stage of technology, only software components can show some degree of adaptiveness, as a result of learning mechanisms.

Many more interesting aspects of agent quality can be defined, like reliability, flexibility, efficiency, etc. We shall not pursue this line here, and shall limit our attention to the three components defined above.

The quality of an agent should be evaluated in quantitative terms. This is relatively easy for performance. In our experiments we have adopted two types of performance indexes:

- *Local performance indexes* (or *learning indexes*), that measure the effectiveness of the learning process (that is, the correspondence between what is taught and what is learned).
- *Global performance indexes*, that measure the correspondence of the robot's behaviors with the target behavior.

In general, we define local performance as the ratio of "correct" actions to the total number of actions performed over a predefined time interval; actions are considered correct if they are rewarded by the trainer. The definition of global performance, on the other hand, strictly depends on the specific target behavior; for a food hoarding task, for instance, such a measure might be defined as the number of food pieces collected and brought to the nest on a predefined time interval.

In fact, the problem of defining performance can be dealt with in a fairly general way within the reinforcement learning paradigm. For ease of explanation, let us consider a very simple example: a mobile robot whose target behavior is to reach and touch a moving light as many times as possible. For any time instant t, the agent's global performance $G(t)$ can be measured as

$$G(t) = \frac{1}{t} \sum_{i=0}^{t} result(t),$$

where $result(t)$ is 1 if the robot touches the light at instant t, and 0 otherwise. The function $G(t)$ can be used to specify the robot's target behavior: for example, we might say that the value $G(t)$ must be as large as possible, and in any case greater than a predefined threshold.

If the robot is trained through a delayed reinforcement method, it will typically receive a reward each time it touches the light. However, if immediate reinforcement is used, like in our experiments, the robot will not be trained to *touch* the light, but rather to *approach* it; this is feasible, because we know that a moving agent will finally touch an object that it steadily approaches. With reference to the light-approaching behavior, we can define a local performance function $l(t)$ as

$$l(t) = -\Delta\, dist(t) = dist(t) - dist(t+1),$$

which measures the decrease of distance between the robot and the light as a result of the robot's action at instant t. In principle, the function $l(t)$ can be used to compute the reinforcement $r(t)$ to be assigned at instant t:

$$r(t) = l(t).$$

In practice, however, reinforcements often do not coincide with a measure of local performance, but are only related to it. We have empirically found that in general learning is sped up if poor performance is punished and good performance is strongly rewarded. In any case, the function ρ relating reinforcement to local performance,

$$r(t) = \rho(l(t)),$$

must be an increasing function;[7] in other words, better performance must receive higher reinforcement. Typically, the ρ function might be a step function like the one depicted in Figure 2.3.4.

---

[7] A numeric function $f(x)$ is *increasing* if $x_1 \bullet x_2$ implies $f(x_1) \bullet f(x_2)$.

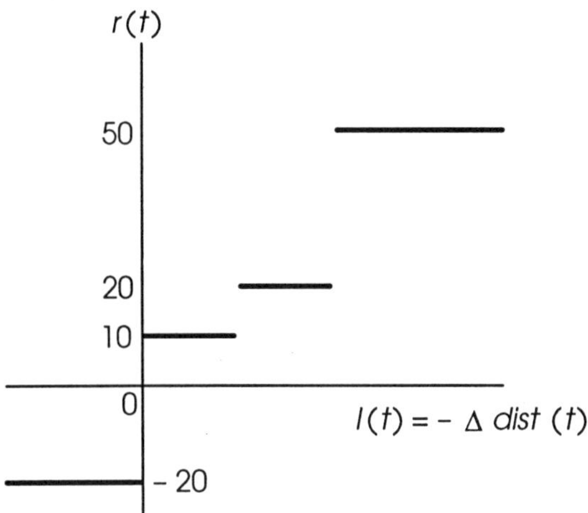

Figure 2.3.4 *Reinforcement computed as an increasing function of local performance.*

It is interesting to note that the three functions $G(t)$, $l(t)$ and $r(t)$ provide three different views of the agent's performance. To allow for a comparison, let us define two cumulative functions associated to l and r:

$$L(t) = \frac{1}{t} \Sigma_{i=0}^{t} l(t),$$

$$R(t) = \frac{1}{t} \Sigma_{i=0}^{t} step(r(t)),$$

where $step(x)$ is 1 if $x > 0$, and 0 otherwise. We can now run a test session of N cycles, and compute the values of $G(N)$, $L(N)$ and $R(N)$. What will these values tell us?

High values of G mean that the agent is performing well its global target behavior, consisting of touching the light. Therefore, the function G captures the point of view of the robot's *customer*. High values of L mean that is effective in approaching the light; the function L captures the point of view of the robot *designer*, who decided to implement light touching in terms of light approaching. Finally, high values of R mean that the robot is learning what it is taught, and this captures the point of view of the robot *trainer*.

The three points of view are obviously related, but they do not coincide. In fact, it is possible to have high values of L and low values of G: this means that the robot designer did a poor job, and decided to realize the global target behavior through local behaviors that actually do not guarantee success (for example, following a mouse would be a very poor strategy to catch it — traps are much more effective). In turn, high values of R tell us that the agent is learning what the reinforcements tell it to do; but reinforcements might tell the wrong thing. For example, the trainer might erroneously reward the agent of our example when it does not approach the light: in this case we would have a high value of R and a low value for G at the same time. We conclude that the three function G, L and R are all necessary for an adequate evaluation of the agent's performance.

Performance is not the only quality aspect that one would like to measure. The functions we have previously analyzed also tell us about the agent's adaptiveness: the increase of performance over time, as an effect of learning, is in fact a sign that the agent has adaptive capacities. In particular, the experiments reported about AutonoMouse II can be viewed as an inquiry in the adaptive capacities of LCS-based agents.

On the contrary, we performed very few experiments to study the robustness of our agents. In the context of our research, an agent would be robust if it were capable of keeping a high level of performance in presence of changes in the agent-environment interaction, without resorting to learning. In other words: while adaptiveness is an effect of learning, robustness — if present — would be a result of the agent's architecture (and in particular of the learned behavioral modules).

Certainly, LCS have some intrinsic robustness, in particular as an effect of their redundancy: learned behavior modules are not minimal, and code the same behavioral rule in several copies and in several versions. For example, an agent that in a given situation has to move forward will learn to do so, but will also learn that turning slightly right or slightly left is not too bad. Such suboptimal rules would turn out to be very useful in cases in which moving straight ahead is physically impossible.

The agent's architecture and its learning capacities thus appear to bear the fundamental responsibility for the agent's quality. Much more research in both directions will have to be done before really high-quality artificial agents can be realized.

2.4 The Concept of Adaptiveness

Literally speaking, "adaptive" means "capable of adaptation". Contrary to the term "adaptable", which has both active and passive acceptations (meaning both "able to adapt" and "able to be adapted"), "adaptive" has an inherent active flavor: for example, an adaptive controller would be one that can tune its parameters on line to control a time-variant process.

Biologists distinguish among different kinds of adaptation.[8] The two kinds which are relevant for us here are *evolutionary* (or *philogenetic*) *adaptation*, concerning the way in which species adjust to environmental conditions through evolution, and *ontogenetic adaptation*, that is, the process by which an individual adjusts to its environment during its lifetime. As far as behavior is concerned, ontogenetic adaptation is a result of *learning*.

Let us first analyze evolutionary adaptation. Many researchers, including us, have shown that evolutionary computation is a suitable paradigm to develop the behavior of artificial agents. In practical applications, in fact, artificial evolution mingles with individual learning, in that "reproduction" only occurs at the software level; evolutionary procedures can thus be viewed as a class of machine learning methods. What characterizes evolutionary methods is the presence of "discovery" operators, like mutation and crossover, and of a process of selection based on an evaluation of the agent's behavior. Given the analogy with natural evolution, the result of such evaluation is usually called *fitness*.

According to the approach adopted, fitness can apply to different entities: to the whole behavior exhibited by the agent, to a single behavior module, or to a highly specific behavior rule. In all cases, however, fitness will always be a function of the actual behavior produced by the agent in its environment.

---

[8] See for example the entry ADAPTATION in *The Oxford Companion to Animal Behaviour* (McFarland, 1981).

In the realm of organisms, we say that an individual has high fitness if it is highly effective in spreading its offspring; that the world is mainly inhabited by organisms with high fitness is therefore almost tautological. The interesting problem for biologists is then to find out which features of the individual essentially contribute to its overall fitness (or, in other words, which features have high adaptive value).

In the realm of artificial agents, the relationship between fitness and reproductive success is reversed: *first*, the fitness of an individual is computed as a function of its interaction with the environment; *second*, the fittest individuals are caused to reproduce. However, this pattern is not exclusive of artificial systems: it is applied by breeders (of cattle, horses, dogs, etc.) to produce breeds with predefined features.

In fact, we contend that the best metaphor of evolutionary computation is not biological evolution, but breeding. This change of perspective is not without consequences. For example, it is typical of breeding that highly disadaptive features can be selected: The survival of pure-breed animals is often more problematic than that of mongrels. Analogously, applying evolutionary methods to the development of task-oriented behavior may easily result into a robot with low survival capacity. In both animal breeding and evolutionary robotics, the fault is not in the evolutionary method itself; rather, it stems from the definition of a fitness function which is not enough comprehensive. This suggests that, as far as possible, the fitness function used to develop robot behavior should take into account the overall quality of the agent, and not performance alone — confirming our previous intuition that quality is the artificial counterpart of biological fitness.

An important difference between the natural and the artificial is that in animals learning is sharply different from evolution. Moreover, the capacity of individual learning in organisms is itself a product of evolution; we must therefore expect to find such a capacity where it has adaptive value. In the realm of the artificial, on the contrary, there is no sharp conceptual separation between individual learning and evolution. In our experiments, for example, we have implemented individual learning of new behaviors in term of the evolution of a population of behavior rules: the ontogenetic adaptation of our agents is actually the result of a process of "filogenetic adaptation" taking place at a finer grain size.

Machine learning techniques can achieve adaptation in two basically different ways, that we can respectively call *parameter setting* and *structural learning*. In ALECSYS, for example, the Bucket Brigade algorithm is used to compute classifier strength (parameter setting), and GA is used to create new classifiers (structural learning). Many well-known learning algorithms, like Back-propagation and Simulated Annealing, can only be used for parameter setting. On the contrary evolutionary computation methods, like GAs, are widely used both for parameter setting and for structural learning.

There is no doubt that automatic parameter setting methods are going to be useful, if not essential, for developing artificial agents, because agents will have to adapt to a world that designers can model only with some approximation. To this purpose, a variety of known learning methods can be used, including evolutionary strategies.

The most stimulating applications of evolutionary strategies, however, are the ones intended to bring about new structures, like behavior rules, neural network topologies, articulation of a system into modules, etc. In the following, we shall direct our attention to such applications.

2.5 The Evolutionary Development of Artificial Agents

From the point of view of structural design, the main interest of evolutionary computation is that it allows us to deal with a larger design space. If we dub *rational design* the conceptual space that is searched by human designers, we can say that evolutionary strategies can search in the space of *nonrational design*.[9] The relevant question is then: is there any practical justification to search such a space? Or, in other words: what are the limitation of rational design that we would like to overcome by enlarging the spectrum of possibilities? Before we try to answer this question, we need to characterize human design better.

---

[9] We prefer the term "*nonrational* design" to "*irrational* design", because in everyday language the latter term has a negative connotation, while the former is more neutral.

We think that the main qualifying aspect of rationally designed systems is that they are *modular*. Modularity is what makes a complex system still easy to conceive, to understand, to modify, etc. *Divide et impera* is perhaps the most fundamental engineering motto.

A system is modular when it is built up from *modules*, that is from subsystems that are both *highly cohesive* and *loosely coupled* (see for example Ghezzi, Yazayeri & Mandrioli, 1991). High cohesion is an intramodular property: it means that the subsystem has a well-identified function, and contains only components that operate to realize such a function. Loose coupling is an intermodular property: it means that the complexity of the interfaces between subsystems is negligible with respect to the internal complexity of the modules.

The virtues of modularity are manifold. Modular systems are easier to understand, maintain and modify; in general, they are less prone to errors and easier to debug. It is important to note, however, that these properties are not directly related to the intrinsic performance of the system — in principle, a highly modular system may be less efficient than a less modular counterpart. The advantages of modularity concern the relationships between an artificial system and the human beings involved in its design, implementation and maintenance. It is true, however, that most artificial systems that are not modular are so because they have grown in a chaotic way, and thus they often behave rather poorly.

According to classical engineering methodologies, lack of modularity is to be avoided. As regards Nature, there is often sharp disagreement as to how modular biological systems are (see for example Fodor, 1985). Clearly, nobody wants to claim that natural systems show no articulation in subsystems. However, such subsystems do not seem to be structured in a modular way (at least under the definition of module that we gave above): it is almost commonplace that living organisms tend to act as a whole, and this implies very strong coupling among subsystems, and thus a low degree of modularity.

Given our previous considerations, the lack of modularity of natural systems is easy to understand. As we have remarked, modularity does not directly improve performance, but it affects the relationship between artificial systems and humans. Clearly, Nature optimizes fitness, not understandability by humans! Observing natural systems, it seems reasonable to assume, at least as a working hypotheses, that their high degree of fitness might profit from their nonmodular organization.

Now, two very important questions must be asked. To which extent is nonmodular design an interesting option for the development of artificial systems? And how can nonmodular systems actually be designed and implemented?

That a high degree of modularity is not always a right (or possible) choice can be clearly seen by analyzing AI programs. In fact much of AI, and in particular Knowledge Engineering, could be viewed as the engineering of low-modularity software systems. Consider for example the programming paradigm of production systems: the interactions among production rules in any large production system are strong and, as any AI programmer knows, often difficult to control. That the royal road of modularity is abandoned mainly by those who aim at building "intelligent" systems is indeed an interesting fact.

Even if nonmodular systems can be very effective, to work properly they have to solve a number of hard problems. In our opinion, these are the main ones:

- *Problems with input information.* While modular systems implement a rational preselection of useful input, nonmodular systems often have to deal with highly redundant input information.
- *Problems of interference among subsystems.* In nonmodular systems, the interaction among subsystems can be very complex. This may lead to useful emergent properties, but also to improper behavior.
- *Problems of action focusing.* Nonmodular systems may find it difficult to focus their action in a coherent way.

If this is true, we should be able to identify specific solutions to these problems in natural agents. In our opinion, this is precisely the role of such important biological mechanisms as *attention*, *inhibition*, and *motivation*: the role of attention is to deal with highly redundant input information; of inhibition, to solve conflicts arising from interference among subsystems; of motivation, to focus the system's activity toward specific goals.

In modular systems, these mechanisms are relatively marginal. In fact, attention, inhibition and motivation are not recognized as important architectural concepts in traditional software design. However, complex concurrent system do make use of mechanisms, like interrupts, that are clearly related to inhibition; moreover, inhibition plays a fundamental role in the subsumption architecture, proposed by Brooks (1991) as a basis for behavior based robotics.

Again, it is interesting to look at production systems which, as we have already remarked, have a low degree of modularity. Production systems of the OPS5-type (Brownston *et al.*, 1985) indeed deal with the problems we have pointed out. For example, the "recency principle" can be viewed as a mechanism to focus the interpreter's attention toward recently acquired information; inhibition among production instances is virtually implemented in the selection strategies applied to the conflict set; and context based metaprogramming is analogous to a motivation mechanism.

However, examples of nonmodular artificial systems are the exception, and not the rule. In spite of many interesting ideas from AI, the *divide et impera* strategy has strong and valid rationality motivations. Is there any concrete need to depart from such a principle?

In fact, we cannot always be rational. Rationality presupposes knowledge: where we do not know enough, no rational methodology can lead us to make the right decisions. And the development of an autonomous agent is a striking example of a case where we do not know enough: the real world is too complex and unpredictable to allow for exhaustive modeling. So far, we have experimented with very simple agents in fairly stable environments, and therefore we have been allowed to put enough rationality in the design of our robots. But the analysis carried out in this paper leads us to expect that such an approach cannot scale up to really complex agents interacting with natural environments.

Of course, we have also to keep in mind that a methodology for BE must be technologically feasible. Evolutionary computation is highly time consuming; given that physical robots move rather slowly, to save time it should be carried out in simulated environments as far as possible. On the other hand, strong adaptation to a real environment can only be achieved in the environment itself, given that simulations environments are too idealized. This dilemma must be solved in order to work out a feasible engineering methodology.

One possible way out, that we intend to pursue in the near future, is to develop artificial agents in simulated environments as far as possible, and then to refine them by additional learning and/or evolution in the real world. In fact, we have already applied this methodology with some success, for example in the CRAB experiment. How far this approach can be pushed is however an open research issue.

2.6 Conclusions

In this paper we have briefly sketched our previous experience with the evolutionary development of artificial agents. We have then tried to reflect on such experience, drawing some conclusions and suggesting directions for future research.

Artificial agents participate of a double nature. As artificial systems, they have to be designed and built by human beings; as agents that must survive in a natural environment, they are close relatives of animals. Therefore, Behavior Engineers will have to produce a new synthesis of two realms, the one of Nature and the one of the Artificial, which are still far apart.

In the last fifteen years or so, models and technologies inspired by biological processes have received increasing attention. It seems to us that evolutionary computation in particular might open a full new range of possibilities for the designs of complex artifacts, and of artificial agents in particular.

Acknowledgments

This work has been partially supported by a MURST (Italian Ministry for University and Scientific and Technological Research) "60%" grant for the years 1992-94 to Marco Colombetti and by an Individual CEC Human Capital and Mobility Programme Fellowship to Marco Dorigo for the years 1994-1996. AutonoMouse II was designed and built by Graziano Ravizza. AutonoMouse V was designed and built by Franco Dorigo. We gratefully acknowledge the cooperation of Giuseppe Borghi (for the research activity on HAMSTER) and Mukesh Patel (for the research activity on CRAB).

Bibliography

Asimov, I. (1950). *I, Robot.* Gnome Press.

Brooks, R.A. (1991). Intelligence without representation. *Artificial Intelligence*, 47 (1-3), 139–159.

Brownston, L., F. Farrell, E. Kant & N. Martin (1985). *Programming expert systems in OPS5: An introduction to rule-based programming.* Addison-Wesley, Reading, MA.

Colombetti, M., & M. Dorigo (1994). Training agents to perform sequential behavior. Adaptive Behavior, 2 (3), 247–275.

Colombetti, M., M. Dorigo & G. Borghi (1996). Behavior Analysis and Training: A methodology for Behavior Engineering. *IEEE Transactions on Systems, Man, and Cybernetics-Part B*, 26 (3), in press.

Dorigo, M. (1992). Using transputers to increase speed and flexibility of genetics-based machine learning systems. *Microprocessing and Microprogramming Journal*, 34, 147–152.

Dorigo, M. (1993). Genetic and Non-Genetic Operators in Alecsys, *Evolutionary Computation Journal*, 1 (2), 151–164.

Dorigo, M., (1995). ALECSYS and the AutonoMouse: Learning to control a real robot by distributed clàssifier systems. *Machine Learning,* 19 (3), 209–240.

Dorigo, M., & M. Colombetti (1994a). Robot shaping: developing autonomous agents through learning. *Artificial Intelligence*, 71 (2), 321–370.

Dorigo, M., & M. Colombetti (1994b). The role of the trainer in reinforcement learning. *Proceedings of MLC-COLT '94 Workshop on Robot Learning*, S. Mahadevan *et al.* (Eds.), New Brunswick, NJ, 37–45.

Dorigo, M. & U. Schnepf (1993). Genetics-based machine learning and behavior based robotics: A new synthesis. *IEEE Transactions on Systems, Man, and Cybernetics*, 23 (1), 141–153.

Dorigo M. & E. Sirtori (1991). ALECSYS: A Parallel Laboratory for Learning Classifier Systems, *Proceedings of the Fourth International Conference on Genetic Algorithms*, San Diego, California, R.K. Belew & L.B. Booker (Eds.), Morgan Kaufmann, 296–302.

Fodor, J. (1985). The modularity of mind. Focal article with commentary, *Behavioral and Brain Sciences*, 8, 1–42.

Ghezzi, C., M. Jazayeri & D. Mandrioli (1991). *Fundamentals of Software Engineering*, Prentice-Hall, Englewood Cliffs, NJ.

Griffin, D.R. (1984). *Animal thinking.* Harvard University Press, Cambridge, MA.

Holland, J.H. (1980). Adaptive algorithms for discovering and using general patterns in growing knowledge bases, *International Journal of Policy Analysis and Information Systems,* 4 (2), 217–240.

Latombe, J.-C. (1991). *Robot motion planning.* Kluwer, Dordrecht, NE.

Lin, L-J. (1993). Hierarchical learning of robot skills by reinforcement., *Proceedings of 1993 IEEE International Conference on Neural Networks*, IEEE, 181–186.

Mahadevan, S., & J. Connell (1992). Automatic programming of behavior-based robots using reinforcement learning, *Artificial Intelligence*, 55 (2), 311–365.

McFarland, D. (Ed.) (1981). *The Oxford Companion to Animal Behaviour.* Oxford University Press, Oxford, UK.

Mondada F., E. Franzi & P. Ienne (1994). Mobile Robot Miniaturization: A Tool for Investigation in Control Algorithms. *Experimental Robotics III: Proceedings of the 3rd International Symposium on Experimental Robotics*, T. Yoshikawa and F. Miyazaki (Eds.), Springer–Verlag, 501–513.

Patel, M.J., M. Colombetti & M. Dorigo (1995). Evolutionary learning for intelligent automation: A case study. *Intelligent Automation and Soft Computing*, 1 (1), 29–42.

Prato Previde, E., M. Colombetti, M.D. Poli & E. Cenami Spada (1992). The mind of organisms: Some issues about animal cognition. Focal article with commentary, *International Journal of Comparative Psychology*, 6 (2), 79–119.

Robosoft SA (1991). Robuter™ User's Manual V3.1, Asnières, France.

Searle, J.R. (1992). *The rediscovery of the mind.* MIT Press, Cambridge, MA.

Wilson, S. (1987). Classifier systems and the Animat problem, *Machine Learning*, 2 (3), 199–228.

Chapter 3

A General Method for Incremental Self-improvement and Multi-agent Learning

J. Schmidhuber

I describe a novel paradigm for reinforcement learning (RL) with limited computational resources in realistic, non-resettable environments. The learner's policy is an arbitrary modifiable algorithm mapping environmental inputs and internal states to outputs and new internal states. Like in the real world, any event in system life and any learning process computing policy modifications may affect future performance and preconditions of future learning processes. There is no need for pre-defined "trials". At a given time in system life, there is only one single training example to evaluate the current long-term usefulness of any given previous policy modification, namely the average reinforcement per time since that modification occurred. At certain times in system life called checkpoints, such singular observations are used by a stack-based backtracking method which invalidates certain previous policy modifications, such that the history of still valid modifications corresponds to a history of long-term reinforcement accelerations (up until to the current checkpoint, each still valid modification has been followed by faster reinforcement intake than all the previous ones). Until the next checkpoint there is time to collect delayed reinforcement and to execute additional policy modifications; until then no previous policy modifications are invalidated; and until then the straight-forward, temporary generalization assumption is: each modification that until now appeared to contribute to an overall speed-up will remain useful. The paradigm provides a foundation for (1) "meta-learning", and (2) multi-agent learning. The principles are illustrated in (1) a single, self-referential, "evolutionary" system using an assembler-like programming language to modify its own policy, and to modify the way it modifies its policy, etc., and (2) another "evolutionary" system consisting of multiple agents, where each agent is in fact just a connection in a fully recurrent RL neural net.

The biggest difference between time and space is that you can't reuse time.

MERRICK FURST

3.1 Theoretical Considerations

Previous work on reinforcement learning (e.g., [16, 2, 49, 51]) requires strong assumptions about the environment. In many realistic settings, however, these assumptions do not hold. In particular, any event/action/experiment occurring early in the life of a learning system may influence events/actions/experiments at any later time. To address these important but previously mostly ignored issues, this paper describes a novel, general framework for single-life reinforcement learning with limited computational resources in rather general environments. The focus is on theoretical considerations. However, experiments in sections 3.3 and 3.4 will serve to illustrate the basic concepts.

Scenario. Consider a learning system executing a lifelong action sequence in an unknown environment. For now, it won't even be necessary to introduce a detailed formal model of the environment. Different system actions may require different amounts of execution time (like in scenarios studied in [25, 4], and in references given therein). Occasionally the environment provides real-valued "reinforcement". The sum of *all* reinforcements obtained between "system birth" (at time 0) and time $t > 0$ is denoted by $R(t)$. Throughout its lifetime, the system's goal is to maximize $R(T)$, the cumulative reinforcement at (initially unknown) "death" T. There is only one life. Time flows in *one* direction (no resets to zero). Related, but less general scenarios were studied in papers on "bandit problems" (e.g., [3, 9] and references therein), which also require to wisely use limited resources to perform experiments. See also [10] and references therein for work on finding search space elements with optimal expected utility, subject to the resource constraint of spending only a feasible amount of time on finding such an element.

Policy. The system's current policy is embodied by modifiable parameters of an arbitrary algorithm mapping environmental inputs and internal states to output actions and new internal states. For example, parameters may be bits of machine code, or weights of a neural net. The number of parameters needs not be fixed. For now, we won't need a detailed formal model of the policy.

Policy modification processes (PMPs). Policy parameters are occasionally modified by finite "policy modification processes" (PMPs), sometimes also called "learning processes". Different PMPs may take different amounts of time. The i-th PMP in system life is denoted PMP_i, starts at time $t_i^1 > 0$, ends at $t_i^2 < T$, $t_i^2 > t_i^1$, and computes a policy modification denoted by M_i. Later we will require that a non-zero time-interval passes between t_i^2 and t_{i+1}^1, the beginning of PMP_{i+1}. While PMP_i is running, the system's lifelong interaction sequence with the environment may continue, and there may be reinforcement signals, too. In fact, PMP_i may use environmental feedback to compute modification M_i — for instance, by executing a known reinforcement learning algorithm. Later I will even take advantage of the possibility that PMPs may be generated and executed according to information embedded in the policy itself — this is of interest in the context of "self-modifying" policies that "learn how to learn how to learn ...". For the moment, however, I do not care for what exactly happens while PMP_i is running: in what follows, I won't need a formal model of the PMP details. The following paragraphs are only concerned with the question: how do we measure modification M_i's influence on the remaining system life? In particular, how do we measure whether M_i successfully set the stage for later M_k, $k > i$?

The problem. In general environments, events/actions/experiments occurring early in system life may influence events/actions/experiments at any later time. In particular, PMP_i may affect the environmental conditions for $PMP_k, k > i$. This is not addressed by existing algorithms for adaptive control and reinforcement learning (see, e.g., [16, 2, 49, 51]), and not even by naive, inefficient, but more general and supposedly infallible *exhaustive search* among all possible policies, as will be seen next.

What's wrong with exhaustive search? Apart from the fact that exhaustive search is not considered practical even for moderate search spaces, it also suffers from another, more fundamental problem. Let n be the number of possible policies. For the sake of the argument, suppose that n is small enough to allow for systematic, sequential generate-and-test of all policies within the system life time. Suppose that after all policies have been generated (and evaluated for some time), during the remainder of system life, we keep the policy whose test brought about maximal reinforcement during the time it was tested. In the general "on-line" situation considered in this paper, *this may be the wrong thing to do:* for instance, each policy test may change the environment in a way that changes the preconditions for policies considered earlier. A policy discarded earlier may suddenly be the "best" policy (but will never be considered again). Similar things can be said about almost every other search algorithm or learning algorithm — exhaustive search is just a convenient, very simple, but representative example.

How to measure performance improvements? Obviously, the performance criterion used by naive exhaustive search (and other, less general search and learning algorithms) is not appropriate for the general set-up considered in this paper. We first have to ask: what is a reasonable performance criterion for such general (but typical) situations? More precisely: if we do not make any assumptions about the environment, can we still establish a sensible criterion according to which, at a certain time, (1) the system's performance throughout its previous life always kept improving or at least never got worse, and which (2) can be *guaranteed* to be achieved by the system? Indeed, such a criterion can be defined, as will be seen below. First we will need additional concepts.

Reinforcement/time ratios based on single observations. At a given time t in system life, we essentially have only one single "training example" to evaluate the current long-term usefulness of any given previous PMP, namely the *average reinforcement per time since that learning process occurred.* Suppose PMP_i started execution at time t_i^1 and completed itself at time $t_i^2 > t_i^1$. For $t \geq t_i^2$ and $t \leq T$, the reinforcement/time ratio $Q(i,t)$ is defined as

$$Q(i,t) = \frac{R(t) - R(t_i^1)}{t - t_i^1}.$$

The computation of reinforcement/time ratios takes into account all computation time, including time required by PMPs.

Why measure time starting from the beginning of PMP_i, instead of starting from its end? Later we will see that the first evaluations of PMP_i's performance will be delayed at least until after its end. While PMP_i is still running, it is in a "grace period" which may be used to collect *delayed* reinforcement to justify M_i — this is important when reinforcement signals occur long after policy modifications took place. Indeed, later I will make use of the fact that a "self-modifying" policy may determine the runtimes of its own PMPs, thus in principle being able to *learn* how long to wait for delayed reinforcement.

Currently valid modifications. After t_i^2, PMP_i's effects on the policy will stay in existence until (a) being overwritten by later PMP_k, $k > i$, or until (b) being *invalidated* by the "success-story algorithm" (SSA), the method to be described below. To define *valid modifications*, only (b) is relevant: after t_i^2, the policy modification M_i generated by PMP_i will remain *valid* as long as SSA (see below) does not discard M_i (by restoring the previous policy right before PMP_i started).

Success-story criterion (SSC). At time t, SSC is satisfied if for each PMP_i that computed a *still valid* modification M_i of the system's policy,

(a) $Q(i,t) > \frac{R(t)}{t}$, and

(b) for all $k < i$, where PMP_k computed a still valid M_k: $Q(i,t) > Q(k,t)$.

In words: SSC is satisfied if the beginning of each completed PMP that computed a still valid modification has been followed by long-term reinforcement acceleration — measured up until the current time. *Note that the success of some PMP depends on the success of all later PMPs, for which it is "setting the stage"*. This represents an essential difference to previous performance criteria.

The method to achieve SSC is called "success-story algorithm" (SSA). SSA uses a stack to trace and occasionally invalidate certain policy modifications. Details are next.

Success-story algorithm (SSA). SSA uses an initially empty stack to store information about currently valid policy changes computed by PMPs. Occasionally, at times called *"checkpoints"*, this information is used to restore previous policies, such that SSC holds (later we will see that a "self-modifying" policy can in principle *learn* to set checkpoints at appropriate times). SSA is based on two complementary kinds of processes:

(1) Pushing. Recall that PMP_i starts at time t_i^1 and ends at t_i^2. Let I_i denote a record consisting of the values t_i^1, $R(t_i^1)$ (which will be needed to compute $Q(i,t)$ values at later times t), plus the information necessary to restore the old policy (before modification by PMP_i). I_i is pushed onto the stack (this will consume time, of course). By definition, PMP_i is not finished until the entire pushing process is completed. From now on, the modification M_i will remain *valid* as long as I_i will remain on the stack.

(2) Popping. At certain times called *"checkpoints"* (see below), do:

> **WHILE** no time t is reached such that one of the following conditions (1-3) holds, **DO:** pop the topmost $I_.$-value off the stack, and *invalidate* the corresponding modification $M_.$, thus restoring the corresponding previous policy.
>
> (1) $Q(i,t) > Q(i',t)$, where $i > i'$, and M_i and $M_{i'}$ are the two most recent currently valid modifications (if existing),
>
> (2) $Q(i,t) > \frac{R(t)}{t}$, where M_i is the only currently valid modification (if existing),
>
> (3) the stack is empty.

For all PMP_i, *checkpoints* occur right before time t_i^1, such that, by definition, t_i^1 coincides with the end of the corresponding popping process (note that checkpoints themselves may be set by a "self-modifying" policy that determines beginnings and runtimes of its own PMPs — care has to be taken, however, to avoid PMPs with infinite duration; see section 3.2.2). The time consumed by pushing processes, popping processes, and all other computations is taken into account (for instance, time goes on as popping takes place).

> **Theorem 1.** Whenever popping is finished, SSA will have achieved SSC.
>
> **Proof sketch.** Induction over the stack contents after popping.

Note that SSA does not care for the nature of the PMPs — for all completed PMP_i (based, e.g., on conventional reinforcement learning algorithms), at each "checkpoint", SSA will get rid of M_i if t_i^1 was not followed by long-term reinforcement speed-up (note that before countermanding M_i, SSA will already have countermanded all $M_k, k > i$). No modification M_i is guaranteed to remain valid forever.

Generalization assumption. After popping, *until the next checkpoint*, SSA's straight-forward generalization assumption is: modifications that survived the most recent popping process (because they appeared to contribute to speed-up of average reinforcement intake) will remain useful. In general environments, which other generalization assumption would make sense? Recall that since life is one-way (time is never reset), at each checkpoint the system has to generalize from a *single* experience concerning the usefulness of any given previous learning process: the average reinforcement per time since that learning process occurred. Learning from singular experiences contrasts other, less realistic kinds of reinforcement learning, which, in one way or another, require the assumption that it is possible to collect sufficient statistics from *repeatable* training sequences.

To summarize: SSA again and again (at each checkpoint) implicitly evaluates each still valid policy modification as to whether it has been followed by long-term performance improvement (perhaps because the modification set the stage for later useful modifications). If there is evidence to the contrary, SSA invalidates policy modifications until SSC is fulfilled again. SSA's stack-based backtracking is efficient in the sense that only the two most recent ("topmost") still valid modifications need to be considered at a given time (although a *single* popping process may invalidate *many* modifications). SSA is a general framework — you can use your favorite learning algorithm A to generate the PMP. This makes sense especially in situations where the applicability of A is questionable because the environment does not satisfy the preconditions that would make A sound. SSA can at least guarantee that those of A's policy modifications that appear to have negative long-term effects are countermanded.

Note that a trivial way of satisfying SSC is to never make a policy modification. But any system that cannot let modification probabilities entirely vanish occasionally will execute policy modifications, and keep those consistent with SSC. In this sense, it cannot help but getting better, if the environment does indeed provide a chance to improve performance, given the set of possible actions.

Due to the generality of the approach, no reasonable statements can be made about improvement *speed*, which indeed highly depends on the nature of the environment and the choice of the action set. This lack is shared by almost all other reinforcement learning approaches, though.

Costs of environment-independence. A price to pay for environment-independence is this: the beginning of the time interval considered to measure the current reinforcement/time ratio is marked by the beginning of the PMP that computed the most recent valid policy modification. The length of this time interval may vary unpredictably, because its beginning may wander back in time due to policy restaurations by SSA. In arbitrary environments, SSA cannot guarantee speed-up of reinforcement per *fixed* time interval (no algorithm can).

Benefits of environment independence. Next we will see that SSA provides a novel basis for two notoriously difficult issues in machine learning: (*) Multi-agent learning, (**) "Learning how to learn".

(*) Multi-agent learning. Consider the case where there are multiple, interacting, SSA-learning agents. For each agent, the others are part of the changing (possibly complex) environment. This is the main reason why previous approaches to multi-agent learning are heuristic by nature. Not so with SSA, however: since SSA is environment-independent, each agent will still be able to satisfy its SSC after each checkpoint. In cases where all agents try to speed up the same reinforcement signals, and where no agent can speed up reinforcement intake by itself, this automatically enforces "learning to cooperate" [35, 36, 40]. Section 3.2.3 will illustrate this with an application of a system consisting of multiple agents, where each agent is in fact just a connection in a neural net.

(**) Learning how to learn / Incremental self-improvement. With SSA, the success of PMP_i recursively depends on the success of later PMP_k, $k > i$: the cumulative reinforcement collected after PMP_i includes the cumulative reinforcement collected after PMP_k, $k > i$. In particular, performance improvements include those improvements that make future additional improvements more likely: policy modification M_i can prove its long term usefulness by setting the stage for additional, useful modifications $M_k, k > i$, etc. Now recall that SSA does not care for the nature of the PMPs — they may depend on the system policy itself. If we allow a system's policy to change itself by computing and executing its own PMPs (this is easy to implement, e.g. by using instructions of an assembler-like, "self-referential" programming language as system actions — see section 3.2.2), then SSA will keep only those self-modifications followed by reinforcement speed-ups, in particular those leading to "better" future self-modifications, etc., recursively: embedding the learning mechanism within the system policy immediately and naturally leads to "incremental self-improvement" and "learning how to learn how to learn ..." — there is no circularity involved, and the approach remains sound.

Outline of remainder of paper. The main contribution of this paper is given by what has been said above. The remainder of this paper mainly serves to illustrate the theory. In section 3.2, I will exemplify the ideas in paragraph (**) on incremental self-improvement and describe a particular, concrete, working, "evolutionary" system that implements them. Section 3.3 will then apply this system to various tasks, including a variant of Sutton's maze task [47]. One difference to Sutton's original task is that the policy environment continually changes because of actions generated by the system itself. Section 3.4 will then exemplify the ideas in paragraph (*) on multi-agent learning and also describe a particular, concrete, working, "evolutionary" system that implements them.

With this system, each SSA-learning agent is in fact just a connection in a fully recurrent neural net. Each connection's policy is represented by its current weight. Connections do have a very limited policy space in comparison to typical, more complex agents used in standard AI — but this is irrelevant: SSA does not care for the complexity of the agents. A by-product of this research is a general reinforcement learning algorithm for recurrent nets. Again, an application to a variant of Sutton's maze task will serve to illustrate the operation of the system. In this application, the environment of each connection's policy continually changes, because the policies of all the other connections keep changing.

Note. This paper is based on [32]. In the meantime we have published several additional papers on SSA, e.g., [50, 53, 40, 42].

3.2 SSA for Incremental Self-Improvement

Outline. The "evolutionary" system in this section (see also [32]) implements the ideas from section 3.1, in particular those in paragraph (**) on "incremental self-improvement". To improve/speed up its own (initially very dumb, highly random) learning strategy, the system policy makes use of an assembler-like programming language suitable to modify the policy itself. The policy actually is a set of conditional, modifiable probability distributions (initially maximum entropy distributions) on a set of assembler-like instructions. These distributions are required to compute the probability of the assembler-like instruction to be executed next (the system executes a lifelong sequence of such instructions). The PMP_i from section 3.1 are self-delimiting "sequences of self-modifications" (SSMs). SSMs are special instruction subsequences (generated according to the current policy) that define their own beginning and their own end (by executing special instructions). With the help of special "self-referential" instructions, SSMs can compute almost arbitrary policy modifications (which actually are sequences of probability modifications). Policy modifications can be computed only by SSMs. SSMs affect the probabilities of future SSMs, which affect the probabilities of future SSMs, etc. These recursive effects are automatically taken care of by SSA: following the SSA principle, whenever an SSM computes a policy modification, information required to restore original probability distributions and to compute reinforcement/time ratios for currently valid modifications is pushed on a stack. After each instruction executed outside an SSM, the system runs a popping process (see section 3.1). It can be *guaranteed* that the system, after each action executed outside an SSM, will achieve SSC (→ "learning how to learn"). In principle, the system can learn to deal with arbitrary reward delays by determining the lengths of its SSMs — SSMs define checkpoints (see section 3.1) by themselves.

The system is "evolutionary" in the sense that it lets survive only those (initially highly random) policy modifications that were followed by long-term reinforcement acceleration. The system has been implemented and tested on (non-Markovian) toy tasks in changing environments. The experiments illustrate the theoretical predictions: the system computes action subsequences leading to faster and faster reinforcement intake (section 3.3). Due to the generality of the approach, however, no reasonable statements can be made about improvement *speed*, which indeed highly depends on the nature of the environment and the choice of initial primitive instructions.

Storage. The system's *storage* is a single array of cells. Each cell has an integer address in the interval $[Min, Max]$. Max is a positive integer. Min is a negative integer. a_i denotes the cell with address i. The variable contents of a_i are denoted by $c_i \in [-Maxint, Maxint]$, and are of type integer as well ($Maxint \geq Max$; $Maxint \geq abs(Min)$). Special addresses, $InputStart$, $InputEnd$, $RegisterStart$, and $ProgramStart$, are used to further divide storage into segments: $Min < InputStart \leq InputEnd < 0 = RegisterStart < ProgramStart < Max$. The *input area* is the set of *input cells* $\{a_i : InputStart \leq i \leq InputEnd\}$. The *register area* is the set of *register cells* $\{a_i : 0 \leq i < ProgramStart\}$. "Registers" are convenient for indirect-addressing purposes. The *program area* is the set of *program cells* $\{a_i : ProgramStart \leq i < Max\}$. Integer sequences in the program area are interpreted as executable code. The *work area* is the set of *work cells* $\{a_i : Min \leq i < ProgramStart\}$. Instructions executed in the program area may read from and write to the work area. Both register area and input area are subsets of the work area.

Environmental inputs. At every time step, new inputs from the environment may be written into the input cells.

Primitives. The assembler-like programming language is partly inspired by the one in [33, 38]. There are n_{ops} primitive instructions

($n_{ops} << Maxint$). Each "primitive" is represented by a unique number in the set $\{0, 1, \ldots, n_{ops} - 1\}$ (due to the code being written in C). The primitive with number j is denoted by p_j. Primitives may have from zero to three arguments, each of which has a value in $\{0, 1, \ldots, n_{ops} - 1\}$. The semantics of the primitives and their corresponding arguments are given in Table 3.1. The non-self-referential ("normal") primitives include actions for comparisons, and conditional jumps, for copying storage contents, for initializing certain storage cells with small integers, and for adding, subtracting, multiplying, and dividing. They also include output actions for modifying the environment, and input actions for perceiving environmental states. The "self-referential" primitives will be described in detail below.

Primitive and argument probabilities. For each cell a_i in the program area, there is a discrete probability distribution P_i over the set of possible cell contents. There is a variable *InstructionPointer (IP)* which always points to one of the program cells (initially to the first one). If $IP = i$ and $i < Max - 3$, then P_{ij} denotes the probability of selecting primitive p_j as the next instruction. The restriction $i < Max - 3$ is needed to leave room for the instruction's possible arguments should it require any. Once p_j is selected: $c_i \leftarrow j$. If p_j has a first argument, then $P_{i+1,k}$ is the probability of k being chosen as its actual value, for $k \in \{0, 1, \ldots, n_{ops} - 1\}$. Once some k is selected: $c_{i+1} \leftarrow k$. Analoguously, if p_j has a second argument, then $P_{i+2,l}$ is the probability of l being chosen as its actual value, for $l \in \{0, 1, \ldots, n_{ops} - 1\}$. Once some l is selected: $c_{i+2} \leftarrow l$. And finally, if p_j has a third argument, then $P_{i+3,m}$ is the probability of m being chosen as its actual value, for $m \in \{0, 1, \ldots, n_{ops} - 1\}$. Once some m is selected: $c_{i+3} \leftarrow m$.

Double indexed addressing. Although program cells can take on only few values, the use of double-indexed addressing allows for addressing the entire storage: a parameter in a program cell may point to a work cell with a small address. The content of this work cell, however, does not have essential limits, and may point to any address in storage. See [11, 53, 42, 40, 39], however, for alternative implementations without double indexed addressing.

Current policy. The set of all current P-values defines the system's *current policy.*

Instruction cycle. A single step of the *interpreter* works as follows: if *IP* points to program cell a_i, a primitive and the corresponding arguments are chosen randomly according to the current probability distributions, as already described. They are sequentially written onto the program area, starting from a_i. Syntax checks are performed. Rules for syntactic correctness are given in the caption of Table 3.1. If syntactically correct, the instruction gets executed. This may result in modifications of *IP* and/or environment and/or storage. If the instruction did not change the value of *IP* (e.g. by causing a jump), *IP* is set to the address of the cell following the last argument of the current instruction. If the instruction is syntactically incorrect, *IP* is reset to the first program cell. This *instruction cycle* represents the basic operation of the system.

System life. At time step 0, storage is initialized with zeros. The probability distributions of all program cells are initialized with maximum entropy distributions [44]. That is, all P_{ij} values are initialized to the same value, so that there is no bias for a particular value in any cell. After initialization, the *instruction cycle* is repeated over and over again until system death at time T. Recall that T does not have to be known in advance.

Storage as part of the environment. After initialization at time 0, the storage cells are never re-initialized: the storage has to be viewed as part of the total enviroment of the system policy. The storage is like an external notebook. Notes written into the notebook may influence future actions[1]. Notes may represent useful memories, or may have harmful long term effects.

Self-referential primitives. Two special primitives, *DecP* and *IncP*, may be used to address and modify the current probability distribution of any program cell (see Table 3.1). With the action *DecP*, the P_{ij} value for a particular cell/value pair (a_i, j) can be decreased by some factor in {0.01, 0.02, ..., 0.99}. The probabilities for that cell are then normalized. Likewise, with the action *IncP*, the *complement* $(1 - P_{ij})$ of the P_{ij} value for a particular cell a_i and value j can be decreased by a factor in $\{0.01, 0.02, \ldots, 0.99\}$ (and the cell probabilities are again renormalized). *DecP* and *IncP* have no effect if the indirectly addressed cell contents $c_{c_{a3}}$ (see Table 3.1) are not an integer between 1 and 99,

[1] Leslie Kaelbling sometimes refers to this as *"writing on the walls"* but says that the "real" name is *"stigmergy"* (personal communication, 1994/1995).

or if the corresponding probability modification would lead to at least one P-value below *MinP* (a small positive constant).

The primitive *GetP* can be used to write scaled versions of current probability values into work cells. *GetP* is potentially useful for purposes of introspection.

There is also another self-referential instruction, *EndSelfMod()*, that helps to group a sequence of probability-modifying instructions and other instructions into self-delimiting self-modification sequences (see below).

Primitive	Semantics
Return()	$IP \leftarrow ProgramStart$
Jmp(a1)	$IP \leftarrow c_{a1}$
Jmpleq(a1, a2, a3)	If $c_{c_{a1}} < c_{c_{a2}}$ $IP \leftarrow c_{a3}$
Jmpeq(a1, a2, a3)	If $c_{c_{a1}} = c_{c_{a2}}$ $IP \leftarrow c_{a3}$
Add(a1, a2, a3)	$c_{c_{a3}} \leftarrow c_{c_{a1}} + c_{c_{a2}}$
Sub(a1, a2, a3)	$c_{c_{a3}} \leftarrow c_{c_{a1}} - c_{c_{a2}}$
Mul(a1, a2, a3)	$c_{c_{a3}} \leftarrow c_{c_{a1}} * c_{c_{a2}}$
Div(a1, a2, a3)	$c_{c_{a3}} \leftarrow c_{c_{a1}} / c_{c_{a2}}$ (integer division)
Rem(a1, a2, a3)	$c_{c_{a3}} \leftarrow$ remainder$(c_{c_{a1}} / c_{c_{a2}})$
Inc(a1)	$c_{c_{a1}} \leftarrow c_{c_{a1}} + 1$
Dec(a1)	$c_{c_{a1}} \leftarrow c_{c_{a1}} - 1$
Mov(a1, a2)	$c_{c_{a2}} \leftarrow c_{c_{a1}}$
Init(a1, a2)	$c_{a1-ProgramStart-2} \leftarrow a2$
Output$_i$(...)	i-th problem specific primitive for influencing the environment
Input$_i$(...)	i-th primitive for perceiving environmental input
GetP(a1, a2, a3)	$c_{c_{a3}} \leftarrow round(Maxint * P_{c_{a1},c_{a2}})$
IncP(a1, a2, a3)	$\forall k \neq c_{a2} : P_{c_{a1},k} \leftarrow 0.01 c_{c_{a3}} P_{c_{a1},k}$; $P_{c_{a1},c_{a2}} \leftarrow 1 - 0.01 c_{c_{a3}} (1 - P_{c_{a1},c_{a2}})$
DecP(a1, a2, a3)	$\forall k \neq c_{a2} : P_{c_{a1},k} \leftarrow \frac{1 - 0.01 c_{c_{a3}} P_{c_{a1},c_{a2}}}{1 - P_{c_{a1},c_{a2}}} P_{c_{a1},k}$; $P_{c_{a1},c_{a2}} \leftarrow 0.01 c_{c_{a3}} P_{c_{a1},c_{a2}}$
EndSelfMod()	Enable top level strategy for restoring probabilities (see text)

Table 3.1: *Semantics of primitives and their parameters. The "normal" primitives are shown in the top block; the "self-referential" primitives are shown in the bottom block. Note the extensive use of double-indexed indirect addressing. Results of arithmetic operations leading to underflow/overflow are replaced by $-Maxint/Maxint$, respectively. The same holds for positive and negative divisions by zero.* DecP *and* IncP *have no effect if the indirectly addressed cell contents $c_{c_{a3}}$ are not an integer between 1 and 99, or if the corresponding probability modification would lead to at least one P value below* MinP. **Rules for syntactic correctness:** *IP may point to any program cell a_i, $i < Max - 3$ (enough space has to be left for arguments). Operations that read cell contents (such as* Add, Move, Jumpleq *etc.) may read only from existing addresses in storage. Operations that write cell contents (such as* Add, Move, GetP *etc.) may write only into work area addresses in* $[Min, ProgramStart - 1]$.

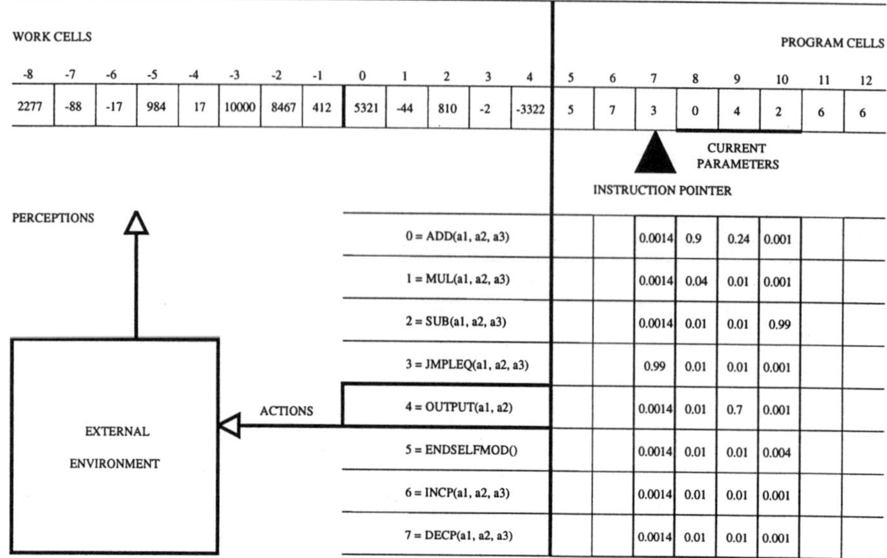

Figure 3.1: *Snapshot of parts of policy and storage (which is part of the policy environment). There are positive and negative addresses. In this hypothetical example, program cells start at address 5. Work cells end at address 4. For each program cell, there is a variable probability distibution on the* n_{ops} *possible cell contents (shown only for cells 7, 8, 9, 10 — for simplicity, in this hypothetical example,* $n_{ops} = 8$*, and there is only one output instruction for manipulating the external environment). IP currently points to cell 7. With high probability (0.99), cell 7 is filled with a 3, which stands for instruction* Jmpleq. Jmpleq *requires 3 parameters: the contents of cells 8, 9, 10 (generated according to the corresponding probability distributions — in the example, the most likely values are chosen). Due to double indexed addressing, the semantics of the current instruction are: if the content of cell 5321 is smaller than the contents of cell -3322, then jump to cell 810.*

Self-delimiting sequences of self-modifications (SSMs). They correspond to the PMP from section 3.1. The beginning of the first *IncP* or *DecP* after an *EndSelfMod()* action or after system "birth" begins an SSM. The SSM ends itself by executing *EndSelfMod()*. Some of the (initially highly random) action subsequences executed during system life will indeed be SSMs. They can compute almost arbitrary sequences of modifications of P_{ij} values, resulting in almost arbitrary modifications of context-dependent probabilities of future action subsequences, including future SSMs. However, due to *MinP* being positive, the probability of selecting and executing a particular instruction at a particular time cannot entirely vanish. In agreement with section 3.1, the i-th SSM is called PMP_i.

Keeping track with a stack. Following the SSA principle, whenever the system uses *IncP* or *DecP* to modify one of its probability distributions, the following values are pushed onto a stack S: the current time, total reinforcement so far, the address of the modified program cell, its old probability distribution right before the current modification (represented by n_{ops} real values), and a pointer to the stack entry corresponding to the first probability modification computed by the current SSM. This information is needed by the SSA popping process to be described later. More formally:

The k-th entry of S, $k \in \{0, 1, \ldots, StackSize\}$, is denoted $S(k)$. $S(k)$ consists of the following variables: $S(k).t$, $S(k).R$, $S(k).address$, $S(k).oldP$ (a vector of n_{ops} variables), and $S(k).first$. The variable sp points to the current topmost stack entry ($sp = 0$ at system startup). The zeroth stack entry, which cannot be popped, is initialized as follows: $S(0).t \leftarrow 0$; $S(0).R \leftarrow 0$; $S(0).first \leftarrow 0$. The remaining values are undefined. If some SSM modifies some probability distribution P_i at time t (by using $IncP$ or $DecP$), sp is incremented, $S(sp).t \leftarrow t$; $S(sp).R \leftarrow R(t)$; $S(sp).address \leftarrow i$; $S(sp).oldP \leftarrow P_i$ *before* the modification (represented by n_{ops} real values). If t marks the beginning of an SSM then $S(sp).first \leftarrow sp$. Otherwise (in between beginning and end of an SSM), $S(sp).first \leftarrow S(sp-1).first$.

SSA popping processes. Popping occurs right before the first pushing process of each SSM, and also after each instruction except when an SSM is running (these are the possible additional checkpoints referred to in section 3.1): "old" probability distributions are successively popped and restored, until SSC (see section 3.1) is satisfied. Of course, the computation time required for pushing and popping probability distributions etc. is taken into account when reinforcement/time ratios are computed. More formally (t denotes the current time):

While $sp \neq 0$ **and**

$$\frac{R(t) - S(S(sp).first).R}{t - S(S(sp).first).t} \leq \frac{R(t) - S(S(S(sp).first - 1).first).R}{t - S(S(S(sp).first - 1).first).t}$$

do: $P_{S(sp).i} \leftarrow S(sp).oldP; \quad sp \leftarrow sp - 1.$

Note: t increases during execution of the while loop.

Lemma 1. According to the SSA principle (section 3.1), after each instruction (except during the execution of an SSM), an SSA popping process ensures that the beginning of each completed SSM that computed still valid probability modifications has been followed by *faster* reinforcement intake than the beginnings of all previous such SSMs.

Proof sketch. Induction over the stack contents after popping, in analogy to proof of Theorem 1, section 3.1.

Arbitrary reward delays. The *EndSelfMod()* instruction allows the system to delay SSA's evaluations of probability modifications arbitrarily (the expectation of the delay remains finite, however, due to $MinP$ being positive). These checkpoint setting capabilities are important, for two reasons: (1) In general, reinforcement events will be separated by long (unknown) time lags. Hence, novel probability modifications are not necessarily bad if they do not lead to immediate reinforcement. In principle, the system itself can learn how much time to spend on waiting for first reinforcement events. (2) Two successive modifications of two particular probability distributions may turn out to be beneficial, while each by itself may be harmful. For this reason, the system is allowed to compute arbitrary sequences of probability modifications, before facing SSA's evaluations.

Delaying evaluations *does* cost time, though, which is taken into account by SSA. In the long run, the system is encouraged to create useful SSMs of the appropriate size.

Accelerating reinforcement intake. Lemma 1 shows: the scheme keeps only modifications caused by SSMs followed by faster and faster reinforcement intake, thus satisfying SSC from section 3.1. Due to non-vanishing probabilities of arbitrary action sequences (recall that *MinP* is positive), the system will eventually discover a way to improve its current performance, if there is any.

Learning how to learn. Performance improvements include improvements that make future improvements more likely: SSMs can prove their long term usefulness by setting the stage for additional, useful SSMs, which potentially include SSMs executing known (and not yet known) learning algorithms. The success of an SSM recursively depends on the success of all later SSMs. SSA automatically takes care of this, thus recursively encouraging "learning how to learn how to learn ...". This represents an essential difference to previous approaches to "continual" learning, see [24].

Improvement speed? Due to the generality of the approach, no reasonable statements can be made about improvement *speed*, which indeed highly depends on the nature of the environment and the choice of initial primitive instructions. This lack is shared by almost all other reinforcement learning approaches, though. Note, however, that unlike previous, less general systems, the novel system in principle can exploit almost arbitrary environmental regularities [14, 5, 45, 21] (if there are any) to speed up performance improvement, simply because it can run almost arbitrary learning algorithms. For instance, in principle, unlike previous evolutionary and genetic algorithms [23, 43, 13, 12, 15], the system can learn to focus its modifications on interfaces between useful "subprograms" (*"divide and conquer"*), instead of mutating the subprograms themselves (if this proves to be beneficial in a given environment), thus creating a higher-level, more abstract search space ($\rightarrow$ directed mutations as opposed to random mutations). Just as evolution "discovered" that having the "genetic crossover operator" was a "good thing", the system is potentially able to discover that various more directed search strategies are "good things". There is just no feasible way of predicting the precise nature of such speed-ups.

How many environments are regular? The last paragraph mentioned that the novel system in principle can exploit almost arbitrary environmental regularities, if there are any. One might ask: how likely is it that a given environment contains regularities at all? How many environments do indeed allow for successful generalization from previous experience? A recent debate in the machine-learning community highlighted a fact that appears discouraging at first glance: in general, generalization cannot be expected, inductive inference is impossible, and nothing can be learned. See, e.g., [8, 26, 52, 31, 38, 37]. Paraphrasing from a previous argument [38, 37]: let the task be to learn some relation between finite bitstrings and finite bitstrings. Somehow, a training set is chosen. In almost all cases, the shortest algorithm computing a (non-overlapping) test set essentially has the same size as the whole test set. This is because most computable objects are irregular and incompressible [14, 5]. The shortest algorithm computing the test set, given the training set, isn't any shorter. In other words, the relative algorithmic complexity of the test set, given the training set, is maximal, and the mutual algorithmic information between test set and training set is zero (ignoring an additive constant independent of the problem — see [14, 5, 45, 21]). Therefore, in almost all cases, (1) knowledge of the training set does not provide any clues about the test set, (2) there is no hope for generalization, and (3) inductive inference does not make any sense. Similarly, almost all possible environments are "hostile" in the sense that they don't provide regularities exploitable by *any* learning algorithm. This may seem discouraging.

Atypical real world. Apparently, however, generalization and inductive inference *do* make sense in the real world! One reason for this may be that the real world is run by a short algorithm. See, e.g., [37]. Anyway, problems that humans consider to be *typical* are *atypical* when compared to the general set of all well-defined problems. Otherwise, things like "learning by analogy", "learning by chunking", "incremental learning", "continual learning", "learning from invariances", "learning by knowledge transfer" etc. would not be possible, and experience with previous problems could not help to sensibly adjust the prior distribution of solution candidates in the search space for a new problem (shift of inductive bias, e.g. [48]).

To repeat: an interesting feature of incremental self-improvement is that its theoretical potential for exploiting environmental regularities, if there are any, exceeds the corresponding potential of previous learning systems.

3.3 Illustrative Experiments

The main purpose of this paper was to describe a theoretically sound principle for environment-independent, "one-way", single-life reinforcement learning. To illustrate basic aspects of the principle, the remainder of this paper will also present a few experiments. These, however, in no way represent a systematic experimental analysis. In fact, many much more complex experiments are described in other recent papers on this subject, e.g., [50, 42, 40].

The experiments in the current section demonstrate that the system from section 3.2 indeed can learn to compute SSMs leading to faster and faster reinforcement intake. The system uses low-level problem-specific instructions in addition to the 17 general, assembler-like instructions mentioned in section 3.2. The instructions reflect the system's initial (weak) bias. Of course, different problem-specific instructions lead to different initial bias and performance (even the primitive *numbers* may influence performance, because numbers of executed primitives appear in the corresponding program cells — later, these numbers may be abused, e.g., as addresses, or as arguments of arithmetic operations). In a given environment, reinforcement intake may be greatly accelerated within a few minutes using one set of instructions. However, the same degree of improvement may require a day of computation time using a different set of instructions. The purpose of this section, however, is *not* to perform a statistically significant experimental evaluation of the system's initial bias, or to study effects of introducing different kinds of initial bias, or to compare the system to other learning systems with different initial bias. Instead, this section's purpose is to illustrate typical aspects of the system's basic (bias independent) mode of operation. See, e.g., [42, 40] for more complex applications.

3.3.1 Writing Variable Sequences

Task. The external environment consists of an array of 30 variables $V_0, V_1, \ldots, V_{29}$. The i-th variable is denoted by V_i. Its current contents are denoted by $C_i \in [-Maxint, Maxint]$. Time is measured in discrete time steps. At time step 0, all variables are initialized with zeros. Every 1000 time steps, *the number of variables whose values equal their*

Primitive	Semantics
Write(a1, a2)	$C_{c_{a2}} \leftarrow c_{c_{a1}}$
Read(a1, a2)	$c_{c_{a1}} \leftarrow C_{c_{a2}}$

Table 3.2: *Semantics of problem specific primitives and their parameters. Again, double-indexed indirect addressing is employed. See text for rules for syntactic correctness. Compare with Table 3.1.*

addresses is counted and written into a special input cell. This number is the current payoff. Then, all variables are re-initialized with zeros. The goal is to maximize cumulative payoff.

Details. In addition to the 17 general primitives from Table 3.1 (not counting input/output primitives), there are two problem-specific primitives. Each has two integer arguments: $Write(a1, a2)$ writes the contents of the storage cell indirectly addressed by the first argument into the variable indirectly addressed by the second argument. $Read(a1, a2)$ writes the contents of the variable indirectly addressed by the second argument into the work cell indirectly addressed by the second argument. See Table 3.2. Between two payoff events, each variable may be written only once (additional write operations have no effect). Write and read operations outside the valid ranges halt the current run.

Since $n_{ops} = 17 + 2 = 19$, all initial probabilities of all possible contents of all program cells are equal to $\frac{1}{19}$. Parameters for storage size etc. are: $Min = -1000$, $Max = 100$, $ProgramStart = bottom(\frac{n_{ops}}{2})$, $MinP = 0.001$, $StackSize = 10,000$, $Maxint = 100,000$. To inform the system about what is going on, the following values are written into special input cells whenever they change: *IP*, *sp*, and the remainder of $t/Maxint$ (integer division, where t denotes the current time).

Measuring time. By definition, each computation that requires the consideration of all n_{ops} probabilities of some program cell (such as selecting an instruction, selecting a parameter, pushing or popping probability distributions, etc.) costs one time step. Other computations do not cost anything. This ensures that measured time is of the order of total cpu-time. The somewhat unelegant way of measuring time was introduced because measuring cpu-time *directly* on our multi-user machine turned out to be somewhat unreliable.

How difficult is this task? For a number of reasons, the task is non-trivial — the system does not appear to have much built-in bias towards the task: (1) Only one of the 19 primitives ($Write$) may affect variable contents at all. But initially, the system does not even have such seemingly trivial knowledge — there is no built-in idea about which actions may lead to payoff. Therefore, it has to find out on its own. (2) The values referred to by the two arguments of $Write$ have to be identical and within the required ranges to lead to a useful result. (3) There are 30 *different* variables with 30 different values. Only one of them, namely V_0, is correctly re-initialized with its own address after each payoff event. (4) The most significant difficulty, however, is the continually changing policy environment.

Changing policy environment. The fact that the external variables are occasionally reset does not imply that the policy environment does not change. In fact, many actions executed by the system change the contents of storage cells, which are *never* reset: as mentioned above, storage cells are like an external notebook and have to be viewed as part of the environment — typically, there are no exactly repeatable trials with identical initial conditions. And the storage cells are not just a negligible nuisance — they are essential for computing parameters for (e.g., self-modifying) instructions. To achieve significant performance improvement, the environmental conditions *have to* change due to actions executed by the system itself. This is an aspect that cannot be dealt with by *any* traditional reinforcement learning system, not even by naive exhaustive search, in a way that is sound.

Comparison. Performance was measured with and without self-modification capabilities. In the latter case, the primitives $IncP$ and $DecP$ had no effect. Both versions were run for $5 * 10^9$ time steps, corresponding to $5 * 10^6$ payoff events. Note that the *optimal* cumulative payoff is $1.5 * 10^8$. This value can be achieved only by a system with "optimal" prior bias — starting at birth, such a system keeps executing optimal actions without having to learn anything.

Results Without Self-Modifications

At system death, total payoff equaled about $7 * 10^6$. Average payoff per payoff event was about 1.4. Most of the total payoff (about $5*10^6$) could be attributed to the fact that V_0 was correctly re-initialized after each payoff event: the system received a little bit of payoff even in cases where it did not execute any *write* operations. As expected, average payoff intake did not significantly increase or decrease during the lifetime of the system. However, this was not *safely* predictable in advance, due to the changing environment.

Results With Self-Modifications

At system death, total payoff was about $1.16 * 10^8$ (recall that the theoretical optimum for a non-learning system with optimal initial bias would be $1.5*10^8$). To find out whether the incremental self-improvement paradigm did indeed lead to incremental self-improvement, let us have a look at the learning history (the results are slightly different from those reported in [32], where a slightly different implementation led to different calls of the random number generator).

Self-generated reduction of numbers of probability modifications. In the beginning, the system computed a lot of probability modifications but later preferred to decrease the number of probability modifications per time interval. After 10^9 time steps, there were about 350,000 probability modifications per 10^8 time steps. After $2 * 10^9$ time steps, there were about 40,000 probability modifications per 10^8 time steps. Towards system death, there were about 20,000 probability modifications per 10^8 time steps. Most of the useful SSMs computed either one or two probability modifications.

Speed-up of payoff intake. After 10^8 time steps, the system already behaved much more deterministically than in the beginning. Average payoff per payoff event had increased from 1.4 to 15.8 (the optimal value being 30.0, of course), and the stack had 70 entries. These entries corresponded to 66 modifications of single cell probability distributions, computed by 45 SSMs — each being more "useful" than all the previous ones. *Storage already looked very messy.* For instance, almost all cells in the work area were filled with (partly big) integers quite different from the initial values. Recall that the storage is never re-initialized and has to be viewed as part of the policy environment.

First maximal payoff. After 1,436,383 payoff events, the system correctly had written *all* 30 variables for the first time, and received maximal payoff 30.0. Due to remaining non-determinism in the system, the current *average* payoff per payoff event (measured shortly afterwards, at time step 1,500,000,000) was about 21.7.

After 3,000,000 payoff events, current average payoff per payoff event was 25.6. But the stack had only 206 entries (corresponding to 174 "useful" SSMs). After 5,000,000 payoff events (at "system death"), the current average was about 26.0, with ongoing tendency to increase. By then, there were 224 stack entries. They corresponded to 192 SSMs, each being more "useful" than all the previous ones.

Temporary speed-ups of performance improvement. Performance did *not* increase smoothly during the lifetime of the system. Sometimes, no significant improvement took place for a time interval comparable to the entire learning time so far. Such "boring" time intervals were somtimes ended by unexpected sequences of rather quick improvements. Then progress slowed down again. Such temporary speed-ups of performance improvement indicate useful shifts of inductive bias, which may later be replaced by inductive bias created by the next "breakthrough".

Evidence of "learning how to learn"? A look at the stack entries revealed that many (but far from all) *useful* probability modifications focused on few program cells. Often, SSMs directly changing the probabilities of future SSMs were considered useful. For instance, 9 of the 224 stack entries at time step $5 * 10^9$ corresponded to "useful" probability modifications of the (self-referential) $IncP$ action of the second program cell. Numerous entries corresponded to "useful" modifications of the *EndSelfMod* probability of various cells. Such stack entries may be interpreted as results of "adjusting the prior on the space of solution candidates" or "fine-tuning search space structure" or "learning to create directed mutations" or "learning how to learn".

3.3.2 A Navigation Task

Non-Markovian variant of Sutton's Markovian maze task [47], with changing policy environment. The external environment consists of a two-dimensional grid with 9 by 6 fields. $F_{i,j}$ denotes the field in the i-th row and the j-th column. The following fields are blocked by obstacles: $F_{3,3}$, $F_{3,4}$, $F_{3,5}$, $F_{6,2}$, $F_{8,4}$, $F_{8,5}$, $F_{8,6}$. In the beginning, an artificial "animat" is placed on $F_{1,4}$ (the start field). In addition to the 17 general primitives from Table 3.1 (not counting input/output primitives), there are four problem-specific primitives with obvious meaning: *one-step-north()*, *one-step-south()*, *one-step-east()*, *one-step-west()*. The system cannot execute actions that would lead outside the grid or into an obstacle. Again, the following values are written into special cells in the input area whenever they change: *IP*, *sp*, $remainder(t/Maxint)$. Another input cell is filled with a 1 whenever the animat is on the goal field, otherwise it is filled with a 0. There is only one way the animat can partially observe aspects of the external world: four additional input cells are rewritten after each execution of some problem-specific primitive — the first (second, third, fourth) cell is filled with $Maxint$ if the field to the north (south, east, west) of the animat is blocked or does not exist, otherwise the cell is filled with $-Maxint$. *Whenever the animat reaches $F_{9,6}$ (the goal field), the system receives a constant payoff (100), and the animat is transferred back to $F_{1,4}$ (the start field).* Parameters for storage size etc. are the same as with the previous task, and time is measured the same way. Clearly, to maximize cumulative payoff, the system has to find short paths from start to goal.

Why this task is non-trivial. Unlike previous reinforcement learning systems, the system does *not* have a smart initial strategy for temporal credit assignment — it has to develop its own such strategies. Unlike with Sutton's original set-up, the system does not see a built-in unique representation of its current position on the grid. Its interface to the environment is non-Markovian [28]. This represents one reason why most traditional reinforcement learning systems do *not* have a sound strategy for solving this task. Another is the changing policy environment. See next paragraph.

Changing policy environment. The fact that the obstacles remain where they are and that the animat is occasionally reset to its start position does not imply that the policy environment does not change. In fact, many actions executed by the system change the contents of storage cells, which are *never* reset: as mentioned above, storage cells

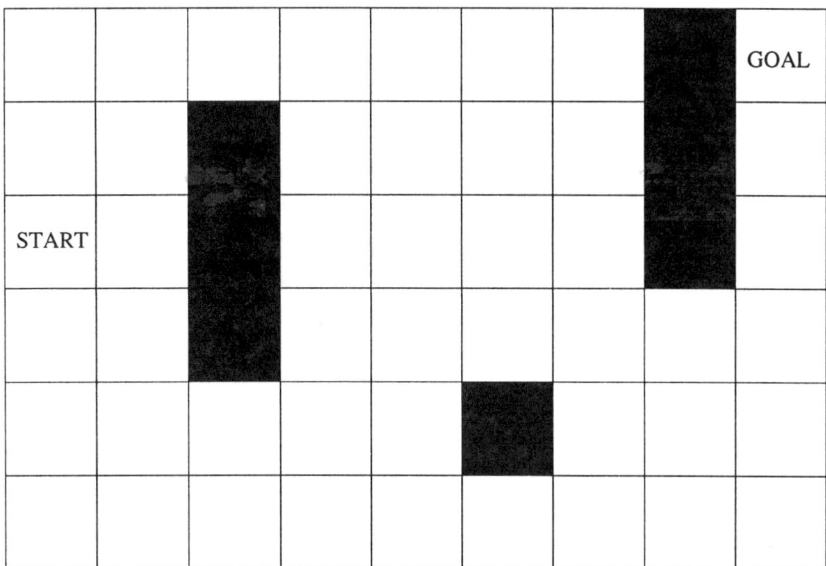

Figure 3.2: *Sutton's partially observable maze. It is a small part of the policy environment, which also includes storage cells with changing contents. See figure 3.1.*

are like an external notebook and have to be viewed as part of the policy environment — there are no exactly repeatable trials with identical initial conditions.

Results without Self-Modifications

As with the previous task, the system was first tested for 10^{10} time steps with self-referential primitives $IncP$ and $DecP$ being switched off. Average trial length (number of time steps required to move from start to goal) was about 12600. This is consistent with results obtained by using Sutton's original set-up.

Results with Self-Modifications

At system death (at time 10^{10}), average trial length (including time required for SSA's pushing and popping processes, of course) was down to 56.6 time steps — more than 200 times faster than without self-improvement, and with ongoing tendency to decrease. Comparable results were obtained with additional runs.

As with the previous task, performance did not improve smoothly. The history of broken records reflects the history of performance improvements (the results from the run reported below are slightly different from those reported in [32], where a slightly different implementation led to different calls of the random number generator).

First, there was a rather quick sequence of improvements which lasted until time $4.6 * 10^7$. By then (after 155,741 payoff events), the shortest trial so far had taken 44 time steps. Then, the "current record" did not improve any more for a comparatively long time interval: $1.14 * 10^8$ time steps — the length of this "boring" time interval by far exceeded the entire previous learning time.

Sudden improvement speed-up. Then, quite unexpected to the observer, the system started to create a new sequence of additional improvements around time step $1.6 * 10^8$. At time $1.6 * 10^8$, the record was down to 42. At time $1.7 * 10^8$, the record was down to 40. At time $1.9 * 10^8$, the record was down to 38. At time $2.0 * 10^8$, the record was down to 36. Then, performance improvement slowed down again.

Similarly, much later, at time $2.4 * 10^9$, the record was 26. Then, not much happened during the next 10^9 time steps. Suddenly, a new sequence of additional improvements started around time step $3.4 * 10^9$. At time $3.429 * 10^9$, the record was down to 24. At time $3.432 * 10^9$, the record was down to 22. At time $3.486 * 10^9$, the record was down to 20. Throughout this flurry of broken records, the number of stack entries steadily increased to 199. Apparently, the system made a little "revolutionary" discovery that permitted a sequence of smoother, additional directed self-mutations.

Final system state. At system death (time step 10^{10}), the record was down to 19. The system's average payoff intake per time interval still had a tendency to increase. All in all, there were nearly $5 * 10^6$ SSMs during system life. The effects of only 200 of them, however, turned out to be worth keeping (the others were countermanded by SSA): these 200 computed a total of 235 valid probability modifications (corresponding to only 235 stack entries). *Why so few?* Again, the reason is: "useful" SSMs are rare, because each has to lead to "better" results (faster reinforcement intake) than all previous ones.

Messy storage environment. In the end, the storage cells (which are part of the environment) looked very messy. Almost all work cells were filled with (partly big) integers quite different from their initial zero values. Still, without storage cells, the system could *not* achieve its dramatic performance improvement. It actually learned to make use of the changing policy environment.

Evidence of "learning how to learn"? As with the previous task, many useful SSMs directly computed valid modifications of probabilities of future SSMs ("learning to learn"). Compare the final paragraph of section 3.3.1.2.

Stability of probability modifications. With the experiments conducted so far, the top level hardly ever countermanded probability modifications other than the 10 most recent valid ones. For instance, once there were 120 stack entries, the 100 oldest stack entries appeared extremely safe and had a good chance to survive the entire system life.

Revolutions. In the tasks above, unexpected temporary speed-ups of performance improvements were observed. Even if the system appears to be stuck for a long time, the external observer never can be sure that it will not suddenly discover a new, "revolutionary" shift of bias that builds the basis for additional, smoother performance improvements. This is analoguous to the history of science itself. Informally, a "revolution" corresponds to a self-improvement with high *"conceptual jump size"* (an expression coined by Solomonoff [46]). One nice thing about open-ended incremental self-improvement is that there is no significant theoretical limit to the nature of the revolutions and to what the system may learn. This is, of course, due to the general nature of the underlying programming language.

Inserting prior bias. The few experiments above were designed to illustrate basic principles of the paradigm. They were based on low-level, assembler-like instructions (making even apparently simple tasks difficult — additional experiments using such low-level instructions can be found in [11, 53, 40, 42]). They are certainly not meant to convince the reader that from now on, he should combine the incremental self-improvement paradigm with the low-level programming language from section 3.2 and apply it to real world problems: of course, with large scale problems, it is desirable to *insert prior knowledge* into the system (if such knowledge is indeed available). With incremental self-improvement, *a priori* knowledge resides in the programmer's selection of primitives with problem-specific built-in bias (and in the payoff function he chooses). There is no reason why certain primitives should not be complex, time consuming programs by themselves, such as statistic classifiers, neural net learning algorithms, logic programs, etc. For instance, using different primitives for the navigation task from section 3.3.2 can greatly reduce the time required to achieve near-optimal trials. This paper, however, is not a study of the effects of different kinds of initial bias.

3.4 SSA for Recurrent Neural Nets: a Multi-Agent Perspective

Now we attack the non-Markovian maze task from section 3.3.2 with multiple, very simple, non-self-modifying, learning agents. Each agent is in fact just a connection (whose current weight represents its current policy) in a fully recurrent neural net. A by-product of this research is a general reinforcement learning algorithm for such nets.

Viewing each connection as a separate agent may seem unconventional: standard AI research is used to more complex agents with full-sized knowledge bases etc. For the purposes of this paper, however, this is irrelevant: SSA does not care for the complexity of the agents.

Again, it should be emphasized that the following preliminary experiment in no way represents a systematic experimental analysis. The only purpose of the current section is to illustrate paragraph (*) (in the theoretical section 3.1).

Basic set-up. There is a fully recurrent neural net with 5 input, 4 output, and 5 hidden units. The variable activation of the i-th unit is denoted o_i (initialized at time 0 with 0.0). $w_{ij} \in [-2.0, 2.0]$ denotes the real-valued, randomly initialized weight (a variable) on the connection (i, j) from unit j to i. There is a lifelong sequence of **"cycles"**. A cycle involves the following computations: the activation of the first (second, third, fourth) input unit is set to 0.0 if the field to the north (south, east, west) of the animat is blocked or does not exist, and set to 1.0 otherwise. Each noninput unit i updates its variable activation

o_i (initialized at time 0 with 0.0) as follows: $o_i \leftarrow 1.0$ with probability $f(net_i)$, $o_i \leftarrow 0.0$ otherwise, where $f(x) = \frac{1}{1+e^{-x}}$, and the net_i (initially 0) are sequentially updated as follows: $net_i \leftarrow net_i + \sum_j w_{ij} o_j$. If i stands for an output unit, then i's current *value* is defined as $v_i \leftarrow o_i + 0.05$. For each output unit j, there is an action a_j (possible actions are *one-step-north*, *one-step-south*, *one-step-east*, *one-step-west*). a_j is selected with a probability proportional to $v_j / \sum_i v_i$. The selected action gets executed. Whenever the animat hits the goal, there is constant reinforcement 1.0, the animat is transferred back to the start position (but the activations and *net*-values of the recurrent net are not reset), and the activation of the fifth input unit is set to 1.0 (0.0 otherwise).

Weight stacks. The current weight of a connection represents its current policy. For each connection (i, j), there is a stack. Following the SSA principle (section 3.1), whenever a weight is modified (see below), the following values are pushed onto (i, j)'s stack: the current time, the total cumulative reinforcement so far, and the weight before the modification.

Weight restauration. After the goal is hit, or if the goal has not been hit for 10,000 cycles (in this case the animat is transferred back to the start position), right before the next cycle, each connection sequentially pops entries from its stack and restores the corresponding previous weight values, until its SSC (see section 3.1) is satisfied.

Weight modification. So far, preliminary experiments were conducted only with very simple weight modification processes (corresponding to the PMP_i from section 3.1). Weight modification is executed after each weight restauration (see above), and works as follows. For each weight w_{ij} do: with small probability (0.05), replace w_{ij} by a randomly chosen value in $[-2.0, 2.0]$. Of course, many alternative weight modification processes are possible, but this is irrelevant for the purposes of this paper.

Measuring time. By definition, each computation involving some weight — such as pushing, popping, computing unit activations etc.— costs one time step. Other computations do not cost anything. Still, measured time is of the order of total cpu-time.

Where is the changing environment? Although the animat is occasionally reset to its start position, the recurrent net activations and the *net*-values are not: the past may influence the future. Apart from this, each single connection's environment continually changes, simply because all the other connections in its environment keep changing. However, all connections receive the same global reinforcement signal. Hence, for each connection, the only way to speed up its *local* reinforcement intake is to contribute to speeding up *global* reinforcement intake. Since no connection can solve the task by itself, this enforces learning to cooperate.

Results without SSA. Again, for purposes of comparison, the system was first run with different weight initializations, and the weight changing mechanism being switched off. Often, the average number of cycles required to reach the goal exceeded 100,000 cycles.

Among the different weight initializations, one was picked that led to an average trial length of 2660 cycles (measured over 20,000,000 cycles). This initialization was used for SSA (see below), because the corresponding average trial length is of the same order of magnitude as the one obtained by using Sutton's original set-up.

Results with SSA. With multi-weight SSA being switched on, after about 10,000 "trials" (more precisely: 11,339,740 cycles — about $2,2 * 10^9$ time steps), the average trial length was down to 89. This corresponds to a speed-up factor of about 30. The shortest trial ever took 14 cycles, which is the theoretical optimum for Sutton's task. In the end, no weight stack had more than 7 entries (each followed by faster reinforcement intake than all the previous ones).

Ongoing work. It is intended to replace the random weight modification process by a process that may be strongly influenced by the current weights themselves. Following [30], the idea is to use activation patterns across special output units to address and modify the network's own weights. Then the recurrent net will be theoretically able to evolve its own weight modification strategies, to replace the random mutations by more directed self-mutations.

3.5 History of Ideas / Previous Work

In what follows, I will briefly describe earlier work and the train of thought leading to this paper.

Meta-evolution. My first attempts to come up with schemes for "true"[2] self-referential learning based on universal languages date back to 1987. They were partly inspired by a collaboration with Dickmanns and Winklhofer [7]. We used a genetic algorithm (GA) to evolve variable length programs for solving simple tasks (the system was implemented in PROLOG). Today, this approach would be classified as "Genetic Programming", e.g. [15]. [7] was in fact one of the first two papers on using GP-like algorithms to evolve assembler-like computer programs (but Cramer's work preceded ours [6]). We applied our system to simple tasks, including the "lawnmower problem" (later also studied by Koza, 1994). Since our programming language was general (for instance, we allowed for programs with loops etc.), our approach had at least the same potential as the one based on Koza's so-called "automatically defined functions". However, in subsequent work (1987 — 1995), we found GP unsatisfactory. One reason was: GP's way of constructing new code from old code does not improve itself — it always remains limited to the initial crossover and mutation mechanisms. This created a desire to improve the trivial mutation and crossover strategies used to construct new programs from old ones. In 1987, I developed an algorithmic scheme (called *"meta-evolution"*) for letting more sophisticated strategies be learned by a potentially infinite hierarchy of higher level GAs whose domains were to construct construction strategies. *Meta-evolution* recursively creates a growing hierarchy of pools of programs — higher-level pools containing program modifying programs being applied to lower-level programs and being rewarded based on lower-level performance. Details in [27].

---

[2] I am not talking about fixed learning algorithms for adjusting the parameters of others. For instance, GAs are sometimes used to adjust learning rates of gradient based neural nets, etc. Or a neural net is used to compute the weights of another neural net. In the literature, one can find quite a few approaches of this kind (too many to cite them all — I settle by citing none, not even my own). Although such approaches sometimes may have their merits, they do not deserve the attribute "self-referential" — the additional level typically just defers the credit assignment problem. However, there were a few apparently more general approaches. For instance, Lenat [17] reports that his EURISKO system was able to discover certain heuristics for discovering heuristics. His approach, however, as well as all other previous approaches I am aware of, were either quite limited (many essential aspects of system behavior being unmodifiable), and/or lacked a sound, convincing global credit assignment strategy (as embodied by the SSA pushing and popping processes).

Collapsing meta-levels. The explicit creation of "meta-levels" and "meta-meta-levels" seemed unnatural, however. For this reason, alternative systems based on "self-referential" languages were explored, the goal being to collapse all meta-levels into one [27]. At that time, however, no convincing global credit assignment strategy was provided.

Self-referential neural nets. Later work presented a neural network with the potential to run its own weight change algorithm [30, 29]. With this system, top-level credit assignment is performed by gradient descent. This is unsatisfactory, however, due to problems with local minima, and because repeatable training sequences are required. In general, this makes it impossible to take the entire learning history into account.

Algorithmic probability / Universal search. Levin's universal search algorithm is theoretically optimal for certain "non-incremental" search tasks with exactly repeatable initial conditions. See Levin [19, 20]; see also Adleman [1]. There were a few attempts to extend universal search to incremental learning situations, where previous "trials" may provide information about how to speed up further learning, see e.g. [46, 22, 31]. For instance, to improve future performance, Solomonoff [45, 46] describes more traditional (as opposed to self-improving) methods for assigning probabilities to successful "subprograms". Alternatively, one of the actually implemented systems in [31] simply keeps successful code in its program area. This system was a conceptual starting point for the one in the current paper. With first attempts (in September 1994), the probability distributions underlying the Turing machine equivalent language required for universal search were modified heuristically. One strategy was to slightly increase the context-dependent probabilities of program cell contents used in successful programs, and then continue universal search based on the new probability distributions. With a number of experiments, this actually led to good results (at first glance, more impressive results than those in the current paper, at least if one does not take the lack of bias into account, as one should always do). The system, however, was unsatisfactory, precisely because there was no principled way of adjusting probability distributions. This criticism led to the ideas expressed in the current paper.

Meta-version of universal search. Without going into details, Solomonoff [46] mentions that self-improvement may be formulated as a time-limited optimization problem, thus being solvable by universal search. However, the straight-forward meta-version of universal search (generating and evaluating probability distributions in order of their Levin complexities [19]) just defers the credit assignment problem to the meta-level, and does *not* necessarily make optimal incremental use of computational resources and previous experience[3]. In fact, just like exhaustive search, but unlike SSA, universal search by itself cannot properly deal with changing environments. However, variants of universal search may be used as the parameter modification algorithms executed by PMPs (see section 3.1 and recent work with Marco Wiering [50, 42]).

3.6 Conclusion

It is easy to show that there can be no algorithm for general, unknown environments that is guaranteed to continually increase reinforcement intake per *fixed* time interval. For this reason, the reinforcement acceleration criterion (SSC) relaxes standard mesures of performance improvement, by allowing for consideration of *arbitrary* time intervals. The success-story algorithm (SSA) is guaranteed to achieve lifelong performance improvement according to this relaxed criterion. Since SSA takes into account all recursive long-term effects of policy modifications on all later policy modifications, and since it does not care for the nature of the policy modification processes, it provides a sound theoretical framework for "meta-learning", "meta-meta-learning", etc. Since SSA is environment-independent, it also provides a sound theoretical framework for "multi-agent learning", where each SSA-learning agent is part of the environment of the other agents.

There are many different ways of implementing SSA. Two of them are described in this paper. The first leads to a "self-referential" sys-

[3]Solomonoff appears to be well aware of problems with the meta-version: at the end of his 1990 paper, he refers to self-improvement as a "more distant goal": *"The kind of training needed involves more mathematics and work on various kinds of optimization problems — ultimately problems of improving computer programs."* Another "more distant goal" mentioned by Solomonoff is to let the system work *"on an unordered batch of problems — deciding itself which are the easiest, and solving them first"*. Note that SSA addresses both goals, without depending on a meta-version of universal search.

tem using assembler-like primitive instructions to modify its own policy — the system's learning mechanism is embedded within the system, and accessible to self-manipulation. The second implementation leads to a general reinforcement learning algorithm for recurrent nets. Alternatively, however, the PMP from section 3.1 may be designed to execute arbitrary, conventional or non-conventional learning or search algorithms.

Other SSA applications. In recent work [50, 42], we combine SSA and Levin search (LS) [18, 20] to solve partially observable Markov decision problems (POMDPs). POMDPs received a lot of attention in the reinforcement learning community. LS is theoretically optimal for a wide variety of search problems including many POMDPs. We show that that LS can solve partially observable mazes (POMs) involving many more states and obstacles than those solved by various previous authors (here, LS also can easily outperform Q-learning). We then note, however, that LS is not necessarily optimal for "incremental" learning problems where experience with previous problems may help to reduce future search costs. For this reason, we introduce a heuristic, adaptive extension of LS (ALS) which uses experience to increase probabilities of instructions occurring in successful programs found by LS. To deal with cases where ALS does not lead to long term performance improvement, we use SSA as a safety belt. Experiments with additional POMs demonstrate: (a) ALS can dramatically reduce the search time consumed by successive calls of LS. (b) Additional significant speed-ups can be obtained by combining ALS and SSA.

In other recent work [53], we use SSA for a multi-agent system with agents much more complex than the ones in section 3.4. In fact, each agent uses incremental self-improvement as described in section 3.2. Experiments demonstrate the multi-agent system's effectiveness. For instance, a system consisting of three co-evolving agents chasing each other learns rather sophisticated, stochastic predator and prey strategies. Additional applications of SSA to quite challenging, complex multiagent tasks are described in [41, 40].

3.7 Acknowledgements

I am grateful to Ray Solomonoff, Peter Dayan, Mike Mozer, Don Matthis, Clayton McMillan, and various NIPS*94 participants, for valuable comments/discussions on the first version of [32]. Many thanks to Sepp Hochreiter, Gerhard Weiß, Martin Eldracher, Margit Kinder, and Daniel Prelinger, for critical remarks on earlier drafts, and to Leslie Kaelbling, David Cohn, Tommi Jaakkola, and Andy Barto, for useful comments on later versions. Also, thanks to Marco Dorigo, Luca Gambardella, Rafal Salustowicz, Cristina Versino, and Marco Wiering, for hepful remarks on [34]. I am particularly indebted to Mark Ring for extensive and constructive criticism. The recent collaboration with Jieyu Zhao was supported by SNF grant 21-43'417.95 "Incremental Self-Improvement" and SNF grant 2100-49'144.96 "Long Short-Term Memory".

Bibliography

[1] L. Adleman. Time, space, and randomness. Technical Report MIT/LCS/79/TM-131, Laboratory for Computer Science, MIT, 1979.

[2] A. G. Barto. Connectionist approaches for control. Technical Report COINS 89-89, University of Massachusetts, Amherst MA 01003, 1989.

[3] D. A. Berry and B. Fristedt. *Bandit Problems: Sequential Allocation of Experiments.* Chapman and Hall, London, 1985.

[4] M. Boddy and T. L. Dean. Deliberation scheduling for problem solving in time-constrained environments. *Artificial Intelligence*, 67:245–285, 1994.

[5] G.J. Chaitin. On the length of programs for computing finite binary sequences: statistical considerations. *Journal of the ACM*, 16:145–159, 1969.

[6] N. L. Cramer. A representation for the adaptive generation of simple sequential programs. In J.J. Grefenstette, editor, *Proceedings of an International Conference on Genetic Algorithms and Their Applications*, Hillsdale NJ, 1985. Lawrence Erlbaum Associates.

[7] D. Dickmanns, J. Schmidhuber, and A. Winklhofer. Der genetische Algorithmus: Eine Implementierung in Prolog. Fortgeschrittenenpraktikum, Institut für Informatik, Lehrstuhl Prof. Radig, Technische Universität München, 1987.

[8] T. G. Dietterich. Limitations of inductive learning. In *Proceedings of the Sixth International Workshop on Machine Learning, Ithaca, NY*, pages 124–128. San Francisco, CA: Morgan Kaufmann, 1989.

[9] J. C. Gittins. *Multi-armed Bandit Allocation Indices.* Wiley-Interscience series in systems and optimization. Wiley, Chichester, NY, 1989.

[10] R. Greiner. PALO: A probabilistic hill-climbing algorithm. *Artificial Intelligence*, 83(2), 1996.

[11] S. Heil. Universelle Suche und inkrementelles Lernen, diploma thesis, 1995. Fakultät für Informatik, Lehrstuhl Prof. Brauer, Technische Universität München.

[12] F. Hoffmeister and T. Bäck. Genetic algorithms and evolution strategies: Similarities and differences. In R. Männer and H. P. Schwefel, editors, *Proc. of 1st International Conference on Parallel Problem Solving from Nature, Berlin.* Springer, 1991.

[13] J. H. Holland. *Adaptation in Natural and Artificial Systems.* University of Michigan Press, Ann Arbor, 1975.

[14] A.N. Kolmogorov. Three approaches to the quantitative definition of information. *Problems of Information Transmission*, 1:1–11, 1965.

[15] J. R. Koza. *Genetic Programming II – Automatic Discovery of Reusable Programs.* MIT Press, 1994.

[16] P. R. Kumar and P. Varaiya. *Stochastic Systems: Estimation, Identification, and Adaptive Control.* Prentice Hall, 1986.

[17] D. Lenat. Theory formation by heuristic search. *Machine Learning*, 21, 1983.

[18] L. A. Levin. Universal sequential search problems. *Problems of Information Transmission*, 9(3):265–266, 1973.

[19] L. A. Levin. Laws of information (nongrowth) and aspects of the foundation of probability theory. *Problems of Information Transmission*, 10(3):206–210, 1974.

[20] L. A. Levin. Randomness conservation inequalities: Information and independence in mathematical theories. *Information and Control*, 61:15–37, 1984.

[21] M. Li and P. M. B. Vitányi. *An Introduction to Kolmogorov Complexity and its Applications.* Springer, 1993.

[22] W. Paul and R. J. Solomonoff. Autonomous theory building systems, 1991. Manuscript, revised 1994.

[23] I. Rechenberg. Evolutionsstrategie - Optimierung technischer Systeme nach Prinzipien der biologischen Evolution. Dissertation, 1971. Published 1973 by Fromman-Holzboog.

[24] M. B. Ring. *Continual Learning in Reinforcement Environments.* PhD thesis, University of Texas at Austin, Austin, Texas 78712, August 1994.

[25] S. Russell and E. Wefald. Principles of Metareasoning. *Artificial Intelligence*, 49:361–395, 1991.

[26] C. Schaffer. Overfitting avoidance as bias. *Machine Learning*, 10:153–178, 1993.

[27] J. Schmidhuber. Evolutionary principles in self-referential learning, or on learning how to learn: the meta-meta-... hook. Institut für Informatik, Technische Universität München, 1987.

[28] J. Schmidhuber. Reinforcement learning in Markovian and non-Markovian environments. In D. S. Lippman, J. E. Moody, and D. S. Touretzky, editors, *Advances in Neural Information Processing Systems 3*, pages 500–506. San Mateo, CA: Morgan Kaufmann, 1991.

[29] J. Schmidhuber. A neural network that embeds its own meta-levels. In *Proc. of the International Conference on Neural Networks '93, San Francisco.* IEEE, 1993.

[30] J. Schmidhuber. A self-referential weight matrix. In *Proceedings of the International Conference on Artificial Neural Networks, Amsterdam*, pages 446–451. Springer, 1993.

[31] J. Schmidhuber. Discovering problem solutions with low Kolmogorov complexity and high generalization capability. Technical Report FKI-194-94, Fakultät für Informatik, Technische Universität München, 1994. Short version in A. Prieditis and S. Russell, eds., Machine Learning: Proceedings of the Twelfth International Conference, Morgan Kaufmann Publishers, pages 488–496, San Francisco, CA, 1995.

[32] J. Schmidhuber. On learning how to learn learning strategies. Technical Report FKI-198-94, Fakultät für Informatik, Technische Universität München, 1994. Revised 1995.

[33] J. Schmidhuber. Discovering solutions with low Kolmogorov complexity and high generalization capability. In A. Prieditis and S. Russell, editors, *Machine Learning: Proceedings of the Twelfth International Conference*, pages 488–496. Morgan Kaufmann Publishers, San Francisco, CA, 1995.

[34] J. Schmidhuber. Environment-independent reinforcement acceleration. Technical Report Note IDSIA-59-95, IDSIA, June 1995. Invited talk at Hongkong University of Science and Technology.

[35] J. Schmidhuber. A general method for multi-agent learning in unrestricted environments. In *Adaptation, Co-evolution and Learning in Multiagent Systems, Technical Report SS-96-01*, pages 84–87. American Association for Artificial Intelligence, Menlo Park, Calif., 1996.

[36] J. Schmidhuber. Realistic multi-agent reinforcement learning. In G. Weiss, editor, *Learning in Distributed Artificial Intelligence Systems. Working Notes of the 1996 ECAI Workshop.* 1996.

[37] J. Schmidhuber. A computer scientist's view of life, the universe, and everything. In C. Freksa, M. Jantzen, and R. Valk, editors, *Foundations of Computer Science: Theory, Cognition, Applications*, volume 1337, pages 201–208. Lecture Notes in Computer Science, Springer, Berlin, 1997.

[38] J. Schmidhuber. Discovering neural nets with low Kolmogorov complexity and high generalization capability. *Neural Networks*, 10(5):857–873, 1997.

[39] J. Schmidhuber. What's interesting? Technical Report IDSIA-35-97, IDSIA, 1997.

[40] J. Schmidhuber, J. Zhao, and N. Schraudolph. Reinforcement learning with self-modifying policies. In S. Thrun and L. Pratt, editors, *Learning to learn*, pages 293–309. Kluwer, 1997.

[41] J. Schmidhuber, J. Zhao, and M. Wiering. Simple principles of metalearning. Technical Report IDSIA-69-96, IDSIA, 1996.

[42] J. Schmidhuber, J. Zhao, and M. Wiering. Shifting inductive bias with success-story algorithm, adaptive Levin search, and incremental self-improvement. *Machine Learning*, 28:105–130, 1997.

[43] H. P. Schwefel. Numerische Optimierung von Computer-Modellen. Dissertation, 1974. Published 1977 by Birkhäuser, Basel.

[44] C. E. Shannon. A mathematical theory of communication (parts I and II). *Bell System Technical Journal*, XXVII:379–423, 1948.

[45] R.J. Solomonoff. A formal theory of inductive inference. Part I. *Information and Control*, 7:1–22, 1964.

[46] R.J. Solomonoff. A system for incremental learning based on algorithmic probability. In E. P. D. Pednault, editor, *The Theory and Application of Minimal-Length Encoding (Preprint of Symposium papers of AAAI 1990 Spring Symposium)*, 1990.

[47] R. S. Sutton. Integrated modeling and control based on reinforcement learning and dynamic programming. In D. S. Lippman, J. E. Moody, and D. S. Touretzky, editors, *Advances in Neural Information Processing Systems 3*, pages 471–478. San Mateo, CA: Morgan Kaufmann, 1991.

[48] P. Utgoff. Shift of bias for inductive concept learning. In R. Michalski, J. Carbonell, and T. Mitchell, editors, *Machine Learning*, volume 2, pages 163–190. Morgan Kaufmann, Los Altos, CA, 1986.

[49] C. J. C. H. Watkins and P. Dayan. Q-learning. *Machine Learning*, 8:279–292, 1992.

[50] M.A. Wiering and J. Schmidhuber. Solving POMDPs with Levin search and EIRA. In L. Saitta, editor, *Machine Learning: Proceedings of the Thirteenth International Conference*, pages 534–542. Morgan Kaufmann Publishers, San Francisco, CA, 1996.

[51] R. J. Williams. Simple statistical gradient-following algorithms for connectionist reinforcement learning. *Machine Learning*, 8:229–256, 1992.

[52] D. H. Wolpert. The lack of a priori distinctions between learning algorithms. *Neural Computation*, 8(7):1341–1390, 1996.

[53] J. Zhao and J. Schmidhuber. Incremental self-improvement for life-time multi-agent reinforcement learning. In Pattie Maes, Maja Mataric, Jean-Arcady Meyer, Jordan Pollack, and Stewart W. Wilson, editors, *From Animals to Animats 4: Proceedings of the Fourth International Conference on Simulation of Adaptive Behavior, Cambridge, MA*, pages 516–525. MIT Press, Bradford Books, 1996.

Chapter 4

Teacher: A Genetics-Based System for Learning and for Generalizing Heuristics

B. W. Wah and A. Ieumwananonthachai

In this chapter, we present the design of Teacher (an acronym for TEchniques for the Automated Creation of HEuRistics), a system for learning and for generalizing heuristics used in problem solving. Our system learns knowledge-lean heuristics whose performance is measured statistically. The objective of the design process is to find, under resource constraints, improved heuristic methods (HMs) as compared to existing ones. Teacher addresses five general issues in learning heuristics: (1) *decomposition* of a problem solver into smaller components and *integration* of HMs designed for each together; (2) *classification* of an application domain into subdomains so that performance can be evaluated statistically for each; (3) *generation* of new and improved HMs based on past performance information and heuristics generated; (4) *evaluation* of each HM's performance; and (5) *performance generalization* to find HMs that perform well across the entire application domain. Teacher employs a genetics-based machine learning approach and divides the design process into four phases. In the classification phase, the application domain is divided into subspaces (based on user requirements) and problem subdomains (based on the performance behavior of HMs). In the learning phase, HMs are generated and evaluated under resource constraints with a goal of discovering improved HMs. In the performance-verification phase, good HMs from the learning phase are further evaluated to acquire more accurate and more complete performance information. Finally, in the performance-generalization phase, HMs most likely to provide the best performance over the entire application domain are selected. We conclude the chapter by showing some experimental results on heuristics learned for two problems used in circuit testing.

4.1 Process of Designing Heuristics

A *heuristics-design process* is a process for *learning* improved heuristic methods (HMs) for a problem solver. These HMs, when used to solve an application problem, can provide better and/or less costly solutions.

The design of heuristics is an important issue in machine learning. Today, many application problems are too complex for us to find optimal algorithms analytically. Rather, we rely on heuristics designed by experts to find high quality solutions. The effectiveness of these heuristics, however, depends on the domain knowledge and past experience of these experts. When little domain knowledge is available, as in the applications we study in this chapter, it is important to develop automated learning methods for generating improved heuristics systematically, evaluating their performance on realistic test cases, and generalizing their performance to test cases not seen in learning.

The goal of this chapter is to present, for a given application domain, a system that can *find improved HMs over existing HMs with respect to some average objective measures.* The applications we are interested in have the following characteristics:

- a large number, and possibly infinitely many, test cases;
- a knowledge-lean application domain with little domain knowledge to relate the controls of HMs to their performance;

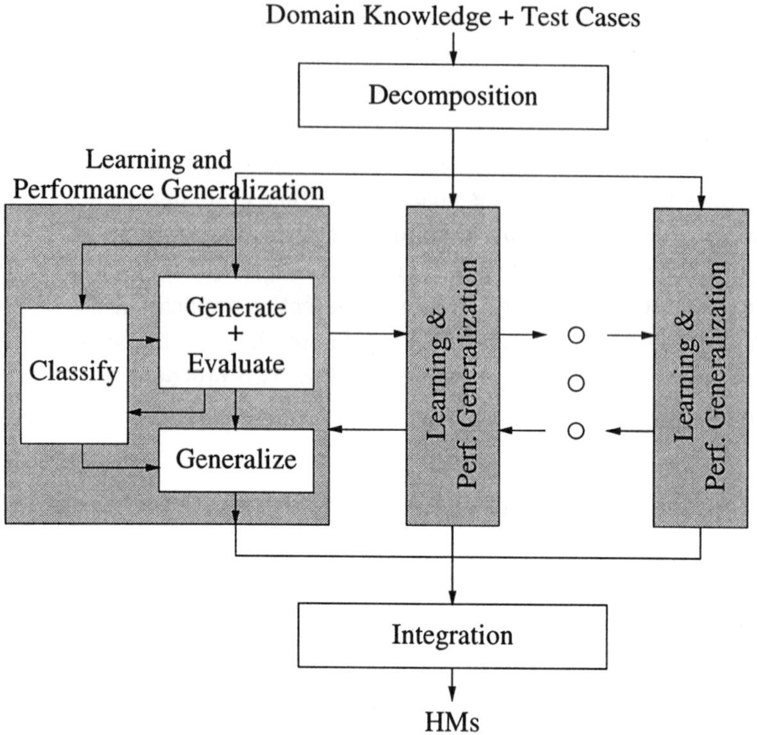

Figure 4.1: A general model of the heuristics-design process.

- performance-related HMs whose performance can be evaluated by the cost of applying them and the quality of the solutions found;
- HMs that are too costly to be tested extensively; and
- a large (and possibly infinite) pool of possible HMs.

There are five major issues in developing HMs for these applications as outlined in Figure 4.1.

(1) **Decomposition and integration of problem-solver components.** For a complex problem solver with multiple heuristic components, there are many combinations of heuristics that can be developed. Oftentimes, it is not possible to find improved heuristics for all the components simultaneously.

A feasible approach is to improve these heuristics in a piecewise fashion. This involves decomposing the problem solver into a number of groups with a smaller number of components in each, designing improved heuristics for each group, and integrating improved heuristics from each group into the problem solver.

There are several difficulties with this approach. First, it is hard to find the best way to group heuristics components in order to have the best overall performance. Second, heuristics in a problem solver may interact with each other, and the design of heuristics for one group may depend on the heuristics designed for others. Without the domain knowledge on the effects of heuristics in one group on others, it is hard to design heuristics for these groups independently.

One simple approach that minimizes the interactions is to design heuristics for different groups sequentially. In this approach, we first design an improved HM_A for group A. This is followed by the design of HM_B for Group B after HM_A is in place. The process is then repeated until HMs for all groups have been designed.

(2) **Classification of application domain**. When the performance of an HM is *nondeterministic* and the cost for evaluating it on a test case is expensive, we can only afford to evaluate each HM on a small number of test cases. In general, it is valid to estimate the true performance of an HM based on a subset of tests when the performance values are independent and identically distributed (IID).

We have found that HMs can behave differently on different subsets of test cases of an application [29]. When this happens, it is necessary to partition the application domain into smaller subsets (called subdomains) so that each can be evaluated independently.

In this chapter, we define a *problem subdomain* as a subset of the application domain so that performance values of HMs, when evaluated on test cases in the subdomain, satisfy the IID property.

Sometimes, it may be more efficient to have different groups of subdomains solved by different HMs. In this case, subdomains may need to be partitioned into groups and an HM be learned for each. We refer to this partitioning of the application domain as the *classification problem.*

(3) **Generation of heuristics**. This refers to the generation of improved HMs based on HMs generated already. This issue has been studied extensively in machine learning. Section 4.2 overviews the pre-

vious work in this area.

The generation of improved HMs is difficult for knowledge-lean problem solvers as there are no models that relate the specifications of an HM to its performance. In this case, the problem solver must be treated as a black box, and heuristics generation have to rely on weak (domain-independent) methods.

(4) **Evaluation of Heuristics.** To obtain improved HMs, we must be able to compare their performance. The performance of HMs is generally obtained by evaluating them on one or more test cases. When the performance of an HM is nondeterministic, this process may need to be repeated multiple times.

The key issue is to be able to compare the performance of different heuristics using a small number of tests. This is especially important in our research since we are dealing with heuristics that are expensive to evaluate.

(5) **Generalization of Performance on Heuristics Learned.** When the performance of an HM is nondeterministic and varies across different test cases, only a subset of test cases are usually used in evaluating its performance. However, we expect the HM selected to be generalizable; that is, it must perform well not only on test cases tested during learning but also on test cases not seen in learning. We call this the *performance-generalization problem* in this chapter.

Performance generalization is difficult when the application domain is large, and HMs have different (and possibly inconsistent) performance behavior across different regions (or subdomains) in the application domain.

The next section presents an overview of the work in automated learning of heuristics, which has been studied extensively in artificial intelligence. There has also been some work on the evaluation and generalization of heuristics in genetics-based learning [31, 33, 71]. The remaining issues on decomposition/integration and classification have been mostly ignored in the literature since they exist only in complicated application problems. Unfortunately, many real-world applications may fit in this category, and it is highly desirable to have some solutions to address these issues.

The approach presented in this chapter addresses all these issues except decomposition and integration. We currently require the decomposition/integration process to be performed manually by designers, who develop improved heuristics for each group sequentially. This is necessary because decomposition and integration cannot be studied until all the other issues have been addressed and a good system for designing improved heuristics for each component has been developed. We plan to address this issue in our future work.

We present in Section 4.4 the design of Teacher, a system that implements our heuristics-design process. Our system has four phases of operation, each of which is isolated to deal with a unique design issue. The first phase dealing with the classification issue is discussed in Section 4.5. Section 4.6 presents the second phase that addresses the generation of good heuristics for a subdomain and their evaluation. The operation in this phase is the one referred to by most researches as the learning process. Our approach in this phase is based on the genetics-based machine learning paradigm presented in Section 4.3. Section 4.7 discusses the third phase that deals with the verification of performance of heuristics. Section 4.8 presents the final phase that deals with the performance-generalization issue. In Section 4.9, we report our experience on learning HMs for two problems used in circuit testing.

4.2 Background on Heuristics Learning

In this section, we present a brief survey on the automated learning of heuristics. We first present a classification of the approaches in heuristics learning. This is followed by examples on the strengths and weaknesses of various learning methods. Finally, we summarize how our work is related to previous approaches and the type of application problems we have studied.

4.2.1 Classification of heuristics-learning methods

Learning is carried out for application domains that are either knowledge-rich or knowledge-lean. In a *knowledge-rich domain*, there is domain knowledge on a world model that relates the controls/inputs of an HM to its performance. Such a model can reduce learning time tremendously because new HMs can be derived with very little or no testing of previous HMs. In contrast, when the domain is *knowledge-lean*, there

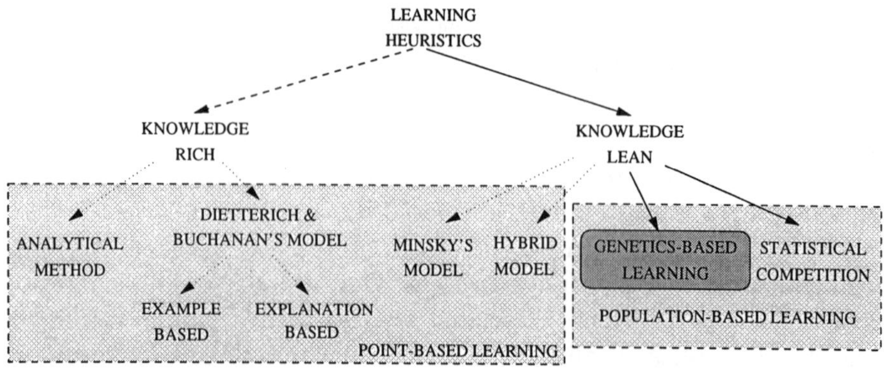

Figure 4.2: Classification of methods for learning heuristics.

is no world model, and heuristics derived must be tested to find their performance. These are the domains that we study in this chapter.

Figure 4.2 shows a classification of the methods for learning heuristics. We classify these methods based on the number of heuristics maintained by each during the design process—whether it is *point based* or *population based* [1, 69].

Point-Based Learning Paradigm. In this paradigm, a learning system maintains one incumbent HM that is modified in place by the learning system. Since each modification of the HM destroys the original HM, there must be high confidence that the new HM is better than the old one. This learning paradigm works well for learning knowledge-rich heuristics because the world model can be used to guide the generation of improved HMs [41, 45].

There are three models in traditional machine-learning studies that fit in this paradigm. Fundamental work in this area was addressed by Mitchell [46, 59], Minsky [42], and Dietterich and Buchanan [19]. The basic principle is based on a generate-and-test paradigm that generates plausible HMs, performs limited tests, and modifies the HMs according to the feedback signals obtained. Each of these models are described briefly in this section. Many existing machine-learning systems fit in one of these models.

A general point-based learning paradigm used by the three point-based models is shown in Figure 4.3 [69]. The general model includes the Learning Performance Database and Preprocessor, Credit Assign-

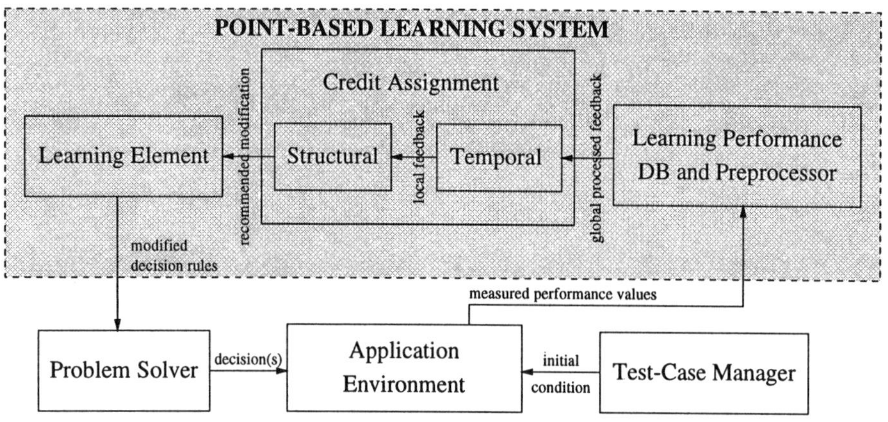

Figure 4.3: A general point-based learning model.

ment unit, and Learning Element. The problem solver and its initial conditions are shown as components outside the learning system.

The *Learning Performance Database and Preprocessor* captures the effects of decisions made by the problem solver on the application environment. The preprocessed data are used for *credit assignments* that include both *temporal* and *structural* credit assignments. The *Learning Element* then modifies the HM based on recommended actions from the Credit Assignment unit.

Population-Based Learning Paradigm. In contrast to the point-based approach, a population-based paradigm maintains multiple competing HMs and tries to find the best HM within the pool. During learning, new HMs are added to the pool and poor ones removed. This paradigm is useful for learning knowledge-lean heuristics, as the weak methods used in generating new HMs do not have to depend on a good world model [12,26]. Moreover, it is not necessary for every new HM to perform well since a number of alternative HMs are generated.

One important characteristic of the population-based approach is the potential need for scheduling the available computational resources among competing HMs. Related issues on scheduling are presented in Sections 4.3 and 4.6.

4.2.2 Learning knowledge-rich heuristics

Several general methods have been proposed for learning knowledge-rich heuristics. These include analytic methods, learning by examples, and explanation-based learning. Learning by examples and explanation-based learning are examples of Dietterich and Buchanan's model of learning.

Analytic Method. An *analytic method* is based on comprehensive analysis on the problem solver with respect to its particular representation [18,20]. This approach is knowledge-intensive and very application-specific.

Dietterich and Buchanan's Model. This point-based learning model [8,19,69] and similar models proposed by Smith et al. [60] and Langley [37] belong to a class of models for learning HMs of target problems with well-defined objectives. They learn by supervised learning with *prescriptive feedback* that carries explicit information to guide the modification of the HM tested. This learning model fits within the framework of the general point-based model shown in Figure 4.3.

Learning by examples narrows the scope of possible heuristics by specialization and generalization [45]. *Explanation-based learning* exercises domain knowledge to explain the relationship between an HM and its performance [43,44].

In learning knowledge-rich heuristics, extensive domain knowledge must be available. As our focus is on learning heuristics without such knowledge, methods developed for learning knowledge-rich heuristics cannot be used.

4.2.3 Learning knowledge-lean heuristics

Several general methods have been proposed for learning knowledge-lean heuristics. These include Minsky's learning model, hybrid point-based learning model, genetics-based learning, and statistical methods.

Minsky's Model. This model [42, 69] is an older and perhaps less restricted model of point-based learning systems. It applies well for learning HMs of target applications with undefined objectives in knowledge-lean environments, which tend to produce evaluative and possibly delayed feedback signals.

An *evaluative feedback* carries only implicit information about the desired behavior but explicit evaluation of the observed behavior. Such behavior is *a posteriori*, being measured or generated after the behavior has occurred. It requires a critic [73] that has some prior knowledge of the objective function and can assess the goodness of external states or sequences thereof. Scalar evaluative feedback signals are called *reinforcements* [42] and learning from such signals, *reinforcement learning.*

In order to simplify temporal credit assignment, the Markovian property has to be satisfied, namely, the current state of the system depends only on the last action performed by the HM and not on the sequence of actions before it. This property is generally hard to satisfy in complex applications. Examples of systems in this class include Klopf's drive reinforcement model [35] and Sutton and Barto's reinforcement model [64].

Hybrid Learning Model. This point-based learning model [69] combines aspects of Dietterich and Buchanan's model and Minsky's model. It uses an approximate temporal model instead of the Markovian model. It is intended for dealing with a knowledge-lean learning environment with an ill-defined objective, evaluative feedback, and a non-Markovian temporal scope.

Examples of this type of learning systems include EURISKO [38], Samuel's Checker Player [56,57], Williams' REINFORCEMENT model [74], classifier system (the Michigan approach) [28], and the truck-backer-upper problem of Widrow et al. [48]. This type of learning does not address the lack of domain knowledge for structural credit assignment.

Genetics-Based Machine Learning. This is a population-based approach based on generate-and-test and the application of genetic algorithms [22, 23] to machine-learning problems. In generate-and-test methods, new heuristics to be tested are generated by applying operators to existing heuristics that perform well [12, 26]. The new heuristics are potentially better as they were generated from heuristics that perform well. The reproduction operators applied include crossover and mutation. More details about this approach are presented in Section 4.3.

Examples of genetics-based machine learning include genetic programming [36] and the Pittsburgh approach to classifier systems [26].

Statistical Competition. One form of statistical competition uses statistics to translate data into concepts so that concept learning can be applied [52]. Another form uses statistics to decide which heuristics to test more, given a pool of candidate heuristics [14,30]. This method is especially useful for learning heuristics whose exact performance cannot be determined by a limited number of tests.

This approach is limited in its usefulness as it only tests a a fixed pool of heuristics and excludes the introduction of new heuristics based on past evaluations.

4.2.4 Summary

In learning knowledge-lean heuristics, genetics-based machine learning is the most suitable approach. The two point-based learning models for learning knowledge-lean heuristics are too restricted and cannot be applied for the type of applications we address in our research. Minsky's model requires a Markovian temporal model that is hard to satisfy in general, and the hybrid model requires some domain knowledge for structural credit assignment. The statistical competition approach can only handle a fixed pool of heuristics and does not allow incremental improvements through mutations and crossovers.

We have adopted a genetics-based learning approach that can operate in a knowledge-lean environment and can generate new and potentially improved heuristics based on past performance information. Since tests are expensive, we have incorporated some aspects of statistical competition to improve resource scheduling in our learning framework. In the next section, we examine the genetics-based approach in more details and identify some key issues to be studied. Section 4.6 presents the architecture of a population-based learning system.

4.3 Background on Evolutionary Computing

Genetics-based machine learning, the approach we have selected for our heuristics-design process, is a part of a bigger field called evolutionary computing [27,62].

Evolutionary computing (EC) include *genetic algorithms (GAs)*, *evolutionary programming (EP)*, *evolution strategies (ES)*, *classifier systems (CFSs)*, *genetic programming (GP)*, and several other problem-solving strategies. They are based on the means of natural selection, the survival of the fittest and the theories of evolution [27]. They provide the evolution of individual structures through the processes of selection, mutation, and reproduction. These processes depend on the perceived performance of the individual structures as defined by an environment [62].

In this section, we first present a brief overview of genetic algorithm (GA) before proceeding to genetics-based machine learning, an extension of genetic algorithms to machine-learning problems.

4.3.1 Genetic algorithms

Genetic algorithms (GAs) are adaptive methods that may be used to solve search and optimization problems. Since the development of GA by Holland [28], GAs have been extensively studied [15, 22, 25]. They are based on the genetic processes of biological organisms described first by Charles Darwin in *The Origin of Species.* Populations of competing individuals evolve over many generations according to the principle of natural selection and "survival of the fittest."

Genetic algorithms work with a *population* of "individuals" and a set of biologically based operators (such as mutation and crossover). Each individual represents a possible solution to a given problem. Based on the theory of evolution, only the most suited elements in a population are likely to survive and generate offsprings [22].

In GAs, each individual is represented as a string of binary values (0 or 1). This uniform representation is application-independent, allowing various studies to focus on the general approach.

A *fitness level* is assigned to each individual based on how good the problem has been solved. Those with high fitness levels will reproduce by recombining with other individuals in the population. New offsprings generated share some features taken from each parent. Those with low fitness levels are less likely to be selected for reproduction and so die out.

A new generation is, therefore, produced by selecting the best individuals from the current *generation* and mating them to produce a new set of offsprings. Over many generations, good characteristics are spread throughout the population. This process allows the most promising ar-

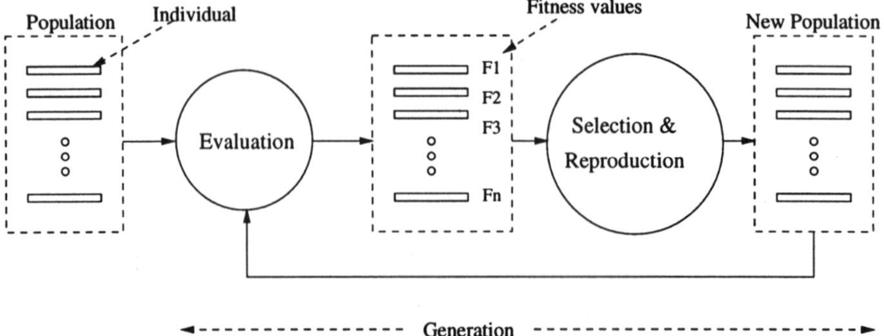

Figure 4.4: General model of the evolution process in a genetics-based approach.

eas of the search space represented by the population to be explored [9].

Figure 4.4 shows the overall process within GAs. The process can be viewed as iterating over two different steps: (1) evaluation of individuals of a population in the current generation, and assigning fitness levels to each individual, and (2) generation of a new population for a new generation by selecting existing individuals based on their fitness values and by using selected individuals to reproduce.

In most traditional GAs, the fitness of each individual is exact and can be computed with negligible costs. However, there are cases in which there are "noises" in the evaluation process, resulting in multiple evaluations and in uncertainties over the fitness of each individual [4, 21, 24]. This condition can significantly increase the amount of fitness evaluations performed during each generation. Such is the case in the applications we have studied. Here, the performance of an HM on a test case is governed by a statistical distribution, and testing the HM once is equivalent to drawing a random value from the distribution.

There are many issues in genetic algorithms that have been and continue to be studied, including issues on representation, population size, fitness evaluation, selection of individuals for reproduction, and reproduction methods [9, 10, 16, 62].

4.3.2 Genetics-based machine learning

Genetics-based machine learning is an extension of genetic algorithms (GAs) to solve machine-learning problems [22]. The term is used in this chapter to cover applications of the idea behind genetic algorithms in order to develop HMs used in a problem-solving process.

Genetics-based machine learning is based on the same idea of evolution and natural selection as in genetic algorithms (see Figure 4.4). Such a system maintains a population of individuals, evaluates their fitness values, and generates a new population by selecting existing individuals for reproduction based on their fitness values. However, the representation of HMs is generally more complex [22, 36]. Some example representations of an individual include an if-then rule [22], a set of rules [34], a Lisp expression [36], and a vector of numbers [70].

Genetics-based learning applied to learn improved HMs are more complex computationally as compared to genetic algorithms. First, because the structure of each individual can be complex, reproduction operators, such as mutation and crossover, can also be more complex. In addition, more domain knowledge may be needed in order to create knowledge-intensive reproduction [10,22], such as those used in GIL [34]. Second, since the evaluation of an HM on a test case is non-deterministic (or noisy), evolutionary computing applied to learn improved HMs must also deal with "noisy" conditions. This means that the fitness of each individual may not be exact, and that multiple evaluations of each individual may be necessary.

Existing work in genetics-based machine learning can be divided into two approaches: (a) treating the entire population as the HM to be learned and (b) treating each individual as a complete HM.

(A) *Population as HM.* This approach, known as the Michigan approach in the genetic algorithm community [15, 75], treats each individual in the current population as a component contributing to the entire population. It requires all components of a solution to be homogeneous across the population. To achieve better performance for the entire population, there must be cooperation among individuals. This is similar to the hybrid point-based learning paradigm discussed earlier. It requires credit assignments to apportion credits or debits to various contributing individuals in an episode. The most common credit assignment strategy is the *bucket brigade* algorithm [22].

Examples of this approach include most classifier systems such as CS-1 [22] and CFS-C [53]. This approach can be applied in online learning to improve a problem solver during the problem-solving process.

(B) *Individual as HM.* This approach, known as the Pittsburgh approach in the genetic algorithm community [15,75], treats each individual as a solution that competes with other individuals in the population. In this case, each individual can be entirely different from one another, leading to more complex systems as compared to the Michigan approach.

This approach does not require credit assignments to apportion credits or debits, since each performance feedback is directed to only one individual. However, feedbacks usually come less often to each individual, leading to more evaluations in order to reach a final result.

Examples of this type of approach include the Pittsburgh approach [15,75] to classifier system (such as LS-1 [61], GABIL [17], and GIL [34]) and genetic programming (GP) [36].

This approach is more suitable for our system because HMs in our applications are usually nonuniform with different structures and do not have good models of interactions among their components to allow credit assignments.

There are some systems that use a hybrid of the Michigan and the Pittsburgh approaches. In this case, each individual is treated as a potential solution with components that can contribute to the problem-solving process. It is also necessary to use credit assignment within each individual to assign credits/debits to each component. An example of this hybrid approach is SAMUEL [26].

In summary, genetics-based learning can be used to learn knowledge-lean HMs in the applications that we study in this chapter. A population of HMs can be maintained, each will be tested, evaluated, mutated, and crossed over with other HMs to form new HMs in the next generation. Existing genetics-based methods, however, do not address the issues when performance data of HMs do not belong to one common statistical distribution and when tests are expensive to conduct. When HMs behave differently across different subsets of test cases of an application, it is possible for an HM to perform well in one subset but poorly in another. Hence, the generalization of test results to test cases not evaluated must be considered. The problem is further complicated when tests are expensive to carry out. In this case, the learning system must decide how many HMs to be tested and the amount of testing to be carried out on each. These issues are addressed in Teacher described in the next section.

4.4 The Teacher System

In this section, we discuss Teacher, a genetics-based learning system we have developed in the last six years [69]. Its objective is to learn, under limited computational resources, good HMs for solving application problems and to generalize the HMs learned to unlearned subdomains. We choose to use the average metric for comparing HMs, and examine the spread of performance values when HMs have similar average performance. When there are multiple objectives in comparing HMs, we constrain all but one objectives during learning and optimize the unconstrained objective. Our learning system is capable of proposing more than one HMs, showing trade-offs among these objectives.

4.4.1 Key characteristics of Teacher

Our present prototype is unique as compared to other genetics-based learning studies because it combines the following three features.

- Our learning environment is noisy so that the performance of each HM may have to be evaluated using multiple tests.

- We consider applications in which HMs behave differently in different subdomains (Section 4.1). Existing methods generally ignore this problem and focus on only one set of statistically related test cases.

- We assume that the cost of evaluating an HM on a test case is expensive. In the applications presented in Section 4.9, a fast workstation takes a few days to perform one to two thousand tests. Hence, it is not feasible to perform millions of tests as assumed in other genetics-based learning systems [36]. For simplicity, we consider logical time in this chapter in which one unit of time is needed for each test of an HM.

These conditions are more realistic for complicated real-world applications for which we want to design improved heuristics.

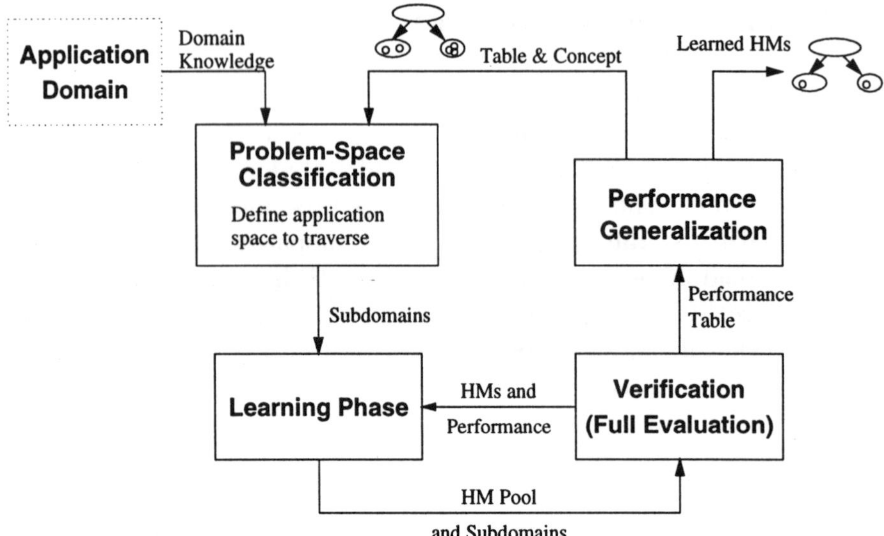

Figure 4.5: Organization of the heuristics-design process in Teacher.

4.4.2 Four phases of Teacher

The operations of Teacher are divided into four phases: classification, learning, performance verification, and performance generalization. Each phase is designed to independently deal with a separate issue discussed in Section 4.1.

Currently, the classification phase is performed manually while the other three phases are automated [32]. We have plans to incorporate strategies for automated classification, decomposition and integration of HMs in Teacher in the future. Figure 4.5 shows the overall design process in Teacher. We describe the objectives and the key issues of each phase in this section and our solutions to these issues in the following sections.

Classification phase

This first phase of the design process partitions test cases in an application into distinct subsets. Its goal is to partition a target application domain into smaller subsets in order to (a) identify different regions within the application domain that may require different HMs, and (b) make sure that performance values from test cases used in learning are representative and can be used for statistical estimation of the true performance of unseen test cases.

There are two steps in this phase.

(a) *Subspace classification.* Within an application domain, different regions may have different characteristics, each of which can best be solved by a unique HM [51]. Hence, regions should be identified whenever possible so that unique HMs can be developed. This involves partitioning the application domain into a small number of distinct subspaces so that improved HMs are learned for each.

We define an *application subspace* as a user-defined partition of an application domain so that HMs for one subspace can be learned independently of HMs in other subspaces. Subspace partitioning is important when test cases in an application have vastly different behavior.

(b) *Subdomain classification.* A *problem subdomain* in this chapter is defined as a subset of the application domain (or application subspace) so that the performance of HMs in each subdomain can be estimated statistically based on a subset of test cases in this subdomain. In other words, the performance values of an HM in a subdomain are *independent and identically distributed* (IID), but may not be IID across subdomains. Since the performance distribution of an HM may be different across different subdomains, the performance of HMs cannot be compared or combined across subdomains in a learning experiment.

Learning phase

The goal in this phase is to find effective HMs for each of a limited set of subdomains. Besides being the most complicated phase in the design process, it is the only phase in which new HMs are introduced and tested under resource constraints. Figure 4.6 shows the tasks in the learning, performance-verification, and performance-generalization phases.

To perform learning, the system first selects a subdomain, generates good HMs (or uses existing HMs from users or previous learning experiments) for this subdomain, and schedules tests of the HMs based on the available computational resources. When learning is completed, the resulting HMs need to be fully verified, as HMs found during learning

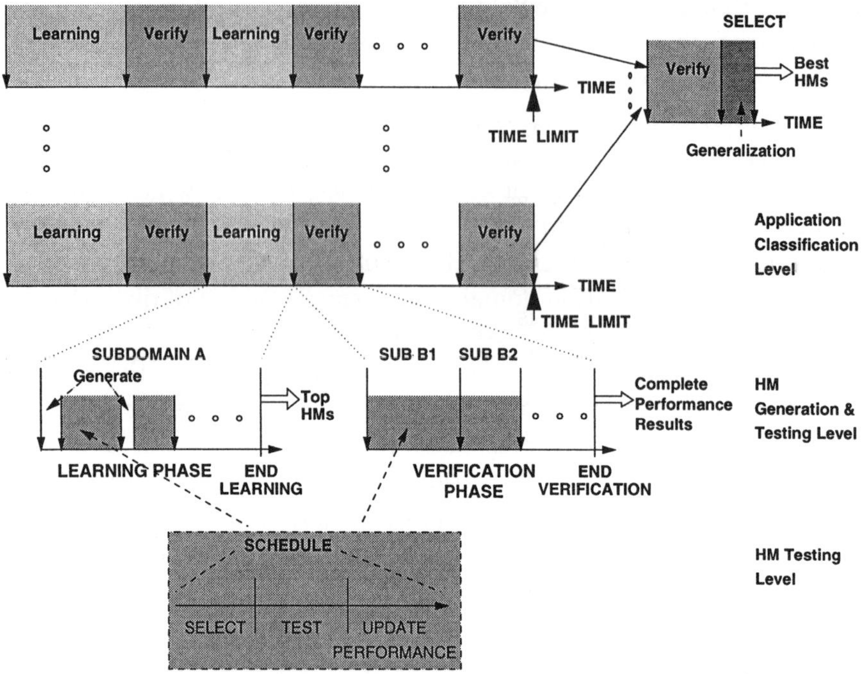

(a) The learning, performance-verification and performance-generalization process.

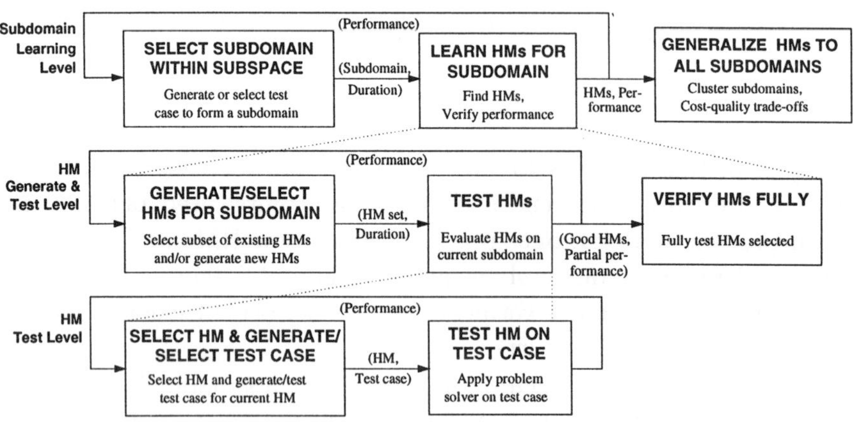

(b) The actions in each phase of Teacher.

Figure 4.6: The process and actions in each phase in Teacher.

may not be tested adequately. Note that learning is performed on one subdomain at a time.

There are three key issues in this phase.

(a) *Heuristics generation.* This entails the generation of good HMs, given the performance information of "empirically good" HMs. As discussed in Section 4.2, we use weak genetics-based operators here [12,36].

(b) *Performance evaluation.* This is related to the performance evaluation of HMs during learning, given that there may be multiple performance measures, that there is no defined relationship among them, and that HMs may have different performance across different subdomains.

(c) *Resource scheduling.* Given the performance information of HMs under consideration, resource scheduling entails the selection of HMs for further testing, the termination of the current generation, and the initiation of the next generation. These problems are important when limited computational resources are available and tests of HMs are expensive and noisy. We schedule computational resources rationally by choosing (i) the number of tests on each HM, (ii) the number of competing HMs to be maintained at any time, and (iii) the number of problem subdomains to be used for learning and for generalization. We have studied two related issues in resource scheduling in genetics-based learning algorithms: *sample allocation* and *duration scheduling* [2,4,6,30,70].

Performance-verification phase

The goal of this phase is to fully evaluate the set of HMs with good performance found at the end of previous learning phases. As mentioned previously, the performance of HMs evaluated during learning is only estimated based on incomplete and possibly inadequate performance data. In order to select HMs that can be generalized to unlearned subdomains, we need to carry out full evaluation of each HM selected at the end of a learning phase. This involves evaluating each selected HM fully on all subdomains from all learning phases and any additional subdomains provided by users. The main potential issue in this phase is the scheduling of limited computational resources to test a given set of HMs.

Performance-generalization phase

The goal of the last phase is determine which HMs found in previous learning phases perform consistently well on all subdomains, including those not studied in learning. This notion of performance generalization is slightly different from that in point-based learning, as we generalize the performance of HMs found to unseen test cases rather than generalizing the HMs found to better HMs. There are two key issues to be studied here.

(a) *Performance of HMs across different subdomains.* As discussed in Section 4.1, HMs may have different performance behavior in different subdomains; hence, performance values of an HM from different subdomains cannot be combined directly. Oftentimes, an HM may perform well in some subdomains but worse in others. One approach we have studied is to find HMs that are consistently better than others with a high probability across all the subdomains [33, 71].

(b) *Cost-quality trade-offs.* This involves determining efficient HMs that perform well in an application. Should there be multiple HMs to be applied (at a higher total cost and better quality of results), or should there be one HM that is costly to run but generates high-quality results? Some results on these trade-offs are shown in Section 4.9.

4.5 Strategies in the Classification Phase

Recall from the last section that quantitative comparison of performance is difficult when test cases are of different behavior. Hence, before learning begins, the application domain should be broken into smaller subspaces and subdomains.

In subspace partitioning, the attributes needed for partitioning may not be defined, or the number of attributes may be too large. When this happens, non-parametric clustering methods, such as those based on neural networks, may have to be used. Another possibility is to always apply multiple HMs for each test case, resulting in a higher computational cost for a better solution.

We show two examples to demonstrate the idea of application subspaces.

Example 1. Consider solving a vertex-cover problem that finds the minimum number of nodes to cover all the edges in a graph. In designing a decomposition HM to decide which vertex to be included in the covered set, previous experience on other optimization problems indicates that HMs for densely connected graphs are generally different from those for sparsely connected ones. Consequently, the application domain of all graphs can be partitioned (in an ad hoc fashion) into a small number of subspaces based on graph connectivities. □

Example 2. As another example, in generating test patterns for testing VLSI circuits, previous experience shows that sequential circuits require tests that are different from those of combinatorial circuits. Hence, we can partition the application domain into two subspaces, one for sequential circuits and another for combinatorial circuits. However, we are not able to partition the subspace of sequential circuits into smaller subspaces as it is not clear which attributes (like the length of the longest path, the number of flip flops, etc.) should be used in this partitioning. □

In our current implementation, subspace partitioning is guided by common-sense knowledge or by user experience in solving similar application problems. It requires knowing one or more attributes to classify test cases and is driven by a set of decision rules that identify the subspace to which a test case belongs. When such attributes cannot be identified, we simply assume that the entire application domain is in one subspace.

In classifying test cases in a subspace into subdomains, some domain knowledge, such as previous experience on similar problems, may be required. After subdomains have been classified, it is important to test the HMs in each subdomain to make sure that their performance data are IID. Examples of methods for testing for identical distributions are Kolmogorov-Smirnov two-sample test [29, 47, 50], Mann-Whitney test [68] and Wald-Wolfowitz two-sample runs test [47]. On the other hand, testing for independence is difficult, if not impossible [68]. Currently, there do not exist methods to guarantee that all performance values are independent. However, it is possible to evaluate the randomness of *a given sequence of test cases*, which is a necessary condition for data to be independent. For instance, test of randomness can be found by computing the total number of runs up and down [47, 72], the total number of runs above and below the median [68,72], and the total num-

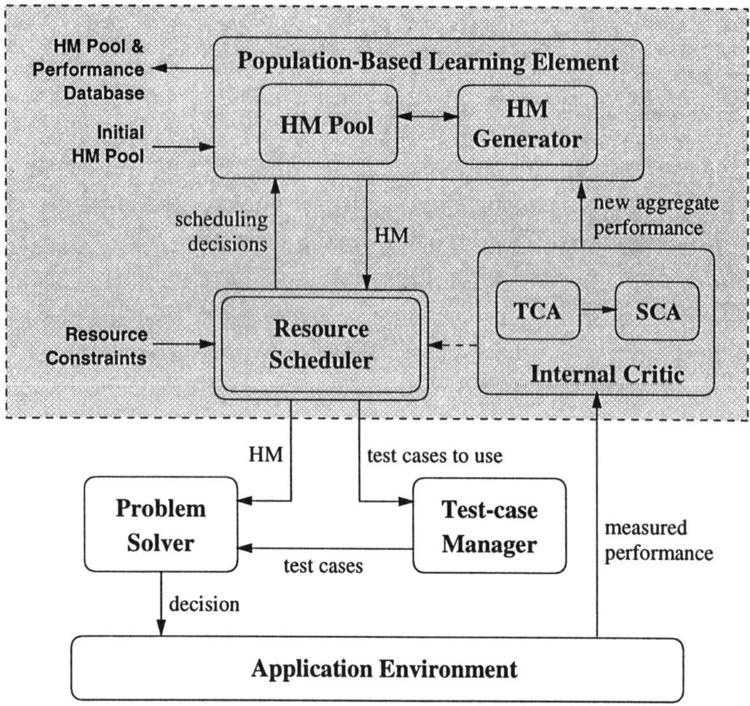

Figure 4.7: Architecture of population-based learning for one subdomain.

ber of runs above and below the mean [47]. Other randomness tests include Kendall's Rank Correlation Coefficient Test [72] and Circular Serial Correlation Coefficient Test [72]. Results on applying these tests are discussed in the references [29].

Continuing with Example 1 on the vertex-cover problem, a problem subdomain can be defined as a collection of random graphs with a certain degree of connectivity. As another example, in generating test patterns for testing VLSI circuits (Example 2), each circuit may be treated as an individual subdomain, as we do not know the best set of attributes to group different circuits into subdomains.

4.6 Learning Heuristics in One Subdomain

In this section, we present our approach to learn improved HMs under resource constraints for a single subdomain. Figure 4.7 shows the architecture of our resource-constrained learning system for one subdomain [69]. This population-based learning system is based on the genetics-based machine-learning paradigm. There are five main components in the system:

(a) *Resource Scheduler* that determines the best way to use the available computational resources,

(b) *Internal Critic* that provides feedback, based on measured performance, to indicate how well a particular HM has performed,

(c) *Population-Based Learning Element* that generates new HMs and maintains a pool of existing ones and their past performance,

(d) *Test-Case Manager* that generates and maintains a database of test cases used in HM evaluation, and

(e) *Problem Solver* that evaluates an HM using a test case.

In this research, we assume that the application-specific Problem Solver and Test-Case Manager are user-supplied. The remaining three components are designed to deal with the three key issues in Section 4.4: heuristics generation, performance evaluation, and resource scheduling.

Problem Solver

This component is simply the target problem solver whose heuristics we want to improve. The performance of applying a problem solver on a test case is in terms of the quality of the solution found and the cost of the problem-solving process.

In our learning strategy, the problem solver accepts (a) the specification of the HM to be used in problem solving, and (b) the test case to be solved. It also has a mechanism to return the measured performance of the problem-solving process as feedback to the learning system.

Test-Case Manager

This provides test cases to be used in learning. These test cases are either generated randomly or retrieved from a database.

In our current implementation, each HM is evaluated on a predefined sequence of user-specified test cases. When a test case is requested for testing a particular HM, the Test-Case Manager returns the first test case in the sequence that has not been evaluated by the chosen HM. This strategy allows performance data of two HMs to be normalized against each other and is useful when performance data have large variances.

Population-Based Learning Element

The *Population-Based Learning Element* maintains a pool of active HMs. At the end of each generation, a new set of HMs are generated to replace existing HMs. Several top active HMs are usually retained along with the new HMs while other HMs are removed from the active pool.

The Population-Based Learning Element in Teacher generates new HMs using weak domain-independent operators, such as crossover, mutation, and hill-climbing. These are traditional operators used in genetic algorithms for generating new HMs [12, 25]. The process for selecting existing HMs for reproduction is also the same as in traditional genetics-based machine learning.

More advanced generation methods that require additional domain knowledge are left for future study. They are currently not necessary because our application domains are knowledge lean.

Internal Critic

In general, this performs credit assignment [63] that apportions credit and blame on components of an HM using results obtained in testing (see Figure 4.3). Credit assignments can be classified into temporal credit assignment (TCA) and structural credit assignment (SCA). TCA is the first stage in the assimilation of feedback and precedes SCA. TCA divides feedback between the current and the past decisions. Methods for TCA depend on whether the state space is Markovian: non-Markovian representations often require more complex TCA procedures. The second stage is SCA that translates the (temporally local but structurally global) feedback associated with a decision point into modifications associated with various parameters of the decision process.

Since the knowledge-lean applications considered here does not have a world model that relates states, decisions, and feedback signals generated by the learning system or measured in the environment, credit assignment has a much weaker influence on performance improvement. Note that the lack of a world model for credit assignment is the main reason for maintaining competing HMs in our learning system.

In our current prototype, the Internal Critic normalizes the performance value of an HM on a test case against the performance value of the same test case evaluated by the baseline HM. It then updates the performance metrics of the candidate HM. This step is similar to updating fitness values in classifier-system learning.

We have chosen to use a fixed baseline HM during each learning phase and compare different HMs based on their estimated average normalized performance. This baseline HM is usually the best existing HM before learning begins.

Our approach in normalization may cause performance anomalies. For instance, different ways of normalization may lead to different ordering of HMs by their performance data. Anomalies in ordering may also happen when baselines are changed. Strategies to address some of these anomalies have been presented elsewhere [29, 69, 70].

Although anomalies may happen, it is not critical to have perfect ordering of HMs during learning, as the HMs will eventually be evaluated fully in the Performance Verification Phase.

Resource Scheduler

This schedules tests of HMs based on the available computational resources. It is critical when tests are computationally expensive. There are two problems in scheduling during each learning phase.

The *sample-allocation problem* involves the scheduling of tests of HMs in a generation, given a fixed number of tests in the generation and HMs to be tested. This problem is known in statistics as the (sequential) *allocation problem* [11, 67] and the scheduler, the *local scheduler*.

The *duration-scheduling problem* involves deciding when to terminate an existing generation and to start a new one. The part of the resource scheduler that deals with this problem is known as the *global scheduler.*

These two problems, as well as the scheduling of tests under multiple performance objectives, are presented elsewhere [3, 5, 7, 30, 69, 70]

4.7 Strategies in Performance Verification

In this phase, we like to find more complete performance information about the HMs we have generated during the learning phase(s). This is necessary for two reasons. First, the performance information obtained during each learning phase pertains to only one subdomain and is usually incomplete due to resource constraints. Second, the performance-generalization phase (to be described in the next section) requires performance information of each HM on every subdomain. Hence, we need to evaluate thoroughly the HMs selected at the end of learning.

The operations in this phase (see Figure 4.8) are very similar to those in the learning phase except for the following differences. (a) A fixed pool of HMs is maintained in this phase and no new HMs are generated. (b) More than one subdomains of test cases can be maintained by the Test-Case Manager. (c) The performance of HMs from different subdomains is evaluated separately and independently by the Internal Critic. (d) Resource scheduling in this phase has a different goal of minimizing uncertainties in the performance of all HMs across all subdomains. (e) Only temporal credit assignment is done in the Internal Critic since we do not use structural credit assignment to modify the HMs tested.

Currently, our prototype does not address the issue on resource scheduling in this phase. It evaluates each HM fully on all test cases in each problem subdomain. Such a strategy may be inefficient because it tests good HMs as well as poor HMs to the same extent. We plan to study resource scheduling in the future.

4.8 Strategies in Performance Generalization

As discussed in Section 4.4.2, an application domain (or application subspace) can have many subdomains, and HMs may behave differently

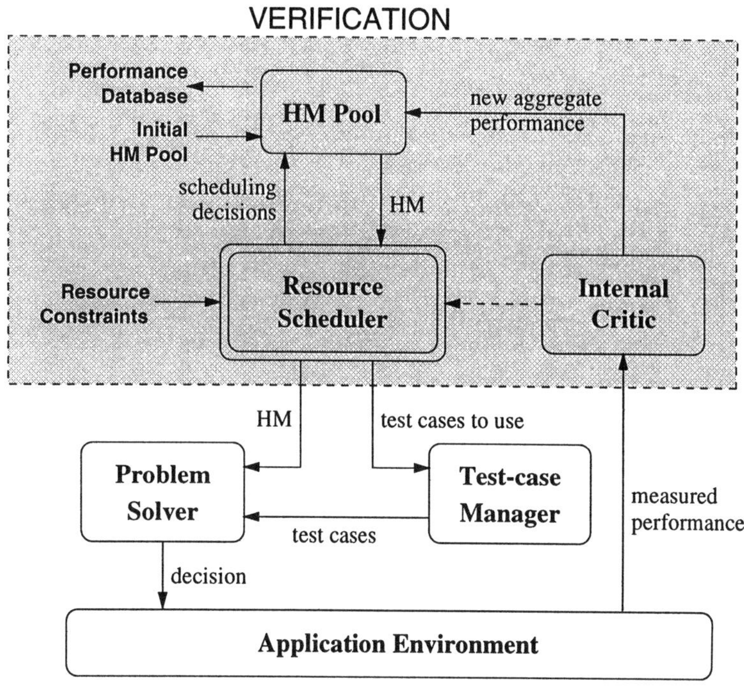

Figure 4.8: General model for performance verification of HMs learned.

in different subdomains. As a result, it is possible for an HM to perform well across all the subdomains, but its performance data from different subdomains cannot be aggregated statistically. Our objective in generalization is, therefore, to find one or more HMs in a given application domain that has a high probability of performing better than other competing HMs on a randomly chosen test case in the problem domain.

The performance-generalization process is difficult because (a) performance data from different subdomains must be treated separately and independently, and (b) there are usually many more subdomains than the ones we can test. Since we may not be able to characterize the subdomains we test to be representatives of the entire application domain, the process is heuristic in nature.

Example 3. To illustrate the difficulties in performance general-

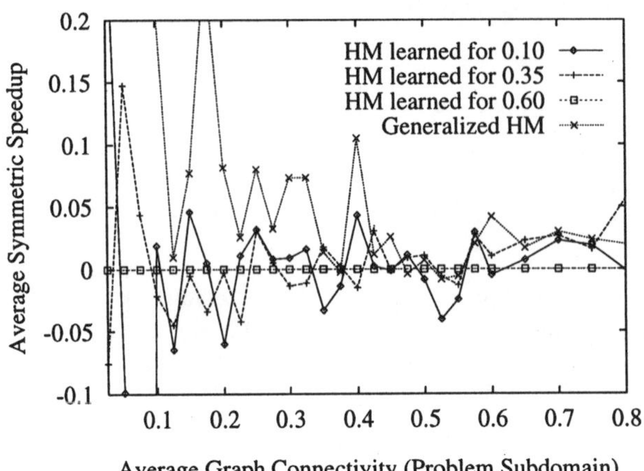

Figure 4.9: Average symmetric speedups (over 15 test cases) of three decomposition HMs to solve the vertex-cover problem, where subdomains are manually selected based on graph connectivity. The HM learned for 0.6 connectivity is the same as the baseline HM.

ization, we show in Figure 4.9 the average symmetric speedups[1] of four decomposition HMs used in a branch-and-bound search to solve vertex-cover problems. We treat all test cases as belonging to one subspace, and graphs with the same degree of connectivity are grouped into a subdomain. We apply genetics-based learning to find the five best HMs for each of three subdomains with connectivities 0.1, 0.35, and 0.6.

Figure 4.9 shows the performance of the best HMs learned in each subdomain across all the subdomains. We have also identified a single

[1]The symmetric-improvement measure, S^{sym+}, is defined as follows [29,69,70]:

$$S^{sym+} = \begin{cases} S^+ - 1 & \text{if} \quad S^+ \geq 1 \\ 1 - \dfrac{1}{S^+} & \text{if} \quad 0 \leq S^+ < 1 \end{cases},$$

where S^+ is the improvement ratio of the new HM with respect to the original baseline HM. Symmetric improvement ratios have the properties that they range from negative infinity to positive infinity, and that the baseline has a value of zero. On the other hand, improvement ratios range from zero to positive infinity, and the baseline HM has a value of one.

generalized HM among the fifteen HMs learned and show its performance in Figure 4.9. We find that the generalized HM is not the top HM learned in each subdomain, indicating that the best HM in each subdomain may be too specialized. We have also found that performance generalization is possible in terms of average performance. We must point out that the average performance should not be used as the sole indicator, as performance variances may differ from one subdomain to another. □

Our current work on generalization is to ensure that HMs generated in learning perform well across multiple subdomains. This is done by testing each HM on multiple subdomains in a generation and by selecting those that perform well across all the subdomains to be candidates for reproduction in the next generation. Our preliminary results indicate the need of a better fitness function to measure the merits of HMs that do not perform well across all the subdomains. Our current fitness function, based on the minimum average performance across all the tested subdomains, is too weak and may prune all the candidate HMs in a generation.

4.9 Experimental Results

Teacher has been applied in learning improved process-placement strategies on a network of workstations [40], more efficient process-placement strategies on distributed-memory multicomputers [30], more robust parameters in a stereo-vision algorithm [58], smaller feed-forward neural networks [65,66], improved heuristics for a branch-and-bound search [39, 76], better and less costly strategies in circuit testing [33, 70, 71] and cell placement and routing [33, 70, 71], and improved parameters in channel equalization [31, 33].

In this section, we report our experience in applying Teacher to learn improved HMs in two problem solvers, CRIS [55] and GATEST [54], for circuit testing. These are two genetic-algorithm software packages for generating patterns to test sequential VLSI circuits. In our experiments, we used sequential circuits from the ISCAS89 benchmarks [13] plus several other larger circuits. Since these circuits are from different applications, it is difficult to classify them by some common features. Consequently, we treat each circuit as an individual subdomain. As we like to find one common HM for all circuits, we assume that all circuits are from one subspace.

4.9.1 CRIS

CRIS [55] is based on continuous mutations of a given input test sequence and on analyzing the mutated vectors to select a new test sequence. Hierarchical simulation techniques are used in the system to reduce memory requirements, thereby allowing its application to large VLSI circuits. The package has been applied successfully to generate test patterns that can detect nearly all the detectable faults (high fault coverage) for large combinatorial and sequential circuits.

CRIS in our experiments is treated as a problem solver in a black box, as we have minimal knowledge in its design. An HM targeted for improvement is a set of eight parameters used in CRIS (see Table 4.1). Note that parameter P_8 is a random seed, implying that CRIS can be run multiple times using different random seeds in order to obtain better fault coverages. (In our experiments, we used a fixed sequence of ten random seeds from Table 4.2.)

A major problem in using the original CRIS is that it is hard to find proper values for the seven parameters (excluding the random seed) for a particular circuit. The designer of CRIS manually tuned these parameters for each circuit, resulting in HMs that are hard to generalize. This tuning was done because the designer wanted to obtain the highest possible fault coverage for each circuit, and computation cost was only a secondary consideration. Note that the times for manual tuning were exceedingly high and were not reported in the reference [55].

Our goal is to develop one common HM that works across all the benchmark circuits and that has similar or better fault coverages as compared to those of the original CRIS. The advantage of having one HM is that it can be applied to new circuits without further tuning.

4.9.2 GATEST

GATEST [54] is another test-pattern generator based on genetic algorithms. It augments existing techniques in order to reduce execution times and to improve fault coverages. The genetic-algorithm component evolves candidate test vectors and sequences, using a fault simulator to

Table 4.1: Parameters in CRIS treated as an HM in learning and in generalization. (The type, range, and step of each parameter were recommended to us by the designer of CRIS. The default parameters were not given to us as they are circuit dependent.)

Parameter	Type	Range	Step	Definition	Learned Value
P_1	integer	1-10	1	related to the number of stages in a flip-flop	1
P_2	integer	1-40	1	related to the sensitivity of changes of state of a flip-flop (number of times a flip-flop changes its state in a test sequence)	12
P_3	integer	1-40	1	selection criterion — related to the survival rate of a candidate test sequence in the next generation	38
P_4	float	0.1-10.0	0.1	related to the number of test vectors concatenated to form a new test sequence	7.06
P_5	integer	50-800	10	related to the number of useless trials before quitting	623
P_6	integer	1-20	1	number of generations	1
P_7	float	0.1-1.0	0.1	how genes are spliced in the genetic algorithm	0.1
P_8	integer	any	1	seed for the random number generator	-

Table 4.2: Sequence of random seeds used in learning experiments for CRIS, GATEST, and TimberWolf.

Sequence of Random Seeds				
61801	98052	15213	48823	55414
60203	43212	08540	94702	92715

compute the fitness of each candidate test. To improve performance, the designers manually tuned various genetic-algorithm parameters in the package, including alphabet size, fitness function, generation gap, population size, and mutation rate as well as selection and crossover schemes. High fault coverages were obtained for most of the ISCAS89 sequential benchmark circuits [13], and execution times were significantly lower in most cases than those obtained by HITEC [49], a deterministic test-pattern generator.

The entire genetic-algorithm process was divided into four phases, each with its own fitness function that had been manually tuned by the designers. The designers also told us that Phase 2 of their package had the largest impact on performance and recommended that we improved it first. As a result, we treated GATEST as our problem solver, and the fitness function (a symbolic formula) in Phase 2 as our HM. The original form of this fitness function is

$$fitness_2 = \#\_faults\_detected + \frac{\#\_faults\_propagated\_to\_flip\_flops}{(\#\_faults)(\#\_flip\_flops)} \tag{4.1}$$

In learning a new fitness function, we have used the following variables as possible arguments of the function: *#_faults*, *#_faults_detected*, *#_circuit_nodes*, *#_flip_flops*, *#_faults_propagated_to_flip_flops*, and *sequence_length*. The operators allowed to compose new fitness functions include $+$, $-$, $*$, and $/$.

4.9.3 Experimental results

In our experiments, we chose five circuits as our learning subdomains. In each of these subdomains, we used Teacher to test CRIS 1000 times with different HMs, each represented as the first seven parameters in Table 4.1. At the end of learning, we picked the top 20 HMs and evaluated them fully by initializing CRIS by ten different random seeds (P_8 in Table 4.1 with values from Table 4.2). We then selected the top five HMs from each subdomain, resulting in a total of 25 HMs supplied to the generalization phase. We evaluated the 25 HMs fully (each with ten random seeds) on the five subdomains used in learning and five new subdomains. We then selected one generalized HM to be used across all ten circuits. Since there is no incumbent HM, we use the median performance value of each test case as the baseline performance for that test case. The elements of the generalized HM found are shown in Table 4.1.

For GATEST, we applied learning to find good HMs for six circuits (s298, s386, s526, s820, s1196, and s1488 in the ISCAS89 benchmark). We then generalized the best 30 HMs (five from each subdomain) by first evaluating them fully (each with ten random seeds from Table 4.2) on the six subdomains and by selecting one generalized HM for all circuits. Since there is an incumbent HM, we use the performance of the incumbent HM as our baseline for improvement. The final fitness function we got after generalization is

$$\begin{aligned} fitness_2 &= 2 \times \#\_faults\_propagated\_to\_flip\_flops \\ &\quad - \#\_faults\_detected \end{aligned} \tag{4.2}$$

Table 4.3 shows the results after generalization for CRIS and GATEST. For each circuit, we present the average and maximum fault coverages (over ten random seeds) and the corresponding computational costs. These fault coverages are compared against the published fault coverages of CRIS [55] and GATEST [54] as well as those of HITEC [49]. Note that the maximum fault coverages reported in Table 4.3 were based on ten runs of the underlying problem solver, implying that the computational cost is ten times the average cost.

Table 4.4 summarizes the improvements of our learned and generalized HMs as compared to the published results of CRIS, GATEST, and HITEC. Each entry of the table shows the number of times our HM wins, ties, and loses in terms of fault coverages with respect to the method(s) in the first column. Our results show that our generalized HM based on CRIS as the problem solver is better than the original CRIS in 16 out of 21 circuits in terms of the maximum fault coverage and better than 11 out of 21 circuits in terms of the average fault coverage. Furthermore, our generalized HM based on GATEST as the problem solver is better than the original GATEST in 7 out of 19 circuits in terms of both the average and the maximum fault coverages. Note that the average fault coverages of our generalized HM are better than or equal to the original GATEST in all subdomains used in the heuristics-design process. Our results show that our generalization procedure can discover good HMs that work better than the original HMs.

Table 4.3: Performance of HMs in terms of computational cost and fault coverage for CRIS and GATEST. (Learned subdomains for CRIS are marked by "*" and generalized subdomains by "+"). Performance of HITEC is from the literature [49, 55]. Costs of our experiments are running times in seconds on a Sun SparcStation 10/51; costs of HITEC are running times in seconds on a Sun SparcStation SLC [54] (a computer around 4-6 times slower than a Sun SparcStation 10/51).

Circuit ID	Total Faults	Fault Coverage				Cost		CRIS Gen. HM			GATEST Gen. HM		
		HITEC	CRIS	Avg. GATEST	Max. GATEST	HITEC	Avg. GATEST	Avg. FC	Max. FC	Avg. Cost	Avg. FC	Max. FC	Avg. Cost
*s298	308	86.0	82.1	85.9	86.0	15984.0	128.6	84.7	86.4	10.9	85.9	86.0	126.4
s344	342	95.9	93.7	96.2	96.2	4788.0	134.8	96.1	96.2	21.8	96.2	96.2	133.3
s349	350	95.7	–	95.7	95.7	3132.0	136.9	95.6	95.7	21.9	95.7	95.7	128.3
+s382	399	90.9	68.6	87.0	87.5	43200.0	203.3	72.4	87.0	7.2	87.0	87.5	208.9
s386	384	81.7	76.0	76.9	77.9	61.8	67.6	77.5	78.9	3.5	78.6	79.3	78.6
*s400	426	89.9	84.7	85.7	86.6	43560.0	229.3	71.2	85.7	8.4	85.7	86.6	215.1
s444	474	87.3	83.7	85.6	86.3	57960.0	259.4	79.8	85.4	9.3	85.6	86.3	233.8
*s526	555	65.7	77.1	75.1	76.4	168480.0	333.4	70.0	77.1	10.0	75.5	77.3	302.7
s641	467	86.5	85.2	86.5	86.5	1080.0	181.2	85.0	86.1	19.5	86.5	86.5	195.0
+s713	581	81.9	81.7	81.9	81.9	91.2	219.9	81.3	81.9	23.0	81.9	81.9	256.5
s820	850	95.6	53.1	60.8	68.0	5796.0	266.4	44.7	46.7	51.3	69.3	80.9	225.4
*s832	870	93.9	42.5	61.9	66.8	6336.0	265.8	44.1	45.6	44.6	66.9	72.8	251.0
s1196	1242	99.7	95.0	99.2	99.5	91.8	292.1	92.0	94.1	20.0	99.2	99.4	421.7
*s1238	1355	94.6	90.7	94.0	94.4	132.0	380.5	88.2	89.2	23.0	94.0	94.2	585.2
s1488	1486	97.0	91.2	93.7	96.0	12960.0	512.3	94.1	95.2	85.6	94.3	96.5	553.4
+s1494	1506	96.4	90.1	94.0	95.8	6876.0	510.4	93.2	94.1	85.5	93.6	95.6	584.3
s1423	1515	40.0	77.0	81.0	86.3	–	3673.9	82.0	88.3	210.4	81.3	87.3	4325.7
+s5378	4603	70.3	65.8	69.5	70.1	–	9973.3	65.3	69.9	501.8	69.6	71.9	8875.7
s35932	39094	89.3	88.2	89.5	89.7	13680.0	184316.0	77.9	78.4	4265.7	89.4	89.7	184417.0
am2910	2573	85.0	83.0	–	–	–	–	83.7	85.2	307.6	–	–	–
+div16	2147	72.0	75.0	–	–	–	–	79.1	81.0	149.9	–	–	–
tc100	1979	80.6	70.8	–	–	–	–	72.6	75.9	163.8	–	–	–

Table 4.4: Summary of results comparing the performance of our generalized HMs with respect to those of HITEC, CRIS, and GATEST. (The first number in each entry shows the number of wins out of all applicable circuits, the second, the number of ties, and the third, the number of losses. A second number in the entry on wins indicates the number of circuits in which the test efficiency is already 100%. For these circuits, no further improvement is possible.)

Our HM wins/ties/loses with respect to the following systems	CRIS Generalized HM			GATEST Generalized HM		
	Total	Max. FC	Avg. FC	Total	Max. FC	Avg. FC
HITEC	22	6, 2, 14	4, 0, 18	19	5+2, 2, 10	4+2, 1, 12
Original CRIS	21	16, 1, 4	11, 0, 10	18	18, 0, 0	17, 0, 1
Original GATEST	19	4, 3, 12	3, 0, 16	19	7+2, 7, 3	7+2, 8, 2
Both HITEC and CRIS	21	5, 2, 14	3, 0, 18	18	5+2, 1, 10	3+2, 1, 13
Both HITEC & GATEST	19	3, 3, 13	1, 0, 18	19	3+2, 4, 10	2+2, 2, 13
HITEC, CRIS, & GATEST	18	2, 3, 13	1, 0, 17	18	3+2, 3, 10	1+2, 1, 14

Table 4.4 also indicates that HITEC is still better than our new generalized HM for CRIS in most of the circuits (in 14 out of 21 in terms of the maximal fault coverage and in 17 out of 21 in terms of the average fault coverage). The poor performance of our generalized HM as compared to HITECH is attributed to the limitations in CRIS and by our HM generator. Such limitations cannot be overcome without using HITECH as our problem solver or without using more powerful HM generator.

Finally, we plot the distributions of symmetric fault coverages of our generalized HMs normalized with respect to the average fault coverages of the original CRIS (Figure 4.10) and GATEST (Figure 4.11). These plots clearly demonstrate improvements over the original HMs.

4.10 Conclusions

In this chapter, we have studied the following five issues in learning improved knowledge-lean heuristics using a genetics-based machine learning approach:

- Decomposition of a problem solver into components so that heuristics can be learned for each, and integration of the heuristics

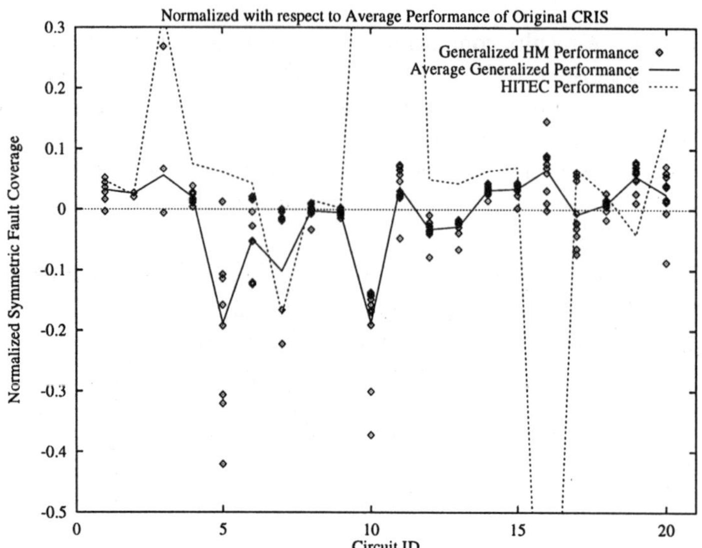

Figure 4.10: Distribution of the normalized symmetric fault coverages of our generalized HM with respect to the average fault coverages of the original CRIS on 20 benchmark circuits (s298, s344, s382, s386, s400, s444, s526, s641, s713, s820, s832, s1196, s1238, s1488, s1494, s1423, s5378, am2910, div16, and tc100 in that order).

learned into the problem solver,

- Partitioning of test cases in an application domain into subdomains so that performance data of heuristics within each subdomain are independent and identically distributed,
- Generation of new heuristics based on performance of existing heuristics evaluated in the past,
- Full evaluation of heuristics to verify their performance,
- Generalization of performance of heuristics to find heuristics that perform well across the entire application domain.

To address these issues, we have developed Teacher, a genetics-based system for learning knowledge-lean heuristics. Teacher has four phases in its operation: (a) classification of test cases into subdomains, (b)

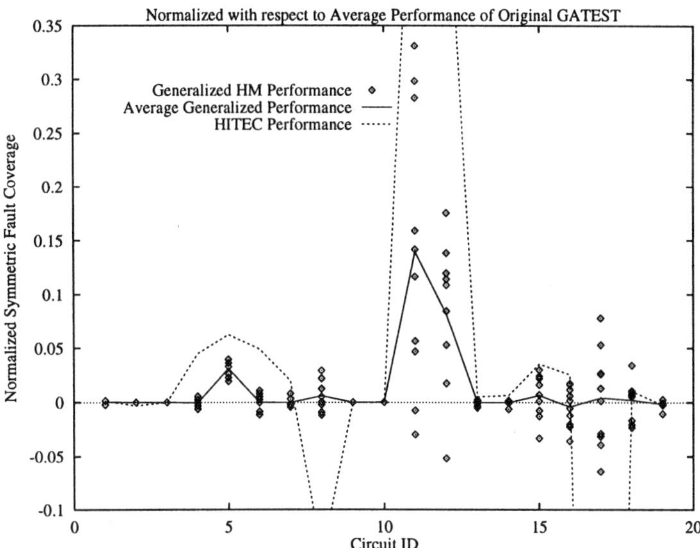

Figure 4.11: Distribution of the normalized symmetric fault coverages of our generalized HM with respect to the average fault coverages of the original GATEST on 19 benchmark circuits (s298, s344, s349, s382, s386, s400, s444, s526, s641, s713, s820, s832, s1196, s1238, s1488, s1494, s1423, s5378, and s35932 in that order).

learning improved heuristics for one subdomain at a time under resource constraints, (c) verification of performance of heuristics learned to augment partial evaluation results obtained during learning, and (d) finding heuristics whose performance behavior can be generalized to subdomains not studied in learning.

Finally, we have shown improved heuristics for two genetic algorithm packages used in VLSI test-pattern generation and have demonstrated that improved heuristics learned can be generalized to new circuits. Our approach allows designers to apply circuit-independent heuristics in these systems, eliminating the time-consuming process to find good heuristics for each circuit.

Acknowledgment

Research was supported partially by National Science Foundation Grants MIP 92-18715 and MIP 96-32316 and by National Aeronautics and Space Administration Contract NAG 1-613.

Bibliography

[1] D. H. Ackley, *A Connectionist Machine for Genetic Hillclimbing.* Boston, MA: Kluwer Academic Pub., 1987.

[2] A. Aizawa and B. W. Wah, "Scheduling of genetic algorithms in a noisy environment," in *Proc. Int'l Conf. on Genetic Algorithms*, (Morgan Kaufman), pp. 48–55, Int'l Soc. for Genetic Algorithms, July 1993.

[3] A. Aizawa and B. W. Wah, "Scheduling of genetic algorithms in a noisy environment," in *Proc. Int'l Conf. on Genetic Algorithms*, (Morgan Kaufman), pp. 48–55, Int'l Soc. for Genetic Algorithms, July 1993.

[4] A. K. Aizawa and B. W. Wah, "Scheduling of genetic algorithms in a noisy environment," *Evolutionary Computation*, vol. 2, no. 2, pp. 97–122, 1994.

[5] A. K. Aizawa and B. W. Wah, "Scheduling of genetic algorithms in a noisy environment," *Evolutionary Computation*, vol. 2, no. 2, pp. 97–122, 1994.

[6] A. N. Aizawa and B. W. Wah, "A sequential sampling procedure for genetic algorithms," *Computers and Mathematics with Applications*, vol. 27, pp. 77–82, May 1994.

[7] A. N. Aizawa and B. W. Wah, "A sequential sampling procedure for genetic algorithms," *Computers and Mathematics with Applications*, vol. 27, pp. 77–82, May 1994.

[8] A. Barr and E. A. Feigenbaum, *The Handbook of Artificial Intelligence.* Vol. 1, 2, and 3, Los Altos, CA: William Kaufmann, 1981.

[9] D. Beasley, D. R. Bull, and R. R. Martin, "An overview of genetic algorithms: Part 1, fundamentals," *Univ. Comput.*, vol. 15, no. 2, pp. 58–69, 1993.

[10] D. Beasley, D. R. Bull, and R. R. Martin, "An overview of genetic algorithms: Part 2, research topics," *Univ. Comput.*, vol. 15, no. 4, pp. 170–181, 1993.

[11] R. E. Bechhofer, "A single-sample multiple decision procedure for ranking means of normal populations with known variances," *Ann. Math. Statist.*, vol. 25, pp. 16–39, March 1954.

[12] L. B. Booker, D. E. Goldberg, and J. H. Holland, "Classifier systems and genetic algorithms," in *Machine Learning: Paradigm and Methods*, (J. Carbonell, ed.), MIT press, 1990.

[13] F. Brglez, D. Bryan, and K. Kozminski, "Combinatorial profiles of sequential benchmark circuits," in *Int'l Symposium on Circuits and Systems*, pp. 1929–1934, May 1989.

[14] S. Chien, J. Gratch, and M. Burl, "On the efficient allocation of resources for hypothesis evaluation: A statistical approach," *IEEE Trans. Pattern Anal. Mach. Intell.*, vol. 17, pp. 652–665, July 1995.

[15] K. DeJong, "Learning with genetic algorithms: An overview," *Machine Learning*, vol. 3, pp. 121–138, Oct. 1988.

[16] K. DeJong and W. Spears, "On the state of evolutionary computation," in *Proc. Fifth Int. Conf. Genetic Algorithms*, pp. 618–623, Int. Soc. for Genetic Algorithms, June 1993.

[17] K. A. DeJong, W. M. Spears, and D. F. Gordon, "Using genetic algorithm for concept learning," *Mach. Learn.*, vol. 13, pp. 161–188, November/December 1993.

[18] R. Desimone, "Learning control knowledge within an explanation-based learning framework," in *Progress in Machine Learning*,

(I. Bratko and N. Lavrac, eds.), pp. 107–119, Cheshire, UK: Sigma Press, 1987.

[19] T. G. Dietterich and B. G. Buchanan, "The role of critic in learning systems," Tech. Rep. STAN-CS-81-891, Stanford Univ., CA, Dec. 1981.

[20] G. W. Ernst and M. M. Goldstein, "Mechanical discovery of classes of problem-solving strategies," *J. of the ACM*, vol. 29, pp. 1–23, Jan. 1982.

[21] J. M. Fitzpatrick and J. J. Grefenstette, "Genetic algorithms in noisy environments," *Machine Learning*, vol. 3, pp. 101–120, Oct. 1988.

[22] D. E. Goldberg, *Genetic Algorithms in Search, Optimization, and Machine Learning.* Addison-Wesley Pub. Co., 1989.

[23] D. E. Goldberg and J. H. Holland, "Genetic algorithms and machine learning," *Machine Learning*, vol. 3, pp. 95–100, Oct. 1988.

[24] D. E. Goldberg, K. Deb, and J. H. Clark, "Genetic algorithms, noise, and the sizing of populations," *Complex Syst.*, vol. 6, pp. 333–362, 1992.

[25] J. J. Grefenstette, "Optimization of control parameters for genetic algorithms," *Trans. on Systems, Man, and Cybernetics*, vol. SMC-16, pp. 122–128, Jan. 1986.

[26] J. J. Grefenstette, C. L. Ramsey, and A. C. Schultz, "Learning sequential decision rules using simulation models and competition," *Machine Learning*, vol. 5, pp. 355–381, 1990.

[27] J. Heitkötter and D. Beasley, eds., *The Hitch-Hiker's Guide to Evolutionary Computation: A List of Frequently Asked Questions (FAQ).* USENET: comp.ai.genetic, 1995. Anonymous FTP: rtfm.mit.edu:/pub/usenet/news.answers/ai-faq/genetic/.

[28] J. H. Holland, *Adaptation in Natural and Artificial Systems.* Ann Arbor, MI: Univ. of Michigan Press, 1975.

[29] A. Ieumwananonthachai, *Automated Design of Knowledge-Lean Heuristics: Learning, Resource Scheduling, and Generalization.* Urbana, IL: Ph.D. Thesis, Dept. of Electrical and Computer Engineering, Univ. of Illinois, May 1996.

[30] A. Ieumwananonthachai, A. Aizawa, S. R. Schwartz, B. W. Wah, and J. C. Yan, "Intelligent process mapping through systematic improvement of heuristics," *J. of Parallel and Distributed Computing*, vol. 15, pp. 118–142, June 1992.

[31] A. Ieumwananonthachai and B. W. Wah, "Statistical generalization of performance-related heuristics for knowledge-lean applications," in *Proc. Int'l Conference on Tools for Artificial Intelligence*, (Houston, TX), pp. 174–181, IEEE, Nov. 1995.

[32] A. Ieumwananonthachai and B. W. Wah, "Teacher – an automated system for learning knowledge-lean heuristics," Tech. Rep. CRHC-95-08, Center for Reliable and High Performance Computing, Coordinated Science Laboratory, Univ. of Illinois, Urbana, IL, March 1995.

[33] A. Ieumwananonthachai and B. W. Wah, "Statistical generalization of performance-related heuristics for knowledge-lean applications," *Int'l J. of Artificial Intelligence Tools*, vol. 5, pp. 61–79, June 1996.

[34] C. Z. Janikow, "A knowledge-intensive genetic algorithm for supervised learning," *Mach. Learn.*, vol. 13, pp. 189–228, November/December 1993.

[35] A. H. Klopf, "Drive-reinforcement learning: A real-time learning mechanism for unsupervised learning," in *Proc. Int'l Conf. on Neural Networks*, pp. 441–445, IEEE, 1987.

[36] J. R. Koza, *Genetic Programming.* Cambridge, MA: The MIT Press, 1992.

[37] P. Langley, "Learning to search: From weak methods to domain-specific heuristics," *Cognitive Science*, vol. 9, pp. 217–260, 1985.

[38] D. B. Lenat, "Theory formation by heuristic search; the nature of heuristics II: Background and examples," *Artificial Intelligence*, vol. 21, pp. 31–59, 1983.

[39] M. B. Lowrie and B. W. Wah, "Learning heuristic functions for numeric optimization problems," in *Proc. Computer Software and Applications Conf.*, (Chicago, IL), pp. 443–450, IEEE, Oct. 1988.

[40] P. Mehra and B. W. Wah, *Load Balancing: An Automated Learning Approach.* World Scientific Publishing Co. Pte. Ltd., 1995.

[41] R. S. Michalski, "Understanding the nature of learning: Issues and research directions," in *Machine Learning: An Artificial Intelligence Approach*, (R. S. Michalski, J. G. Carbonell, and T. M. Mitchell, eds.), pp. 3–25, Los Altos, CA: Morgan Kaufmann, 1986.

[42] M. Minsky, "Steps toward artificial intelligence," in *Computers and Thought*, (E. A. Feigenbaum and J. Feldman, eds.), pp. 406–450, New York: McGraw-Hill, 1963.

[43] S. Minton, J. G. Carbonell, C. A. Knoblock, D. R. Kuokka, O. Etzioni, and Y. Gil, "Explanation-based learning: A problem solving perspective," in *Machine Learning: Paradigms and Methods*, (J. Carbonell, ed.), pp. 63–118, Cambridge, MA: M.I.T. Press, 1990.

[44] T. M. Mitchell, "Learning and problem solving," in *Proc. 8th Int'l Joint Conf. on Artificial Intelligence*, (Los Altos, CA), pp. 1139–1151, William Kaufman, Aug. 1983.

[45] T. M. Mitchell, P. E. Utgoff, and R. B. Banerji, "Learning by experimentation: Acquiring and refining problem-solving heuristics," in *Machine Learning*, (R. S. Michalski, J. G. Carbonell, and T. M. Mitchell, eds.), Tioga, 1983.

[46] T. M. Mitchell, P. E. Utgoff, B. Nudel, and R. Benerji, "Learning problem-solving heuristics through practice," in *Proc. 7th Int'l Joint Conf. on Artificial Intelligence*, (Los Altos, CA), pp. 127–134, William Kaufman, 1981.

[47] H. R. Neave and P. L. Worthington, *Distribution-Free Tests.* London, UK: Unwin Hyman, 1988.

[48] D. Nguyen and B. Widrow, "The truck backer-upper: An example of self-learning in neural networks," in *Proc. Int'l Joint Conf. on Neural Networks*, pp. 357–363, IEEE, 1989.

[49] T. M. Niermann and J. H. Patel, "HITEC: A test generation package for sequential circuits," in *European Design Automation Conference*, pp. 214–218, 1991.

[50] W. H. Press, S. A. Teukolsky, W. T. Vetterling, and B. P. Flannery, *Numerical Recipes in C.* Cambridge, UK: Cambridge University Press, 2nd ed., 1992.

[51] C. L. Ramsey and J. J. Grefenstette, "Case-based initialization of genetic algorithms," in *Proc. of the Fifth Int'l Conf. on Genetic Algorithms*, (Morgan Kaufman), pp. 84–91, Int'l Soc. for Genetic Algorithms, June 1993.

[52] L. A. Rendell, "A new basis for state-space learning systems and a successful implementation," *Artificial Intelligence*, vol. 20, pp. 369–392, 1983.

[53] G. Robertson and R. Riolo, "A tale of two classifier systems," *Machine Learning*, vol. 3, pp. 139–160, Oct. 1988.

[54] E. M. Rudnick, J. H. Patel, G. S. Greenstein, and T. M. Niermann, "Sequential circuit test generation in a genetic algorithm framework," in *Proc. Design Automation Conf.*, ACM/IEEE, June 1994.

[55] D. G. Saab, Y. G. Saab, and J. A. Abraham, "CRIS: A test cultivation program for sequential VLSI circuits," in *Proc. of Int'l Conf. on Computer Aided Design*, (Santa Clara, CA), pp. 216–219, IEEE, Nov. 8-12 1992.

[56] A. L. Samuel, "Some studies in machine learning using the game of checkers," *IBM J. Research and Development*, vol. 3, pp. 210–229, 1959.

[57] A. L. Samuel, "Some studies in machine learning using the game of checkers II–recent progress," *J. of Research and Development*, vol. 11, no. 6, pp. 601–617, 1967.

[58] S. R. Schwartz and B. W. Wah, "Automated parameter tuning in stereo vision under time constraints," in *Proc. Int'l Conf. on Tools for Artificial Intelligence*, pp. 162–169, IEEE, Nov. 1992.

[59] D. Sleeman, P. Langley, and T. M. Mitchell, "Learning from solution paths: An approach to the credit assignment problem," *AI Magazine*, vol. 3, pp. 48–52, 1982.

[60] R. G. Smith, T. M. Mitchell, R. A. Chestek, and B. G. Buchanan, "A model for learning systems," in *Proc. 5th Int'l Joint Conf. on Artificial Intelligence*, (Los Altos, CA), pp. 338–343, William Kaufman, Aug. 1977.

[61] S. F. Smith, "Flexible learning of problem solving heuristics through adaptive search," in *Proc. Int'l Joint Conf. on Artificial Intelligence*, pp. 422–5, Morgan Kaufman, 1983.

[62] W. M. Spears, K. A. DeJong, T. Bäck, D. Fogel, and H. de Garis, "An overview of evolutionary computing," in *Proc. European Conf. on Machine Learning*, (New York, NY), pp. 442–459, Springer-Verlag, 1993.

[63] R. S. Sutton, *Temporal Credit Assignment in Reinforcement Learning*. PhD thesis, Univ. of Massachusetts, Amherst, MA, Feb. 1984.

[64] R. S. Sutton and A. G. Barto, "Toward a modern theory of adaptive networks: Expectation and prediction," *Psychological Review*, vol. 88, no. 2, pp. 135–170, 1984.

[65] C.-C. Teng and B. W. Wah, "An automated design system for finding the minimal configuration of a feed-forward neural network," in *Proc. Int'l Conf. on Neural Networks*, pp. III–1295 – III–1300, IEEE, June 1994.

[66] C.-C. Teng and B. W. Wah, "Automated learning of the minimal configuration of a feed forward neural network," *IEEE Trans. on Neural Networks*, vol. 7, pp. 1072–1085, Sep. 1996.

[67] Y. L. Tong and D. E. Wetzell, "Allocation of observations for selecting the best normal population," in *Design of Experiments: Ranking and Selection*, (T. J. Santner and A. C. Tamhane, eds.), pp. 213–224, New York, NY: Marcel Dekker, 1984.

[68] N. R. Ullman, *Statistics: An Applied Approach.* Lexington, MA: Xerox College Publishing, 1972.

[69] B. W. Wah, "Population-based learning: A new method for learning from examples under resource constraints," *IEEE Trans. on Knowledge and Data Engineering*, vol. 4, pp. 454–474, Oct. 1992.

[70] B. W. Wah, A. Ieumwananonthachai, L. C. Chu, and A. Aizawa, "Genetics-based learning of new heuristics: Rational scheduling of experiments and generalization," *IEEE Trans. on Knowledge and Data Engineering*, vol. 7, pp. 763–785, Oct. 1995.

[71] B. W. Wah, A. Ieumwananonthachai, S. Yao, and T. Yu, "Statistical generalization: Theory and applications (plenary address)," in *Proc. Int'l Conf. on Computer Design*, (Austin, TX), pp. 4–10, IEEE, Oct. 1995.

[72] J. E. Walsh, *Handbook of Nonparametric Statistics.* Vol. 1, Princeton, NJ: D. Van Nostrand Company, Inc., 1962.

[73] B. Widrow, N. K. Gupta, and S. Maitra, "Punish/reward: Learning with a critic in adaptive threshold systems," *Trans. Systems, Man, and Cybernetics*, vol. SMC-3, no. 5, pp. 455–465, 1973.

[74] R. J. Williams, "On the use of backpropagation in associative reinforcement learning," in *Proc. Int'l Conf. on Neural Networks*, pp. 263–270, IEEE, July 1988.

[75] S. W. Wilson and D. E. Goldberg, "A critical review of classifier systems," in *Proc. of the Third Int. Conf. Genetic Algorithms*, pp. 244–255, Int. Soc. for Genetic Algorithms, June 1989.

[76] C. F. Yu and B. W. Wah, "Learning dominance relations in combinatorial search problems," *IEEE Trans. on Software Engineering*, vol. SE-14, pp. 1155–1175, Aug. 1988.

Chapter 5

Automatic Discovery of Protein Motifs Using Genetic Programming

John R. Koza and David Andre

Automated methods of machine learning may prove to be useful in discovering biologically meaningful information hidden in the rapidly growing databases of DNA sequences and protein sequences.
Genetic programming is an extension of the genetic algorithm in which a population of computer programs is bred, over a series of generations, in order to solve a problem. Genetic programming is capable of evolving complicated problem-solving expressions of unspecified size and shape. Moreover, when automatically defined functions are added to genetic programming, genetic programming becomes capable of efficiently capturing and exploiting recurring sub-patterns.
This chapter describes how genetic programming with automatically defined functions successfully evolved motifs for detecting the D-E-A-D box family of proteins and for detecting the manganese superoxide dismutase family. Both motifs were evolved without prespecifying their length. Both evolved motifs employed automatically defined functions to capture the repeated use of common subexpressions. When tested against the SWISS-PROT database of proteins, the two genetically evolved consensus motifs detect the two families either as well, or slightly better

than, the comparable human-written motifs found in the PROSITE database.

5.1 Introduction

The structure and functions of living organisms are primarily determined by proteins (Stryer 1995). Proteins are large polypeptide molecules composed of sequences of up to several thousand amino acid residues. All proteins are composed from the same repertoire of 20 amino acid residues (conventionally denoted by the letters A, C, D, E, F, G, H, I, K, L, M, N, P, Q, R, S, T, V, W, and Y). Subject to only a few minor qualifications, the three-dimensional location of every atom of a protein in a living organism is fully determined by its sequence (its *primary structure*) of amino acid residues (Anfinsen 1973). The protein's three-dimensional structure (its *tertiary structure* or *conformation*), in turn, determines the biological function and activity of the protein within a living organism. Thus, effectively all of the information about the biological function and activity of a protein is contained (albeit deeply hidden) in its primary sequence (i.e., the linear sequence of letters over an alphabet of size 20).

SWISS-PROT is a massive, systematically-collected, periodically-reviewed, annotated database of protein sequences that is maintained by the University of Geneva and the European Molecular Biology Laboratory (Bairoch and Boeckmann 1991). Release 30 (October 1994) of SWISS-PROT, for example, contains 14,147,368 amino acid residues from 40,292 sequences from hundreds of different species. The Human Genome Project and other research efforts in molecular biology are rapidly increasing the number of entries in SWISS-PROT and other databases of protein sequences and genomic DNA sequences. Automated techniques (such as those of machine learning) may prove useful or necessary for analyzing this accumulating data.

Most proteins appear in many different species; however, the primary sequences of the "same" protein in two different species are often not identical. For one thing, the primary sequences of the "same" protein in two different species may differ slightly in length. Moreover, even after using an alignment algorithm (e.g., Smith and Waterman 1981) to align the related sequences of somewhat different lengths, the residues found at a particular aligned position often will still differ. The reason is that only relatively small subsequences of the overall sequence are responsible for the biological function, activity, and structure of the protein. Over millions of years, evolution has substituted dissimilar residues at non-critical positions. Even when one locates the relatively small subsequence of the protein that is responsible for the protein's biological activity, only a few of the residues of the subsequence will prove to be identical (that is, *conserved*) because evolution has also substituted chemically similar residues at these critical positions.

Sometimes, amidst all the differences, it is possible to identify certain high specificity, high sensitivity patterns (called *motifs*, *sites*, *signatures*, or *fingerprints*) in a set of sequences for biologically similar proteins. If a motif is defined well, it will detect a biologically-important common property. The residues in such motifs often prove to be directly responsible for the essential function and activity of the protein.

PROSITE is a database of biologically meaningful patterns found in protein sequences (Bairoch and Bucher 1994). Release 12 (June 1994) of PROSITE, for example, contains 1,029 different motifs. Motifs are entered in the PROSITE database after careful consideration by Amos Bairoch at the University of Geneva and his colleagues. Since the intended primary purpose of PROSITE is to detect families of proteins in computerized databases, a motif is included in PROSITE if it detects most (preferably all) sequences that have a particular biological property (i.e., has few false negatives), while detecting few (preferably zero) unrelated sequences (i.e., has few false positives).

Automated methods of machine learning may be useful in discovering biologically meaningful patterns that are hidden in the rapidly growing databases of genomic and protein sequences. Unfortunately, almost all existing methods of automated discovery require that the user specify, in advance, the size and shape of the pattern that is to be discovered. However, in practice, the discovery of the size and shape of the pattern may, in fact, be *the problem* (or at least a major part of the problem). Moreover, none of the existing methods of automated discovery have a workable analog of the idea of a reusable, parameterized subroutine or subprogram to capture and exploit repeated occurrences of regularities or sub-patterns of the problem environment.

The problem of discovering biologically meaningful patterns in databases can be rephrased as a search for an unknown-sized task-performing computer program (i.e., a composition of primitive functions and terminals). When the motif discovery problem is so rephrased, genetic programming becomes a candidate for solving this problem. Moreover, if it is also desired to reuse regularities in the problem environment, then genetic programming with automatically defined functions becomes a candidate.

Section 5.2 of this chapter provides background on protein databases, motifs, the D-E-A-D box family of proteins, and the manganese superoxide dismutase family. Section 5.3 of this chapter provides background on genetic programming. Section 5.4 identifies the preparatory steps required to apply genetic programming to the D-E-A-D box problem. Section 5.5 describes the implementation of genetic programming on a parallel computer. Section 5.6 presents a genetically consensus evolved motif that is slightly better than the human-written motif found in the PROSITE database for detecting the D-E-A-D box family of proteins. Section 5.7 presents a genetically evolved consensus motif for detecting the manganese superoxide dismutase family that is as good as the human-written motif found in the PROSITE database. Section 5.8 states the conclusion.

5.2 Background on Motifs and Proteins

The D-E-A-D Box Family of Proteins and the Manganese Superoxide Dismutase Family of Proteins will be used to illustrate how genetic programming may be applied to the problem of discovering motifs in protein sequences.

5.2.1 The D-E-A-D Box Family of Proteins

In the "Birth of the D-E-A-D box," Linder et. al. (1989) described a family of proteins (called *helicases*) involved in the unwinding of the double helix of the DNA molecule during the replication of DNA (Chang, Arenas, and Abelson 1990; and Dorer, Christensen, and Johnson 1990; Hodgman 1988).

This family of proteins gets its name from the fact that the amino acid residues D (aspartic acid), E (glutamic acid), A (alanine), and D appear, in that order, at the core of one of its biologically critical subsequences. There are 34 proteins from this family among the 40,292 proteins appearing in Release 30 of SWISS-PROT. Proteins of this family can be detected effectively (but not perfectly) by the following motif of length nine (called ATP_HELICASE_1) that was included by Amos Bairoch at the University of Geneva in the PROSITE database:
`[LIVM]-[LIVM]-D-E-A-D-X-[LIVM]-[LIVM].`

In interpreting this expression, the first pair of square brackets indicates that the first residue of the nine is to be chosen from the set consisting of the amino acid residues L, I, V, and M. The second pair of square brackets indicates that the second residue is chosen (independently from the first) from the same set of four possibilities. Then, the third, fourth, fifth, and sixth residues must be D, E, A, and D, respectively. The `X` in the motif indicates that the seventh residue can be any of the 20 possible amino acid residues. The eighth and ninth residues are chosen from the same set of four, namely L, I, V, and M.

D and E are negatively charged and hence hydrophilic (water-loving) at normal pH values. A is small, uncharged, hydrophobic (water-hating). L (leucine), I (isoleucine), V (valine), or M (methionine) are moderately-sized, uncharged, and hydrophobic. Thus, ignoring the `X`, this motif calls for three hydrophilic residues accompanied, on each side, by two moderately-sized hydrophobic residues.

The above PROSITE expression detects any of $4^4 \infty 20$ = 5,120 different possible sequences of length nine (out of approximately $5 \infty 10^{11}$ possible sequences of length nine). When SWISS-PROT is searched using the above PROSITE motif, there are 34 true positives, 14,147,333 true negatives (among the 40,292 proteins), 1 false positive, and 0 false negatives. This corresponds to a correlation coefficient (Matthews 1975), *C*, of 0.99.

Table 5.1 shows six of the 34 proteins containing the D-E-A-D box motif in the SWISS-PROT database. The table shows the position of the start of the D-E-A-D box motif in its second column. The third column shows the three amino acid residues in the primary sequence before the onset of the motif, the nine residues (in boldface) of the D-E-A-D box itself, and the five residues following the D-E-A-D box.

The number of PROSITE expressions (composed of disjunctions such as shown above) covering exactly nine positions is $(2^{20})^9 \sim 10^{54}$. Since the length of an expression that is capable of detecting a particular family of proteins is, in actual practice, not known in advance, the search space of the motif discovery problem is considerably larger than 10^{54}.

Table 5.1 *Six examples of D-E-A-D box motif.*

Protein	Start	Subsequence
Human Putative ATP Dependent RNA Helicase P54	244	QMI**VLDEADKLL**SQDFV
Rabbit Eukaryotic Initiation Factor 4A	168	KMF**VLDEADEML**SRGFK
Fruit Fly Vasa Protein	397	RFVVLDEADRMLDMGFS
C. Elegans Putative ATP-Dependent RNA Helicase	192	KFL**IMDEADRIL**NMDFE
E. Coli ATP-Dependent RNA Helicase	155	ETL**ILDEADRML**DMGFA
Fruit Fly Putative ATP-Dependent RNA Helicase	303	KFL**VIDEADRIM**DAVFQ

The question arises as to whether it is possible to use an automated machine learning technique to examine a large set of protein sequences and extract biologically meaningful motifs. Such a technique should, of course, not require advance specification of the length of the motif. When this problem is rephrased as a search for an unknown-sized task-performing computer program (i.e., a composition of primitive functions and terminals), genetic programming becomes a candidate for solving this problem. Moreover, if it is also desired to capture regularities in the problem environment (e.g., the repeated use of a subexpression such as `[LIVM]`), then genetic programming with automatically defined functions becomes relevant.

5.2.2 The Manganese Superoxide Dismutase Family of Proteins

The oxygen radicals that are normally produced in living cells have been implicated in many degenerative processes, including cancer and aging. Proteins belonging to the manganese superoxide dismutase family prevent oxidative damage to DNA and other molecules by catalyzing the conversion of these toxic superoxide radicals to oxygen and hydrogen peroxide (Ludwig et al. 1991; Stoddard, Ringe, and Petsko 1990; Bannister, Bannister, and

Rotilio 1987). The four ligands of the manganese atom are conserved in all the known sequences of the manganese superoxide dismutase family. Amos Bairoch selected a short conserved region that includes two of the four ligands, namely one D (aspartic acid) and one nearby H (histidine), to create the following motif of length eight (called SOD_MN) for detecting proteins belonging to this family:
`D-X-W-E-H-[STA]-[FY][FY].`

For example, in human manganese superoxide dismutase (whose length is 198), the above motif correctly identifies the protein as belonging to this family because residues 159 to 166 of this protein are
`DVWEHAYY.`
When it is tested against all of SWISS-PROT, the above motif scored 40 true positives, 14,147,328 true negatives, and 0 false positive and 0 false negatives (for a correlation of 1.00).

The Protein Data Bank (PDB), maintained by the Brookhaven National Laboratory in Upton, New York (Bernstein et al. 1977), is the worldwide computerized repository of the three-dimensional coordinates of the atomic structure of proteins. Proteins from the PDB can be interactively displayed by making a three-dimensional *kinemage* of the protein using the PREKIN software and viewing the kinemage with the MAGE software (Richardson and Richardson 1992). Figure 5.1 shows residues 159 to 166 of human manganese superoxide dismutase (1ABM in the Protein Data Bank) as well as the histidines at positions 26 and 74 of the protein sequence. The manganese is ligated by Asp 159, His 163, His 26, and His 74.

5.3 Background on Genetic Programming

John Holland's pioneering *Adaptation in Natural and Artificial Systems* described how the evolutionary process in nature can be applied to solving problems using what is now called the *genetic algorithm* (Holland 1975). Additional information on recent work in the field of genetic algorithms can be found in Goldberg (1989); Davis (1987, 1991); Michalewicz (1992); Eshelman (1995); Whitley (1992); Maenner and Manderick (1992); Schaffer and Whitley (1992); Albrecht, Reeves, and Steele (1993); Stender (1993);

Buckles and Petry (1992); Stender, Hillebrand, and Kingdon (1994); Forrest (1991); Bauer (1994); and Davidor (1990).

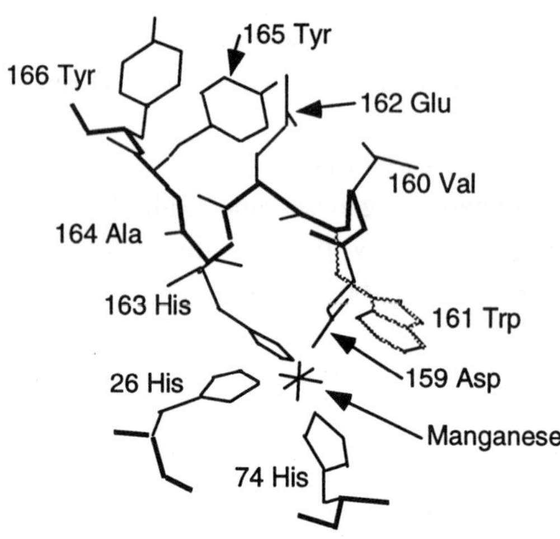

Figure 5.1 *Active site of human manganese superoxide dismutase.*

Genetic programming is an extension of the genetic algorithm in which the genetic population consists of computer programs. Genetic programming starts with a primordial ooze of randomly generated computer programs composed of available primitive programmatic ingredients. The population of programs is then bred over many generations in a domain-independent way using the Darwinian principle of survival of the fittest and an analog of the naturally-occurring genetic operation of crossover (sexual recombination). The crossover operation is designed to create syntactically valid offspring programs from parents that are probabilistically selected based on their fitness at solving the problem at hand. Genetic programming combines the expressive high-level symbolic representations of computer programs with the near-optimal efficiency of learning of the genetic algorithm.

Genetic Programming: On the Programming of Computers by Means of Natural Selection (Koza 1992) provides evidence that genetic programming can solve, or approximately solve, a variety of problems from a variety of fields. These problems include benchmark problems from machine learning and artificial intelligence involving control, robotics, optimization, game playing, symbolic regression, system identification, empirical discovery, and concept learning. Recent work on genetic programming is found in Kinnear 1994 and Angeline and Kinnear 1996. A videotape visualization of a number of applications of genetic programming can be found in Koza and Rice (1992) and Koza (1994).

The sequence of work-performing steps of the to-be-evolved programs are not specified in advance by the user. Instead, the sequence of steps is evolved as a result of the competitive and selective pressures of the evolutionary process and the recombinative role of crossover. Specifically, genetic programming is a domain-independent method that genetically breeds populations of computer programs to solve problems by executing the following three steps:

(1) Generate an initial population of random computer programs composed of the primitive functions and terminals of the problem.
(2) Iteratively perform generations consisting of the following sub-steps until the termination criterion of the problem is satisfied:
   (a) Execute each program in the population and determine how fit it is at solving the problem.
   (b) Create a new generation of the population of programs by applying the following two primary operations to program(s) that are selected from the population with a probability based on fitness (i.e., the fitter the program, the more likely it is to be selected).
      (i) *Reproduction*: Copy a selected program to the new population.
      (ii) *Crossover*: Create two new offspring programs for the new population by genetically recombining randomly chosen parts of two selected programs.
(3) The single best computer program produced anytime during the run is typically designated as the result of the run. This result may be a solution (or approximate solution) to the problem.

5.3.1 Automatically Defined Functions

When humans write programs, they use subroutines to exploit, *by reuse*, the regularities, symmetries, homogeneities, similarities, patterns, and modularities of problem environments. *Genetic Programming II: Automatic Discovery of Reusable Programs* (Koza 1994a) extends genetic programming to evolve multi-part programs consisting of a main program and one or more reusable hierarchically-callable subprograms.

An *automatically defined function* (*ADF*) is a function (i.e., subroutine, DEFUN, procedure, module) that is dynamically evolved during a run of genetic programming and that may be called by a calling program (or subprogram) that is simultaneously being evolved.

When automatically defined functions are being used, a program in the population consists of one (or more) *reusable* function-defining branches along with a main result-producing branch. As a run progresses, genetic programming evolves different main programs in the result-producing branch, different subprograms (i.e., automatically defined functions) in the function-defining branches, and different hierarchical references among the branches. The initial random generation of the population is created so that every individual program in the population has a constrained syntactic structure consisting of a particular architectural arrangement of result-producing branches and function-defining branches. Crossover is then performed in a structure-preserving way so as to preserve the syntactic validity of all offspring by assigning *types* to either entire branches (*branch typing* and *like-branch typing*) or individual points of the overall program (*point typing*).

Genetic programming with automatically defined functions has been shown to be capable of solving numerous problems. More importantly, the evidence so far indicates that, for many problems, genetic programming requires less computational effort (i.e., fewer fitness evaluations to yield a solution with a satisfactorily high probability) with automatically defined functions than without them (provided the difficulty of the problem is above a certain relatively low break-even point). Also, genetic programming usually yields solutions with smaller average overall size with automatically defined functions than without them (again provided that the problem is not too simple). That is, parsimony is an emergent property of automatically defined functions.

Moreover, there is also evidence that genetic programming with automatically defined functions is scalable. For several problems for which a progression of scaled-up versions was studied, the computational effort increased as a function of problem size at a *slower rate* with automatically defined functions than without them. Also, the average size of solutions similarly increased as a function of problem size at a *slower rate* with automatically defined functions than without them. Scalability results from the profitable reuse of hierarchically-callable subprograms within an overall program.

The PROSITE language has no facility for defining and using subroutines; however, the D-E-A-D box motif found in PROSITE database contains a repeatedly used subexpression consisting of four moderately-sized, uncharged, hydrophobic residues (L, I, V, and M). Similarly, the manganese superoxide dismutase motif contains a repeatedly used subexpression consisting of Y and F. Because of this manifest modularity, genetic programming with automatically defined functions may be appropriate for evolving a motif-detecting program for the D-E-A-D box family of proteins.

When genetic programming with automatically defined functions was applied to the problem of identifying transmembrane domains in proteins, the results were slightly better than previous human-written algorithms (Koza 1994c). Genetic programming has also been used to identify omega loops in proteins (Koza 1994c), to predict whether a residue in a protein sequence is in an α-helix (Handley 1993a, 1994a), to predict the degree to which a protein sequence is exposed to solvent (Handley 1994b), to predict whether or not a nucleic acid sequence is an *E. coli* promoter region (Handley 1995a); to predict whether or not a 60-base DNA sequence contains a centrally-located splice site (Handley 1995b); and to classify a nucleic acid subsequence as being an intron or exon (Handley 1995c).

5.4 Preparatory Steps for the D-E-A-D Box Family of Proteins

In applying genetic programming with automatically defined functions to a problem, there are six major preparatory steps, namely determining

(1) the set of terminals for each branch,

(2) the set of primitive functions for each branch,

(3) the fitness measure for evaluating how well a program does at solving the problem,

(4) the parameters and variables for controlling the run,

(5) the criterion for terminating a run and designating the result, and
(6) the architecture of the overall multi-part program.

Figure 5.2 summarizes these six user-supplied inputs to the genetic programming process with automatically defined functions. A run of genetic programming breeds, over a series of generations, a population of computer programs that generally exhibit increasing fitness in grappling with the problem environment. The result of a run of genetic programming is a computer program that may solve, or approximately solve, the user's given problem.

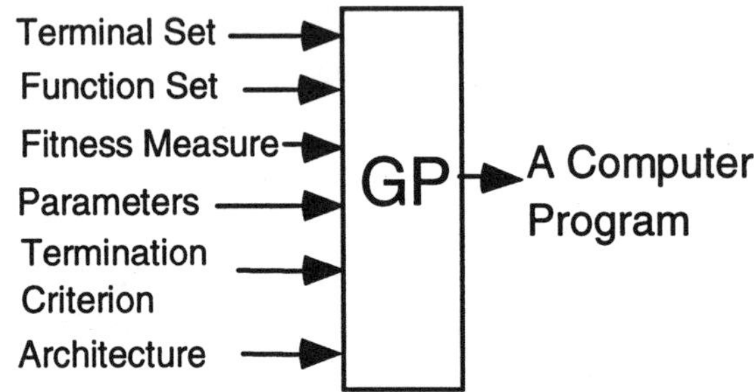

Figure 5.2 *Six major preparatory steps for applying genetic programming with automatically defined functions.*

5.4.1 Terminal Set, Function Set, and Architecture

After analyzing the problem, it seems reasonable that the ingredients of the to-be-evolved computer programs should include 20 zero-argument logical functions capable of interrogating the current position of a protein sequence. For example, `(A?)` is the zero-argument residue-detecting function that returns 1 if the current residue in the sequence is alanine (A) but otherwise returning 0.

The square brackets used in PROSITE expressions are used to form sets of residues. The two-argument disjunctive function `OR` can be used to dynamically define disjunctions of the values returned by the 20 residue-detecting functions.

If the overall architecture of the yet-to-be-evolved motif-detecting program uses automatically defined functions to organize amino acid residues into subsets, then the result-producing branch can be used to perform some operations to reach a conclusion. A two-argument conjunctive function AND can then correspond to the dash of the PROSITE language that is used to lengthen the PROSITE expression. This suggests an overall architecture consisting of several (say, two) automatically defined functions and one result-producing branch.

Specifically, the terminal set, $\mathcal{T}_{\text{adf}}$, for the two function-defining branches (ADF0 and ADF1) contains the 20 zero-argument residue-detecting functions. That is,

$\mathcal{T}_{\text{adf}}$ = {(A?), (C?), (D?), ... , (Y?)}.

The function set, $\mathcal{F}_{\text{adf}}$, for the two function-defining branches is

$\mathcal{F}_{\text{adf}}$ = {OR}.

The terminal set, $\mathcal{T}_{\text{rpb}}$, for the result-producing branch includes the now-defined ADFs, ADF0 and ADF1, and the 20 zero-argument residue-detecting functions.

$\mathcal{T}_{\text{rpb}}$ = {ADF0, ADF1, (A?), (C?), (D?),..., (Y?)}.

The function set, $\mathcal{F}_{\text{rpb}}$, for the result-producing branch is

$\mathcal{F}_{\text{rpb}}$ = {AND}.

Programs consist of two function-defining branches (ADF0 and ADF1) composed of functions from $\mathcal{F}_{\text{adf}}$ and terminals from $\mathcal{T}_{\text{adf}}$, as well as one result-producing branch composed of functions from $\mathcal{F}_{\text{rpb}}$ and terminals from $\mathcal{T}_{\text{rpb}}$. Note that we do not prespecify the length of the motif that is to be evolved. Both the size and content of each branch of the multi-part program is to be evolved by genetic programming.

If the result-producing branch of an overall program returns a logically true value at a particular position in a protein sequence, that position will be identified as the beginning of an occurrence of the motif; otherwise that position will be classified negatively. If a program examines a residue that is beyond the C-terminal (end) of the protein, the position will be classified negatively.

5.4.2 Fitness Measure

The fitness measure must assign a value as to how well a particular genetically-evolved motif-detecting program predicts whether a particular amino acid residue is the beginning of a D-E-A-D box.

Fitness is measured over a number of trials called *fitness cases.* A set of in-sample fitness cases (i.e., the training set) is used to measure the fitness of programs during the evolutionary process. The fitness cases for this problem are individual amino acid residues of proteins. The single residue indicating the start of the occurrence of the motif is a positive fitness case and all other residues are negative fitness cases.

When a genetically evolved motif-detecting program in the population is tested against a particular fitness case, the outcome can be a true positive, a true negative, a false positive (an overprediction) , or a false negative (and underprediction). The sum of the number of true positives (N_{tp}) the number of true negatives (N_{tn}), the number of false positives (N_{fp}), and the number of false negatives (N_{fn}) equals the total number of fitness cases, N_{fc}:

$$N_{fc} = N_{tp} + N_{tn} + N_{fp} + N_{fn}.$$

The set of positive in-sample fitness cases contained all the residues of 26 of the 34 proteins in SWISS-PROT belonging to the D-E-A-D box family. Because of the rarity of the motif among the 14,147,368 residues in SWISS-PROT and in order to save computer time, we constructed the set of negative in-sample fitness cases by extracting 210 30-residue fragments that did not belong to the D-E-A-D box family, did not contain the D-E-A-D box motif, but did contain a sizable partial match with the D-E-A-D box motif (such as all `X-X-D-E-A-D-X-X-X` or `V-X-X-EAD-X-X-X` that are not in the D-E-A-D box family). When we were done, the in-sample fitness cases consisted of 19,200 amino acid residues from 236 proteins (26 residues being positive instances and 19,174 being negative instances of the D-E-A-D box motif).

Correlation is appropriate as a measure of raw fitness for genetic programming in a two-way classification problem. For a two-way classification problem, *correlation*, C, of a genetically evolved motif-detecting program can be computed (Matthews 1975) as

$$C = \frac{N_{tp}N_{tn} - N_{fn}N_{fp}}{\sqrt{(N_{tn} + N_{fn})(N_{tn} + N_{fp})(N_{tp} + N_{fn})(N_{tp} + N_{fp})}}$$

The correlation coefficient indicates how much better a particular predictor is than a random predictor. It may be instructive to view the correlation, C, as the cosine of the angle in a space of dimensionality N_{fc}

between the zero-mean vector (obtained by subtracting the mean value of all components of the vector from each of its components) of correct answers and the zero-mean vector of predictions made by the predicting program. A correlation C of –1.0 indicates that the pair of vectors point in opposite directions in N_{fc}-space (i.e., greatest negative correlation); a correlation of +1.0 indicates coincident vectors (i.e., greatest positive correlation); a correlation C of 0.0 indicates orthogonality (i.e., no correlation).

The *in-sample correlation*, C, is the correlation computed from the set of in-sample fitness cases. The in-sample correlation C lends itself to being the measure of raw fitness for a genetically evolved computer program. Since raw fitness ranges between –1.0 and +1.0 (higher values being better), standardized fitness can then be defined as

$$\frac{1-C}{2}$$

Standardized fitness ranges between 0.0 and +1.0, lower values being better and a value of 0 being best. Specifically, a standardized fitness of 0 indicates perfect agreement between the predicting program and the observed reality; a standardized fitness of +1.0 indicates perfect disagreement; a standardized fitness of 0.50 indicates that the predictor is no better than random.

After a motif-detecting program is evolved using the in-sample fitness cases, the question arises as to how well it generalizes to unseen different fitness cases from the same problem environment. A set of out-of-sample fitness cases consisting of 5,605 amino acid residues from 53 proteins (8 residues being positive instances and 5,597 being negative instances) is used to validate the performance of a genetically-evolved motif-detecting program. For reference, when the D-E-A-D box motif found in the PROSITE database is tested against the out-of-sample fitness cases, there are 8 true positives, 5,596 true negatives, 1 false positive, and 0 false negatives (for a correlation of 0.94). When it is tested against all of SWISS-PROT, it scored 34 true positives, 14,147,333 true negatives, and 1 false positive and 0 false negatives (for a correlation of 0.99).

5.4.3 Parameters

A population size, M, of 256,000 was used. The maximum number of generations, G, was set at 201 (although every run we made yielded a solution long before generation 200). The maximum size (i.e., number of functions and terminals in the work-performing parts of each branch) was 50 points per branch. Minor parameters were chosen as in Koza 1994a.

5.4.4 Termination Criterion and Result Designation

The termination criterion for any one run of this problem is emergence of an evolved program with an in-sample correlation of 1.00 on the in-sample fitness cases. That program is designated as the result of the one run.

5.4.5 Jury Method for Creating a Consensus Motif

Because of the intended purpose of PROSITE (which is purposely oriented toward overfitted descriptions) and because the 1,029 PROSITE motifs partition the existing databases into relatively small subsets, there is a poverty of instances of any given motif in the database. The difficulties of evolving a motif from such an impoverished database can be compensated for by using a jury (Rost and Sander 1993) of at least two evolved results having an in-sample correlation of 1.00. A unanimous jury decision was required in order to classify a position of a protein sequence as the beginning of the motif. Otherwise, the position was classified negatively.

5.5 Implementation of Parallel Genetic Programming

The problem (written in ANSI C) was run on a home-built medium-grained parallel computer system consisting of 64 INMOS transputers (housed on Transtech 4 megabyte TRAMs) arranged in a toroidal mesh with a host PC 486 type computer (running Windows). The so-called *distributed genetic algorithm* or *island model* for parallelization (Tanese 1989, Goldberg 1989) was used. That is, subpopulations (called *demes* after Sewell Wright 1943) were situated at the processing nodes of the system. Population size was Q = 4,000 at each of the D = 64 demes. The initial random subpopulations were created locally at each processing node. Generations were run asynchronously on each node. After a generation of genetic operations was performed locally on each node, four boatloads, each consisting of $B = 8\%$ (the migration rate) of the subpopulation (selected on the basis of fitness) were dispatched to each of the four toroidally adjacent nodes. Details of the parallel implementation of genetic programming can be found in Koza and Andre 1995.

5.6 Results for the D-E-A-D Box Family of Proteins

In one run, the best motif-detecting program (shown below) among the 256,000 random programs of generation 0 scored 20 true positives, 19,152 true negatives, 22 false positives, and 6 false negatives (for an in-sample correlation of 0.60):

```
(PROGN (DEFUN ADF0 ()
            (VALUES (OR (L?) (N?))))
        (DEFUN ADF1 ()
            (VALUES (OR (R?) (V?))))
        (VALUES (AND (V?) (AND (L?) (D?)))))
```

Note that although we program genetic programming in C, the LISP programming language is used to present the genetically evolved programs since LISP highlights the program's tree structure. This best-of-generation program defines the motif, `V-L-D`, of length three. This motif admits no alternatives in any of its three positions and ignores the subsets defined by its two automatically defined functions, `ADF0` and `ADF1`.

In subsequent generations, the programs in the population became more complex and their fitness improved apace. The length of the motifs started to increase (sometimes beyond nine). The result-producing branches started to refer to one or both of their automatically defined functions. The automatically defined functions started to be used two or more times.

On generation 42 of one run, the best-of-generation program (shown below) scored 26 true positives, 19,174 true negatives, and 0 false positives and 0 false negatives (for an in-sample correlation of 1.00):

```
(PROGN (DEFUN ADF0 ()
            (VALUES (OR (OR (OR (OR (W?)(M?))(OR
            (C?)(A?)))(M?))(OR (OR (OR (OR
            (W?)(M?))(OR (M?)(I?)))(L?))(I?)))))
        (DEFUN ADF1 ()
            (VALUES (OR (OR (OR (A?) (E?))(OR (OR
            (OR (OR (A?)(K?))(OR (V?)(N?)))(OR (OR
            (E?)(R?))(OR (OR (A?)(W?))(OR
            (K?)(Q?)))))(OR (V?)(K?))))(OR (OR
            (I?)(C?))(A?))))))
        (VALUES (AND (AND (AND (AND (AND (AND (AND
        (ADF1) (ADF0)) ( AND (D? ) (E? ))) (ADF0))
        (D? )) (ADF1)) (ADF0)) (ADF0)))
```

This best-of-generation program defines the following motif of length nine:
`[VIAEKNRWQC]-[LIMCAW]-D-E-[LIMCAW]-D-[RNEKVIAWQC]-[LIMCAW]-[LIMCAW]`

Note that the common sub-expression `[LIM CAW]` defined in `ADF0` is used a total of four times in the above overall expression. When tested on the 5,605 out-of-sample fitness cases, this expression scored 8 true positives, 5,597 true negatives, and 0 false positives and 0 false negatives (for a correlation of 1.00). When tested against SWISS-PROT, this program scored 34 true positives, 14,147,328 true negatives, and 6 false positives, and 0 false negatives (for a correlation of 0.92).

In another run, the best-of-generation program from generation 64 had an in-sample correlation of 1.00 and defined the following motif of length ten:
`[FVIAC]-[LIM EQDNRSK]-D-E-[AFVIC]-D-[LIMEQDNRSK]-[LIMEQDNRSK] -[LIMEQDNRSK]-[LIMEQDNRSK]`

Note that the common sub-expression `[LIMEQDNRSK]` defined in `ADF1` is used a total of five times in the above overall expression. When tested on the out-of-sample fitness cases, this program has a correlation of 0.94. When tested against SWISS-PROT, this program scored 34 true positives, 14,147,272 true negatives, and 62 false positives, and 0 false negatives (for a correlation of 0.60).

In other runs, 10 additional evolved programs each had an in-sample correlation of 1.00. These 12 results participated in a jury that created a genetically evolved consensus motif of length 10 (shown below) that scored

26 true positives, 19,174 true negatives, 0 false positives, and 0 false negatives (for an in-sample correlation of 1.00):

`[IV]-[LIM]-D-E-[AI]-D-[RNEK]-[LIM]-[LIM]-[LIMEQDNRSK]`

Note that `[LIM]` is used three times in this expression. When tested on the 5,605 out-of-sample fitness cases, this expression scored 8 true positives, 5,597 true negatives, and 0 false positives and 0 false negatives (for a correlation of 1.00). When tested against SWISS-PROT, this program scored 34 true positives, 14,147,334 true negatives, and 0 false positives, and 0 false negatives (for a correlation of 1.00).

Thus, the genetically evolved consensus motif created by the jury scored slightly better than the human-written motif found in the PROSITE database on the problem of detecting the D-E-A-D box family of proteins.

Recalling that the motif found in the PROSITE database for the D-E-A-D box family is

`[LIVM]-[LIVM]-D-E-A-D-X-[LIVM]-[LIVM],`

one can see that the genetically evolved consensus motif differs in the following four ways from the motif found in the PROSITE database.

First, position 7 of the motif has a definite character. The `X` in position 7 of the PROSITE motif is replaced by `[RNEK]` in the consensus motif. Figure 5.3 is a scatter diagram relating the Van der Waals volume (Creighton 1993) and the hydrophobicity values (Kyte and Doolittle 1982) of the 20 amino acids. In this figure, R, N, E, and K are located in the same general area (circled in the lower right) indicating that they are all highly hydrophilic and bulky. Second, the `[LIVM]` in positions 2, 8, and 9 of the PROSITE motif is replaced by the somewhat more precise `[LIM]` in the consensus motif. As can be seen in the circled area at the top right of the figure, residues I, L, and M have virtually identical volumes whereas V has a different volume.

Third, the `[LIVM]` in position 1 of the PROSITE motif is replaced by the somewhat more precise `[IV]` in the consensus motif.

Fourth, the genetically evolved consensus motif specifies that position 10 (beyond the last position specified by the PROSITE motif) contains `[LIMRNEKQDS]`.

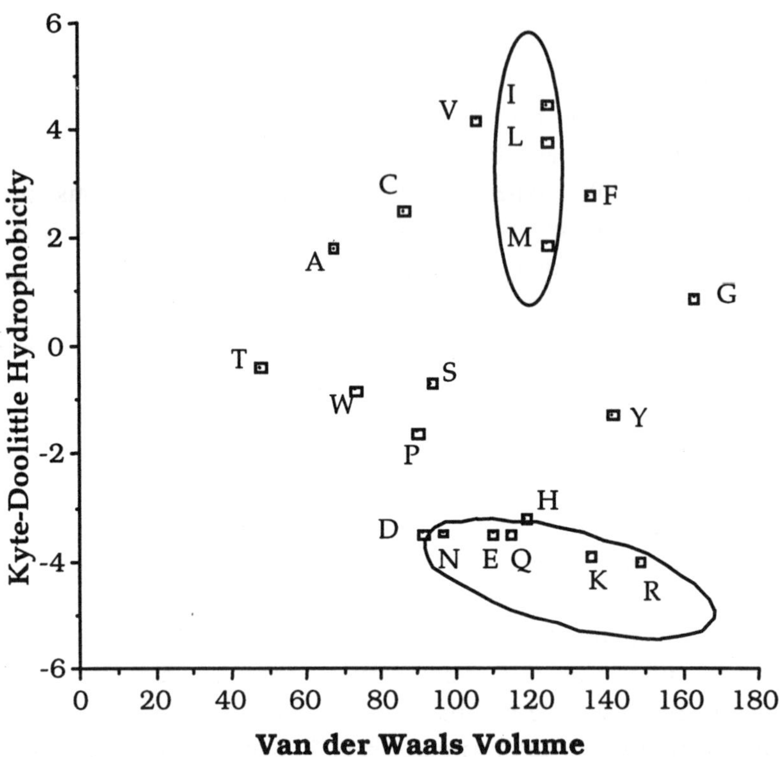

Figure 5.3 *Scatter diagram of hydrophobicity and Van der Waals volume of the 20 amino acid residues.*

5.7 Results for the Manganese Superoxide Dismutase Family of Proteins

The in-sample fitness cases for the problem of detecting the manganese superoxide dismutase family of proteins consisted of 13,518 amino acid residues from 270 proteins (30 residues being positive instances and 13,488 being negative instances). The out-of-sample fitness cases were constructed using the same approach as described above and consisted of 3,280 residues from 53 proteins (10 residues being positive instances and 3,270 being negative instances).

When the manganese superoxide dismutase motif found in the PROSITE database is tested against the out-of-sample fitness cases, there are 10 true positives, 3,270 true negatives, 0 false positive, and 0 false negatives (for a correlation of 1.00). When it is tested against all of SWISS-PROT, it scores a correlation of 1.00.

Three automatically defined functions were used on this problem.

As before, the genetically evolved motifs participated in a jury that created the following consensus motif of length nine that had an in-sample correlation of 1.00:

`D-[VAML]-W-E-H-[SA]-[YFH]-[YFAHS]-[YFADHLIS]`

When tested on the 3,280 out-of-sample fitness cases, this expression had an out-of-sample correlation of 1.00. When tested against SWISS-PROT, this program scored 40 true positives, 14,147,328 true negatives, and 0 false positives, and 0 false negatives (for a correlation of 1.00). That is, the genetically evolved consensus motif created by the jury scored as well as the human-written motif found in the PROSITE database on the problem of detecting the manganese superoxide dismutase family of proteins.

The motif found in the PROSITE database for the manganese superoxide dismutase family is

`D-X-W-E-H-[STA]-[FY][FY].`

The genetically evolved consensus motif differs in the following ways from the motif found in the PROSITE database.

First, the `X` in position 2 of the PROSITE motif is replaced by the set of hydrophobic residues `[VAML]`. As can be seen from figure 5.4, position 2 of the motif (i.e., position 160 of the protein) is buried (in contrast to, for example, electrically charged Glu 162 which is exposed to the solvent). Thus, it is reasonable that whatever appears at position 2 should be hydrophobic.

Second, the `[STA]` in position 6 of the PROSITE motif is replaced by the somewhat more precise `[SA]` in the consensus motif.

Third, the genetically evolved consensus motif specifies that position 9 (beyond the last position specified by the PROSITE motif) contains `[YFADHLIS]`.

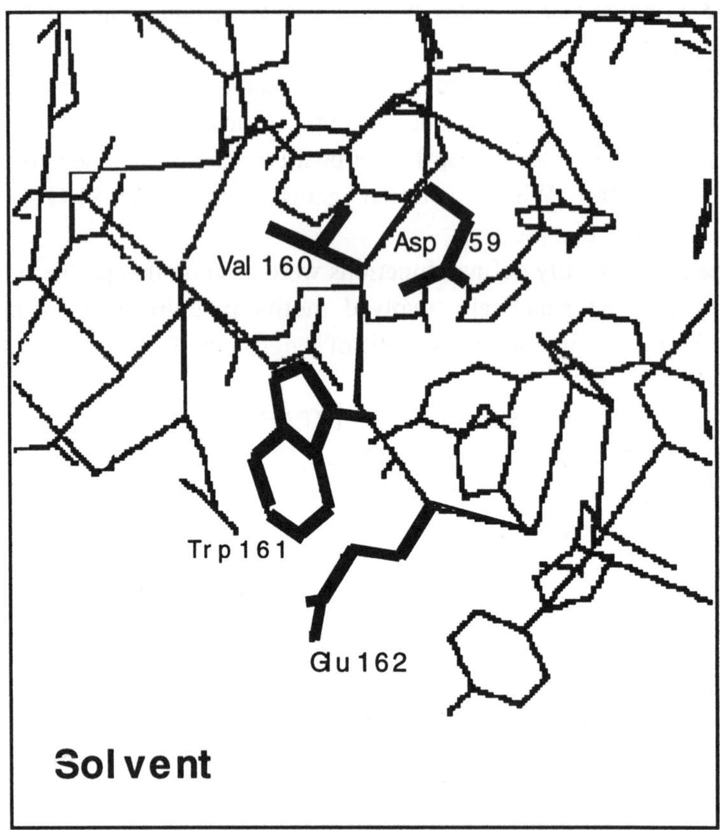

Figure 5.4 *Section of manganese superoxide dismutase showing that position 160 is buried.*

5.8 Conclusions

Genetic programming was successfully used to create motifs for the D-E-A-D box family of proteins and the manganese superoxide dismutase family. Both motifs were evolved without prespecifying their length. Both evolved motifs employed automatically defined functions to capture the repeated use of a common subexpression. When tested against the SWISS-PROT database of proteins, the two genetically evolved consensus motifs detect the two families either as well, or slightly better than, the comparable human-written motifs found in the PROSITE database.

Bibliography

Albrecht, R. F., Reeves, C. R., and Steele, N. C. 1993. *Artificial Neural Nets and Genetic Algorithms*. Springer-Verlag.

Anfinsen, C. B. 1973. Principles that govern the folding of protein chains. *Science* 81: 223-230.

Angeline, Peter J. and Kinnear, Kenneth E. Jr. (editors). 1996. *Advances in Genetic Programming*. Cambridge, MA: The MIT Press.

Bairoch, A. and Boeckmann, B. 1991. The SWISS-PROT protein sequence data bank: current status. *Nucleic Acids Research* 22(17) 3578–3580.

Bairoch, Amos and Bucher, Philipp. 1994. PROSITE: Recent developments. *Nucleic Acids Research* 22(17) 3583-3589.

Bannister Joe V., Bannister, William.H., and Rotilio Giuseppe. 1987. Aspects of the structure, functions, and applications of superoxide dismutase. *CRC Critical Review of Biochemistry* 22:111-154.

Bauer, R. J., Jr. 1994. *Genetic Algorithms and Investment Strategies*. John Wiley.

Bernstein, F. C., Koetzle, T. F., Williams, G. J. B., Meyer, E.J., Jr., Brice, M. D., Rodgets, J. R., Kennard, O. Shimamouchi, T., and Tasumi, M. 1977. The protein data bank: A computer based archival file for macromolecular structures. *Journal of Molecular Biology*. 112: 535-542.

Buckles Bill P. and Petry, Frederick E. *Genetic Algorithms*. Los Alamitos, CA: The IEEE Computer Society Press. 1992.

Chang, Tien-Hsien, Arenas, Jaime, and Abelson, John. 1990. Identification of five putative yeast RNA helicase genes. *Proceedings of the National Academy of Sciences U.S.A.* 87:1571–1575.

Creighton, T. E. 1993. *Proteins: Structures and Molecular Properties*. Second Edition. W. H. Freeman.

Davidor, Yuval. *Genetic Algorithms and Robotics*. Singapore: World Scientific 1990.

Davis, L. (editor). 1987. Genetic Algorithms and Simulated Annealing. Pittman.

Davis, L. 1991. *Handbook of Genetic Algorithms.* Van Nostrand Reinhold.

Dorer, Douglas R., Christensen, Alan C., and Johnson, Daniel H. 1990. A novel RNA helicase gene tightly linked to the *Triplo-lethal* locus of *Drosophila. Nucleic Acids Research* 18(18): 5489–5495.

Eshelman, L. (editor). 1995. *Genetic Algorithms: Proceedings of the Fifth International Conference.* San Francisco, CA: Morgan Kaufmann.

Forrest, Stephanie. *Parallelism and Programming in Classifier Systems.* London: Pittman 1991.

Goldberg, David E. 1989. *Genetic Algorithms in Search, Optimization, and Machine Learning*. Reading, MA: Addison-Wesley.

Handley, Simon. 1993a. Automated learning of a detector for α-helices in protein sequences via genetic programming. In Forrest, Stephanie (editor). *Proceedings of the Fifth International Conference on Genetic Algorithms.* San Mateo, CA: Morgan Kaufmann Publishers Inc. Pages 271-278.

Handley, Simon. 1994a. Automated learning of a detector for the cores of α-helices in protein sequences via genetic programming. *Proceedings of the First IEEE Conference on Evolutionary Computation.* IEEE Press. Volume I. Pages 474–479.

Handley, Simon. 1994b. The prediction of the degree of exposure to solvent of amino acid residues via genetic programming. In Altman, Russ, Brutlag, Douglas, Karp, Peter, Lathrop, Richard, and Searls, David (editors). *Proceedings of the Second International Conference on Intelligent Systems for Molecular Biology.* Menlo Park, CA: AAAI Press. 1994. Pages 156–159.

Handley, Simon. 1995a. Predicting whether or not a nucleic acid sequence is an *E. coli* promoter region using genetic programming. *Proceedings of First International Symposium on Intelligence in Neural and Biological Systems.* Los Alamitos, CA: IEEE Computer Society Press. 122-127.

Handley, Simon. 1995b. Predicting whether or not a 60-base DNA sequence contains a centrally-located splice site using genetic programming. In Rosca, Justinian (editor). Proceedings of the Workshop on Genetic Programming: From Theory to Real-World Applications. University of Rochester. National Resource Laboratory for the Study of Brain and Behavior. Technical Report 95-2. June 1995. Pages 98-103.

Handley, Simon, 1995c. Classifying nucleic acid subsequences as introns or exons using genetic programming. In. Christopher Rawlings, Dominic Clark, Russ Altman, Lawrence Hunter, Thomas Lengauer, and Shoshana Wodak (editors). Proceedings of the Third International Conference on Intelligent Systems for Molecular Biology. Menlo Park, CA: AAAI Press. 1995. Pages 162–169.

Hodgman, T. C. 1988. A new superfamily of replicative proteins. *Nature* 333:2 2–23 and Errata at Nature 333: 578-578.

Holland, John H. 1975. *Adaptation in Natural and Artificial Systems: An Introductory Analysis with Applications to Biology, Control, and Artificial Intelligence.* Ann Arbor, MI: University of Michigan Press. The second edition is currently available from The MIT Press 1992.

Kinnear, Kenneth E. Jr. (editor). 1994. *Advances in Genetic Programming.* Cambridge, MA: The MIT Press.

Koza, John R. 1992. *Genetic Programming: On the Programming of Computers by Means of Natural Selection.* Cambridge, MA: The MIT Press.

Koza, John R. 1994a. *Genetic Programming II: Automatic Discovery of Reusable Programs.* Cambridge, MA: The MIT Press.

Koza, John R. 1994b. *Genetic Programming II Videotape: The Next Generation.* Cambridge, MA: The MIT Press.

Koza, John R. 1994c. Evolution of a computer program for classifying protein segments as transmembrane domains using genetic programming. In Altman, Russ, Brutlag, Douglas, Karp, Peter, Lathrop, Richard, and Searls, David (editors). *Proceedings of the*

Second International Conference on Intelligent Systems for Molecular Biology. Menlo Park, CA: AAAI Press. 1994. Pages 244–252.

Koza, John R. and Andre, David. 1995. *Parallel Genetic Programming on a Network of Transputers*. Stanford University Computer Science Department technical report STAN-CS-TR-95-1542. January 30, 1995.

Koza, John R., and Rice, James P. 1992 .*Genetic Programming: The Movie*. Cambridge, MA: The MIT Press.

Kyte, J. and Doolittle, R. 1982. A simple method for displaying the hydropathic character of proteins. *Journal of Molecular Biology*. 157:105-132.

Linder, P., Lasko, P., Ashburner, M., Leroy, P., Nielsen, P. J., Nishi, J., Schneir, J., and Slonimski, P. P. 1989. Birth of the D-E-A-D box. *Nature* 337: 121–122.

Ludwig, M. I., Metzger, A. I., Pattridge, R. A., and Stallings, W. C. 1991. Manganese superoxide dismutase from *Thermus thermophilus*: A structural model refined at 1.8 Å resolution. *Journal of Molecular Biology* 219: 335-358.

Maenner, R., and Manderick, B. (editors). 1992. *Proceedings of the Second International Conference on Parallel Problem Solving from Nature*. North Holland.

Matthews, B. W. 1975. Comparison of the predicted and observed secondary structure of T4 phage lysozyme. *Biochemica et Biophysica Acta*. 405:442-451.

Michalewicz, Z. 1992. *Genetic Algorithms + Data Structures = Evolution Programs*. Springer-Verlag.

Richardson, D. C. and Richardson, J. S. 1992. The kinemage: A tool for scientific communication. *Protein Science* 1(1) 3–9.

Rost, B. and Sander, C. 1993. Prediction of protein secondary structure at better than 70% accuracy. *Journal of Molecular Biology*. 232: 584–599.

Schaffer, J. D. and Whitley, D. (editors). 1992. *Proceedings of the Workshop on Combinations of Genetic Algorithms and Neural Networks 1992*. Los Alamitos, CA: The IEEE Computer Society Press.

Smith, T. F. and Waterman, M. S. 1981. Identification of common molecular subsequences. *Journal of Molecular Biology*. Volume 147. Pages 195-197.

Stender, J. (editor). 1993. *Parallel Genetic Algorithms*. IOS Publishing.

Stender, J., Hillebrand, and Kingdon, J. (editors). 1994. *Genetic Algorithms in Optimization, Simulation, and Modeling*. Amsterdam: IOS Publishing.

Stoddard, B. I., Ringe, D., and Petsko, G. A. 1990. The structure of iron superoxide dismutase from *Pseudomonas ovalis* complexed with the inhibitor azide. *Protein Engineering* 4: 113–199.

Stryer, Lubert. 1995. *Biochemistry*. W. H. Freeman. Fourth Edition.

Tanese, Reiko. 1989. *Distributed Genetic Algorithm for Function Optimization.* PhD. dissertation. Department of Electrical Engineering and Computer Science. University of Michigan.

Whitley, D. (editor). 1992. *Proceedings of Workshop on the Foundations of Genetic Algorithms and Classifier Systems, Vail, Colorado 1992*. San Mateo, CA: Morgan Kaufmann Publishers Inc.

Wright, Sewall. 1943. Isolation by distance. *Genetics* 28. Page 114–138.

Chapter 6

The Role of Self Organization in Evolutionary Computations

A. C. Tsoi and J. Shaw

This paper is divided into two parts: in part 1, we will consider the role of self organization in evolutionary computations (ECs), and in part 2, we will consider a specific example to illustrate the importance of the information assessment stage in an evolutionary computing system. In part 1, we present a generic EC system, which consists of two stages, viz., the information gathering and assessment stage, and the action stage. Each stage is active in each sampling interval, and the system is allowed to evolve. A number of current EC systems are shown to be modelled by this generic EC system. It is shown then in the information assessment stage, two approaches may be taken, viz., the supervised learning scheme, and the supervised learning scheme. It is argued that in EC systems, the unsupervised learning scheme would be more prevalent. It is also argued that the action stage is problem specific, i.e., it depends on the problem under study.

Part 2 gives a specific illustrative example to show the importance of the information assessment stage in an EC system. This system aims to investigate the behaviour of multiple insects. It is argued that a simple functional model of an insect consisting of a number of instincts arranged in a hierarchy, and a number of associated sensors. it is shown that the information processing stage consists of two parts: a learning vector quantization stage, and a modified hebbian learning stage. It is shown how this combination can be used to overcome the problem that the target output is not given explicitly. Then a number of simulation experiments are shown based first on a single insect, and then on multiple insects. The behaviour of the single insect appears to mimic quite closely the behaviour of a scout ant. The behaviour of the multiple insects appear to exhibit pack group behaviour. This emerging group behaviour appears to be very interesting, as it clearly indicates the role of evolutionary computing in the simulation of complex system behaviours.

6.1 Introduction

Evolutionary computation (EC) is an all encompassing topic. It means different things to many researchers who may have different backgrounds. To-date, EC could encompass the following topics:

1. genetic algorithms and related topics
2. artificial life and related topics
3. heuristic search and computations
4. fuzzy logic and systems
5. adaptive learning systems
6. neural networks
7. autonomous vehicle navigation

While such all encompassing approach could be very useful in assisting the growth of a new inter disciplinary subject, it could also mean confusion to some who may not be so well versed in its deliberations. To many researchers, EC is almost synonymous with "Complex systems" research.

In this paper, we will first give an overview of a generic EC system. We will illustrate this generic EC system with existing examples in EC systems. We will then consider one particular aspect of an approach for EC systems, viz., information assessment, and review one of the approaches available, viz., the learning vector quantization technique in solving this problem. In part 2, we will give an illustrative example of the role of information processing for investigating the behaviour of multiple insects.

6.2 A Generic View of EC system

As indicated previously, EC could mean different things to different researchers. Hence, it would be useful at the beginning to give an overall view of a generic EC system, which captures the essence of what an EC system.

A generic EC system is a computational engine which runs in time, i.e., it evolves in time. At time t, it measures, or observes the system under study, and makes some action, which will be activated in producing more information assessment at time $t+1$. Hence, an EC system consists of the following components:

1. Information gathering and assessment – at time t, it observes the system under study. This can take the form of measurements, observations. The output of this stage is a set of information which embodies the state of the system under study. The EC system will assess the content of this set of information vectors, and make appropriate conclusions about the state of the system.

2. Action — the EC system, after evaluating the information available, will make some actions, to be taken before time $t+1$. These actions include: issuing a command to alter the control variables, alter the genetic code of a genetic algorithm etc. There is no fixed rule about the action plan, except that the EC system will make some action plan before time $t+1$, and this action plan will lead to an activation of the system under study.

Note that there are a number of assumptions underlying this generic view of an EC system. These are:

1. The sampling instant will be long enough so that any action taken before the arrival of time $t+1$ will have reached the steady state.

2. The measurements or observations have been carefully chosen so that they will "reveal" the current state of the system under study.

3. The action will properly excite the system under study, so as to "elucidate" its underlying properties.

These assumptions are meant to exclude pathological cases. For example, it excludes situations when the inappropriate observations are made on the system which do not "reveal" its underlying state. It also excludes the pathological example of issuing inappropriate actions, e.g., a zero action, when an other than zero input is called for.

The system will continue to evolve, i.e., $t = 1, 2, \ldots, T$, when a final time T is reached. Theoretically, T can be infinity, but for practical computations, T is assumed to be finite.

For some EC systems, e.g., a reinforcement learning scheme, the action plan may not be undertaken at every sampling interval, i.e., the EC system may only take action after a number of samples have elapsed.

It is also possible for a different stopping criterion to be formulated, e.g., the EC system may stop evolving when a particular criterion is satisfied. We consider this a degenerate version of EC, as one of the main aims in EC studies is to allow the system to evolve, if necessary, ad infinitum.

6.3 Illustrative Examples From Current EC Applications

In this section, we will give illustrative examples from various current EC systems to indicate the generic EC system as proposed in section 6.2.

6.3.1 Genetic algorithm

In a genetic algorithm, there is often a goal, e.g., the error involved in optimization. The information assessment step includes the evaluation of the error involved in the optimization. The action taken will be to later the genetic code so as to obtain another generation of the population, ready for the evaluation of the goal for the next time step.

6.3.2 Heuristic search techniques

In a heuristic search, one evaluates the goal at every time step, and then based on these evaluations, one decides on where the next search point will be, ready for the next iteration.

6.3.3 Autonomous vehicle navigation

In an autonomous vehicle navigation (AVN) system, the current location of the system with respect to its environment is evaluated via a number of measurements, e.g., visual, ultra sound, laser range finding. Based on these measurements, the vehicle will decide on what to do next, in order to reach a goal, e.g., obstacle avoidance, to reach the end of the journey.

6.3.4 Artificial life

In artificial life experiments, the information gathering and the action stages are blurred together. Often in an artificial life experiment, the evolution program is fixed a priori, and will not be altered, as no external measurements will be taken. This can be considered as a degenerate form of the generic EC system, in that the measurement is taken only initially, and the system is allowed to evolve, without any reference to external measurements. This is possible when there are no constraints being placed on the artificial life experiment. However, if one considers a more general form of artificial life experiment where there are constraints placed on the evolution of life form, then measurements will need to be taken, probably at regular intervals, if not at every time step, and decision on how to continue to evolve the life form will be taken.

Other examples of EC systems which can be easily fit into the generic EC system mode include the adaptive learning systems, neural and fuzzy control systems. These systems, almost by definition, uses the measurements to decide on the next control variable. Hence, we will not describe any of these examples in detail.

6.4 Information Assessment Stage

As indicated previously, in the generic EC system, there are two stages, viz., the information gathering and assessment stage, and the action stage. The action stage is dependent on the system under study, hence it would be rather difficult to give a general description of the procedures involved. On the other hand, the information gathering and assessment stage is reasonably generic, once one separates any hardware aspects of information gathering from the actual processing of the information gathered. The hardware aspect is system dependent, e.g., the type of analog to digital device used, the sampling interval. On the other hand, the information processing of the information gathered can be described in more general theoretical concepts. Hence, we have chosen to consider the information gathering and assessment aspects of an EC system in more detail.

Broadly speaking, there are two ways in which the information gathered can be assessed. These are

1. Supervised learning paradigm [5] – in this case, one can assess the information in accordance with some given target values. Hence, an error function can be formed. This error function is used in formulating an appropriate action plan.

2. Unsupervised learning paradigm [5] — in this case, we are not given any target values, and we have to extract information from the gathered information.

In general, the information assessed using the supervised learning scheme is more precise, as it gives us an idea how far the system is performing as compared with the targets. However, with a number of EC systems, the target often is not given explicitly. For example, in an artificial life experiment, no target state is given. The life form is allowed to evolve, often without any constraints, until a stable population results. As another example, in an AVN system, again often, the target is given, e.g., as reaching the end of a room, or to search for some object. In these cases, the target, while is given, is not in a form which is conducive for an easy formulation in terms of an error function.

As a result, in EC systems, it is conceivable that the unsupervised learning scheme would be more important. For example, in an AVN system, as indicated previously, we are often given a desired end state. However, in reaching the end state, it is not possible to utilize the given end state to formulate an error function. The EC system, often needs to "make sense" of the measurements and/or observations, and then to draw appropriate inference for the next action. These measurements may reveal, e.g., there are obstacles in the environment which the AVN system is operating; they may reveal that the AVN system is far from its target. As a result, appropriate actions need to be taken in order that the target state can be reached. It is for this reason, that in this paper we will concentrate on the unsupervised learning scheme.

Note that the unsupervised learning scheme does not make as "efficient" use of the information available as the supervised learning scheme. This is because of the fact that the supervised learning scheme, an error function, in itself, gives a precise measure of how far the current state is from the target state, is formed. This makes very effective use of the measurements available. On the other hand, the unsupervised scheme, because it does not have any error functions, does not make as efficient use of the measurements.

6.5 Unsupervised Learning Schemes

In this class of algorithms [5], the central problem can be stated as follows:

> Given a set of measurement vectors $\mathcal{S} = \{\mathbf{u}_t, t = 1, 2, \ldots, N\}$, where $\mathbf{u}_t$ is the t th exemplar. In our case, it is assumed to be a $p \times 1$ vector. Can we find a set of M vectors, $M \leq N$, $\mathcal{T} = \{\mathbf{v}_t, t = 1, 2, \ldots, M$, "homogeneous" underlying groupings which may exist in the set S ? The vector $\mathbf{v}_t$ is a $q \times 1$ vector. In our case, M is unknown a priori.

Note that, in general, the fact that M is unknown makes the problem difficult. The EC system needs to discover the number of distinct groupings from the set of given data. "Homogeneity" is a key word here, as without any criterion of homogeneity one may have the situation that $M = N$, and each exemplar $\mathbf{u}_t$ forms a group by itself. While this may occur in practice, it does not aid the information reduction problem, as one ends up with as much information before and after the information assessment process.

The dimension p may not necessarily be the same as q. In fact, if $q < p$, then it is an information reduction process. This is the case where one wishes to extract some features to form a representative set $\mathcal{S}'$ from the set of $\mathcal{S}$. On the other hand, if $p = q$, then this is a clustering problem, i.e., the resulting groupings are "clusters" of the original data set $\mathcal{S}$. In this paper, we will not consider the data reduction problem (feature extraction problem) further, as the techniques used would be quite different from those used in the clustering techniques.

Once the M groupings are found, then they can be used in providing appropriate action plans.

"Homogeneity" within a group is characterized by some "intrinsic" features which vectors of the same group share. Vectors from different groups do not share these common "intrinsic" features.

There are many ways in which "homogeneity" measure can be defined. The common ones include the following measures:

1. Distance measures — a common method is to measure the distance between vectors [5]. Thus, vectors which belong to the same group would have a smaller distance than those vectors which are in different groups. The common distance criteria used include: Euclidean distance measure, spectral distance measure, Mahalanobis distance measure.

2. Entropy measures — this is also quite popular, especially among the classification tree literature [5]. The entropy measure used include: self entropy, cross entropy, information measures, mutual information.

These are not the only ways in which homogeneity can be measured. For example, if data set under study is encoded properly, one may find another way to measure "homogeneity" among the vectors. Consider the following situation: the data vector contains features which describe objects. For example, we may have the data vector describing "chair" and "table". Each vector, i.e., each object is described by a number of attributes, e.g., a chair is one which has four legs, a flat surface, a back, etc. From these description attributes, one could cluster a given set of objects in the universe of "chair" and "table" respectively. Provided there are sufficient number of attributes, it is possible to "cluster" the given set of objects into two "distinct" groups. The "homogeneity" measure here may be something very different from the distance measures or the information measures described previously.

Intrinsic in the description of "homogeneity" measures is the idea of "orderness". By employing either a distance measure, or an information measure, one implicitly wishes to separate the given set of vectors into a number of "ordered" sets. For example, if a distance measure is used to measure homogeneity among a set of given vectors, then one can order the distance of a particular vector with respect to the rest of the set of vectors. The ordering set can then be formed by ordering the distance of this particular vector with the rest of the vectors. The distance among inter group vectors should be smaller than the distance among intra group vectors.

As M is unknown, there are two general approaches in which the number of groups can be obtained.

1. Partitioning techniques [16] – in this class of techniques, one partitions the domain with which the set of vectors into a number of partitions. As the EC system evolves, the number of partitions as well as the partitions themselves will vary.

2. Hierarchical grouping techniques [3] – in this class of techniques, one divides the groups hierarchically and recursively into different number of groups. One may commence by assuming two groups, and then recursively divide the two groups into a number of hierarchical groupings.

Dependent on the application and the given data set, both techniques are capable of finding out the unknown M, as well as performing the clustering operations.

Thus, to summarize the clustering approach, we have the following steps:

1. Choose a criterion to define the "homogeneity" of the set of data being analyzed.

2. Choose either a partition approach or a hierarchical approach to perform the clustering.

A major assumption in many current clustering algorithms is that there is no correlation in time among the set of given vectors $\mathcal{S}$. Thus, the index t indicates the t th exemplar. It does not denote the exemplars in time. However, it would be very interesting to consider clustering of vectors which are correlated in time, for example, in time series analysis. However, currently, very little work is performed on this aspect of clustering.

There are many clustering or self organization techniques available. These include the following:

1. K-mean clustering [3]
2. Fuzzy clustering [4]
3. Learning vector quantization and self organization map [5]
4. Dynamic clustering [8]

Because of space limitations, we will not describe each of these clustering algorithms in detail. Instead, we will describe only one of the algorithms, viz., the learning vector quantization (LVQ) in some detail, as this will be used in the ensuing EC system for information processing purposes.

6.6 Learning Vector Quantization

Learning vector quantization (LVQ) and self organizing maps (SOM) are often associated with Kohonen, in view of his pioneering effort in this area [7]. They are in fact two different methods. The LVQ is a clustering method in that it attempts to cluster a given set of vectors $\mathcal{S}$ into a number of clusters, M. In this case, M is assumed to be given. On the other hand, the self organizing map (SOM) is used to display the topological relationship among a set of vectors in one or two dimensions [8].

For a given set of N vectors $\mathcal{S} = \{\mathbf{u}_t, t = 1, 2, \ldots, N\}$, the problem is cluster them into M clusters. $\mathbf{u}_t$ is a $p \times 1$ vector.As indicated previously,

M is given. Since M is given, it is easiest to use the partitioning method to divide $\mathcal{S}$ into the required M clusters. The LVQ algorithm can be represented [7] as follows:

1. Given a set of unlabelled vectors $\mathcal{S} = \{\mathbf{u}_t, t = 1, 2, \ldots, N\} \subset \mathcal{R}^p$. M is given. The maximum number of iterations T_{max} is given. The error tolerance ϵ ¿ 0 is also given.

2. Initialize the set of clusters $\mathcal{T}_0 = \{\mathbf{v}_t, t = 1, 2, \ldots, M\} \in \mathcal{R}^{Mp}$, and learning rate α_0, with $\alpha_0 \in [0, 1]$.

3. For $n = 1, 2, \ldots, T_{max}$
   For $t = 1, 2, \ldots, N$
   (a) Find

$$\| \mathbf{u}_t - \mathbf{v}_{i,n-1} \| = \min_{1 \leq j \leq M} \{\| \mathbf{u}_t - \mathbf{v}_{j,n-1} \|\}$$

   (b) Update the winner:

$$\mathbf{v}_{i,n} = \mathbf{v}_{i,n-1} + \alpha_n (\mathbf{u}_t - \mathbf{v}_{i,n-1})$$

   (c) Next t

4. Compute the error

$$E = \| \mathcal{T}_n - \mathcal{T}_{n-1} \| = \sum_{r=1}^{M} \| \mathbf{v}_{r,n} - \mathbf{v}_{r,n-1} \|_1 = \sum_{t=1}^{N} \sum_{r=1}^{M} |v_{rt,n} - v_{rt,n-1}|$$

5. If E ¡ ϵ, then stop. Else adjust the learning rate α_n. Next n.

It is known that if the learning rate α_n satisfies the following conditions:

1. $\sum_{n=0}^{\infty} \alpha_n = \infty$, and

2. $\sum_{n=0}^{\infty} \alpha_n^2 < \infty$

then the LVQ algorithm will converge to a unique limit point. Note that this limit point does not mean that the LVQ will give the correct clusters. It will only give the correct clusters if the initial set of clusters are reasonably close to a good set of clusters. This means one needs a good initial estimate of the clusters using other algorithms.

Note that in this algorithm, the distance measure is chosen to be the Euclidean distance. In the update algorithm, we have chosen to update only the 1 nearest neighbor of the winner. This can be extended to a k nearest neighbor if in (2b) instead of the learning rate α_n is replaced by a learning rate distribution $\alpha_{ik,n}$. This learning rate distribution depends on the self organizing map (SOM) concept. At the n th iteration, there is a two dimensional display $\mathbf{d}_{i,n}$ associated with the winner $\mathbf{v}_{i,n}$. Note that $\mathbf{d}_{i,n}$ is a two dimensional vector, whereas $\mathbf{v}_{i,n}$ is a $p \times 1$ vector. The display vector $\mathbf{d}_{i,n}$ as its name indicated, is purely used for display purpose. Then, a topological (spatial) neighborhood $\mathcal{N}(\mathbf{d}_{i,n})$ can be defined centered on the display vector $\mathbf{d}_{i,n}$. Then the learning rate distribution indicates that it is only the vectors $\mathbf{v}_{i,n}$ which falls within the image of the topological neighborhood of $\mathcal{N}(\mathbf{d}_{i,n})$ will be updated. All the other $\mathbf{v}_{i,n}$ vectors outside the image of this topological neighborhood will not be updated.

Similar to the situation on a 1 nearest neighbor update rule, the learning rate distribution would need to decrease to zero in order for the SOM to converge. This means as the SOM is converging, the update neighborhood is getting smaller and smaller until the process converges.

As indicated previously, the LVQ depends on the assumption that M is known a priori. If M is not known a priori, then one needs to resort to more complicated clustering algorithms, e.g., fuzzy clustering, or dynamic clustering algorithms. These more complicated clustering algorithms will not be considered in this paper, as they are not required in the consideration of the EC system which we will use to illustrate the role of self organization in EC systems.

6.7 A Specific Example of Information Gathering and Assessment Used in an EC System

In this section, we will describe a specific example whereby the information gathering and assessment process is used to make decisions in the action in the next time instant in an EC system. In this example, our aim is to study how artificial insects exhibit grouping behaviour. Note that there are many more parts to this system, which could require a much more detailed description of the system. We will only describe in some detail the information gathering and assessment portion of the system, enough to illustrate the importance of information gathering and assessment procedures in EC systems, and we will only describe briefly the other necessary mechanisms to complete the system.

6.7.1 Description of the EC problem

In this section, we will describe the EC system which we wish to investigate. The problem which we wish to investigate can be stated as follows:

> Given a group of insects [1], how would they interact with one another, if the insects are only endowed with a limited number of "instincts", e.g., hunger, avoidance of danger, attraction to the opposite sex, repulsion of the same sex. In particular, we wish to investigate if any group behaviour will emerge.

This problem is important [1], in that it allows us to

1. find out what "minimum" assumptions which need to be given to an artificial insect.
2. investigate how group behaviour may emerge from individual behaviour.

Note that this problem cannot be undertaken using analytical approaches, as it is a multi agent problem. The individual agent, in this case, the artificial insect, may cooperate with one another, or they may be in conflict with one another. Thus, the situation may be analyzed as a team problem, or as a game problem. However, because of the dynamics involved in each insect, it is not possible to analyze such systems analytically. On the other hand, by defining each insect with a set of

[1] Henceforth, we will use the term "insect" as synonymously with "artificial insect". In this paper, we are not studying biological insects at all. Instead, we are studying the behaviour of artificial insects. Hence, there is no danger of confusion in the reader's mind.

assumptions, (resulting in a simulation model), it is possible to study the evolution of complex behaviour from simple systems. In a way, one may consider this problem as similar to an artificial life problem, except that the situation is far more complicated. Here, the individual agent may encounter different constraints, each agent has dynamics, and each agent can interact with other agents or the environment. In an artificial life problem, often the evolutionary program is allowed to evolve with the associated parameters fixed. It often does not allow any measurements during the evolution of the system to be incorporated. It often assumes that the universe with which the life form can evolve is infinite, i.e., there are no external constraints.

6.7.2 Minimum assumptions to be placed on the insect

A biological insect is a very complicated evolving living system [1]. At our current stage of understanding of both the biological functions, or the computer modelling, it is not possible to simulate any biological insects to any degree of biological complexity. Instead, we need to abstract a simulation model which will represent the insect's behaviour.

There are two schools of thought [1]:

1. One school of thought argues that even though it is not possible to simulate fully the biological insect, nevertheless, it may be possible to simulate a simplified version based on current understanding of the biological system. Thus, the followers of this school of thought would attempt to "imitate" the visual aspects of insect, the locomotion aspects etc. Because of the complexity of the individual components concerned, todate, as far as we are aware, there is no known complete simulation of an insect based on this school of thought. Instead, there is much work on individual components of the system, e.g., insect visual system, motion detection, insect locomotion.

2. The second school of thought [2] argues that it is the functional aspect of the insect which is more important. Hence, the followers of this school of thought would build insects which attempt to reproduce the behaviour of insects functionally. For example, one may be interested to build an insect which runs around, scrambles

over the obstacle etc. In this case, as long as the insect can perform these limited tasks, then the mission is achieved [2]. The internal representation of such insects may not bear any relationship with the actual biological insect.

In this paper, we will follow the second school of thought, and would wish to represent an insect functionally, rather than as a biological system.

When one thinks of an insect, there are many behavioral aspects which can be modelled. In this paper, we will model the following insect behaviour:

1. Food finding
2. Avoid obstacles
3. Attraction to insect of the opposite sex
4. Repulsion of insect of the same sex

There are many more other types of behaviour which can be incorporated [10]. For example, one may allow the insect to sound an alarm when a predator is detected. However, this would necessitate some form of sound, or alarm being issued, and similarly a receptive system which can understand such signal. Hence, they will not be considered in this paper.

In view of these behavioral aspects, the insect needs to be given detectors. It would be fair to assume that the insect is given the following sensors:

1. Food detection — the insect must be able to detect food, otherwise it will not be able to detect its presence. However, there are some possible variations in the type of food sensor allowed. For example, whether the insect can determine if food is in the vicinity, or its direction with respect to its current position. In this paper, we will assume that the insect can detect the direction with which food is located. In addition, we will also assume that the insect has "omni" smelling capabilities in the universe which it can travel, i.e., it can smell food anywhere in the universe which it exists. The

second assumption, while unrealistic in real biological insects, will simplify the simulation model.

The food sensor is assumed to be directionally sensitive. We assume that food at right angles to the insect will give a weaker signal than, say, a signal which is at 45° to the insect.

In addition, the insect is assumed to be able to distinguish by smell the sex type of neighboring insects. For example, it can recognize by the smell if an insect of the opposite sex is present. This would simplify the model which we need to use to represent the insect.

To make the model easier to work with, we assume that there is another sensor, separate from the smell sensor, which detects the presence of other insects.

2. Pressure sensors — in order for the insect to detect obstacles, the insect can either be given "sight" or "tactile" capability. Visual system is far more complicated to implement in practice. Hence, we will only give our insects the tactile capability. In particular, if it collides with an obstacle, its pressure sensor will register such contact. We will also assume there are two pressure sensors, both can detect signals from within a given direction. To make the model simple, we will assume that the sensors are mounted in front of the insect, one extends at 45° and the other extends at 135° respectively with respect to a reference direction.

These behavioral types can be "translated" into a number of "instincts" as follows:

1. Instinct 1. Unconditional, do not stop. This instinct basically ensures that the insect will not stay in one place. This is a default position. Without this condition, the insect may stay in one place, when there is no stimulus, e.g., food being detected, available.

2. Instinct 2. Pleasure: change in food sensor level. This instinct allows the insect to detect the presence of food.

3. Instinct 3. Pain: collision detector is active. This indicates that the insect has collided with an obstacle.

4. Instinct 4. Pleasure: detection of the presence of an opposite sex insect.

5. Instinct 5. Pain: detection of the presence of an insect of the same sex.

These instincts are organized in terms of hierarchy, in view of its danger level, or the risk of losing the insect's life. This can be organized as follows:

1. Group 1 — "life threatening". These instincts, if not heeded to could endanger the life of the insect. In this group, we can place the obstacle avoidance instinct, as if this is not heeded to, the insect may damage itself in the process.

2. Group 2 — Necessary, but not necessarily life threatening, at least not in the short term. In this group, we can place the instinct for finding food.

3. Group 3 — Ordinary. This is the default instinct, do not stop.

4. Group 4 — "Fun" or the lack of it. This group includes the instincts for detection of same sex or opposite sex insects.

The hierarchy of the groups will be in descending order. For example, in the presence of two or more detectors being active, the insect will heed to the instincts in a descending order ranging from life threatening to fun. it will deal with the life threatening instincts first until it is inactive before dealing with instincts lower down in the hierarchy.

Thus, our insect will have 6 inputs, each input is associated with a particular instinct on both sides of the insect. In the computer simulation program, it is assumed that the insect will have two outputs, i.e., forward movement, and direction. If we were to construct the insect in hardware (which we had done so, for an insect which is endowed with only one instinct, viz., obstacle avoidance), then we would need the following outputs from this insect model: four outputs for the four set of wheels. These four outputs will be able to drive the insect to go forward, or to turn.

6.7.3 EC system

The EC system which associates with the insect consists of two sections:

1. information gathering and information assessment — the insect needs to make sense of the input measurements from the various sensors, to order them in a hierarchical fashion, and then to "interpret" or infer what are its current options

2. action — the model will give outputs to activate the prime movers which powers the insect to move. In the computer simulation, this is interpret as two outputs, one for the direction and the other to move forward.

The insect will make use of both sections in every sampling time instant. From the sensors, it can infer if it is colliding with an obstacle, or if it can detect the presence of other insects, and their types. It is noted that by choosing to encode the insect behaviour in terms of instincts, we have successfully given a functional model of the insect. This model is biologically motivated, but has nothing to do with the biological counterpart. It is just a convenient way to organize the information and present them to the insect.

Information gathering and information assessment section of the insect model

This is the most important part of our insect model. The insect is given 6 inputs derived from each sensor. The insect is not given any desired outputs, at least not in the usual sense. From these input measurements, the insect will need to infer the following situations:

1. The presence of obstacles

2. The presence of food

3. The presence of other insects and their type, whether one with the same sex, or with an opposite sex.

Note that the insect is not given any visual nor range finding mechanisms. Hence, our insect does not have a "mental" map or model of the universe in which it exists. From these inputs from the sensors, it needs to infer the current state of the environment it exists in. Note that by organizing the instincts in a hierarchy would remove the necessity to give the insect an internal "perception" model. The insect simply considers the inputs in a hierarchy, and deals with the one with the highest order first before considering the inputs lower down in the hierarchy. Thus, it eliminates the need for an internal "mental" model.

Because of the way in which we model the insect, the information assessment section of the insect has two parts:

1. a clustering part which uses learning vector quantization (LVQ) For this stage, the network model is given by

$$\mathbf{z} = F(W_1\mathbf{u} + \tau) \tag{6.1}$$

   where $\mathbf{u}$ is the $p \times 1$ input vector, and $\mathbf{z}$ is a $M \times 1$ vector. W_1 is a $M \times p$ constant matrix. $F(.)$ is a $M \times 1$ vector nonlinearity. In our case, this nonlinearity is a max operator. τ is a $M \times 1$ vector denoting the threshold.

2. a modified hebbian learning based on inputs from the sensors. In this second stage, the neural network model is given by

$$\mathbf{y} = G(W_2\mathbf{z}) \tag{6.2}$$

   where $\mathbf{y}$ is a $L \times 1$ output vector. W_2 is a $L \times M$ matrix.

The second part is necessary, as the LVQ, while giving a set of clusters, does not associate the clusters with a label. Hence, in order to make use of these clusters, a second stage is necessary. We will describe both stages in more detail as follows:

1. LVQ stage — The LVQ stage is exactly the same as described previously, except for two modifications:

   (a) Normalized inputs — we find it is easier to work with normalized inputs. Hence our input is normalized to range between $[0, 1]$. This implies that the difference $\| \mathbf{u}_t - \mathbf{v}_{i,n} \|$ can be evaluated as $cos(\theta)$ where θ is the angle between the two normalized vectors.

(b) In order to make the output of the LVQ section more sensitive, we make the following modifications.

$$y' = \frac{a}{1 + a - y} \tag{6.3}$$

where a is a constant, and y is the original output $cos(\theta)$. The constant a is chosen to be 0.1 in our case. The second modification is that we will introduce a threshold τ for the signal y', i.e.,

$$y' = \begin{cases} y' & \text{if } y' > \tau \\ 0 & \text{otherwise} \end{cases}$$

The weight matrix W_1 is updated by using the LVQ algorithm as shown. This stage attempts to cluster the input vectors into a number of M clusters. Note that while the inputs are clustered into appropriate clusters, these clusters are unlabelled, i.e., they do not convey any interpretation in terms of the state of the system, nor its environments.

2. Modified hebbian learning stage. In this stage, the weight matrix W_2 is updated by a modified hebbian learning rule of the following form:

$$\delta w_{ij} = \eta \zeta z_i y_j \tag{6.4}$$

where η is a learning constant, z_i is the i th input neuron, and y_j, the j th output neuron. ζ is a state dependent variable. The function ζ can be understood as a function of the detected values based on the instincts. Thus, if the detector indicates pain, then ζ is ¡ 0. On the other hand, if the detector indicates pleasure, then ζ is ¿ 0. Normally, $\zeta = \pm 1$, dependent on the detected value of the instincts. Now since we require some time history concerning the past experience of the insect, we will use the following ζ function instead:

$$\zeta = tsin(\sigma t) \tag{6.5}$$

where t is the time that the detector has indicated a negative value, σ is the sweep frequency. The intuition behind this state dependent function is that if the insect registers "pain", it does not know how to free itself out of the pain state. it is possible that it may continue to move itself so that the pain is continuously inflicted. On the other hand, the ζ function shown previously allows the ζ function to swing between positive values and negative values. What this means is that the insect will get out of the "pain" state sooner or later. The parameter σ is a constant, which controls how fast the insect is allowed to swing out of the "pain" state. If σ is too small, then it may reduce the ability of the insect to explore the neighborhood. On the other hand, if σ is too large, then the insect may spend too much time in the "pain" state, and risk the possibility of long term damage.

Thus, the modified hebbian learning rule allows us to update the weight matrix W_2 in accordance with the input from stage 1.

6.7.4 Action

As indicated previously, the action stage is dependent on the particular system under study. In our case, the action results from the outputs of the second stage. These outputs are used to derive the control which powers the locomotion of the insect itself in the case of hardware implementations, or in moving the insect to the next position in the case of software simulation. We will not give details of this part of our experiment.

6.8 Results

In this section, we will present some results of the evolution of the insect behaviour. First, we will give some indicative evolution in the behaviour of a single insect. Then, we will give some indicative evolution of the group behaviour of a group of insects.

6.8.1 Single insect behaviour

In this section, we will denote an insect using the following graphical notation (see figure 6.1). The head of the insect as well as the path which the insect moves will be displayed. The two dots represent the left and right antennae (pressure sensor) respectively.

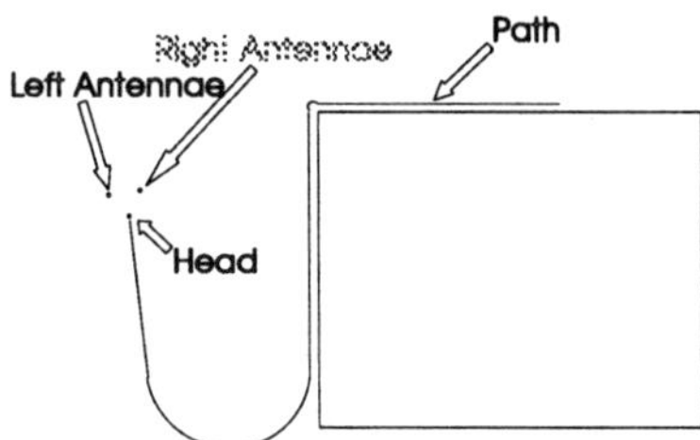

Figure 6.1: A Closeup of the Insect Simulator

Note: For all examples, it is worth to emphasize that the insect starts with no knowledge of its environment. There is no global information assumed. It learns about the environment in which it operates in, and make appropriate decisions based on the output of the sensors, and the hierarchy of instincts as indicated.

In this section, we will give some results on the evolution of the behaviour of a single insect. We will give a number of typical behaviour of the insect under various environmental conditions.

Wall following

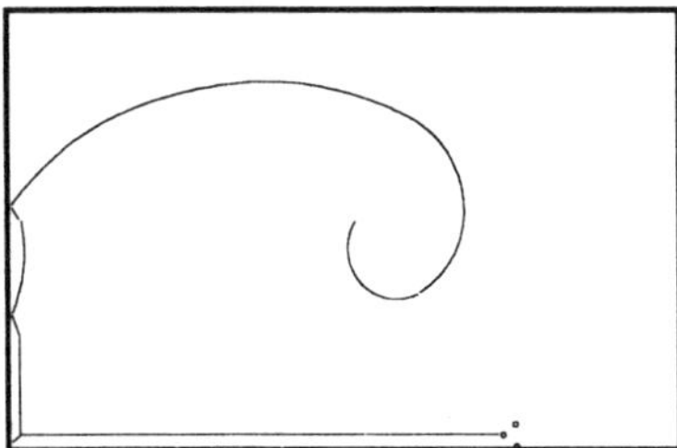

Figure 6.2: The Insect Learning about Walls

Figure 6.2 shows a 'new born' insect. The only obstacles in the area are the walls at the edge of the environment. The insect starts randomly running around. When it hits a wall, the trial and error (the ζ function in the information processing section as described previously) starts. If the insect tries to head more into the wall, nothing will happen, however, when it turns away, the path will change. After 3 hits, the insect seems to have learnt about walls to the right. Walls to the left have not been encountered yet.

Food

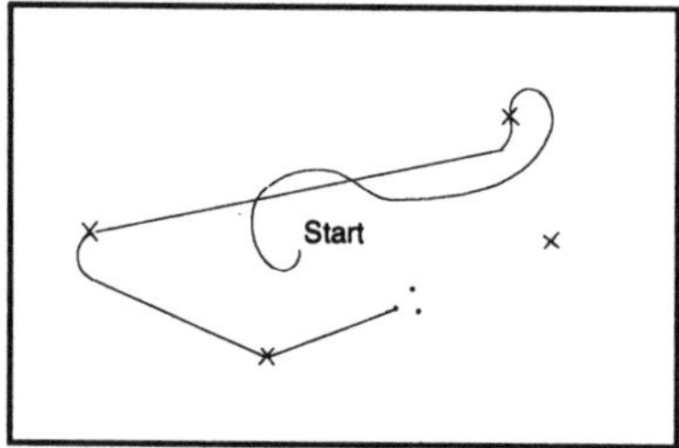

Figure 6.3: The Insect Learning about Food

Figure 6.3 shows the insect in the same space as figure 6.2, however this time, food is present. The insect detects the food but turns away; after a while, it learns to travel towards it (as it learns to associate food with pleasure. The arc is large and inefficient at first, however, as soon as the insect misses the food with the big arc, it is forced to change i.e. the arc narrows. This is equivalent to turning faster. After a while, the insect turns quickly towards the food and heads directly for it. Several contacts are shown. Each is marked with a cross. Each time the food is reached, it disappears and is replaced by another appearance of food at a random location.

Food and walls

Figure 6.4 shows the insect in an environment with both food and walls. The insect learns the food finding as in figure 6.3, but it encounters the wall in the process. Thus both wall and food functions are learnt.

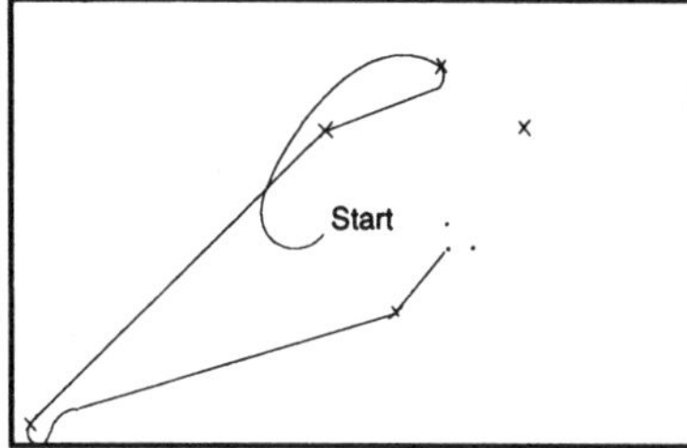

Figure 6.4: The Insect with both Food and Walls

Trapped in a bottle

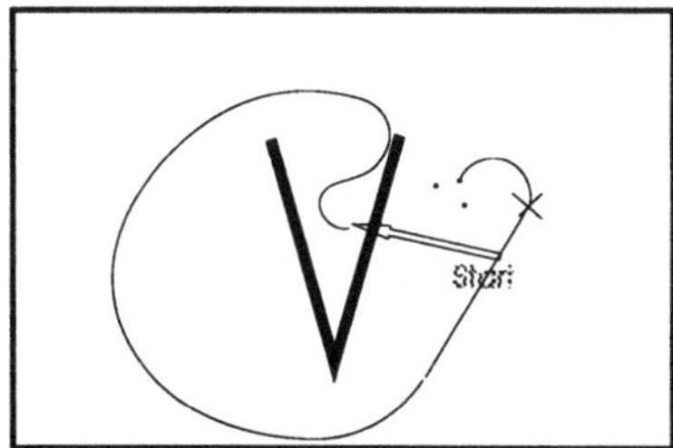

Figure 6.5: The Insect 'Trapped' in a Bottle

Figure 6.5 shows the trained insect 'trapped' in a bottle. It detects food but encounters a wall. It finds its way out of the bottle but forgets about the food. After 'wandering' for a while, it finds the food again and heads towards it. This behaviour is very similar to the scouting behaviour observed in biological insects.

Trapped with two food sources

Figure 6.6 shows the insect of figure 6.5 presented with 2 food sources. It again finds its way out of the bottle; however, food source 2 is detected when food source 1 is lost. After 'devouring' source 2, it detects source 1 again and heads for it.

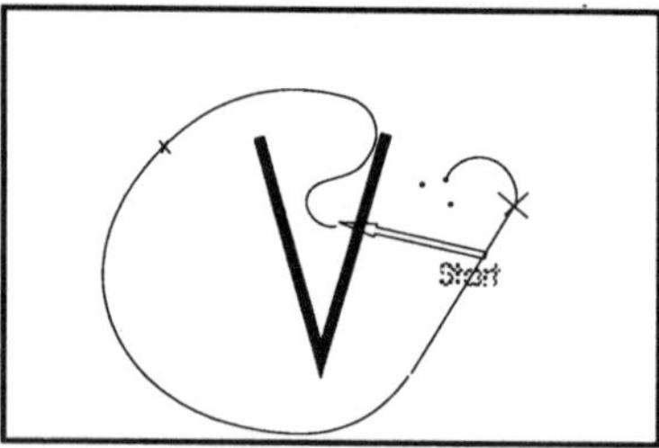

Figure 6.6: Insect in a Bottle with Two Food Sources

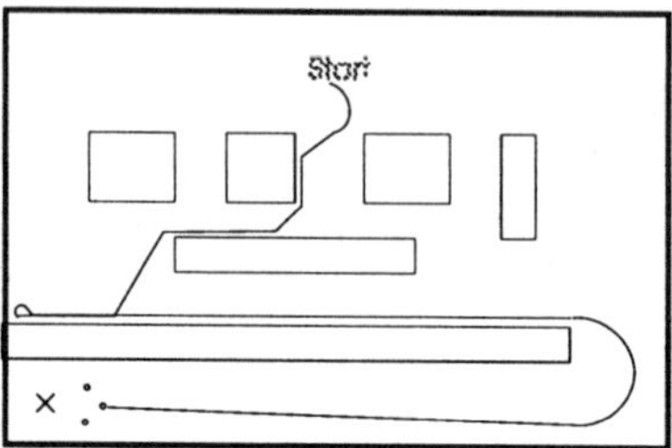

Figure 6.7: The Insect in a Complex Maze

Solving a maze

This is the most complicated task yet. In a pseudo maze the insect heads for the food. It follows the wall and heads for the food only to be denied by a further obstacle. It works its way around the obstacle and re discovers the food. After several attempts, it finally reaches the food. This shows extensive wall following and food finding behaviours.

As can be observed from these figures, the simulated insect seems to have successfully learnt all the behaviours it was originally intended to learn. The simulator is an effective way to test the insect as trained insects can be 'stored' to disk to be recalled at a later stage. A new maze can be constructed and a trained insect recalled to try to solve it as in figure 6.7. The insect behaves similarly to the scout ant observed in biological insects. The performances are also very similar to the performances of ants recorded in [9]. The ants can solve simple mazes, by trying to locate food in a passage in the maze.

Figures 6.8 and 6.9 show problems encountered during training of the insects. Figure 6.8 shows what happens when the jump step (i.e., the step size taken by the software simulator) is too high and figure 6.9 shows the insect trying to solve a maze which is not solvable: the food source cannot be reached.

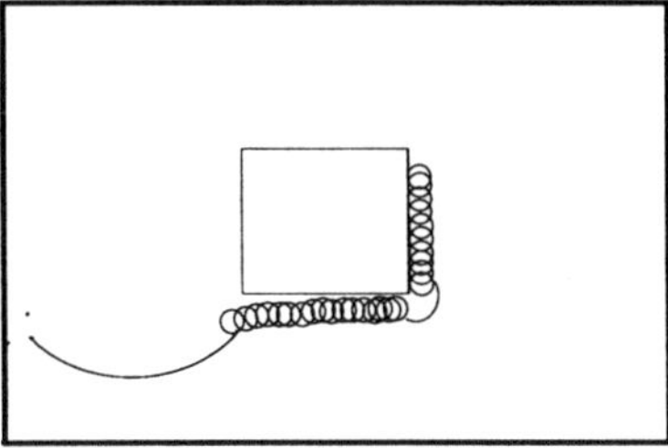

Figure 6.8: Jump Step too high

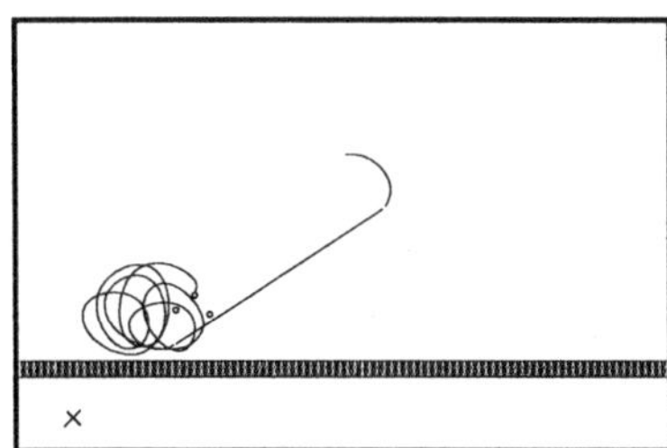

Figure 6.9: An Impossible Maze

Note that the main reason why the artificial insects can learn, even from an initial position of ignorance, e.g., new born, is that they are given instincts. From these imputed instincts, it will be able to learn to associate "food" with "pleasure", and "pain" with "hitting obstacles". By utilizing the ζ function, it also allow considerable experimentation in the association process. Once, the experimentation period is finished, it learns to associate particular stimulus with particular "feeling", it will then remember the experience in the internal neurons. Note that our insects allows continuous adaptation of behaviour, as there is no particular period of training is specified. If a new experience is encountered, it will gradually alter its present "experience" to adapt to the new environment.

6.8.2 Modified sensors

It is the material which is presented in this section which distinguishes our insect reported here from the robots of Brooks [2] and DeWeerth [14]. Hardwired insects perform badly when inputs are amputated (unless of course they are specifically designed to cope with this situation). Our insect can learn to operate with badly working or even missing inputs. If we look at the real insect world, insects also can modify their behaviours so that they can perform with amputated inputs. [12] shows a bee with one of its eyes blackened. Over time, the bee learns to compensate for this loss.

We can experiment with different options in the insect simulator. If we 'amputate' one of the insect's antennae, it can still function. It learns to compensate by making sure it does not turn towards the affected antennae. When the insect hits a wall on the side of the affected antennae, it associates the present input with pain. If that input happens to be the default action, it will ensure that the insect never randomly hits a wall in that direction. Figure 6.10 shows an insect with an amputated right antennae. Notice the default direction is to the left. Left is favored in all directions. The insect only turns very slightly right. This, of course, hampers its performance, however it still finds food and avoids most walls. This shows the generality of the insect model. Faced with a modified task, it attempts to solve it by optimizing what it has still got. It also corresponds well to the bee with the blackened eye in [12].

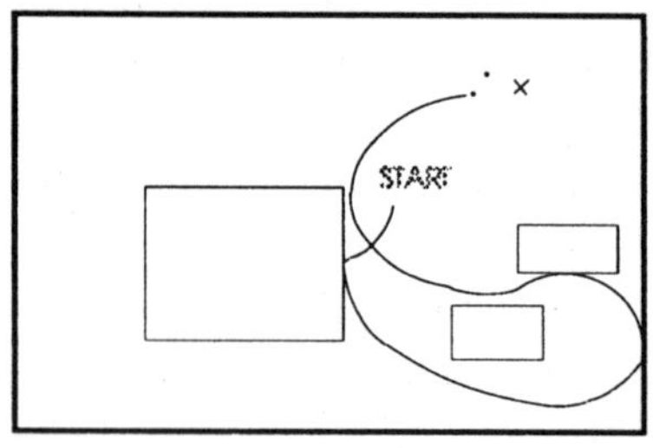

Figure 6.10: Amputated Sensors

6.8.3 Multiple insects

When investigating insect behaviour, two types of behaviour are present. The first is individual behaviour, the second is group behaviour. Section 6.8.1 showed the results which an individual insect exhibits. This is similar to the ant wanderings. Group behaviours are more interesting as they are far more complicated. Unfortunately it is very difficult to accurately model ant group behaviours, however artificial groups behaviours have been created to show that group behaviours are possible using our insect model.

Section 6.8.1 dealt with simulating a single insect. This is relatively simple to perform even on a personal computer. When several insects need to be simulated, each insect needs to get information on its fellow insects. This task is more time consuming. When many thousands of insects are to be simulated, it would be more advisable to use a parallel computer. Consequently, we have used MasPar computer, which consists of 4096 processors to simulate our multiple insect model.

The number of insects present, the proportion of insect types, and the instincts were modifiable. The insects could have the food finding instinct revoked, or the courtship/rival instincts could be removed. The following diagrams depict the results from the evolution of multiple insect behaviour. The insects could either be viewed as a dot, or their traces could be recorded.

Figure 6.11 shows the MasPar simulator simulating only one insect. This can be compared with the sequential simulation in section 6.8.1. This verifies the functioning of the multiple insect model.

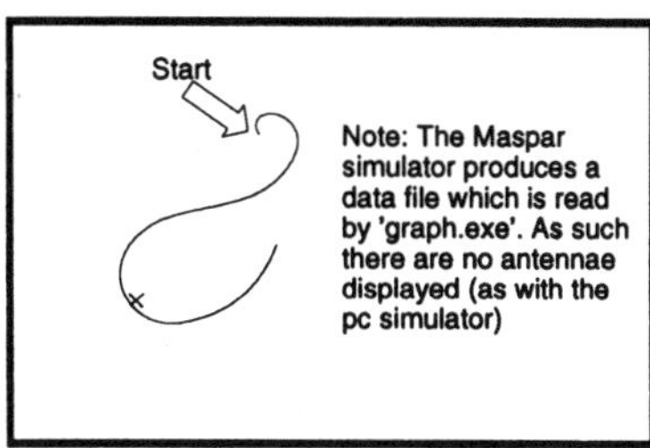

Figure 6.11: A Single Insect simulated using a multiple insect model

Figure 6.12 shows the trace of 5 insects which have just been ‘born’.

In this example, no courtship/rivalry is present, only wall avoiding and food finding instincts are operational. All 5 insects are zeroing in on the food ('x' marks the spot!).

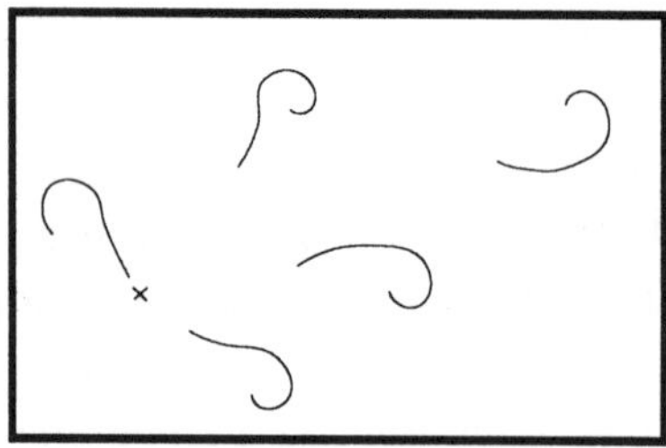

Figure 6.12: 5 'New Born' Insects

Figure 6.13 shows these 5 insects after devouring 2 lots of food and heading towards the third. Note that all insects are now traveling in converging paths directly at the food.

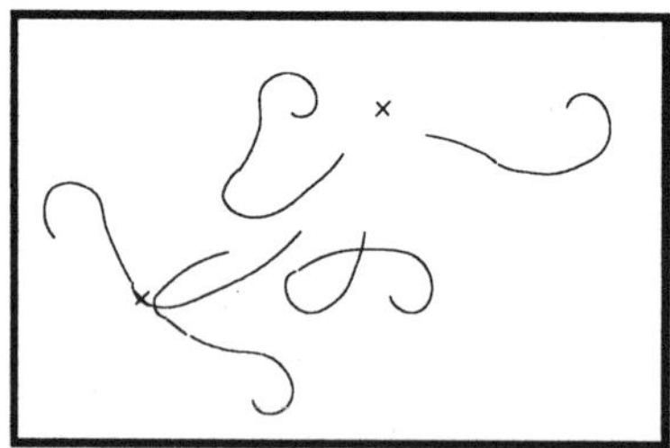

Figure 6.13: 5 Insects Learning to Find Food

Figure 6.14 shows the insects (in dot mode rather than trace) after several successful food 'missions'. They have now converged into a pack. All seem to have fairly similar behaviours and turn rates. Any differences are soon wiped out by the insects converging on the next food source.

Figure 6.15 shows another shot of the pack — after getting the food source on the left, they head right for the next source.

Figure 6.16 shows the pack behaviour for a 10 insect simulation. Once again, the insects are 'running' in a pack.

Figure 6.17 shows 10 insects with the food finding instinct removed, and the rivalry/courtship instinct activated. The group of 5 in the

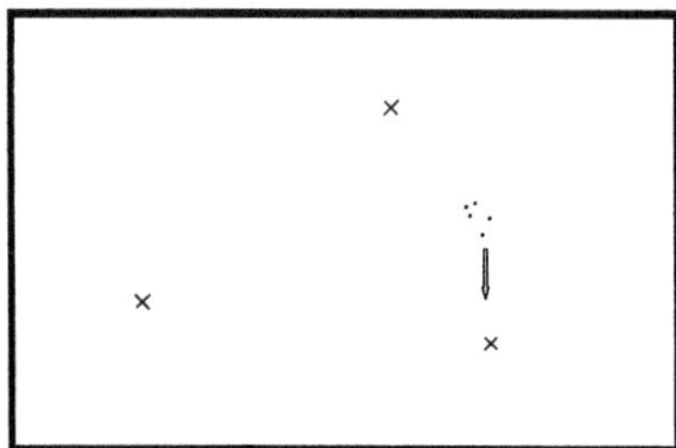

Figure 6.14: 5 Insects — the Pack

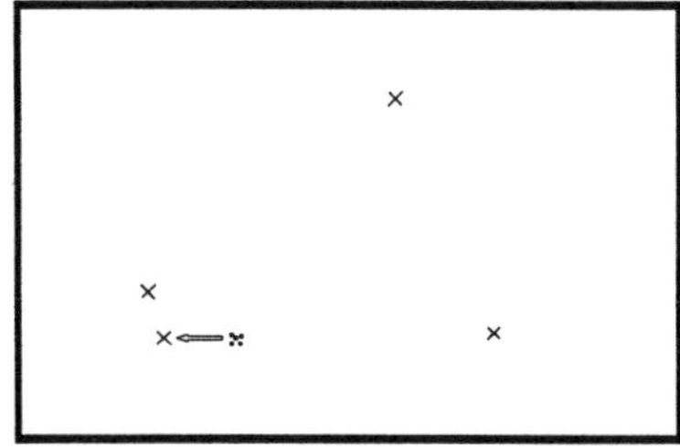

Figure 6.15: 5 Insects — On the Run

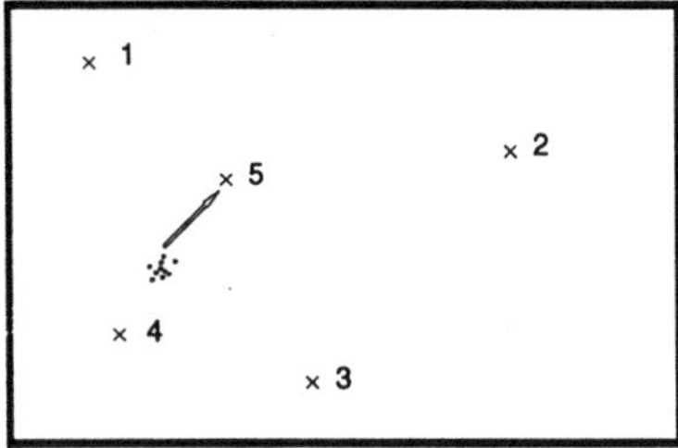

Figure 6.16: 10 Insects

middle are of different types. That means that the linear group goes — type 1, type 2, type 1, etc. Each is following the one in front of it. The first insect (the bottom one) is just running around unaware of all the commotion it is causing behind it. This shows the insects moving in point form.

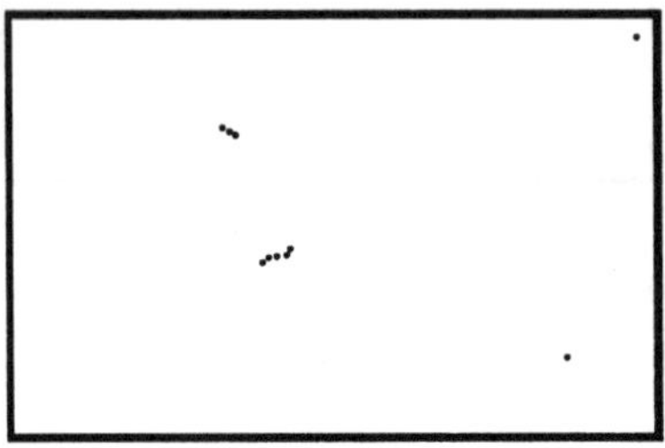

Figure 6.17: 10 Insects out for a walk

Figure 6.18 to 6.22 show this group after a while. One member has left after a 'fight'. A fight occurs when members of the same type vie for the attention of an insect of the opposite type. Figures 6.21 and 6.22 show the group breaking up after it got too tight and 'in fighting' broke out.

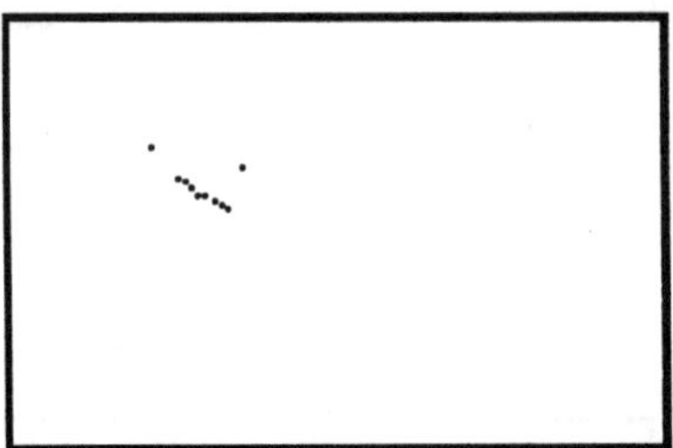

Figure 6.18: Breakup — number 1

Figure 6.23 shows the start of a simulation which joins both food finding and courtship/rivalry. These newly 'born' insects have a ratio of 1:3 — type 1 to type 2. On the left hand side, a union of type 1 and 2 can already be seen.

Figure 6.24 shows the insects forming a food finding pack (food being more important than courtship/rivalry, all hostilities are dropped). This is not yet as tight as the food finding pack of previous figures, however

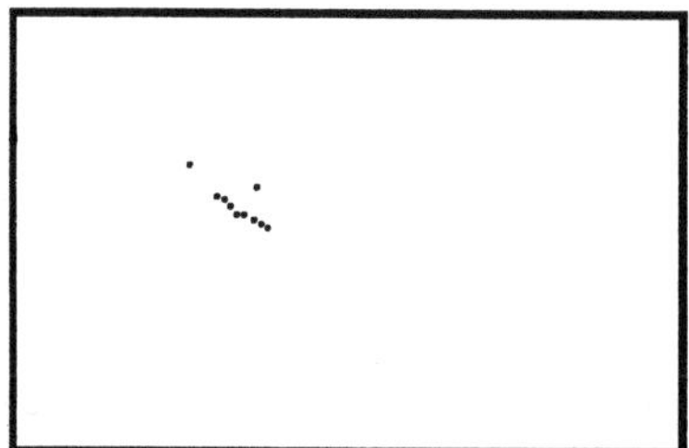

Figure 6.19: Breakup — number 2

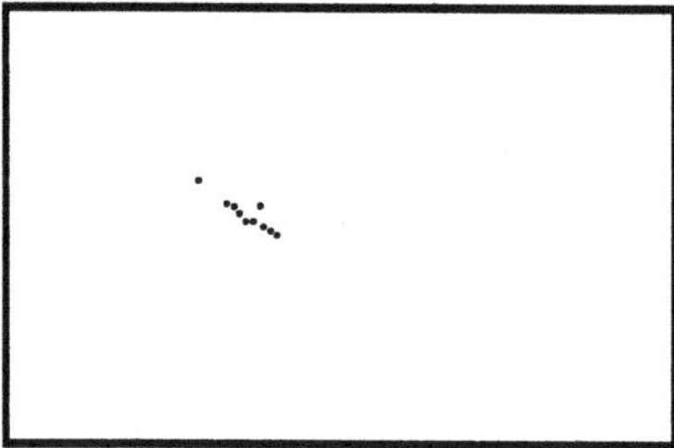

Figure 6.20: Breakup — number 3

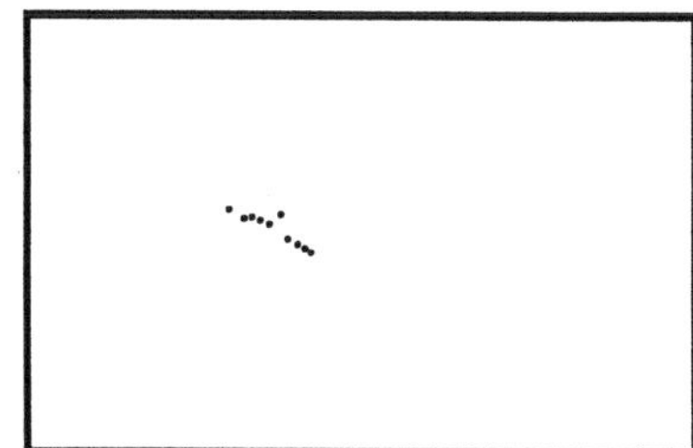

Figure 6.21: Breakup — number 4

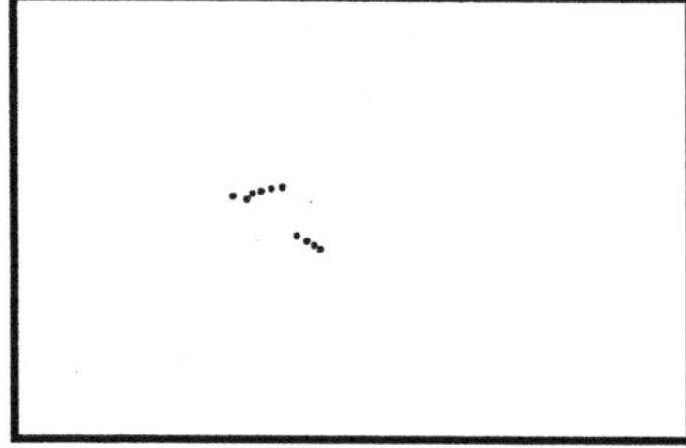

Figure 6.22: Breakup — number 5

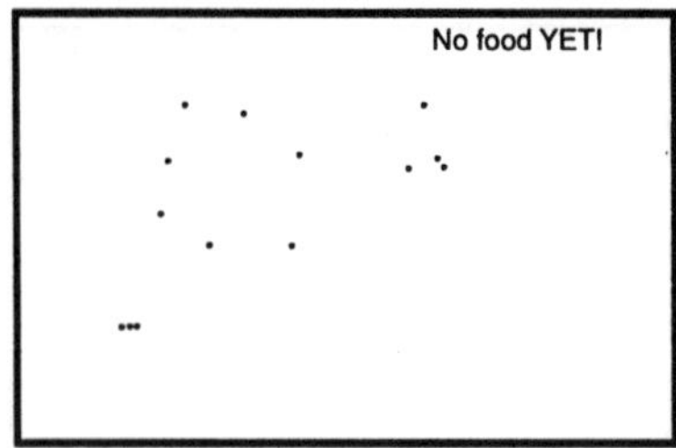

Figure 6.23: 16 Insects — 4 type 1, 12 type 2

as soon as the food is eaten, the insects resume their courtship/rivalry actions.

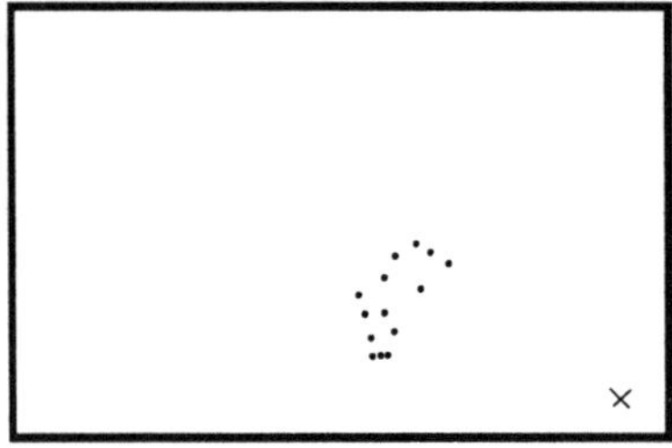

Figure 6.24: 16 Insects Hunting for Food

6.8.4 Analyzing the results

If we analyze the previous section, we can arrive at some simple conclusions.

The pack behaviour results from all insects trying to get the same food. Although it appears as if they travel in packs for some other reason, (e.g. pack instinct) it is only through necessity that this occurs.

Courtship pairs off insects or in some cases causes long chains of insects following the one in front. This ends up in a 'fight' occurring. The one closest will win the 'affections' of the other type of insect. By getting closer than its rival, an insect may take its rival's 'mate'. Figures 6.18 to 6.22 show this occurring.

The following behaviour is observed when the program was run in real time. The insects can be seen to 'run' along in a follow the leader manner until they bunch up. Then the two (or more) suitors circle the insect being fought over. When one gets appreciably closer to the fought over insect, the other rival will give up and either try again later, or go and bother another couple (or a single insect). This apparently complicated behaviour is a result of very simple instincts which are used in slightly different ways in each insect.

The learning mechanism is never the same in two insects - not only is it 'genetic' (the insect make up which is of course identical), but also the environment in which it learns. The behaviours are very similar, however the slight differences are detectable.

When both instincts are active, a very complicated set of behaviours emerges. Whilst tracking down food, type 1 insects will happily 'pack' with other type 1 (similarly with type 2). However when the food is 'eaten', they tend to revert back to trying to find a mate (of the opposite type). This induces all of the fighting and follow the leader antics previously mentioned.

All these complex behaviours have been produced from very simple rules (instincts). With the correct instincts, very complicated behaviours can be created.

Note that none of these emerging behaviour can be analyzed in an analytic model. It can only be obtained by the simulation described. It would be very interesting to attempt to give the insects other instincts, and observe if different group behaviour would emerge.

6.9 Conclusions

In this paper, we have considered a number of issues in an EC system. First, we presented a generic view of an EC system, indicating that generically, an EC system can be divided into two parts: (1) information gathering and assessment stage, and (2) action stage. It is further argued that the information gathering and assessment stage can be considered using two approaches, the supervised learning scheme and the unsupervised learning scheme. it is further argued that in an EC system, unsupervised learning scheme may be most prevalent. It is also argued that in general, the action stage is problem dependent. It is shown how various EC systems, e.g., autonomous vehicle navigation, can be understood using this generic view of an EC system.

In order to illustrate the points made, an EC system, viz., the behaviour of multiple insects is considered. In pursuing this EC system, some details of a functional model of an insect is presented. It is argued that by using a hierarchy of instincts, it is possible to model the insect functionally, i.e., not according to biological understanding at all. It is shown that in this case, the information gathering and assessment stage takes the form of two stages: the learning vector quantization stage, and the modified hebbian learning stage. By using these two stages, it is argued that the insect model can interpret the sensory detection obtained by interacting with the environment.

Two typical sets of experiments with the proposed EC system are then presented. it is shown that in the single insect experiments, it appears that the proposed insect model has "captured" most of the essence of the behaviour of a simple insect. Then, we have shown a number of evolutions of the behaviour of multiple insects. It is shown that the multiple insects exhibit pack behaviour, a fact which cannot be predicted from using a single insect model. This pack behaviour has arisen because of the interaction of the multiple agents involved in the EC system.

There are many further problems which can be considered under this methodology. For example, it may be useful to include some kind of instinct which informs the insect of the presence of predators, and to warn other fellow insects of the danger in surrounding areas. This may give rise to further complex behaviour which may have arisen from simple insect models.

Our multiple insect model may be viewed as a complicated artificial life experiment, whereby we impose constraints on the evolution of the life form. The life form itself has a functional model. In addition, the life form is endowed with a number of sensors. It is shown, that such simple assumptions on individual agents, when allowed to interact with the environment, and the other agents, can give rise to very complicated behaviour. Such behaviour is almost impossible to come from analytical studies.

Bibliography

[1] Beer, R. D. *Intelligence as Adaptive Behavior.* Academic Press: Boston. 1990.

[2] Brooks, R. A. "A robot that walks: Emergent behaviors from a carefully evolved network." *Neural Computation*, Vol 1, No 2, pp 253 - 263, 1989.

[3] Duda, R. Hart, P. *Pattern classification and scene analysis.* New York: Wiley, 1973.

[4] Gath, I., Geva, A. "Unsupervised optimal fuzzy clustering". *IEEE Trans pattern Analysis Machine Intelligence.* Vol PAMI 11, pp 773 - 781, 1989.

[5] Hertz, J., Frogh, A. Palmer, R. G. *Introduction to The Theory of Neural Computation.* Addison-Wesley:Redwood City, Calif. 1991.

[6] Hebb, D. O, *Neurocomputing Foundations of Research* pp 43 - 57, MIT Press: Cambridge. 1988.

[7] Kohonen, T. *Self Organising and Associative Memory* Springer-Verlag: Berlin; New York, 1984

[8] Pal, N. Bezdeck, J., Tsao, E. "Generalized clustering networks and Kohonen self organizing scheme". *IEEE Trans Neural Networks.* Vol 4, pp 549, 557, 1993.

[9] Chauvin, R *The World of Ants.* Victor Gollancz LTD: London. 1970.

[10] Stokes, D. W. *A Guide to Observing Insect Lives.* Little, Brown and Company: Boston, 1982

[11] Walker, S. *Learning and Reinforcement.* Methuen: London, 1975.

[12] Matthews, R. W., Matthews, J. R *Insect Behaviour.* John Wiley and Sons: New York, 1978.

[13] Karadaglis, C. "Modelling Biological Nervous Systems - Insect Locomotion." *Proceedings of the Second Australian Conference on Neural Networks 1991.* pp 67 - 70, 1991.

[14] DeWeerth, S. P. "An Analog VLSI Framework for Sensory-Motor Feedback." *Proceedings of the Second Australian Conference on Neural Networks 1991.* pp 26 - 29, 1991.

[15] Dethier, V. G. "Feeding Behaviour." *Insect Behaviour.* Addlard and Son: Surrey, 1966.

[16] Weiss, S., Kulikowski, C. *Computer Systems that learn.* San Mateo: Morgan Kaufmann. 1991.

Chapter 7

Virus-Evolutionary Genetic Algorithm and Its Application to Traveling Salesman Problem

T. Fukuda, N. Kubota, and K. Shimojima

7.1 Introduction

Living things evolve in order to adapt to its external environments. If it is possible to simulate evolution in a living world on a computer, we realize an adaptive system like living things in nature. Evolutionary algorithm is a stochastic optimization method simulated the process of evolution in nature. The three main categories of evolutionary algorithms are Genetic Algorithm(GA) by Holland [1], Evolutionary Programming(EP) by Fogel [2], and Evolution Strategy(ES) by Rechenberg [3]. These algorithms are fundamentally iterative generation and alternation process to operate on a population of candidate solutions. These algorithms can be classified into two types from the viewpoint of a representation method. In the EP and ES, individuals represent candidate solutions by means of integer or real variables, neither string nor bit, that is, the EP and the ES operate on the phenotype directly, not the genotype. Therefore, The EP and the ES are often applied for continuous parameter optimization problems. The main operator is mutation using a Gaussian noise with zero mean. On the other hand, the GA works on string or bit. The main operator is a crossover between individuals. Fogel reported that the EP outperformed the GA for numerical optimization problem [4]. However, the GA has an advantage of symbolic processing.

The GA, in general, simulates the survival of fittest by natural selection in the Darwin's theory of evolution [5]. With a progress of molecular biology, various types of evolutionary theories have been proposed [5]~[8]. One of them is the virus theory of evolution, which is based on the view that the virus transduction is a key mechanism for transporting segments of DNA across species. GAs based on evolutionary theory instead of Neo-Darwinism, have been hardly presented in conventional researches of GAs. Therefore, this chapter proposes a new algorithm, which we call VEGA: Virus-Evolutionary Genetic Algorithm based on the virus theory of evolution. The VEGA has two types of populations: a host population and a virus population. The virus population has two virus operators. One is a reverse transcription operator to transcribe a virus genes onto the chromosome of a host individual. The other is a transduction operator to create a new virus by transducing from host individual. These virus operators make it possible to transmit some segments of DNA among individuals in the host population. The VEGA is applied to the traveling salesman problem as a conventional optimization problem in order to show the effectiveness of the proposed algorithm.

This chapter is organized as follows. Section 7.2 presents the new evolutionary algorithm based on the virus theory of evolution. The virus infection operator is defined and incorporated into the GA. Section 7.3 presents an application to a traveling salesman problem as a NP-hard problem. The effectiveness of the proposed algorithm is shown through numerical simulations.

7.2 Virus-Evolutionary Genetic Algorithm

7.2.1 Genetic Algorithm

The first genetic algorithm was devised as an adaptation process [1], and later, the GAs were used as optimization methods [9]. The GA has been demonstrated the effectiveness in various optimization problems [9]~[17]. The GAs work on a set of solutions, which called population, with reproduction to copy strings and recombination to exchange segment of strings. An individual has one or some chromosomes of strings. In general, a string stands for a potential solution by the binary notation. A population of the next generation is generated by the reproduction according to the individual fitness value, and some new individuals are generated by crossover and mutation operator. In the GA, the operation for strings is called a genetic operator. The main genetic operators are reproduction, crossover, and mutation. Reproduction operator creates the population to the next generation by selecting individuals from the current population according to the probability based on individual fitness. Crossover operator creates new individuals(offspring) by combining segments on the string of parents. Mutation operator replaces a character on the string with another one.

In the stochastic proportional selection, an individual with a higher fitness can reproduce more offsprings. The selection would have to realize two different aims. One is to select individuals with high fitness value in order to select good solution candidates. The other is to maintain genetic diversity in population in order to generate new offsprings with new genotype. It is difficult to realize these two aims, because there is a trade-off between these aims. Premature convergence is one of genetic drifts and occurs when a population lacks genetic diversity in early generation. In fact, the premature convergence is a phenomenon that a certain individual with a high fitness value occupies the population, though the individual is far from the optimal solution. As a result, the premature convergence may mislead the evolution of the population toward the wrong direction instead of the optimal solution. GA should maintain genetic diversity within a population not to occur the premature convergence. Because the standard proportional selection such as the roulette wheel selection, is dependence on fitness values among individuals, GA can regulate selection by using a selection pressure.

The convergence of the population is controllable with varying selection pressure [9]. For example, the selection pressure is lower in early generations, and higher in late generations. To vary the selection pressure is able to switch between global search and local search.

Other methods are fitness scaling, ranking selection and so on [9]. The fitness scaling is used as a method to extend or reduce the difference between fitness values. There are three fundamental methods of fitness scaling such as a linear scaling, a sigma truncation, and an exponential scaling. The ranking selection is a strategy based on the rank sorted according to individual fitness. This strategy selects individuals by the number of the its reproduction into the next generation based on the ranking.

7.2.2 Virus Theory of Evolution

How have living things evolved in nature? Though the fact of evolution is certain, nobody can maybe explain the process of evolution. One of the most important evolutionary theory in biology is Darwin's theory of evolution [5]. Evolution means change of living things as a result of natural selection through generations. Darwin called evolution 'descent with modification'. Evolutionary modification in living things depends on an environmental change and a random genetic innovation. Evolution is mainly controlled by natural selection. Natural selection is the process that the best adapted individuals to the environment tend to survive and reproduce more offsprings to the next generation. The Darwin's theory of evolution by natural selection explained evolutionary change and adaptation, however the theory lacked a theory of heredity. Since then, Neo-Darwinism is based on the Darwin's theory and the Mendel's atomistic theory of heredity. However, the Neo-Darwinism can not explain well the process of evolution from the viewpoint of the evidences of evolution discovered so far. Four main points which take place in nature, do not fully explained by Neo-Darwinism as follows:

- The rapid evolution of species
- The rapid extinction of species
- The evolution progressing in a specific direction

- The parallel segregation

Recent progress of molecular biology results in proposals of various theories of evolution. Therefore, there are other evolutionary theories such as, neutral theory of molecular evolution, Imanishi's evolutionary theory, serial symbiosis theory, and virus theory of evolution. Most of evolutionary theories can not explain evolutionary mechanisms, though them explain the fact of evolution is certain.

The virus theory of evolution is based on the view that virus transduction is a key mechanism for transporting segments of DNA across species [7]. Virus is a minute particle which consists of a core of nucleic acid, which may be DNA or RNA, surrounded by a protein coat. Here the transduction means the genetic modification of a bacterium by genes from another bacterium carried by a bacteriophage [8]. Most of viruses in nature can easily cross species barriers and are often transmitted directly from individuals of one phylum to another. And this is the most significant difference between virus theory of evolution and other theories of evolution. Furthermore, whole virus genomes may be incorporated into germ cells and transmitted from one generation to the next one as horizontal inheritance. Therefore, the virus theory of evolution has a possibility of explaining the punctuational evolution in nature, which is difficult to explain with other theories of evolution.

To summarize, the virus infection enables rapid and horizontal propagation in the host population and the heredity enables vertical propagation of the genetic information from ancestor to descendant.

7.2.3 Virus-Evolutionary Genetic Algorithm Architecture

In this section, we propose a virus-evolutionary genetic algorithm(VEGA) incorporated the virus infection, that simulates the evolution with both horizontal propagation and vertical inheritance. As mentioned in Section 7.2.2 a virus has an ability to transmit segments of DNA between species. We define virus population as the species of virus which exists in nature. Therefore, the VEGA is composed of two populations: a host population and a virus population. Here the host population is defined as a set of candidate solutions. The infection of the virus population realizes the horizontal propagation in the host population.

In applying the GAs to optimization problems, it is important to use a roulette-based selection strategy because this kind of selection strategy expresses the survival of the fittest well. However, it is difficult to maintain genetic diversity by the roulette-based selection because of plural times of the selection of same individuals, and the lack of genetic diversity causes a premature local convergence. In order to incorporate the virus infection mechanism into the GA, we adopt a steady state genetic algorithm(SSGA) [17], for the SSGA exchanges only a little individuals in a population per generation. The SSGA is a technique to operate with the crossover of only one pair in the population every generation and realizes a slower evolution than other GAs. We use SSGA to perform virus infection every i-th generations. The procedure is shown as follows:

```
begin
    Initialization
    repeat
        for i:=1 to Interinfection_time do
            begin
            Crossover
            Mutation
            Selection
        end
        Virus_infection
    until Termination_condition = True
end.
```

First, in the initialization, individuals in the host population are randomly generated, and then the virus population is generated as the substring or segment of string from the host population. Interinfection_time is defined as an interval time of virus infections. Crossover, Mutation, and Selection are genetic operators correspondent to its optimization problem. Assuming that the string length of host individual, which is predefined. And the length of each virus individual, which is a variable, is extending with evolution of the host population. The most significant feature of the VEGA is to partially increase of only the segment of DNA in the host population as the result of the reverse transcription, not to increase a whole chromosome in the host population.

7.2.4 Virus Infection Operators

In this subsection, we define the virus infection operators in order to incorporate into the VEGA. There are many characteristics about virus infection. However, in this chapter we assume that the main process of a virus infection is horizontal propagation of a segment of DNA among individuals in the host population. A virus can transduce the genes from a host individual and transcribe to another host individual. The VEGA has two virus infection operator as follows.

- Reverse transcription operator: Virus transcribes its genes on the chromosome of host individual (Figure 7.1).

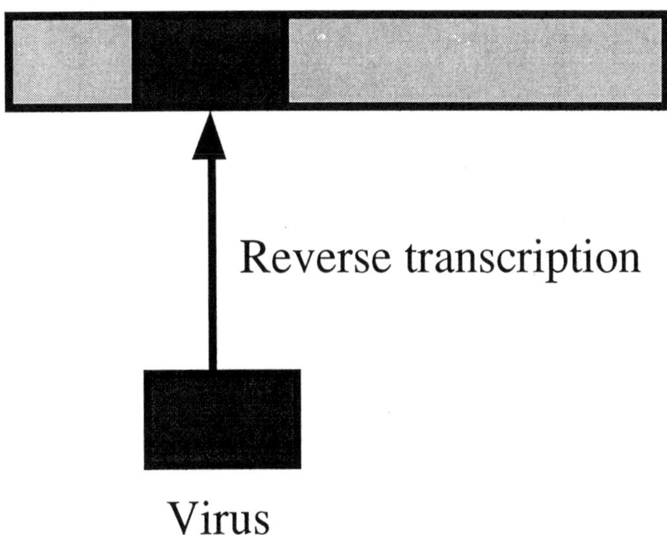

Figure 7.1: Reverse transcription operator

- Transduction operator: Virus transduces the segment of DNA from host individual. As its fundamental operation, virus transduces a segment in addition/reduction to some genes on the host chromosome (Figure 7.2).

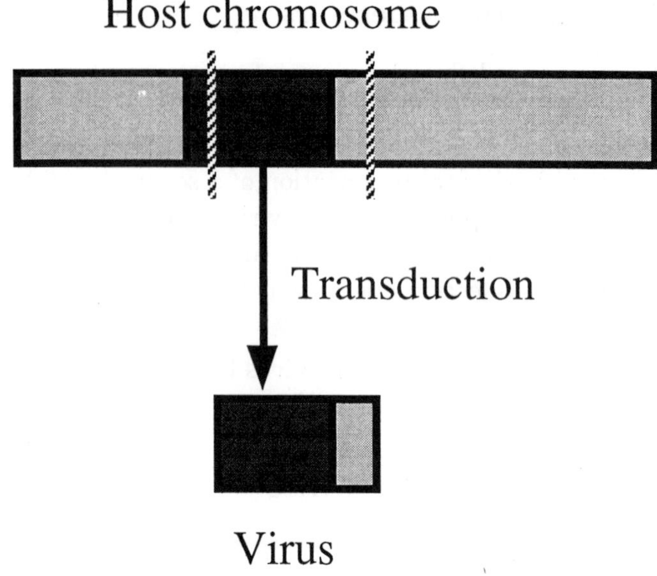

Figure 7.2: Transduction operator

Each virus has the parameter $fitvirus_i$ as a strength about the virus infection. The number of infection times of each virus is controlled under $fitvirus_i$. Assuming that $fithost_j$ is a fitness value before the infection and $fithost'_j$ is a fitness value after the infection. The $fitvirus_{i,j}$ represents difference between $fithost_j$ and $fithost'_j$, which is equal to the value obtained by infecting to the host individual:

$$fitvirus_{i,j} = fithost'_j - fithost_j \tag{7.1}$$

$$fitvirus_i = \sum_{j \in S} fitvirus_{i,j} \tag{7.2}$$

where i is the virus number and S is a set of the host individuals which is infected by the virus i. The virus which can improve the performance of the host population, has a high possibility of surviving to the next generation. Furthermore, each virus has an life power as follows:

$$life_{i,t+1} = r \times life_{i,t} + fitvirus_i \tag{7.3}$$

where t and r means the generation and the life reduction rate, respectively.

The procedure of virus infection is shown in Figure 7.3. First, a virus randomly selects a individual out of the host population and does the reverse transcription to the individual. The number of virus infection times is dependent on its ability to increase $life_{i,t}$. If $life_{i,t}$ becomes to negative, the virus individual randomly selects a new host individual and transduces a new segment with the transduction operator from the host individual. If not, the virus individual transduces a partially new segment from the transcribed host individual with the transduction.

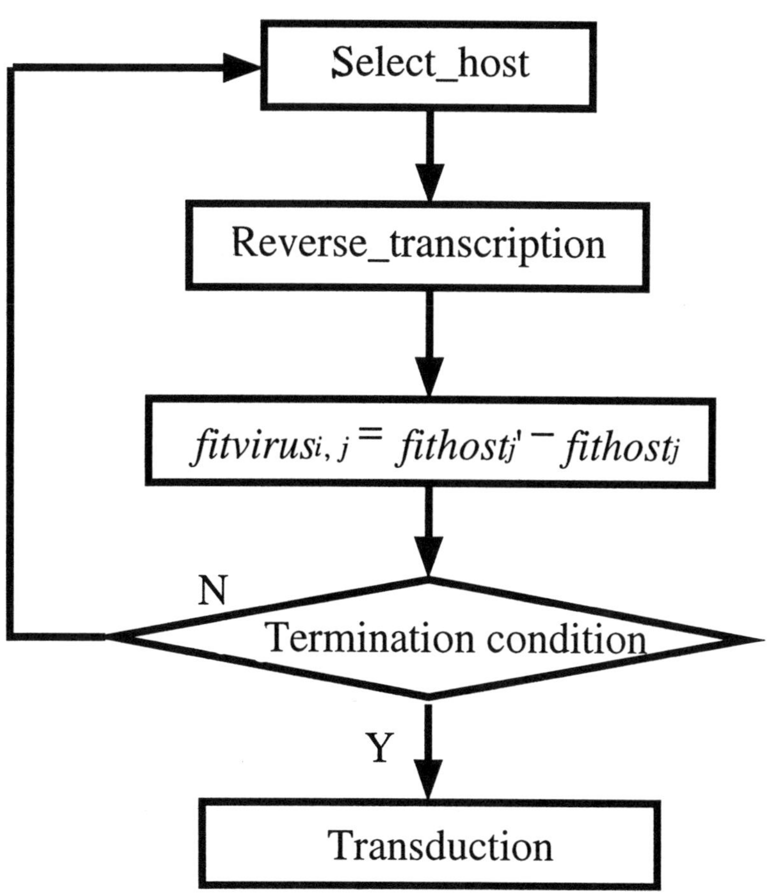

Figure 7.3: The procedure of virus infection

7.3 Numerical Simulation

7.3.1 Traveling Salesman Problem

A traveling salesman problem (TSP) is well-known as a NP-hard problem [18]. In the TSP, a traveling salesman must visit each of n cities exactly once. The objective of the TSP is to minimize the fitness value of a round tour which is expressed by eq.(7.4). We assume a permutation of the city number stands for a tour of the travel. For example, a permutation 4312 is a tour 4-3-1-2-4. The cost of a tour depends on the link costs $c_{x,y}$ from x to y where $c_{x,y}$ is the length between x and y. Consequently, we can calculate the total cost of tour as follows:

$$fitness\ value = \sum_{i=1}^{n-1} c_{x_i x_{i+1}} + c_{x_n x_1} \quad (7.4)$$

where x_i is the i-th city number on the permutation.

We apply the GA to a TSP as an example of combinatorial optimization problems. The genotype is defined as the positive number between 1 and n. The gene means the city number and the overlapping of the same number is not permitted on the chromosome. The proposed VEGA employs partially matched crossover (PMX) and cycle crossover [9] as a crossover operator for the TSP. The PMX and the cycle crossover operators are satisfied with constraints of a permutation problems. First, the PMX and the cycle crossover randomly select two individuals P1 and P2 for mating. Figure 7.4 illustrates the procedure of the PMX. The PMX starts with choosing randomly two break-points as a crossing site. The PMX chooses substrings between two break-points in both the parents. The PMX searches the genes of the P1 for the same gene as the i-th gene on the P2, then exchanges the searched gene with the i-th gene on the P1. Figure 7.5 illustrates the procedure of a cycle crossover. The cycle crossover chooses a starting point, not crossing site. The cycle crossover makes a closed round of substring. The cycle crossover starts with choosing a starting point x on the P1. The cycle crossover chooses the same gene on the P1 as the x-th gene on the P2. The cycle crossover repeats this process until the chosen gene returns to the first chosen character on the P1. The cycle crossover exchanges the round of substring between P1 and P2. Consequently, the cycle crossover can obtain a closed round of substring.

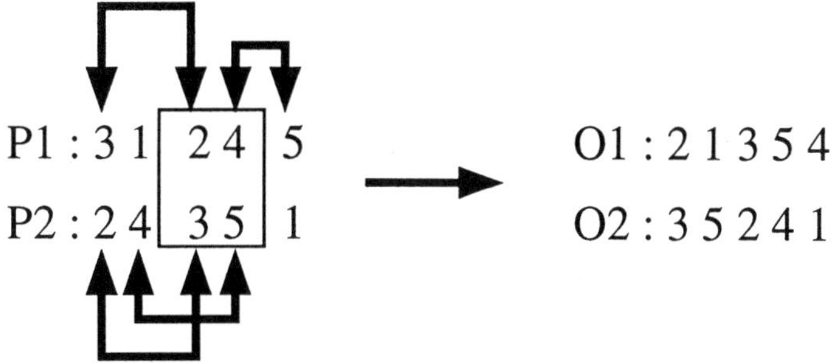

Figure 7.4: An example of PMX operator

Figure 7.5: An example of cycle crossover operator

The proposed GA employs a mutation operator to exchange of two genes chosen randomly, and furthermore, employs a inversion operator. As a selection method, the VEGA and the SSGA employ 'delete least fitness' method, which we call, the individual with the least fitness is exchanged from the population for new generated individuals. However, the selection deletes the individual with the highest fitness, since the objective of TSP is to minimize a fitness value of a round tour. Figure 7.6 shows the reverse transcription operator in the case of TSP. The reverse transcription operator performs like a PMX. The reverse transcription operator starts with choosing randomly starting point. The reverse transcription operator searches the genes of the host for the same gene as the i-th gene on the virus, then exchanges the searched gene with the i-th gene on the host.

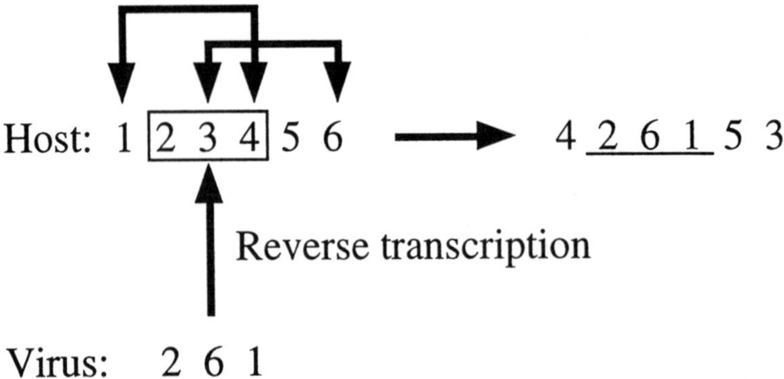

Figure 7.6: Reverse transcription operator in the case of TSP

7.3.2 Simulation Results

In the numerical simulation, we use the SSGA, the VEGA, and the standard GA(SGA) which employed the roulette wheel selection. Here we apply to a plane TSP with 25 cities and 3 dimensional lattice TSP with 27 cities and 64 cities. The position of each city shifts a little randomly from regular lattice position. Table 7.1 shows the parameter of the VEGA, the SSGA, and the SGA.

The typical simulation result of the plane TSP with 25 cities is shown in Figure 7.7 and the results of 20 trials are shown in Table 7.2. In early generations, the VEGA is the latest to reduce the length of a round tour, since there are little virus to be effective for a host individual. In the last generation, the VEGA reduces the length without trapping to the local minima. In the average, the VEGA obtains more feasible solution than others. Furthermore, the VEGA is superior to other methods in the comparison of the average computational time took to fulfill the aspiration level, where the value of 1.0 is defined as the time required for the VEGA to fulfill the aspiration level.

The typical solutions of 3D-lattice TSP are shown in Figure 7.8 and Figure 7.9 and the results of 20 trials are shown in Table 7.3. In the 27 cities, though both the SSGA and the VEGA obtained the optimal solution, the VEGA is superior to the SSGA in the average. Moreover, in the case of the large number of combination in the TSP (64 cities), the VEGA obtains more feasible solution obviously than the SSGA.

Table 7.1: Parameter of VEGA, SSGA, and SGA

Virus_population_size		10
Life_reduction_rate(r)		0.9
Population_size ;	SGA:	100
	SSGA,VEGA:	200
Crossover_rate		0.8
Inversion_rate		0.2
Mutation_rate		0.001
Generation (SGA)		3000

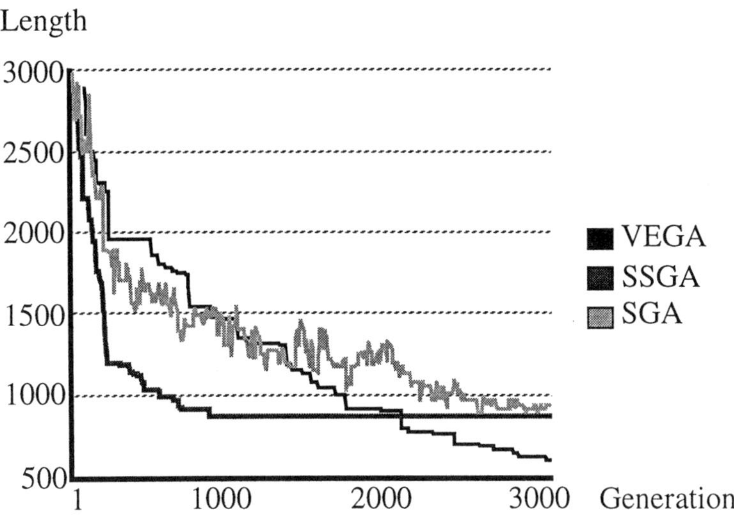

Figure 7.7: Simulation result of 25-city TSP

Table 7.2: Simulation results of 20 trials of 25-city TSP

	SGA	SSGA	VEGA
Min_tour	614	614	610
Mean_tour	954	854	683
Max_tour	1288	1020	749
Time	2.2	1.9	1.0

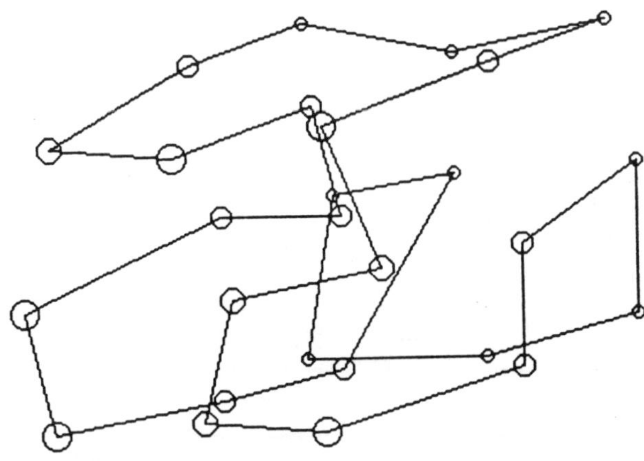

Figure 7.8: Simulation result of 3D-lattice TSP of 27 cities

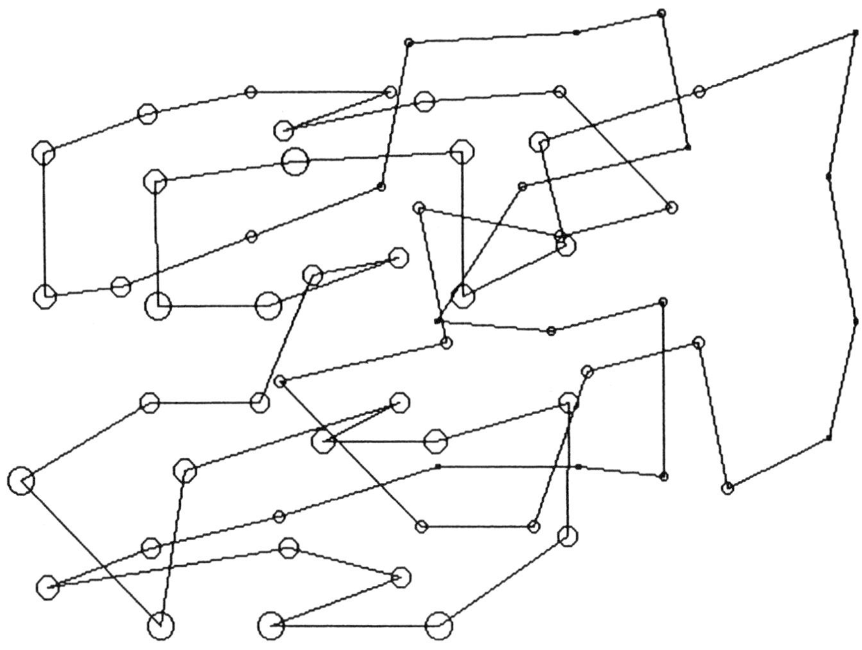

Figure 7.9: Simulation result of 3D-lattice TSP of 64 cities

Table 7.3: Simulation results of 20 trials of 3D TSP

		SSGA	VEGA
	Min_tour	688	688
27-city	Mean_tour	770	714
	Max_tour	872	749
	Min_tour	1720	1620
64-city	Mean_tour	1828	1740
	Max_tour	1926	1850

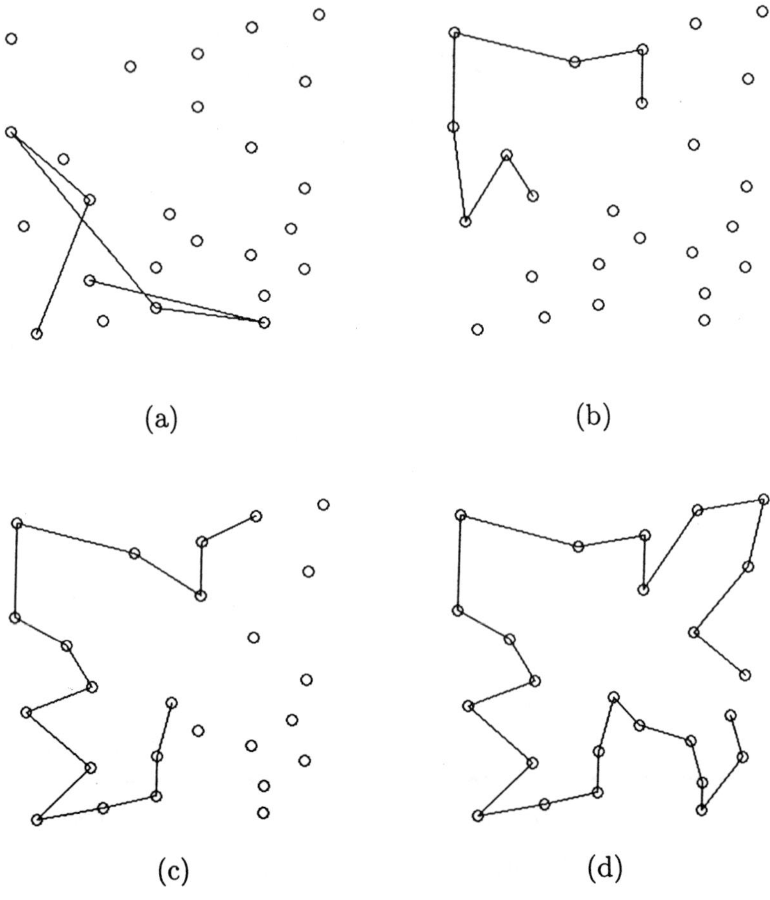

Figure 7.10: Evolutionary transition of virus individual

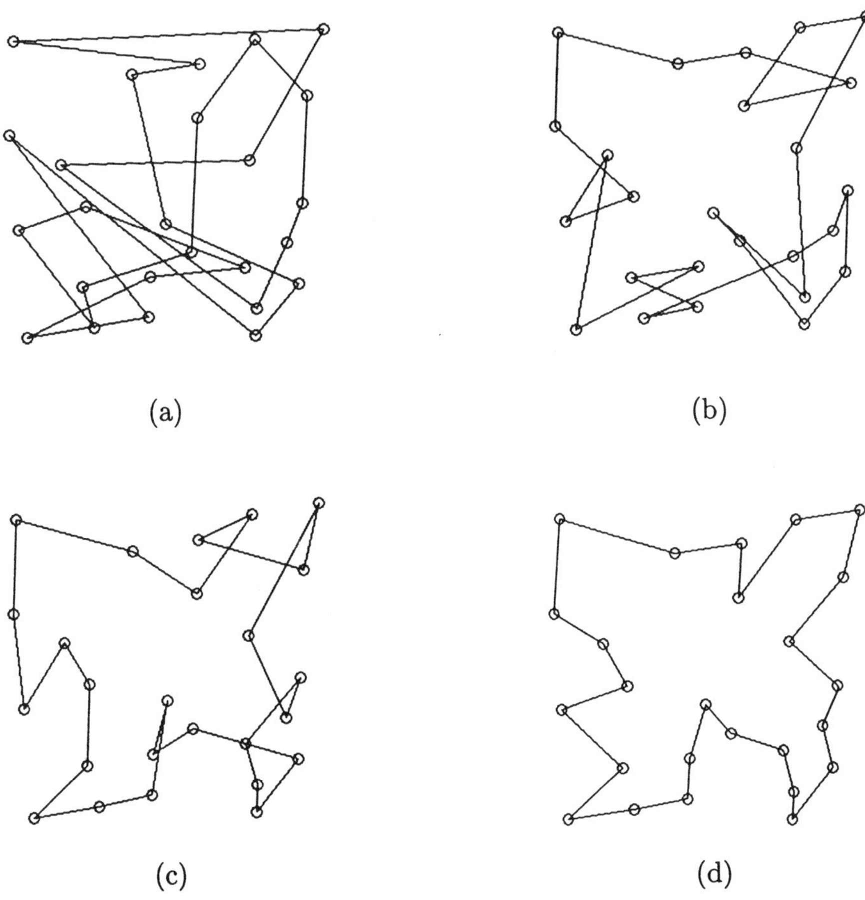

Figure 7.11: Evolutionary transition of host individual

Furthermore, we discuss whether VEGA possesses the effective schema or not. The evolutionary transitions are shown in Figure 7.10 and Figure 7.11 as the result of the 25 cities TSP. Figure 7.10 shows the evolutionary transitions of the virus individual with the highest fitness and Figure 7.11 shows evolutionary transitions of the host individual. In early generations(a), it seemed that the virus does not possess the effective schema. Next, the virus begins to possess the effective schema with short length as generation is passed. The virus possesses the longer length schema generation by generation, and at last(d) the virus possesses the almost optimal solution. In the comparison of phenotype between the virus and the host, the almost similar phenotype in them is formed at the almost same generation. This shows the fact that there is coevolution between the host population and the virus population, since virus individuals propagate their segments into the host individuals.

7.4 Conclusions

This chapter proposed a virus-evolutionary genetic algorithm, VEGA, which is based on the virus theory of evolution. The VEGA has two essentials, one is a horizontal propagation of genetic information, the other is a vertical propagation of genetic information. The horizontal propagation contributes to increase a schema possessed population, the vertical propagation contributes to create new individuals and reproduce a population with higher fitness.

The VEGA has two populations: the virus population and the host population. Virus population effects host population with virus operators. The virus operators are transduction and reverse transcription as processes peculiar to virus. The transduction operator can transduce the genetic information from a host individual and the reverse transcription operator can transcribe the genetic information into a host individual. Therefore, these operators can partially exchange a genetic information in a host population.

The proposed algorithm is applied to the traveling salesman problem. We show the effectiveness of the VEGA in the TSP since the virus operator propagates horizontally a schema in the population. Furthermore, we show viruses with effective schemata are generated by interaction between host and virus population through generation.

The VEGA is not incorporated the characteristic of a virus such as the selection ability of host species, however the VEGA realizes both vertical and horizontal propagation of genetic information. As future subjects, we must extend the schema theorem under virus infection and apply to the deceptive problem. Furthermore, we must extend evolutionary algorithm which are capable to explain evolution in nature well.

Bibliography

[1] J. H. Holland, "Adaptation in Natural and Artificial Systems," *University of Michigan Press*, 1975.

[2] L. J. Fogel, "Evolutionary Programming in Perspective," *Computational Intelligence Imitating Life*, pages 135-146, 1994.

[3] I. Rechenberg, "Evolution Strategy," *Computational Intelligence Imitating Life*, pages 147-159, 1994.

[4] D. B. Fogel, "A Comparison of Evolutionary Programming and Genetic Algorithms on Selected Constrained Optimization Problems," *Simulation*, , **64**:6, 399-406, 1995.

[5] M. Ridley, "Evolution," *Blackwell Scientific Publications*, 1993.

[6] B. Halstead, "Anti-Darwinism Theory in Japan," *Nature*, **317**:587-589, 1985.

[7] N. Anderson, "Evolutionary Significant of Virus Infection," *Nature*, **227**:1346-1347, 1970.

[8] S. B. Primrose and N. J. Dimmock, "Introduction to Modern Virology," *Blackwell Scientific Publications*, 1980.

[9] D. E. Goldberg, "Genetic Algorithm in Search, Optimization, and Machine Learning," *Addison Wesley*, 1989.

[10] N. Kubota, T. Fukuda, et al, "Genetic Algorithm with Age Structure and Its Application to Self-Organizing Manufacturing System," *Proc. of 1994 IEEE Symposium on Emerging Technologies and Factory Automation*, pages 472-477, 1994.

[11] H. Tamaki, H. Kita, et al, "A Comparison Study of Genetic Codings for the Traveling Salesman Problem," *Proc. of The First IEEE Conference on Evolutionary Computing*, **1**:1-6, 1994.

[12] T. N. Bui, B. Moon, "A New Genetic Approach for the Trveling Salesman Problem, " *Proc. of The First IEEE Conference on Evolutionary Computing*, **1**:7-12, 1994.

[13] A. Homaifar, S. Guan, G. E. Liepins, "A New Approach on the Traveling Salesman Problem by Genetic Algorithms," *Proc. of the Fifth International Conference on Genetic Algorithms*, pages 460-466, 1993.

[14] A. T. Rahmani, N. Ono, "A Genetic Algorithm for Channel Routing Problem," *Proc. of The Fifth International Conference on Genetic Algorithms*, pages 494-498, 1993.

[15] N. Baba, N. Kubota, "Collision Avoidance Planning of a Robot Manipulator by Using Genetic Algorithm -A Consideration for the Problem in which Moving Obstacles and/or Several Robots Are in the Workspace-, " *Proc. of The First IEEE Conference on Evolutionary Computing*, **2**:714-719, 1994.

[16] K. Shimojima, T. Fukuda, F. Arai, Y. Hasegawa, "Unsupervised/Supervised Learning for RBF-Fuzzy Inference -Adaptive Rules and Membership Function and Hierarchical Structure by Genetic Algorithm-," *Proc. of the IEEE World Wisemen/women Workshop*, pages 97-104, 1994.

[17] G. Syswerda, "A Study Reproduction in Generational and Steady-State Genetic Algorithms, Foundations of Genetic Algorithms, " *Morgan Kaufmann*, pages 94-101, 1991.

[18] J. G. Ecker, M. Kuperschmid, "Introduction to Operations Research, " *John Wiley & Sons*, 1988.

Chapter 8

Hybrid Evolutionary Optimization Algorithm for Constrained Problems

J.-H. Kim and H. Myung

8.1 Introduction

Although evolutionary computation techniques have proved useful in general function optimization, they appear particularly apt for addressing nonlinearly constrained optimization problems [1, 2, 3]. Constrained optimization problems present the difficulties of potentially nonconvex or even disjoint feasible regions. Classic linear programming and nonlinear programming methods are often either unsuitable or impractical when applied to these constrained problems. Difficulties arise because either the amount of computation required quickly becomes unmanageable as the size of the problem increases, or the constraints violate the required assumptions, e.g., differentiability or convexity. Unfortunately, the real world often poses such problems.

Evolutionary computation techniques can be constructed to cope effectively with the above difficulties. However, no well-established guidelines on how to deal with unfeasible solutions have been offered.

Some recent developments in constraint handling techniques in evolutionary computation have been described in [4, 5, 6]. These can be classified into several categories, such as methods based on (1) penalty functions [5, 7, 8], (2) specialized operators [9], (3) the assumption of the superiority of feasible solutions over unfeasible solutions [10], (4) multi–objective optimization techniques [11], (5) co–evolutionary models [12], (6) cultural algorithms [13], and (7) repair algorithms [3, 14].

Each of these methods, of course, has its own merits and drawbacks for nonlinear programming problems; however, they appear unlikely to provide exact solutions for heavily constrained problems, i.e., the problems with many nonlinear constraints. Most of them depend on the heuristics in applying evolutionary operators and do not provide the condition(s) for convergence to the optimum. Despite significant time and effort spent on constrained optimization problems, still there is no generally useful method for a given nonlinear programming problem.

In this paper, let us first consider a hybrid scheme. Intuitively, a two–stage procedure, which consists of the evolutionary algorithm as the first stage to overcome multiple minima and a traditional optimization method as the second stage to accelerate local convergence. This procedure may provide more rapid and robust convergence on many function optimization problems than either method alone.

The rationale behind the scheme is that an evolutionary optimization algorithm is unlikely to be the best optimization procedure for any specific function in terms of efficiency, convergence rate, solution accuracy, etc.; its robustness comes at the sacrifice of domain specificity. For example, if the function to be minimized is a quadratic bowl, then Newton–Gauss optimization will generate the minimum point in one iteration from any starting location. In turn, Newton–Gauss will generally fail to find the minima of multimodal surfaces because it relies heavily on gradient and higher–order statistics of the function to be minimized.

Regarding the hybridization of different algorithms, there have been some attempts to combine evolutionary and classic search methods in the hope of generating a more useful hybridization. Three such attempts are illustrated in [15, 16, 17]. Waagen et al. [15] combined an evolutionary programming optimization procedure with the direction set method of Hooke–Jeeves. Belew et al. [16] used a genetic algorithm to provide initial weight values for a neural network, with the weights then subsequently optimized using back propagation and a conjugate gradient method. Recently, Renders and Flasse [17] designed hybrid methods combining principles from genetic algorithms and hill-climbing in order to find a better compromise to the trade-off of global versus local search. These hybrid methods involve two interwoven levels of optimization, namely evolution by genetic algorithms and individual learning by quasi-Newton methods, which cooperate in a global process of optimization. But all of these approaches considered unconstrained problems, i.e., all solutions were feasible.

A hybrid method for general constrained problems which consists of evolutionary and deterministic optimization procedures was proposed in [18, 19]. The hybrid algorithm relies on an initial stochastic optimization in the form of evolutionary programming (EP) followed by deterministic optimization using a Lagrange multiplier method offered by Maa and Shanblatt [20]. This hybrid appeared to offer a potentially robust yet rapid method for addressing difficult nonlinear constrained optimization problems.

Although the hybrid of evolutionary and deterministic optimization procedures [18, 19] applied to a series of nonlinear and quadratic optimization problems has proved useful when addressing heavily constrained problems in terms of computational efficiency and solution accuracy, the hybrid method offers an exact solution only when the mathematical form of the function to be minimized/maximized and its gradient information are known. The method makes use of the gradient of the objective function, and of the penalty function measuring a degree of constraint violation. Even if these functions are known, the hybrid method cannot be applied when a gradient does not exist. To overcome such limitations, a two–phase evolutionary programming (TPEP) method based on the hybrid method [21] has been developed.

The TPEP is based on the concept of the two–phase optimization neural network operating under different dynamics as the phase is changed by a predetermined timing switch in continuous time [20]. The two–phase neural network guarantees a global minimizer to a convex program, as it satisfies the Kuhn-Tucker optimality condition in the second phase.

The TPEP uses a standard EP as the first phase and the EP formulation of the augmented Lagrangian method [22] as the second phase. The augmented Lagrangian is used as an objective function in the second phase, with elitist selection based on a deterministic ranking. By updating Lagrange multipliers in the augmented Lagrangian function and therefore putting gradual emphasis on violated constraints, the trial solutions are driven to the optimal point where all constraints are satisfied. In general, the TPEP could be considered as a discrete-time version of the two-phase neural network.

We describe the constrained optimization problems and some mathematical preliminaries in Section 8.2. The hybrid EP is described in Section 8.3 together with the computer simulations, and the TPEP is described in Section 8.4. To indicate the potential usefulness of the proposed schemes, computer simulations for some test cases are presented in Section 8.5. Finally conclusions are given in Section 8.6.

8.2 Constrained Optimization Problem

The following notation and convention are used throughout the paper. $\vec{X} \subset R^n$ is said to be *convex* iff any $\vec{x_l}, \vec{x_r} \in \vec{X}$ implies $[\vec{x_l}, \vec{x_r}] \subset \vec{X}$, where $[\vec{x_l}, \vec{x_r}] = \{\vec{x} \in R^n | \vec{x} = \lambda\vec{x_l} + (1-\lambda)\vec{x_r}, 0 \leq \lambda \leq 1\}$. Let $\vec{X} \subset R^n$ be a nonempty *convex set*; then $f : \vec{X} \longrightarrow R$ is said to be convex iff $f(\lambda\vec{x} + (1-\lambda)\vec{y}) \leq \lambda f(\vec{x}) + (1-\lambda)f(\vec{y})$ for any $\vec{x}, \vec{y} \in \vec{X}$ and for $0 \leq \lambda \leq 1$. The function $f : \vec{X} \longrightarrow R$ is *concave* if $-f$ is convex. An *affine* function $f : \vec{X} \longrightarrow R$ is a function which is convex and concave.

The general constrained optimization problem (P) for continuous variables is defined as:

$$\text{Minimize } f(\vec{x}) \text{ subject to constraints}$$

$$g_1(\vec{x}) \leq 0, \cdots, g_r(\vec{x}) \leq 0, \qquad h_1(\vec{x}) = 0, \cdots, h_m(\vec{x}) = 0, \tag{8.1}$$

where f and the g_i's are functions on R^n and the h_j's are functions on R^n for $m \leq n$, $\vec{x} = [x_1, \cdots, x_n]^T \in R^n$, and $\vec{x} \in \mathcal{F} \subseteq \mathcal{S}$. A vector $\vec{x}$ is called a *feasible solution* to (P) if and only if $\vec{x}$ satisfies the $r+m$ constraints of (P). When the collection of feasible solutions is empty, (P) is said to be *infeasible*. The set $\mathcal{S} \subseteq R^n$ defines the *search* space and the set $\mathcal{F} \subseteq \mathcal{S}$ defines a *feasible* part of the search space. Usually, the search space $\mathcal{S}$ is defined as an n-dimensional rectangle in R^n:

$$x_l(i) \leq x_i \leq x_u(i), \qquad 1 \leq i \leq n$$

where $x_l(i)$ and $x_u(i)$ are lower and upper bounds for a variable x_i, respectively, whereas the feasibility set $\mathcal{F}$ is defined by the search space $\mathcal{S}$ and the above constraints expressed by (8.1).

There have been several attempts to solve the nonlinear programming problem above by using evolutionary computation techniques, but most of these were applied to the case of $\mathcal{S} \cap \mathcal{F} = \mathcal{S}$, i.e., the set of constraints is empty [5]. Several test functions used during the last 20 years considered only domains of n variables; for example, the five test functions proposed in [23], as well as many others [24, 25, 26].

Recently, several methods for handling infeasible solutions for continuous numerical optimization problems have emerged for the case of $\mathcal{F} \subsetneq \mathcal{S}$ [1, 7, 10, 27]. Some of them are based on penalty functions. However, they differ in how the penalty function is designed and applied to infeasible solutions. They commonly use the cost function f to evaluate a feasible solution, i.e.,

$$\Phi_f(\vec{x}) = f(\vec{x}), \quad \text{for } \vec{x} \in \mathcal{F},$$

and the constraint violation measure $\Phi_u(\vec{x})$ for the $r+m$ constraints, usually defined as [28, 20, 29, 3, 5],

$$\Phi_u(\vec{x}) = \sum_{i=1}^{r} g_i^+(\vec{x}) + \sum_{j=1}^{m} |h_j(\vec{x})|,$$

or

$$\Phi_u(\vec{x}) = \frac{1}{2}\left[\sum_{i=1}^{r}(g_i^+(\vec{x}))^2 + \sum_{j=1}^{m}(h_j(\vec{x}))^2\right],$$

where $|\cdot|$ is an absolute value of the argument, and

$$g_i^+(\vec{x}) = \max\{0,\ g_i(\vec{x})\}.$$

In other words, $g_i^+(\vec{x})$ is the magnitude of the violation of the ith constraint in (P), where $1 \le i \le r$. Then the total evaluation of an individual $\vec{x}$, which can be interpreted as the error (for a minimization problem) or fitness (for a maximization problem) of an individual $\vec{x}$ to (P), is obtained as

$$\Phi(\vec{x}) = \Phi_f(\vec{x}) + s\Phi_u(\vec{x}),$$

where s is a *penalty parameter* of a positive or negative constant for the minimization or maximization problem, respectively. By associating a penalty with all constraint violations, a constrained problem is transformed to an unconstrained problem such that we can deal with candidates that violate the constraints to generate potential solutions without considering the constraints.

A primary concern in using the penalty function approach is assigning penalty parameters to the constraints. There are several methods depending on the choice of the penalty parameter [1, 7, 8, 10]. For example, Homaifar et al. [7] establishes a family of intervals for every constraint that determines the appropriate penalty values. In contrast, the pressure on infeasible solutions may be increased by a time-dependent component of the penalty term, as in [8]. That is, the penalty component is not constant but increases with the generation number. The other methods [1, 10] also focus on how to design the penalty parameter.

The following theorems provide a guideline to the above methods on how the penalty parameter should be selected. Theorems 1 and 2 are known as the Kuhn-Tucker optimality theorem [30] and the penalty function theorem [22], respectively.

Theorem 1 *Let (P) be a convex program and $\bar{x}$ be a feasible solution to (P). Suppose that each g_i and h_j is differentiable at $\bar{x}$. Assume further that $\bar{x}$ is a regular point. Then $\bar{x}$ is an optimal solution to (P) iff there exists $\lambda = [\lambda_1 \dots \lambda_r]^T$ and $\mu = [\mu_1 \dots \mu_m]^T$ together with $\bar{x}$ that satisfy*

$$\text{1)}\quad \lambda_i \geq 0, g_i(\bar{x}) \leq 0, \text{ and } \lambda_i g_i(\bar{x}) = 0, i = 0, \dots, r \text{ and}$$

$$\text{2)}\quad \nabla f(\bar{x}) + \sum_{i=1}^{r} \lambda_i \nabla g_i(\bar{x}) + \sum_{j=1}^{m} \mu_j \nabla h_j(\bar{x}) = 0.$$

(P) is said to be a *convex program* if f and the g_i's are convex functions, and the h_j's are affine functions on R^n. If (P) is a convex program, its feasibility set is necessarily convex. For a feasible solution $\vec{x}$, the *binding set* at $\vec{x}$ is the set $I = \{i | g_i(\vec{x}) = 0\}$. A feasible solution $\vec{x}$ is said to be a *regular point* if the gradients, $\nabla g_i(\vec{x}), \nabla h_j(\vec{x}), i \in I, 1 \leq j \leq m$, are linearly independent.

The variables λ_i and μ_j are known as Lagrange multipliers. The above theorem will be used in Section 8.3.2.

Theorem 2 *Let $\{s_t\}_1^\infty$ be a nonnegative, strictly increasing sequence tending to infinity. Define the function*

$$L(s,\vec{x}) = f(\vec{x}) + \frac{s}{2}\left[\sum_{i=1}^{r}(g_i^+(\vec{x}))^2 + \sum_{j=1}^{m}(h_j(\vec{x}))^2\right] . \tag{8.2}$$

Let the minimizer of $L(s_t,\vec{x})$ be $\vec{x}_t$. Then any limit point of the sequence $\{\vec{x}_t\}_1^\infty$ is an optimal solution to (P). Furthermore, if $\vec{x}_t \to \bar{x}$ and $\bar{x}$ is a regular point, then $s_t g_i^+(\vec{x}_t) \to \lambda_i$ and $s_t h_j(\vec{x}_t) \to \mu_j$, which are the Lagrange multipliers associated with g_i and h_j, respectively.

From the penalty function theorem above, the minimum of $L(s,\vec{x})$ is equivalent to the minimum of $f(\vec{x})$ when $s \to \infty$. For a finite value of s, the value of $f(\vec{x})$ evaluated at the minimizer of $L(s,\vec{x})$ might be less than the value evaluated at the exact solution. Furthermore, for fixed s, the minimum of $L(s,\vec{x})$ might occur in the infeasible region. This is because at the minimizer of $L(s,\vec{x})$, the second term on the right–hand side of (8.2) might be positive, which implies a constraint violation.

8.3 Hybrid Evolutionary Programming

Let us assume hereafter the same notations are used as in the previous section.

8.3.1 First Stage of the Hybrid EP

Hybrid evolutionary programming (EP) combines a standard EP and the second phase of the two–phase optimization neural network [20]. EP takes the place of the first phase of the search, providing the potential for nonconvex optimization, and the second phase of a two–phase optimization neural network is subsequently applied to rapidly generate a precise solution under the assumption that the evolutionary search has generated a solution near the global optimum.

EP is implemented as follows:

1. A population of N_{p1} trial solutions is initialized. Each solution is taken as a pair of real-valued vectors, $(\vec{x}^i, \vec{\sigma}^i)$, $\forall i \in \{1, 2, \cdots, N_{p1}\}$,

with their dimensions corresponding to the number of variables, n, to be optimized. The initial components of each $\vec{x}^i$, $\forall i \in \{1, 2, \cdots, N_{p1}\}$ are selected in accordance with a uniform distribution ranging over a presumed solution space. The values of $\vec{\sigma}^i$, $\forall i \in \{1, \cdots, N_{p1}\}$, the so-called *strategy parameters* [31], are initially set to the constant vector $\vec{\sigma}_1$.

2. The fitness score for each solution $\vec{x}^i$ is evaluated in the light of an objective function $\Phi_1(\vec{x}^i)$. For the constrained optimization problems studied here, $\Phi_1(\vec{x}^i)$ is defined as:

$$\Phi_1(\vec{x}^i) = f(\vec{x}^i) + \frac{s_t}{2}\left[\sum_{k=1}^{r}(g_k^+(\vec{x}^i))^2 + \sum_{j=1}^{m}(h_j(\vec{x}^i))^2\right] \tag{8.3}$$

where $\{s_t\}_1^\infty$ can either be fixed or increased with time.

3. From each of the N_{p1} parents $(\vec{x}^i, \vec{\sigma}^i)$, one offspring is generated by:

$$\sigma_j^i[t] = \sigma_j^i[t-1] \cdot \exp(\tau' \cdot N^i(0,1) + \tau \cdot N_j^i(0,1))$$
$$x_j^i[t] = x_j^i[t-1] + \sigma_j^i[t] \cdot N_j^i(0,1),$$

$\forall i \in \{1, 2, \cdots, N_{p1}\}$, $\forall j \in \{1, 2, \cdots, n\}$, where $x_j^i[t]$ denotes the jth parameter in the ith vector among N_{p1} vectors at the kth generation and $N^i(0,1)$ denotes a realization of a Gaussian-distributed one-dimensional random variable with mean zero and standard deviation 1. $N_j^i(0,1)$ indicates that the random variable is sampled anew for each value of the counter j. The scaling factors τ, τ' are robust exogenous parameters, which are usually set to $\left(\sqrt{2\sqrt{n}}\right)^{-1}$ and $\left(\sqrt{2n}\right)^{-1}$ [32].

4. The fitness score for each offspring, $\Phi_1(\vec{x}^i)$, is determined.

5. A selected number of pairwise comparisons over all the $2N_{p1}$ solutions are conducted. For each solution, N_c randomly selected opponents are chosen from among all parents and children with equal probability. In each comparison, if the conditioned solution offers at least as good performance as the randomly selected opponent, it receives a "win."

6. The N_{p1} best solutions out of all the $2N_{p1}$ solutions based on the number of wins received are selected to be the parents for the subsequent generation.

7. The algorithm proceeds to step 3 unless the best solution does not change for a prespecified interval of generations.

Specifically, the EP procedure of the first stage stops if the following condition is satisfied: For the best solution at generation t, $\vec{x}^1[t]$, and generation $t-1$, $\vec{x}^1[t-1]$, $|\vec{x}_j^1[t] - \vec{x}_j^1[t-1]|/|\vec{x}_j^1[t]| \leq \rho = \rho_1$ for a sufficiently small positive value ρ_1 and all j for successive $N_g = N_{g1}$ generations.

8.3.2 Second Stage of the Hybrid EP

In the field of artificial neural networks (ANNs), constrained or unconstrained optimization problems have been studied [20, 33, 34, 35, 36, 37] to achieve the exact solutions based on mathematical formulation. ANNs have demonstrated potential for solving such problems efficiently. Among such networks, the first for solving mathematical programming problems was proposed in [33], where a linear programming problem was mapped into a closed–loop network. When a constraint violation occurred, the magnitude and the direction of the violation were fed back to adjust the states of the neurons of the network such that the overall energy function of the network was always decreasing, until it achieved a minimum. When it attained the minimum, the states of the neurons were assumed to be the minimum solution to the original problem. However, the network of [33] has a shortcoming in that the equilibrium point may not be a solution to the original problem because it fails to satisfy the Kuhn–Tucker optimality conditions for a minimizer. Even if it is a solution, it is often a local minimum, not a global minimum.

An improved network was developed in [34], which extended the results of [33] to the general nonlinear programming problem. The energy function for the network is a Lyapunov function, which guarantees that the network converges to a stable equilibrium point without oscillation. From the viewpoint of optimization theory, the Kennedy and Chua network [34] satisfies both the Kuhn–Tucker optimality conditions and the penalty function theorem. Under proper assumptions, it was shown that the network is completely stable. Moreover, the equilibria of the network are in a neighborhood of the set of the minimizers of the original problem, and the distance between the equilibria and the minimizers may be made arbitrarily small by selecting a sufficiently large penalty parameter.

But the shortcoming of the network of [34] is that its equilibrium point may converge to only an approximate solution that is outside the feasible region when the solutions of the constrained problems are on the boundary of the feasible region. This is explainable by applying the penalty function theorem with a finite penalty parameter. For applications in which an infeasible solution cannot be tolerated, the usefulness of this technique may be compromised. For these situations, a two–phase network formulation of a Lagrange multiplier method was proposed [20] as an alternative approach to the solution infeasibility problem inherent in the Kennedy and Chua network [34].

A two–phase optimization neural network operates under different dynamics as the phase is changed by a predetermined timing switch. In the second phase, it satisfies the Kuhn–Tucker optimality conditions such that the equilibrium point is precisely a global minimizer to a convex program. This means that it can achieve an exact solution with a smaller penalty parameter than the usual gradient method.

Their approach consists of two phases in search [20]:

(i) the first phase (for $0 \leq t < t_1$):

$$\dot{\vec{x}} = -\nabla f(\vec{x}) - s_t \left[\sum_{i=1}^{r} g_i^+(\vec{x}) \nabla g_i(\vec{x}) + \sum_{j=1}^{m} h_j(\vec{x}) \nabla h_j(\vec{x}) \right] \tag{8.4}$$

where t_1 is a predetermined switching time, s_t is a sufficiently large positive real number and $g_i^+ = \max(0, g_i)$.

(ii) the second phase (for $t \geq t_1$):

$$\begin{aligned} \dot{\vec{x}} &= -\nabla f(\vec{x}) - \left[\sum_{i=1}^{r} \nabla g_i(\vec{x})(s_t g_i^+(\vec{x}) + \lambda_i) \right. \\ & \left. \quad + \sum_{j=1}^{m} \nabla h_j(\vec{x})(s_t h_j(\vec{x}) + \mu_j) \right] \end{aligned} \tag{8.5}$$

The Lagrange multipliers are updated as $\dot{\lambda}_i = \epsilon s_t g_i^+$, and $\dot{\mu}_j = \epsilon s_t h_j$, where ϵ is a small positive constant. For this network there is no restriction on the initial condition of $\vec{x}$, while the initial values of vectors λ and μ are set to zero.

According to the penalty function theorem, the solution found by the first phase might not be equivalent to the minimum of $f(\vec{x})$ unless the penalty parameter s_t goes to infinity [20]. Thus the use of the second phase optimization might be required for any finite value of s_t.

The system is in equilibrium when $g_i^+(\vec{x}) = 0$, $h_j(\vec{x}) = 0, \lambda > 0$, and $\nabla f + \sum_i \nabla g_i \lambda_i + \sum_j \nabla h_j \mu_j = 0$. This satisfies the optimality conditions of the Kuhn-Tucker theorem, and an equilibrium point of the two-phase network is the precise global minimizer to a convex program (P).

For problems where infeasible solutions cannot be tolerated, e.g., owing to physical operational limits, a two–phase neural network which can obtain both the exact solution for the constrained optimization problem and the corresponding Lagrange multiplier associated with each constraint can be very useful. Owing to this utility, the second phase of the two-phase neural network [20] is employed as a second stage of the hybrid EP.

The problem of two–phase optimization neural network is that the performance strongly depends on the initial condition. In the hybrid EP, the first stage plays the role of providing a good initial solution vector to reach the global optimal.

After halting the first stage of the hybrid EP, the second phase optimization was applied to the best evolved solution of the first stage (EP) and iterated until the system was in equilibrium. The stopping criteria for the second stage was the same as that of the first stage except that $\rho = \rho_2 \leq \rho_1$ and $N_g = N_{g2} \geq N_{g1}$ to obtain exact solutions.

8.3.3 Simulation Results

Simulations have been conducted to compare the hybrid EP with three other methods, (1) EP alone (wholly stochastic), (2) TP (two–phase) optimization (wholly deterministic), and (3) NS–EP (EP with a non–stationary penalty function [8]).

To compare the computational efficiency of each algorithm, the computation time (T_C) required to meet the stopping criteria was defined as:

$$T_C = \begin{cases} N_{p1} \cdot (T_{EP} - N_{g1}) + T_{TP} - N_{g2} & \text{for Hybrid EP} \\ N_{p1} \cdot (T_{EP} - N_{g1}) & \text{for EP alone, NS–EP} \\ T_{TP} - N_{g2} & \text{for TP alone} \end{cases}$$

where N_{p1} is the population size in the first stage, T_{EP} is the number of generations consumed in the first stage (EP alone), and T_{TP} is the number of time steps consumed in TP optimization. The specific parameter values for each phase are shown in Table 8.1.

Table 8.1: Stopping criteria for each algorithm. ρ and N_g are used in the stopping condition described at the end of Section 3.1 and 3.2. TP and NS–EP stand for two–phase optimization and EP with a non–stationary penalty function method, respectively.

Algorithm	ρ	N_g
1st stage of Hybrid EP	10^{-4}	200
2nd stage of Hybrid EP	10^{-8}	300
EP alone	10^{-8}	300
TP	10^{-8}	300
NS–EP	10^{-8}	300

In the nonstationary penalty parameter (NS–EP) method, the penalty parameter s_t is increased with time in accordance with the penalty function theorem. We set $s_t = s_0 + k_s \cdot N_G$ where s_0 is an initial penalty parameter, k_s is the increasing rate of penalty parameter, and N_G is the current number of generations. In applying NS–EP, the parameter settings of $s_0 = 10$ and $k_s = 3$ were used.

Each algorithm was applied to the following constrained optimization problems:

Problem #1:
Minimize $f(x) = x_1^2 + x_2^2 + x_1 x_2 + 3x_1 + 3x_2$

subject to constraints g_1 to g_4 and h_1:

$$
\begin{aligned}
g_1(x) &= \frac{5}{12}x_1 - x_2 - \frac{35}{12} \leq 0 \\
g_2(x) &= \frac{5}{2}x_1 + x_2 - \frac{35}{2} \leq 0 \\
g_3(x) &= -x_1 - 5 \leq 0 \\
g_4(x) &= x_2 - 5 \leq 0 \\
h_1(x) &= x_1 - 3 = 0.
\end{aligned}
$$

Problem #2:
Minimize $f(x) = (x_1 - 2)^2 + (x_2 - 1)^2$
subject to constraints:

$$
\begin{aligned}
g_1(x) &= \frac{{x_1}^2}{4} + {x_2}^2 - 1 \leq 0 \\
h_1(x) &= x_1 - 2x_2 + 1 = 0.
\end{aligned}
$$

Problem #3:
Minimize $f(x) = x_1^2 + 2x_2^2 - 0.3\cos(3\pi x_1) - 0.4\cos(4\pi x_2) + 0.7$
subject to constraints:

$$
\begin{aligned}
g_1 &= x_1 - 1 \leq 0 \\
g_2 &= 0.1 - x_1 \leq 0 \\
g_3 &= x_2 - 1 \leq 0 \\
g_4 &= 0.1 - x_2 \leq 0.
\end{aligned}
$$

Problem #4:
Minimize $f(x) = 5.3578547x_3^2 + 0.8356891x_1x_5 + 37.293239x_1 - 40792.141$
subject to constraints:

$$
\begin{gathered}
0 \leq p_1(x) \leq 92 \\
90 \leq p_2(x) \leq 100 \\
20 \leq p_3(x) \leq 25 \\
78 \leq x_1 \leq 102 \\
33 \leq x_2 \leq 45 \\
27 \leq x_3, x_4, x_5 \leq 45.
\end{gathered}
$$

where

$$p_1(x) = 85.334407 + 0.0056858x_2x_3 + 0.00026x_1x_4 - 0.0022053x_3x_5$$
$$p_2(x) = 80.51249 + 0.0071317x_2x_5 + 0.0029955x_1x_2 + 0.0021813x_3^2$$
$$p_3(x) = 9.300961 + 0.0047026x_3x_5 + 0.0012547x_1x_3 + 0.0019085x_3x_4 .$$

Problem #1 is a quadratic programming problem, whereas Problems #2, #3, and #4 are nonlinear programming problems. Problem #1 was taken from [20], and Problems #2 and #4 were taken from [7]. The function $f(x)$ in Problem #3 is known to be the Bohachevsky function [15], which has multiple minima. In each case, $s_t = 100$, $\epsilon = 0.01$, $\vec{\sigma}_1 = 5.0$, and the population size was varied with 10 trials at settings of $N_{p1} = 10, 20, 30, 40$, and 50. There was little change in the results with respect to the population size variation. For brevity, the results depicted below are for $N_{p1} = 40$ with 100 trials.

All the results are briefly reviewed below and summarized in Table 8.2, which shows the mean of the best results averaged over 100 independent trials.

Problem #1:

The best evolved solution in the first phase of the hybrid EP was (2.91860, -1.80223), and the second-phase optimization drove the best evolved solution to the point (2.99999, -1.66667), which was essentially the same as the exact solution (3.00000, -1.66667). Comparisons in Table 8.2 indicate that the hybrid EP offers better performance than EP alone or NS–EP considering the value of the objective function as well as the degree of constraint satisfaction (See g_1 and h_1). But the TP optimization gave the same performance as that of the hybrid EP with less computation time.

Problem #2:

The exact solution to this problem is (0.82288, 0.91144). The hybrid EP could offer better solutions than EP alone or NS–EP. Again, the TP optimization was better than the hybrid EP in the light of the computation time.

Problem #3:

As in Problems #1 and #2, the hybrid EP offered better solutions than EP alone or NS–EP. As expected, TP optimization often fell in local minima such as (0.61861, 0.1) and (0.1, 0.93333) as shown in Table 8.3.

Table 8.2: Results of Hybrid EP, EP alone, TP, and NS–EP on four problems. This shows mean of the best solution averaged over 100 independent trials with $N_{p1} = 40$. The symbol '—', stands for 'T_C was over 100,000,000'. Note that '$*$' can be found in Table 8.3.

Prob. #		*Exact*	*Hybrid EP*	*EP alone*	*TP*	*NS-EP*
1	Φ	10.77778	10.77770	10.40117	10.77770	10.77754
	f	10.77778	10.77770	10.03940	10.77770	10.77733
	x_1	3.00000	2.99999	2.91862	2.99999	2.99996
	x_2	-1.66667	-1.66667	-1.72526	-1.66667	-1.66670
	g_1	-3.33333	0.00000	0.02469	0.00000	0.00002
	g_2	-11.66667	-11.66669	-11.92877	-11.66669	-11.66682
	g_3	-8.00000	-7.99999	-7.91860	-7.99999	-7.99995
	g_4	-6.66667	-6.66667	-6.72525	-6.66667	-6.66670
	h_1	0.00000	-0.00001	-0.08140	-0.00001	-0.00005
	T_C		20,215	4,325	10,462	1,154,238
2	Φ	1.39345	1.39344	1.36462	1.39344	1.39344
	f	1.39345	1.39344	1.33669	1.39344	1.39342
	x_1	0.82288	0.82289	0.84692	0.82290	0.82292
	x_2	0.91144	0.91144	0.91570	0.91143	0.91143
	g_1	0.00000	0.00000	0.01784	0.00001	0.00002
	h_1	0.00000	0.00002	0.01550	0.00001	0.00002
	T_C		18,452	4,830	16,436	457,224
3	Φ	0.43006	0.42999	0.30295		0.42992
	f	0.43006	0.42999	0.20963		0.42980
	x_1	0.10000	0.10000	0.07924	$*$	0.09998
	x_2	0.10000	0.09999	0.06213		0.09996
	T_C		26,248	4,203		707,312
4	Φ	-30954.484	-30959.815	-32165.790	-30959.815	
	f	-30954.484	-30959.815	-32770.630	-30959.815	
	x_1	78.00000	78.00000	77.49607	78.00000	
	x_2	33.00000	32.99999	34.87640	32.99999	
	x_3	27.75000	27.75343	25.19989	27.75342	
	x_4	45.00000	45.00000	45.14013	45.00000	—
	x_5	43.00000	42.90258	26.69770	42.90254	
	p_1	88.82230	88.82858	89.75740	88.82859	
	p_2	100.00000	100.00001	96.63433	100.00001	
	p_3	20.00000	19.99999	17.08602	19.99999	
	T_C		110,459	9,435	102,745	

Table 8.3: Results of TP on the Problem #3 for ten sampled trials. The global optimum is (0.1, 0.1).

Trial	$\Phi(x)$	$f(x)$	x_1	x_2	T_C
1	2.00817	2.00817	0.09998	0.93338	19,873
2	0.70918	0.70918	0.61861	0.09997	23,994
3	0.70918	0.70918	0.61861	0.09997	23,995
4	2.28750	2.28750	0.61861	0.93338	224
5	0.70918	0.70918	0.61861	0.09997	23,981
6	0.70918	0.70918	0.61861	0.09997	23,979
7	2.28750	2.28750	0.61861	0.93338	235
8	2.00817	2.00817	0.09998	0.93338	19,873
9	0.60349	0.60349	0.09998	0.46953	19,868
10	2.00817	2.00817	0.09998	0.93338	19,871

On the other hand, the hybrid EP discovered an exact global minimum. This suggests that the hybrid EP might be particularly useful in solving optimization problems with multiple local minima.

Problem #4:

The hybrid EP is seen to improve on evolved solutions in that the constraints are satisfied to a greater degree. NS–EP could not converge to any solution until $T_C = 100,000,000$. Here again, the TP optimization showed an advantage over the hybrid EP in the sense of computation time.

The simulation results suggest that the hybrid EP can be used to advantage on nonlinear constrained optimization problems regardless of unimodal or multimodal functions. The second–stage of the hybrid EP, which is the second phase of the TP optimization, could consistently improve on the solution offered by its first phase. It should be noted that in multimodal function optimization problems, the first stage of the hybrid EP overcame the difficulties of the nonconvex optimization problems which the TP optimization could not solve, and the second stage drove the trial solutions offered by the first stage to the exact solutions. Basically, the dynamic penalty method (NS–EP) could improve the performance of the EP. As can be seen in Table 8.2, NS–EP provided a better solution than EP alone for most problems. A proper designing of the penalty parameter may not require such a high computation time. But it is not easy to design the appropriate increasing rate of the penalty parameter. In this respect, the hybrid EP has potential for easy implementation.

8.4 Two–Phase Evolutionary Programming

The hybrid EP method described in the previous section could offer an exact solution when the mathematical formulation of the function to be minimized/maximized and its gradient were known [18, 19]. However, the exact function form and its gradient information are difficult to obtain in most practical problems. Even if we know the objective functions, we cannot apply the hybrid EP when a gradient does not exist. As an example, if a gradient of $(g_i^+(\vec{x}))^2$ does not exist, equation (8.5) is not meaningful since the term $\nabla g_i(\vec{x})(sg_i^+(\vec{x}))$ is derived from it. In the simple case that the $g_i(\vec{x})$'s are linear constraints, such as $g(\vec{x}) = Dx - b$, where D is $r \times n$ constant matrix and $b \in R^r$, $(g_i^+(\vec{x}))^2$ is continuously differentiable so that the equation (8.5) is meaningful. In most cases, $\nabla((g_i^+(\vec{x}))^2)$ does not exist, and the hybrid EP may fail to find an optimal solution. To cope with such problems, a two–phase EP (TPEP) approach is proposed in this section. Before describing the TPEP, we briefly introduce the augmented Lagrangian method which will be used in the second phase of the TPEP.

8.4.1 Augmented Lagrangians

The augmented Lagrangian method is one of the most effective general classes of nonlinear programming methods, which can be viewed as a combination of the penalty function and the local duality method [22, 38, 29].

The augmented Lagrangian for the constrained problem is

$$\Phi_2(\vec{x}) = f(\vec{x}) + \frac{s_t}{2}\left[\sum_{k=1}^{r}(g_k^+(\vec{x}))^2 + \sum_{j=1}^{m}(h_j(\vec{x}))^2\right] + \sum_{k=1}^{r}\lambda_k g_k^+(\vec{x}) + \sum_{j=1}^{m}\mu_j h_j(\vec{x}). \tag{8.6}$$

As compared with equation (8.3), the last two terms of the right-hand side are added to put gradual emphasis on any violated constraints. A typical step of the augmented Lagrangian method starts with $\lambda_k[t], k = 1, \cdots, r$ and $\mu_j[t], j = 1, \cdots, m$. Then $\vec{x}[t]$ is found as the minimum point of equation (8.6). Next $\lambda_k[t]$ and $\mu_j[t]$ are updated to $\lambda_k[t+1]$ and $\mu_j[t+1]$, respectively. A standard method for the update is

$$\lambda_k[t+1] = \lambda_k[t] + \epsilon s_t g_k^+(\vec{x}[t]) \quad \text{and}$$
$$\mu_j[t+1] = \mu_j[t] + \epsilon s_t h_j(\vec{x}[t])$$

where ϵ is a small positive constant.

The augmented Lagrangian method can be considered as a discrete-time version of the second phase of the two-phase neural network.

8.4.2 TPEP method

The first phase of this method uses the standard EP, just as the hybrid EP does. After the first phase is halted, satisfying the halting condition described in the previous section, the EP formulation of the augmented Lagrangian method as a second phase is applied to the best evolved solution. In the light of the solution accuracy, the success rate, and the computation time, the elitist EP with deterministic ranking strategy is considered for the EP formulation of the augmented Lagrangian method. In other words, the second phase initializes a population of N_{p2} trial solutions using the best solution found in the first phase, and employs the modified elitist EP, that is, the best solution always survives in the subsequent generation through a deterministic ranking strategy. By putting emphasis on violated constraints in the objective function whenever the best solution does not fulfill the constraints, the trial solutions are driven to the optimal point where all constraints are satisfied. The algorithm is implemented as follows:

1. A population of $N_{p2} < N_{p1}$ trial solutions is initialized. Each solution is taken as a pair of real-valued vectors, $(\vec{x}^i, \vec{\sigma}^i)$, $\forall i \in \{1, 2, \cdots, N_{p2}\}$, with their dimensions corresponding to the number of variables, n, to be optimized. All vectors are initialized to be the same as the best evolved solution after the first phase. The values of $\vec{\sigma}^i$, $\forall i \in \{1, \cdots, N_{p2}\}$, are reset to $(\vec{\sigma}_2 + \vec{\sigma}_\epsilon)$, where $\vec{\sigma}_2$ is

the strategy parameter of the best evolved solution after the first phase and $\vec{\sigma}_\epsilon$ is a positive constant vector. Set $t = 0$, and the Lagrange multipliers for the best solution are initialized to zero:

$$\lambda_k = 0, k = 1, \cdots, r, \quad \text{and} \quad \mu_j = 0, j = 1, \cdots, m.$$

2. The fitness score for each solution $\vec{x^i}$ is evaluated in the light of the augmented Lagrangian $\Phi_2(\vec{x^i})$. For the constrained optimization problems studied here, $\Phi_2(\vec{x^i})$ is defined as:

$$\begin{aligned}\Phi_2(\vec{x^i}) &= \Phi_1(\vec{x^i}) + \sum_{k=1}^{r} \lambda_k g_k^+(\vec{x^i}) + \sum_{j=1}^{m} \mu_j h_j(\vec{x^i}) \\ &= f(\vec{x^i}) + \frac{s_t}{2}\left[\sum_{k=1}^{r}(g_k^+(\vec{x^i}))^2 + \sum_{j=1}^{m}(h_j(\vec{x^i}))^2\right] \\ &+ \sum_{k=1}^{r} \lambda_k g_k^+(\vec{x^i}) + \sum_{j=1}^{m} \mu_j h_j(\vec{x^i}) \end{aligned} \qquad (8.7)$$

3. Increase t by 1, and from each of the N_{p2} parents $(\vec{x^i}, \vec{\sigma^i})$, one offspring is generated by:

$$\begin{aligned}\sigma_j^i[t] &= \sigma_j^i[t-1] \cdot \exp(\tau' \cdot N^i(0,1) + \tau \cdot N_j^i(0,1)) \\ x_j^i[t] &= x_j^i[t-1] + \sigma_j^i[t] \cdot N_j^i(0,1),\end{aligned}$$

$\forall i \in \{1, 2, \cdots, N_{p2}\}$, $\forall j \in \{1, 2, \cdots, n\}$.

4. The fitness score for each offspring, $\Phi_2(\vec{x^i}[t])$, is determined.

5. Deterministic ranking over all the $2N_{p2}$ solutions is conducted.

6. The N_{p2} best solutions out of all the $2N_{p2}$ solutions based on the rank are selected to be the parents for the subsequent generation.

7. The Lagrange multipliers for the objective function Φ_2 are updated as follows:

$$\begin{aligned}\lambda_k[t] &= \lambda_k[t-1] + \epsilon s_t g_k^+(\vec{x^1}[t-1]) \\ \mu_j[t] &= \mu_j[t-1] + \epsilon s_t h_j(\vec{x^1}[t-1]) \qquad \forall k,\ j\end{aligned} \qquad (8.8)$$

where ϵ is a small positive constant. It should be noted that the Lagrange multipliers are updated at the best solution $\vec{x}^1$. In this step, the penalty parameter can be increased in an appropriate manner.

8. The algorithm proceeds to step 3 unless the best solution does not change for a prespecified interval of generations.

The rationale for choosing an elitist selection method is described in the following. If the solution obtained after the first phase lies in the global optimization region, which is a moderate assumption, the second phase does not require as large a population because of the reduced search space. Thus, N_{p2} is to be chosen small compared to N_{p1}. Due to the small population size and the reduced search space, the deterministic ranking strategy is applied to ensure that the best available solution always survives into the next generation. $\vec{\sigma_2}$ is a very small positive value obtained from the best evolved solution of the first phase. To reflect the violated constraints which have not yet been satisfied in the first phase, we introduce $\vec{\sigma_\epsilon}$ in the second phase which is larger than $\vec{\sigma_2}$ and might be interpreted as a strategy parameter resetting. Using Lagrange multipliers while evaluating the objective function Φ_2, the violated constraints are emphasized through generations according to (8.8) where ϵ is chosen to be a small positive constant. If the value of ϵ is too large, the Lagrange multipliers may diverge. But if it is chosen too small, the convergence speed may be too small. The proper choice depends on the geometry or the complexity of the problem and cannot be generalized. By emphasizing the violated constraints, the second phase eventually drives the solution to satisfy the constraints. The stopping criteria for the second phase is the same as that of the first phase except for the values of $\rho = \rho_2 \leq \rho_1$ and $N_g = N_{g2} \geq N_{g1}$. For more rigorous explanation about the TPEP algorithm, please refer to the mathematical analysis in a continuous-time domain in the Appendix.

The following points should be checked before selecting the second phase method: (1) the usefulness of the deterministic ranking, (2) the form of the objective function, and (3) even the necessity of the first phase. And by what method should the population of the second phase inherit from that of the first phase? Should all population vectors of the second phase be initialized to be the same as the best evolved solution after the first phase or inherit the superior N_{p2} individuals out of N_{p1} individuals of the first phase? How many individuals are necessary for the second phase to reduce the computation time? Computer simulation comparisons are made in Section 8.5 to provide reasonable answers to these questions.

8.5 Simulation Results and Discussion

In Section 8.4, a TPEP was designed with the following characteristics: (1) the first phase is used, (2) Φ_2 (= Φ_{21}) is used as an objective function of the second phase, (3) the population size in the second phase is less than that of the first phase ($N_{p2} < N_{p1}$), (4) a deterministic ranking strategy is used in the second phase, (5) the population of the second phase is initialized by the best evolved individual of the first phase, and (6) the penalty parameter is increased with generation in the second phase. To answer questions raised in the previous section, several variants of the TPEP in Section 8.4 could be designed by the following frameworks:

(1) Use of the first phase (use or do not use).

(2) The form of the objective function in Step 2 of the second phase:

$$\Phi_{21}(\vec{x}^i) \equiv \Phi_1(\vec{x}^i) + \sum_{k=1}^{r} \lambda_k g_k^+(\vec{x}^i) + \sum_{j=1}^{m} \mu_j h_j(\vec{x}^i)$$

or

$$\Phi_{22}(\vec{x}^i) \equiv f(\vec{x}^i) + \sum_{k=1}^{r} \lambda_k g_k^+(\vec{x}^i) + \sum_{j=1}^{m} \mu_j h_j(\vec{x}^i).$$

(3) The size of the population in Step 1 of the second phase ($N_{p2} = N_{p1}$ or $N_{p2} < N_{p1}$).

(4) The method of ranking (stochastic or deterministic) in Step 5 of the second phase.

(5) The method of inheritance from the first phase (initialize N_{p2} individuals of the second phase by recruiting superior N_{p2} individuals

Table 8.4: Description of several variants of a two–phase EP. The meaning of each framework can be found in the text, earlier in this Section. The blank and 'S_2' denote the use of Scheme 1 and Scheme 2, respectively, in the parenthesis in each framework.

	Algorithm #						
Framework	1	2	3	4	5	6	7
(1)		S_2					
(2)			S_2				
(3)				S_2	S_2	S_2	S_2
(4)					S_2	S_2	S_2
(5)						S_2	S_2
(6)							S_2

out of N_{p1} individuals of the first phase, or by the best evolved solution of the first phase) in Step 1 of the second phase.

(6) The value of the penalty parameter in Steps 2 and 7 of the second phase (stationary or increasing).

From the above frameworks, we can obtain 64 (=2^6) kinds of algorithms according to the combinations of the above schemes. But by the sequential comparisons of the algorithms, we can reduce the number of combinations to seven. In other words, the comparison between Algorithms #1 and #2 indicates whether or not it is useful to use the first phase, and by the comparison result, we can reduce the number of combinations. As Table 8.4 shows, each algorithm consists of combinations of Scheme 1 or Scheme 2. For example, Algorithm #3 consists of schemes such as: (1) the first phase is used, (2) Φ_{22} is used in the second phase, (3) $N_{p1} = N_{p2}$ is used in the second phase, (4) stochastic ranking strategy is used in the second phase, (5) inherit superior N_{p2} out of N_{p1} after the first phase, and (6) the penalty parameter is fixed. Each algorithm was designed to investigate which scheme is effective with respect to the solution accuracy, the success rate , and the total computation time . The success rate (R_S) is the ratio of the number of trials by which the algorithm succeeds to discover the exact global optimum and the total number of trials (for each algorithm, 100 trials were performed in our experiments). This success rate can be used to measure the convergence stability of the algorithm, i.e., how consistently the solution converges to the exact global optimum. To compare the computational efficiency of each algorithm, the computation time (T_C) required to meet the stopping criteria was defined as:

$$T_C = \begin{cases} N_{p2} \cdot (T_2 - N_{g2}) & \text{if the 1st phase is not used} \\ \sum_{i=1}^{2} N_{pi} \cdot (T_i - N_{gi}) & \text{if the 1st/2nd phase are used} \end{cases}$$

where T_i is the number of generations consumed in the ith phase, N_{pi} is the population size in the ith phase, and N_{gi} is the generation tolerance of the ith phase. T_i is set to zero before starting each phase. The specific parameter values for each phase are shown in Table 8.5.

The seven variants of the two–phase EP were compared for the following six test problems which include quadratic and nonlinear functions with several linear and nonlinear constraints. All problems were taken from [3]. Problems #1 to #6 were the test cases for GENOCOP II system [2, pp. 144-147] developed to solve nonlinear optimization problems. Problem #7 is the nondifferentiable and deceptive [39] optimization problem and was used to compare various genetic algorithm-based optimization techniques [3, p. 75].

Problem #1:
Minimize $f(\vec{x}) = 100(x_2 - x_1^2)^2 + (1 - x_1)^2$,
subject to nonlinear constraints:

$$\begin{aligned} c_1 &: \; x_1 + x_2^2 \geq 0, \\ c_2 &: \; x_1^2 + x_2 \geq 0, \end{aligned}$$

and bounds:

$$-0.5 \leq x_1 \leq 0.5 \text{ and } x_2 \leq 1.0.$$

The known global solution is $\vec{x}^* = (0.5, 0.25)$, and $f(\vec{x}^*) = 0.25$.

Problem #2:
Minimize $f(\vec{x}) = -x_1 - x_2$,
subject to nonlinear constraints:

Table 8.5: The specific parameter values for each phase

Par.	Value	Meaning
N_{p1}	40	Population size in the 1st phase
N_{p2}	40	Population size in the 2nd phase (Alg. #1-3)
	10	Population size in the 2nd phase (Alg. #4-7)
$\vec{\sigma}_1$	5.0	Initial perturbation in the 1st phase
$\vec{\sigma}_\epsilon$	0.01	Added perturbation in the 2nd phase
N_c	10	Num. of competing opponents in the ranking
ρ_1	10^{-4}	Error tolerance of the 1st phase
ρ_2	10^{-8}	Error tolerance of the 2nd phase
N_{g1}	200	Generation tolerance of the 1st phase
N_{g2}	2000	Generation tolerance of the 2nd phase
ϵ	0.1	Learning rate of the Lagrange multiplier
s_k	s_0	Penalty parameter (except for Alg. #7)
	s_0+ $\log(k+1)$	Penalty parameter in the 2nd phase (Alg. #7)
s_0	100.0	Initial penalty parameter (except for Prob. #4)
	10.0	Initial penalty parameter in the 2nd phase (Prob. #4)

$$\begin{aligned} c_1 &: \ x_2 \leq 2x_1^4 - 8x_1^3 + 8x_1^2 + 2, \\ c_2 &: \ x_2 \leq 4x_1^4 - 32x_1^3 + 88x_1^2 - 96x_1 + 36, \end{aligned}$$

and bounds:

$$0 \leq x_1 \leq 3 \text{ and } 0 \leq x_2 \leq 4.$$

The known global solution is $\vec{x}^* = (2.3295, 3.1783)$, and $f(\vec{x}^*) = -5.5079$.

Problem #3:
Minimize $f(\vec{x}) = (x_1 - 10)^3 + (x_2 - 20)^3$,
subject to nonlinear constraints:

$$\begin{aligned} c_1 &: \ (x_1 - 5)^2 + (x_2 - 5)^2 - 100 \geq 0, \\ c_2 &: \ -(x_1 - 6)^2 - (x_2 - 5)^2 + 82.81 \geq 0, \end{aligned}$$

and bounds:

$$13 \leq x_1 \leq 100 \text{ and } 0 \leq x_2 \leq 100.$$

The known global solution is $\vec{x}^* = (14.095, 0.84296)$, and $f(\vec{x}^*) = -6961.81381$.

Problem #4:
Minimize $f(\vec{x}) = 0.01x_1^2 + x_2^2$,
subject to nonlinear constraints:

$$\begin{aligned} c_1 &: \ x_1 x_2 - 25 \geq 0, \\ c_2 &: \ x_1^2 + x_2^2 - 25 \geq 0, \end{aligned}$$

and bounds:

$$2 \leq x_1 \leq 50 \text{ and } 0 \leq x_2 \leq 50.$$

The global solution is $\vec{x}^* = (\sqrt{250}, \sqrt{2.5}) = (15.811388, 1.581139)$, and $f(\vec{x}^*) = 5.0$.

Problem #5:
Minimize $f(\vec{x}) = (x_1 - 2)^2 + (x_2 - 1)^2$,
subject to a nonlinear constraint:

$$c_1 \ : \ -x_1^2 + x_2 \geq 0,$$

and a linear constraint:

$$x_1 + x_2 \leq 2.$$

The global solution is $\vec{x}^* = (1.0, 1.0)$ and $f(\vec{x}^*) = 1.0$.

Problem #6:
Minimize $f(\vec{x}) = e^{x_1 x_2 x_3 x_4 x_5}$,
subject to:

$$x_1^2 + x_2^2 + x_3^2 + x_4^2 + x_5^2 = 10, \quad x_2 x_3 - 5x_4 x_5 = 0, \quad x_1^3 + x_2^3 = -1,$$
$$-2.3 \leq x_i \leq 2.3, i = 1, 2, \quad -3.2 \leq x_i \leq 3.2, i = 3, 4, 5.$$

The global solution is $\vec{x}^*$ = (-1.717143, 1.595709, 1.827247, -0.7636413, -0.7636450) and $f(\vec{x}^*) = 0.0539498473$.

Problem #7:
Minimize $f(x) = -x \cdot \text{sgn}(x)$,
subject to: $-1.0 \leq x \leq 2.0$.
The global solution is $x^* = 2.000$ and $f(x) = -2.000$.

In each problem, the constraints were transformed to the form of (8.1) before solving the problem, and 100 independent trials were carried out. The results are summarized in Tables 8.6 and 8.7, where the best (b), median (m), and the worst (w) results (out of 100 independent runs), the success rate (R_S), and the computation time (T_C) are reported. The best solution obtained from each algorithm was an exact global optimum except for Problem #6. But each algorithm showed different performance with respect to R_S and T_C.

For Problem #7, all the algorithms could find the optimal solution. The only difference was the computation time.

Algorithm #1 provided acceptable results for all test problems. But R_S was not equal to 1.0 for Problems #2, #4, and #6, which indicates convergence instability, i.e., the algorithm did not converge to the global optimum consistently.

Algorithm #2 was applied to see if the first phase was necessary. Without the first phase, T_C was reduced greatly for most of the problems, however, the convergence stability was very poor for Problems

Table 8.6: Experimental results for six test problems. For each algorithm, we report the best (b), median (m), and the worst (w) results (out of 100 independent runs), the success rate (R_S) and the computation time (T_C).

Prob. #	Exact opt.		Algorithm # 1	2	3
1	0.25	b	0.25	0.25	0.25
		m	0.25	0.25	0.25
		w	0.25	0.25	0.25
		R_S	1.00	1.00	1.00
		T_C	11,134	6,809	10,870
2	-5.50801	b	-5.50801	-5.50801	-5.50801
		m	-5.50801	-5.50801	-5.50679
		w	-5.50679	-5.50802	-4.41998
		R_S	0.98	0.99	0.97
		T_C	9,530	6,165	10,466
3	-6961.81388	b	-6961.81388	-6961.81388	-6961.81388
		m	-6961.81388	-6961.89225	-6961.81388
		w	-6961.81388	-6961.05124	-6961.81388
		R_S	1.00	0.98	1.00
		T_C	49,459	46,060	64,012
4	5.00000	b	5.00000	5.00000	5.00000
		m	5.00003	5.12323	5.00002
		w	5.00048	5.49622	5.00005
		R_S	0.73	0.06	0.72
		T_C	16,992	3,991	14,691
5	1.00000	b	1.00000	1.00000	1.00000
		m	1.00000	1.00000	1.00000
		w	1.00000	1.00000	1.00439
		R_S	1.00	1.00	0.97
		T_C	9,265	6,146	9,183
6	0.05395	b	0.05603	0.05507	0.05507
		m	0.06178	0.05596	0.05596
		w	0.99657	0.87683	0.46182
		R_S	0.11	0.13	0.32
		T_C	39,383	42,234	30,304
7	-2.000	b	-2.000	-2.000	-2.000
		m	-2.000	-2.000	-2.000
		w	-2.000	-2.000	-2.000
		R_S	1.00	1.00	1.00
		T_C	272,224	274,640	3,592

Table 8.7: Continuation of Table 8.6.

Prob. #		Algorithm # 4	5	6	7
1	b	0.25	0.25	0.25	0.25
	m	0.25	0.25	0.25	0.25
	w	0.25	0.25	0.25	0.25
	R_S	1.00	1.00	1.00	1.00
	T_C	11,994	11,392	10,428	4,658
2	b	-5.50801	-5.50801	-5.50801	-5.50801
	m	-5.50801	-5.50801	-5.50801	-5.50801
	w	-5.50801	-5.50801	-5.50801	-5.50801
	R_S	1.00	1.00	1.00	1.00
	T_C	7,027	6,693	3,732	3,659
3	b	-6961.81388	-6961.81388	-6961.81388	-6961.81388
	m	-6961.81388	-6961.81388	-6961.81388	-6961.81388
	w	-6961.69408	-6961.81388	-6961.81388	-6961.81388
	R_S	0.99	1.00	1.00	1.00
	T_C	22,612	22,832	22,701	21,739
4	b	5.00000	5.00000	5.00000	5.00000
	m	5.00002	5.00002	5.00003	5.00007
	w	5.00005	5.00082	5.00173	5.00021
	R_S	0.83	0.90	0.76	0.72
	T_C	16,803	14,724	17,298	19,139
5	b	1.00000	1.00000	1.00000	1.00000
	m	1.00000	1.00000	1.00000	1.00000
	w	1.00000	1.00000	1.00000	1.00000
	R_S	1.00	1.00	1.00	1.00
	T_C	4,872	4,819	3,968	3,730
6	b	0.05502	0.05502	0.05490	0.05400
	m	0.05522	0.06178	0.05550	0.05621
	w	0.42744	0.42744	0.43889	0.56568
	R_S	0.39	0.40	0.50	0.55
	T_C	40,423	36,428	30,166	11,210
7	b	-2.000	-2.000	-2.000	-2.000
	m	-2.000	-2.000	-2.000	-2.000
	w	-2.000	-2.000	-2.000	-2.000
	R_S	1.00	1.00	1.00	1.00
	T_C	81,752	78,988	81,147	78,255

#4 ($R_S = 0.06$) and #6 ($R_S = 0.13$). From this result we can induce that the use of the first phase increases the chances for stabilizing the convergence of the solution for these problems.

Algorithm #3 showed similar performance to Algorithm #1 except for Problems #5 ($R_S = 0.97$) and #6 ($R_S = 0.32$). The objective function without the squared penalty term $\frac{s_k}{2}[\sum(g_k^+(\vec{x}^i))^2 + \sum(h_j(\vec{x}^i))^2]$ also caused convergence instability. Using Φ_{22}, the value of the objective function increases/decreases in a sudden fashion when the evolved solution is far from the feasible region. The squared penalty term plays a role of stabilizing the Lagrange penalty term $\sum \lambda_k g_k^+(\vec{x}^i) + \sum \mu_j h_j(\vec{x}^i)$. This result encourages the use of Φ_{21} in the second phase instead of Φ_{22}.

Algorithm #4 used a smaller population size in the second phase than in the first phase ($N_{p2} = 10$). N_{p2} individuals of the second phase were initialized by recruiting superior N_{p2} individuals out of N_{p1} individuals of the first phase. As can be seen from the results for Problems #2, #3, and #5, this algorithm shows greatly reduced T_C compared to Algorithm #1 without sacrificing the convergence stability. This might be the expected result because Algorithm #4 uses $N_{p2} < N_{p1}$.

Algorithm #5 is the same as Algorithm #4 except the use of a deterministic ranking strategy. This shows slightly better results than Algorithm #4. Moreover, the CPU time was somewhat reduced because of the use of the deterministic ranking.

In Algorithm #6, the initial population in the second phase was initialized to be the same as the best evolved solution after the first phase. Except for Problem #4, T_C was reduced to some degree without reducing R_S compared to Algorithm #5. Compared with Algorithm #5, it was better to have diversity in the initial population of the second phase than to initialize with only the best solution found after the first phase for Problem #4. But in general, the scheme of initializing by the best could reduce T_C without reducing R_S.

Algorithm #7 used a nonstationary (increasing) penalty parameter in the second phase of Algorithm #6. Increasing the penalty parameter by $s_k = s_0 + \log(k+1)$ led to the greatly reduced T_C except for Problem #4. But in general, there is no rule for designing the penalty parameter to accelerate the convergence. With the properly designed penalty parameter, NS–EP in Section 3.3 could have resulted in a shorter computation time.

It should be noted that for Problems #2 and #3, all seven algorithms provided a better solution than the previous known solution as well as the solution obtained by the GENOCOP II system [3]. The solution found for Problem #2 is: $\vec{x}^* = (2.32952, 3.17849)$, and $f(\vec{x}^*) = -5.50801$, which is lower than the previous known solution (-5.5079) and feasible, and the solution for Problem #3 is: $\vec{x}^* = (14.09500, 0.842961)$, and $f(\vec{x}^*) = -6961.81388$, which is lower than the previous known solution (-6961.81381) and feasible. As for Problems #4 and #6, all algorithms resulted in small convergence stability, i.e., $R_S \leq 1.0$ because of the small feasible solution space [5].

It may be difficult to provide a complete analysis of each algorithm based on the seven test problems. But the simulation results can provide some guidelines to obtain an algorithm that is more efficient with respect to the computation time, the convergence stability, and the success rate. To summarize, the following statements could be made: (1) the use of the first phase and the use of the Φ_{21} improved the convergence stability (increasing the success rate), and (2) the smaller population size in the second phase ($N_{p2} < N_{p1}$), the use of a deterministic ranking method (reducing the CPU time), inheritance from the best evolved solution after the first phase, and increasing the penalty parameter in the second phase all reduced the computation time. Coinciding with Algorithm #7, the TPEP in Section 8.4 was designed to include all these features.

The TPEP was also compared with the hybrid EP and EP alone. 100 trials were performed with EP alone and the hybrid EP for the same seven problems above. The specific parameter values for EP alone were: $\rho = 10^{-8}, N_g = 2000$, and $s_k = 100.0$ except for Problem #4 where $s_k = 10.0$, and for the hybrid EP: $\rho_1 = 10^{-4}, N_{g1} = 200, \rho_2 = 10^{-8}, N_{g2} = 2000, s_k = 10.0$, and $\epsilon = 0.001$. The results are reported in Table 8.8. As mentioned previously, the hybrid EP method could not give satisfactory results when the inequality penalty term $(g_i^+(x))^2$ was not differentiable. For Problems #1, #2, and #4, the hybrid EP could offer a converged solution near an optimum whereas it did not even converge for Problems #3, #5, and #6. The hybrid EP could not find an exact optimum for Problems #1 and #2, although it could offer converged values. However, the hybrid EP could consistently offer an exact optimum ($R_S = 1.0$) for Problem #4, for which the TPEP had lower convergence stability ($R_S = 0.72$). For Problem #6, the hybrid

EP as well as the TP method diverged because of the large value of the gradient of the function f. Because of the nondifferentiable and deceptive properties of Problem #7, the second stage of the hybrid EP could not be applied. The result is only from the first stage. EP alone and the hybrid EP could not offer an optimal solution whereas the TPEP could. EP alone sometimes resulted in the near-optimal solution, e.g., $\Phi = 0.05380, f = 0.05365$ slightly violating equality constraints, but not frequently ($R_S = 0.167$). Only the TPEP could give reasonable solutions satisfying all the constraints with a reasonable success rate (R_S= 0.55).

8.6 Conclusions

In this paper, we have proposed two evolutionary programming techniques for nonlinear constrained optimization problems. The first method, a hybrid EP, could only handle specific types of inequality constraints such as linear inequalities, while the second method, the TPEP, could consistently offer an exact feasible solution for other types of constraints. Using Lagrange multipliers and putting gradual emphasis on violated constraints in the objective function whenever the best solution does not satisfy the constraints, the TPEP drives the solution to the optimal point where all constraints are satisfied. Generally speaking, TPEP was shown to be more applicable to problems with various types of constraints than the hybrid EP. On the other hand, for problems having a moderate type of constraint such as a linear inequality, the hybrid EP guarantees an accurate solution with less computation time and more convergence stability than the TPEP. We can conclude that the proper application of either TPEP or hybrid EP, depending on the type of constraints, may offer reasonable results with respect to the solution accuracy, convergence stability, and the computation time for constrained problems similar to those studied here.

Appendix

With a simple calculation of the time derivative of the objective function in the TPEP method, the usefulness of the elitist selection and the aug-

Table 8.8: Results of TPEP, hybrid EP, and EP alone. This shows mean of the best solutions averaged over 100 independent trials. The symbol '∗' and '—', mean that 'the method diverged' and 'the result didn't converge to an exact optimum'. In Problem #7, the result for the hybrid EP was obtained using only the first stage because the second stage could not be applied due to the nondifferentiable function f.

Prob. #		*Exact*	*TPEP*	*Hybrid EP*	*EP alone*
1	Φ	0.25000	0.25000	0.83636	0.24510
	f	0.25000	0.25000	0.83636	0.24029
	R_S		1.00	—	—
	T_C		4,658	7,667	5,014
2	Φ	-5.50801	-5.50801	-5.42623	-5.51096
	f	-5.50801	-5.50801	-5.42623	-5.51392
	R_S		1.00	—	—
	T_C		3,659	8,081	4,392
3	Φ	-6961.81388	-6961.81388	∗	-10330.13591
	f	-6961.81388	-6961.81388	∗	-12069.74762
	R_S		1.00	—	—
	T_C		21,739	—	14,049
4	Φ	5.00000	5.00000	5.00000	4.99800
	f	5.00000	5.00000	5.00000	4.99600
	R_S		0.72	1.00	—
	T_C		19,139	13,130	78,851
5	Φ	1.00000	1.00000	∗	0.99559
	f	1.00000	1.00000	∗	0.99122
	R_S		1.00	—	—
	T_C		3,730	—	4,251
6	Φ	0.05395	0.05400	∗	0.43321
	f	0.05395	0.05400	∗	0.42771
	R_S		0.55	—	—
	T_C		11,210	—	318,080
7	Φ	-2.000	-2.000	-2.005	-2.005
	f	-2.000	-2.000	-2.010	-2.010
	R_S		1.00	1.00	1.00
	T_C		78,255	678	1,448

mented Lagrangian can be demonstrated. For rigorous mathematical formulation, we employ the continuous-time analysis.

The augmented Lagrangian objective function for the ith individual is:

$$\begin{aligned}\Phi_2(\vec{x}^i) &= \Phi_1(\vec{x}^i) + \sum_{k=1}^{r} \lambda_k g_k^+(\vec{x}^i) + \sum_{j=1}^{m} \mu_j h_j(\vec{x}^i) \\ &= f(\vec{x}^i) + \frac{s_t}{2}\left[\sum_{k=1}^{r}(g_k^+(\vec{x}^i))^2 + \sum_{j=1}^{m}(h_j(\vec{x}^i))^2\right] \\ &\quad + \sum_{k=1}^{r} \lambda_k g_k^+(\vec{x}^i) + \sum_{j=1}^{m} \mu_j h_j(\vec{x}^i).\end{aligned}$$

Taking the time derivative gives:

$$\begin{aligned}\frac{d\Phi_2(\vec{x}^i)}{dt} &= (\frac{\partial f}{\partial \vec{x}^i})^T \frac{\partial \vec{x}^i}{\partial t} + s_t\left[\sum_{k=1}^{r} g_k^+ (\frac{\partial g_k}{\partial \vec{x}^i})^T \dot{\vec{x}}^i + \sum_{j=1}^{m} h_j (\frac{\partial h_j}{\partial \vec{x}^i})^T \dot{\vec{x}}^i\right] \\ &\quad + \sum_{k=1}^{r} \dot{\lambda}_k g_k^+ + \sum_{j=1}^{m} \dot{\mu}_j h_j + \left(\sum_{k=1}^{r} \lambda_k \nabla g_k + \sum_{j=1}^{m} \mu_j \nabla h_j\right)^T \dot{\vec{x}}^i \\ &= (\nabla f(\vec{x}^i))^T \dot{\vec{x}}^i + \left[\sum_{k=1}^{r} \nabla g_k (s_t g_k^+ + \lambda_k) + \sum_{j=1}^{m} \nabla h_j (s_t h_j + \mu_j)\right]^T \dot{\vec{x}}^i \\ &\quad + \epsilon s_t \left(\sum_{k=1}^{r} (g_k^+)^2 + \sum_{j=1}^{m} h_j^2\right) \\ &= G^T(\vec{x}^i)\dot{\vec{x}}^i + \epsilon s_t \left(\sum_{k=1}^{r} (g_k^+)^2 + \sum_{j=1}^{m} h_j^2\right)\end{aligned}$$

where $G(\vec{x}^i) = \nabla f(\vec{x}^i) + \sum_{k=1}^{r} \nabla g_k (s_t g_k^+ + \lambda_k) + \sum_{j=1}^{m} \nabla h_j (s_t h_j + \mu_j)$. Note that in the second equality, $\dot{\lambda}_k = \epsilon s_t g_k^+$, $\dot{\mu}_j = \epsilon s_t h_j$ were used. By the elitist selection scheme, the objective function of the best solution is always non-increasing, i.e., $d\Phi_2(\vec{x}^1)/dt \leq 0$. We are now ready to derive useful properties of the TPEP. Before going further, let us introduce following theorem and lemma, known as Lyapunov Theorem for local stability and Barbalat's Lemma [40].

Theorem 3 *If, in a ball B_r, there exists a scalar function $\Phi(\vec{x})$ with continuous first partial derivatives such that* (1) *$\Phi(\vec{x})$ is positive definite (locally in B_r), and* (2) *$\dot{\Phi}(\vec{x})$ is negative semi-definite (locally in B_r), then the equilibrium point is stable.*

Lemma 1 *If the differential function $\Phi(t)$ has a finite limit as $t \to \infty$, and if $\dot{\Phi}$ is uniformly continuous, then $\dot{\Phi}(t) \to 0$ as $t \to \infty$.*

We assumed that the first phase of the TPEP drove the best solution to the global optimization region, i.e., near the global optimum. In the same context, we can make the objective function Φ_2 locally positive definite by adding a constant to Φ_2. Then by the Lyapunov Theorem for local stability, it can be said that the TPEP algorithm gives a stable equilibrium point. In addition, by Barbalat's Lemma, the derivative of the objective function tends to zero ($\dot{\Phi}_2 \to 0$).

Since $d\Phi_2(\vec{x}^1)/dt$ is always not greater than 0, $\dot{\vec{x}}^1 \to 0$ yields

$$\frac{d\Phi_2(\vec{x}^1)}{dt} \longrightarrow \epsilon s_t \left(\sum_{k=1}^{r} (g_k^+)^2 + \sum_{j=1}^{m} h_j^2 \right) \leq 0$$

$$\Leftrightarrow g_k^+ = h_j \equiv 0 \qquad \text{for all} \quad k, j,$$

which means perfect constraint satisfaction. In the classical gradient method [34], $\dot{\vec{x}} = -G^T(\vec{x})$ was designed to make $d\Phi_2(\vec{x})/dt \leq 0$ and to make the solution satisfy the Kuhn-Tucker optimal conditions. In the TPEP method, the solution is feasible, however, the optimality of the solution cannot be guaranteed.

If $\dot{\vec{x}}^1 \nrightarrow 0$ and if the solution is feasible, i.e., satisfies all the constraints, then

$$\frac{d\Phi_2(\vec{x}^1)}{dt} \to G^T(\vec{x}^1)\dot{\vec{x}}^1 \to 0$$

$$\Leftrightarrow G^T(\vec{x}^1) \to 0$$

$$\Leftrightarrow \nabla f(\vec{x}^1) + \sum_{k=1}^{r} \lambda_k \nabla g_k + \sum_{j=1}^{m} \mu_j \nabla h_j \to 0$$

This satisfies the Kuhn-Tucker optimality condition [20, 28, 29], and the solution can be said to be optimal.

To summarize, the TPEP algorithm gives a stable solution with the following important properties: (1) if $\dot{\vec{x}}^1 \to 0$, then the constraint satisfaction is achieved, however, the optimality of the solution may not be guaranteed, and (2) if $\dot{\vec{x}}^1 \nrightarrow 0$ and if the solution is feasible, then the best solution is optimal.

Bibliography

[1] Z. Michalewicz and N. Attia, "Evolutionary optimization of constrained problems," in *Proc. of the Third Annual Conference on Evolutionary Programming* (A. V. Sebald and L. J. Fogel, eds.), (River Edge, NJ), pp. 98–108, World Scientific, 1994.

[2] Z. Michalewicz, "Evolutionary operators for continuous convex parameters spaces," in *Proc. the Third Annual Conference on Evolutionary Programming* (A. V. Sebald and L. J. Fogel, eds.), (River Edge, NJ), pp. 84–97, World Scientific, 1994.

[3] Z. Michalewicz, *Genetic Algorithms + Data Structures = Evolution Programs.* Berlin: Springer-Verlag, 1996. Third, Revised and Extended Edition.

[4] Z. Michalewicz, "A survey of constraint handling techniques in evolutionary computation methods," in *Proc. of the Fourth Annual Conference on Evolutionary Programming* (J. R. McDonnell, R. G. Reynolds, and D. B. Fogel, eds.), (Cambridge, MA), pp. 135–155, MIT Press, 1995.

[5] Z. Michalewicz, "Genetic algorithms, numerical optimization, and constraints," in *Proc. of the Sixth International Conference on Genetic Algorithms* (L. J. Eshelman, ed.), (Los Altos, CA), pp. 151–158, Morgan Kaufmann, 1995.

[6] Z. Michalewicz and M. Schoenauer, "Evolutionary algorithms for constrained parameter optimization problems," *Evolutionary Computation*, vol. 4, no. 1, pp. 1–32, 1996.

[7] A. S. Homaifar, H.-Y. Lai, and X. Qi, "Constrained optimization via genetic algorithms," *Simulation*, vol. 62, pp. 242–254, 1994.

[8] J. A. Joines and C. R. Houck, "On the use of non-stationary penalty functions to solve nonlinear constrained optimization problems with gas," in *Proc. of IEEE Conference on Evolutionary Computation*, pp. 579–584, June 1994.

[9] Z. Michalewicz and C. Janikow, "Handling constraints in genetic algorithms," in *Proc. of the Fourth International Conference on Genetic Algorithms* (R. Belew and L. Booker, eds.), (Los Altos, CA), pp. 151–157, Morgan Kaufmann, 1991.

[10] D. Powell and M. M. Skolnick, "Using genetic algorithms in engineering design optimization with non-linear constraints," in *Proc. of the Fifth International Conference on Genetic Algorithms* (S. Forrest, ed.), (Los Altos, CA), pp. 424–430, Morgan Kaufmann, 1993.

[11] N. Srinivas and K. Deb, "Multiobjective optimization using nondominated sorting in genetic algorithms," tech. rep., Department of Mechanical Engineering, Indian Institute of Technology, Kanput, India, 1993.

[12] J. Paredis, "Co-evolutionary constraint satisfaction," in *Proc. of the Third Conference on Parallel Problem Solving from Nature*, (New York), pp. 46–55, Springer-Verlag, 1994.

[13] R. G. Reynolds, "An introduction to cultural algorithms," in *Proc. of the Third Annual Conference on Evolutionary Programming* (A. V. Sebald and L. J. Fogel, eds.), (River Edge, NJ), pp. 131–139, World Scientific, 1994.

[14] Z. Michalewicz and G. Nazhiyath, "Genocop III: A co-evolutionary algorithm for numerical optimization problems with nonlinear constraints," in *Proc. of IEEE International Conference on Evolutionary Computation*, (Piscataway, NJ), pp. 647–651, IEEE Press, 1995.

[15] D. Waagen, P. Dercks, and J. McDonnell, "The stochastic direction set algorithm: A hybrid technique for finding function extrema," in *Proc. of the First Annual Conference on Evolutionary Programming* (D. B. Fogel and W. Atmar, eds.), (La Jolla, CA), pp. 35–42, Evolutionary Programming Society, 1992.

[16] R. K. Belew, J. McInerney, and N. N. Schraudolph, "Evolving networks: Using the genetic algorithm with connectionist learning," in *Artificial Life II* (C. G. Langton, C. Taylor, J. D. Farmer, and S. Rasmussen, eds.), (Reading, MA), pp. 511–547, Addison-Wesley, 1991.

[17] J.-M. Renders and S. P. Flasse, "Hybrid methods using genetic algorithms for global optimization," *IEEE Trans. on Systems, Man, and Cybernetics - Part B: Cybernetics*, vol. 26, pp. 243–258, April 1996.

[18] H. Myung, J.-H. Kim, and D. B. Fogel, "Preliminary investigations into a two-stage method of evolutionary optimization on constrained problems," in *Proc. of the Fourth Annual Conference on Evolutionary Programming* (J. R. McDonnell, R. G. Reynolds, and D. B. Fogel, eds.), (Cambridge, MA), pp. 449–463, MIT Press, 1995.

[19] H. Myung and J.-H. Kim, "Hybrid evolutionary programming for heavily constrained problems," *BioSystems*, vol. 38, pp. 29–43, 1996.

[20] C. Y. Maa and M. A. Shanblatt, "A two-phase optimization neural network," *IEEE Trans. Neural Networks*, vol. 3, no. 6, pp. 1003–1009, 1992.

[21] J.-H. Kim and H. Myung, "A two–phase evolutionary programming for general constrained optimization problem," in *Proc. of the Fifth Annual Conference on Evolutionary Programming* (L. J. Fogel, P. J. Angeline, and T. Bäck, eds.), (Cambridge, MA), pp. 295–304, MIT Press, 1996.

[22] D. G. Luenberger, *Introduction to Linear and Nonliner Programming*. Reading, MA: Addison-Wesley, 1973.

[23] K. A. De Jong, *An Analysis of the Behavior of a Class of Genetic Adaptive system.* PhD thesis, Department of Computer and Communication Sciences, University of Michigan, Ann Arbor, MI, 1975.

[24] D. B. Fogel and L. C. Stayton, "On the effectiveness of crossover in simulated evolutionary optimization," *BioSystems*, vol. 32, pp. 171–182, 1994.

[25] A. H. Wright, "Genetic algorithms for real parameter optimization," in *Foundations of Genetic Algorithms, First Workshop on the Foundations of Genetic Algorithms and Classifier Systems* (G. Rawlins, ed.), (Los Altos, CA), pp. 205–218, Morgan Kaufmann, 1991.

[26] L. J. Eshelman and J. D. Schaffer, "Real-coded genetic algorithms and interval schemata," in *Foundations of Genetic Algorithms-2* (D. Whitley, ed.), (Los Altos, CA), pp. 187–202, Morgan Kaufmann, 1993.

[27] M. Schoenauer and S. Xanthakis, "Constrained GA optimization," in *Proc. of the Fifth International Conference on Genetic Algorithms* (S. Forrest, ed.), (Los Altos, CA), pp. 573–580, Morgan Kaufmann, 1993.

[28] D. G. Luenberger, *Linear and Nonliner Programming.* Reading, MA: Addison-Wesley, 2nd ed., 1989.

[29] D. P. Bertsekas, *Constrained Optimization and Lagrange Multiplier Methods.* New York: Academic Press, 1982.

[30] R. T. Rockafellar, *Convex Analysis.* Princeton, NJ: Princeton University Press, 1979.

[31] N. Saravanan and D. B. Fogel, "Evolving neurocontrollers using evolutionary programming," in *Proc. of the First IEEE Conference on Evolutionary Computation* (Z. Michalewicz, H. Kitano, D. Schaffer, H.-P. Schwefel, and D. B. Fogel, eds.), (Orlando, Florida), pp. 217–222, IEEE Press, June 1994.

[32] T. Bäck, G. Rudolph, and H.-P. Schwefel, "Evolutionary programming and evolution strategies: Similarities and differences," in *Proc. of the Second Annual Conference on Evolutionary Programming* (D. B. Fogel and W. Atmar, eds.), (San Diego, CA), pp. 11–22, Evolutionary Programming Society, February 1993.

[33] D. W. Tank and J. J. Hopfield, "Simple 'neural' optimization networks: An A/D converter signal decision circuit, and a linear programming circuit," *IEEE Trans. Circuits and Syst.*, vol. CAS-31, pp. 533–541, 1986.

[34] M. P. Kennedy and L. O. Chua, "Neural networks for nonlinear programming," *IEEE Trans. Circuits and Syst.*, vol. 35, no. 6, pp. 554–562, 1988.

[35] S. Zhang, X. Zhu, and L.-H. Zou, "Second-order neural nets for constrained optimization," *IEEE Trans. Circuits and Syst.*, vol. 3, no. 6, pp. 1021–1024, 1992.

[36] S. Zhang and A. G. Constantinides, "Lagrange programming neural networks," *IEEE Trans. Circuits and Syst.*, vol. 39, pp. 441–452, 1992.

[37] C. B. Feng and Y. Zhao, "Time-varying nonlinear programming and its realization via neural networks," in *Proc. of ACC*, vol. 2, pp. 978–982, 1992.

[38] G. N. Vanderplaats, *Numerical Optimization Techniques for Engineering Design.* McGraw-Hill Inc., 1984.

[39] D. E. Goldberg, *Genetic Algorithms in Search, Optimization and Machine Learning.* Reading, MA: Addison Wiley, 1989.

[40] J.-J. E. Slotine and W. Li, *Applied Nonlinear Control.* Englewood Cliffs, NJ: Prentice-Hall International, Inc., 1991.

Chapter 9

CAM-BRAIN — The Evolutionary Engineering of a Billion Neuron Artificial Brain

H. de Garis

This chapter describes an ambitious eight year research project which aims to implement a cellular automata based artificial brain with a billion neurons by 2001, which grows/evolves at (nano-)electronic speeds inside a Cellular Automata Machine — ATR's so-called "CAN-Brain Project." The states of the cellular automata (CA) cells and the CA state transition rules can be stored cheaply in gigabytes of RAM. By using state of the art cellular automata machines, e.g., MIT's "CAM8" machine ($40,000, which can update 200 million CA cells a second) it is technically feasible by the end of 1995 to evolve artificial nervous systems containing a hundred thousand neurons, and within a few years, a million neurons. By the end of the current research project, i.e., 2001, it should be possible using nano-scale electronics to grow/evolve artificial brains containing a billion neurons and upwards. This is our aim.

9.1 Introduction

Following on from the abstract above, to understand how CAs can be used to grow/evolve neural networks, imagine a 2D CA trail which is 3 cells wide (e.g., Figure 9.2). Down the middle of the trail, send growth signals. When a growth signal hits the end of the trail, it makes the trail extend, or turn left, or right, or split, etc., depending upon the nature of the signal. It is a human programmer who hand codes the CA rules which make these extensions, turns, splits etc. happen. The CA rules themselves are not evolved. It is the *sequence* of these signals (fed continuously over time into an initialized short trail) that is evolved. This sequence of growth signals is the "chromosome" of a genetic algorithm, and it is this sequence that maps to a cellular automata network. When trails collide, they form"synapses" (e.g., Figure 9.7). Once the CA network has been formed in the initial "growth phase," it is later used in a second "neural signaling phase." Neural signals move along CA-based axons and dendrites, and across synapses etc. The CA network is made to behave like a conventional artificial neural network. The outputs of some of the neurons of the complex recurrent networks which result can be used to control complex time dependent behaviors whose fitness can be measured. These fitness values can be used to drive the evolution. By growing/evolving thousands of neural net modules and their interconnections in an incremental evolutionary way, it will be possible to build artificial brains. We expect that within a few years, a new field will be established, based partly on this work, called simply "Brain Building." According to the CAM developers at MIT, it is likely that the next generation of CAMs will achieve an increase in performance of the order of thousands, within 5 years. However, to be able to evolve a billion neuron artificial brain by 2001, a "nano-CAM" machine will need to be developed. To this end, we are collaborating with an NTT researcher who has developed a nanoscale electronics device, who wants to combine them to behave like molecular scale cellular automata machines.

In the summer of 1994, a two dimensional CAM-Brain simulation was completed which required 11,000 hand crafted state transition rules. It was successfully applied to the evolution of maximizing the number of synapses, outputting an arbitrary constant neural signal value, outputting a sine wave of a desired arbitrary period and amplitude and to the evolution of a simple artificial retina which could output the vector velocity of a "white line" which "moved" across an array of "detector" neurons. Work on the 3D simulation should be completed in 1995, and is expected to take about 150,000 hand crafted CA rules. The Brain Builder Group of ATR took possession of one of MIT's CAM8 machines in the fall of 1994. At the time of writing(August 1995) the porting of the 2D rules from a Sparc20 workstation to the CAM8 is nearing completion. (See Section 8 on future work). If the porting of the rules of the 3D simulation to this machine is not possible, then a "SuperCAM" machine will be designed specifically for CAM-Brain, with the collaboration of the Evolutionary Technologies (ET) group of NTT, with whom our Brain Builder group of ATR's Evolutionary Systems (ES) group collaborates closely. (Again see Section 8).

The following paragraphs now present the CAM-Brain Project in more detail. As mentioned in the extended abstract, the "CAM-Brain Project" is an 8 year research project at ATR labs in Kyoto, Japan, which intends to build an artificial brain containing billions of artificial neurons. The complexity of such an artificial brain will make it largely undesignable, so a (directed) evolutionary approach called "evolutionary engineering" is being used. Neural networks based on cellular automata [1], can be grown and evolved at electronic speeds inside state of the art cellular automata machines, e.g. MIT's "CAM8" machine, which can update 200 million cells per second [2, 3]. Since RAM is cheap, gigabytes of RAM can be used to store the states of the CA cells used to grow the neural networks. CA based neural net modules are evolved in a two phase process. Three cell wide CA trails are grown by sending a sequence of growth signals (extend, turn left, turn right, fork left, fork right, T fork) down the middle of the trail. When an instruction hits the end of the trail it executes its function. This sequence of growth instructions is treated as a chromosome in a Genetic Algorithm [4] and is evolved. This sequence maps to a CA network. When trails collide, they form "synapses". Once the CA network is grown, it is used as a neural network in a second neural signaling phase. Some of the neural signals can be tapped to control some process and the fitness of the control can be measured. This fitness is used to drive the evolution. Once gigabytes of RAM and electronic evolutionary speeds can be used, genuine brain building, involving millions and later billions of artificial neurons, becomes realistic, and should become concrete within a year or two. The CAM-Brain Project should revolutionize the fields of neural networks and artificial life, and in time help create a new specialty called "Brain Building," with its own conferences and journals.

This chapter consists of the following sections. Section 9.2 describes briefly the idea of "Evolutionary Engineering," of which the CAM-Brain Project is an example. Section 9.3 describes how neural networks can be based on cellular automata [1], and evolved at electronic speeds. Section 9.4 presents some of the details of CAM-Brain's implementation. Section 9.5 shows how using cellular automata machines will enable millions of artificial neural circuits to be evolved to form an artificial brain. Section 9.6 discusses changes needed for the 3D version of CAM-Brain. Section 9.7 deals with recent work. Section 9.8 outlines future work, and section 9.9 summarizes.

9.2 Evolutionary Engineering

Evolutionary Engineering is defined to be "the art of using evolutionary algorithms (such as genetic algorithms [4]) to build complex systems." This chapter reports on the idea of evolving cellular automata based neural networks at electronic speeds inside cellular automata machines. This idea is a clear example of evolutionary engineering. Evolutionary engineering will be increasingly needed in the future as the number of components in systems grows to gargantuan levels. Today's nano-electronics for example, is researching single electron transistors (SETs) and quantum dots. Probably within a decade or so, humanity will have full blown nanotechnology (molecular scale engineering), which will produce systems with a trillion trillion components [5]. The potential complexities of such systems will be so huge, that designing them will become increasingly impossible. However what is too complex to be humanly designable, might still be buildable, as this paper will show. By using evolutionary techniques (i.e. evolutionary engineering), it is often still possible to build a complex system, even though one does not understand how it functions. This arises from the notion of the "complexity independence" of evolutionary algorithms, i.e. so long as the (scalar) fitness values which drive the evolution keep increasing, the internal complexity of the evolving system is irrelevant. This means that it is possible to successfully evolve systems which function as desired, but which are to complex to be designable. The author believes that this simple idea (i.e. the complexity independence of evolutionary algorithms) will form the basis of most 21st century technologies (dominated by nanotechnology [5]). Thus, evolutionary engineering can "extend the barrier of the buildable," but may not be good science, because its products tend to be black boxes. However, confronted with the complexity of trillion trillion component systems, evolutionary engineering may be the only viable method to build them.

9.3 Cellular Automata Based Neural Networks

Building an artificial brain containing billions of artificial neurons is probably too complex a task to be humanly designable. The author felt that brain building would be a suitable task for the application of evolutionary engineering techniques. The key ideas are the following. Use evolutionary techniques to evolve neural circuits in some electronic medium, so as to take advantage of electronic speeds. The medium chosen by the author was that of cellular automata [1], using special machines, called "Cellular Automata Machines (CAMs)," which can update hundreds of millions of CA cells a second [2, 3]. CAMs can be used to evolve the CA based neural networks at electronic speeds. The states of the cellular automata cells can be stored in RAM, which is cheap, so one can have gigabytes of RAM to store the states of millions of CA cells. This space is large enough to contain an artificial brain. MIT's Information Mechanics Group (Toffoli and Margolus) believe that within a few years it will be technically possible to update a trillion CA cells in about 0.1 nanoseconds [2, 3]. Thus, if CA state transition rules can be found to make CA behave like neural networks, and if such CA based networks prove to be readily evolvable, then a potentially revolutionary new technology becomes possible. The CAM-Brain Project is based on the above ideas and fully intends to build artificial brains before the completion of the project in 2001. The potential is felt to be so great that it is likely that a new specialty will be formed, called "Brain Building."

For the first 18 months of the CAM-Brain Project, the author simulated a two dimensional version of CAM-Brain on a Sparc 10 workstation, hand coding over 11,000 (eleven thousand) CA state transition rules to get the CA-based neural nets to evolve. This work was completed in the summer of 1994. The 2D version was used briefly (before work on the 3D version was started) to undertake some evolutionary tests, whose results will be presented in the next section. The 2D version served only as a feasibility and educational device. Since trails are obliged to collide in 2D, the 2D version was not taken very seriously. Work was begun rather quickly on the more interesting 3D version almost immediately after the 2D version was ready. Proper evolutionary tests will be undertaken once the 3D version is ready, which should be by early 1995. To begin to understand how cellular automata [1], can be used as the basis for the growth and evolution of neural networks, consider Figure 9.1 which shows an example of a 2D CA state transition rule, and Figure 9.2 which shows a 2D CA trail, 3 cells wide. All cells in a CA system update the state of their cells synchronously. The new state of a given cell depends upon its present state and the states of its nearest neighbors. Down the middle of the 3 cell wide CA trail, move "signal or growth cells" as shown in Figure 9.2.

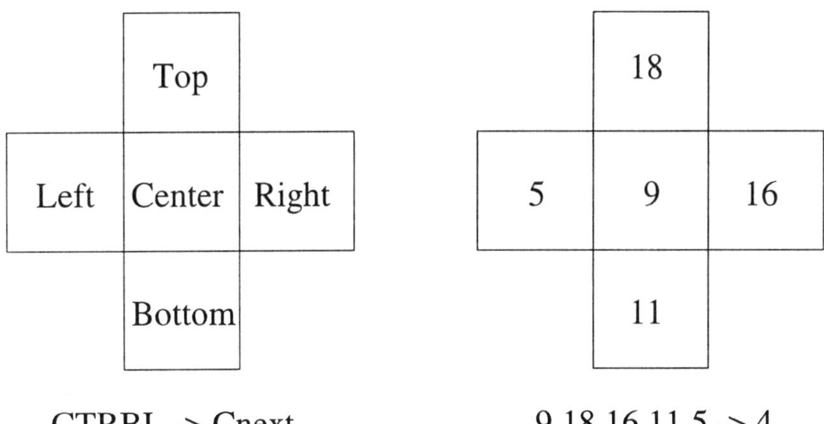

Figure 9.1: A 2D CA State Transition Rule

As an example of a state transition rule which makes a signal cell move to the right one square, consider the right hand most signal cell in Figure 9.2, which has a state of 5. The cell immediately to its right

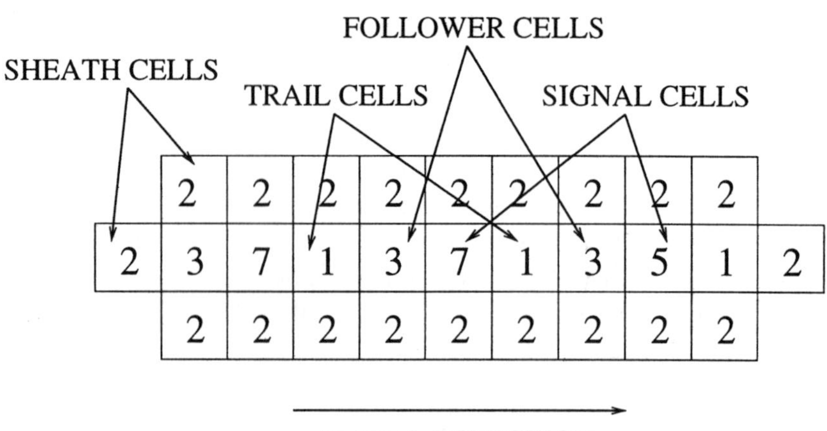

Figure 9.2: Signal Cells Move Along a Cellular Automata Trail

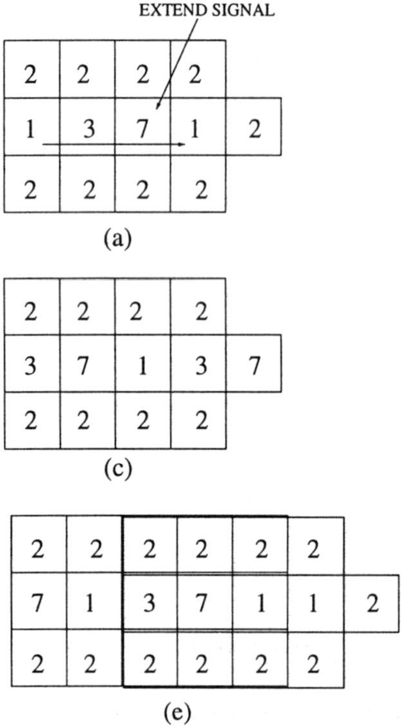

EXTEND SIGNAL

2	2	2	2	
1	3	7	1	2
2	2	2	2	

(a)

2	2	2	2	
7	1	3	7	2
2	2	2	2	

(b)

2	2	2	2	
3	7	1	3	7
2	2	2	2	

(c)

2	2	2	2	2	
1	3	7	1	3	11
2	2	2	2	2	

(d)

2	2	2	2	2	2	
7	1	3	7	1	1	2
2	2	2	2	2	2	

(e)

Figure 9.3: Extend the Trail

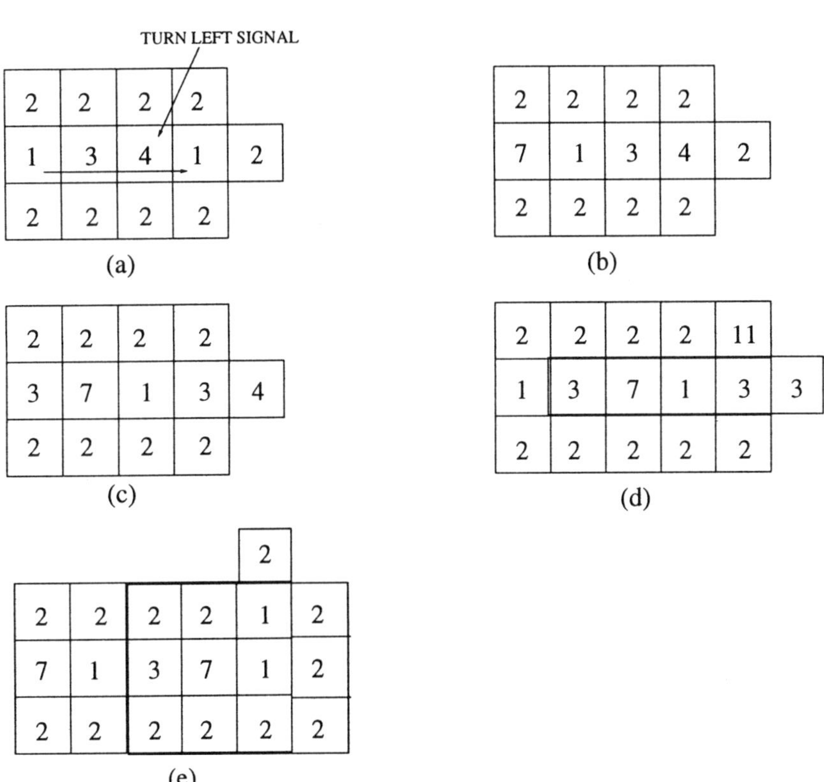

Figure 9.4: Turn Trail Left

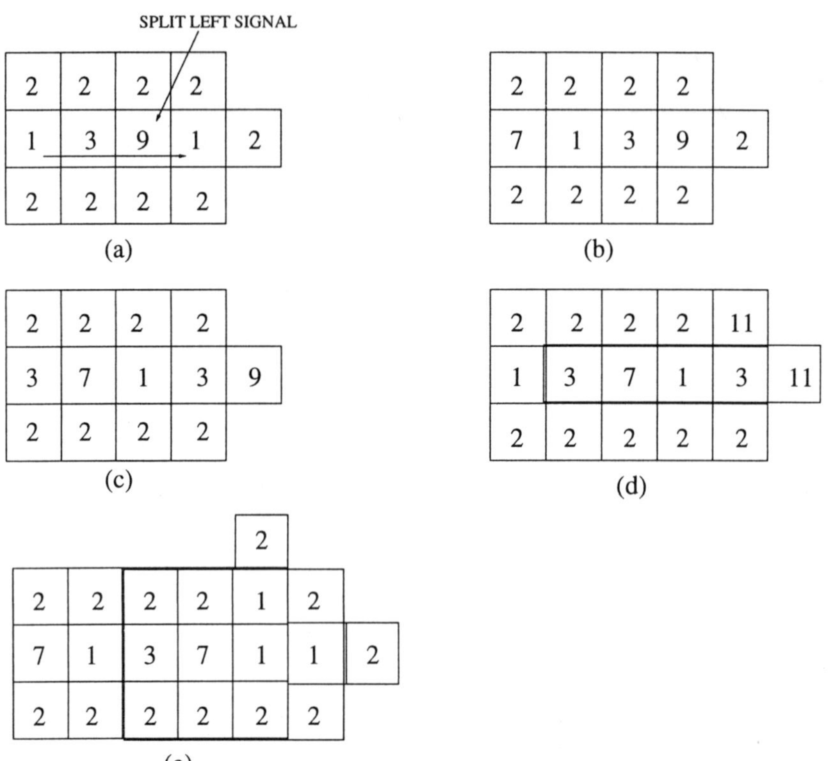

Figure 9.5: Split Trail Left

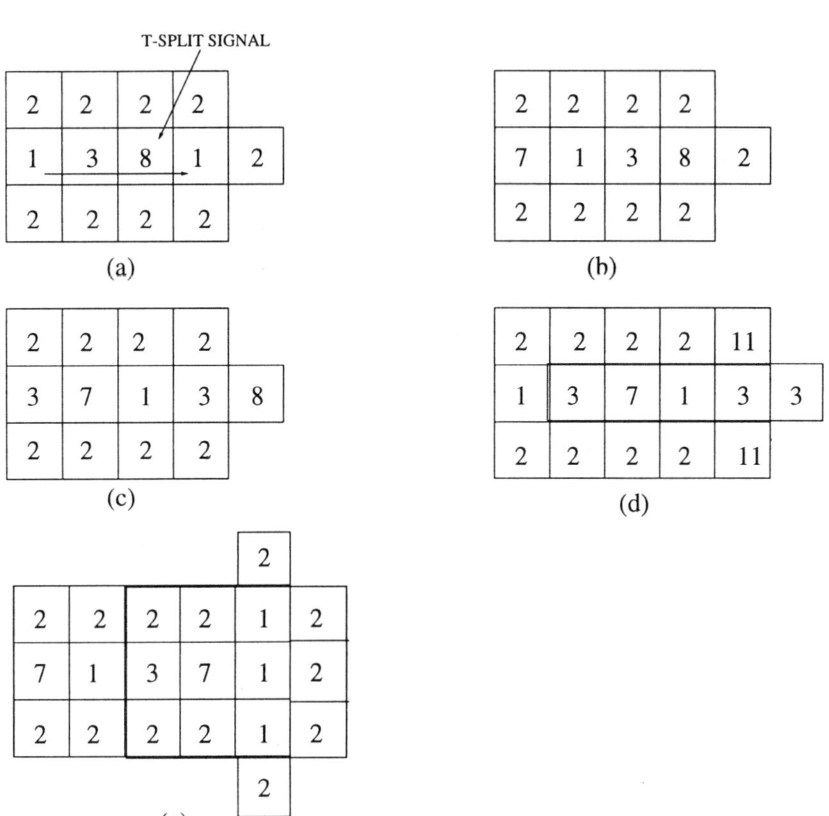

Figure 9.6: T-Split Trail

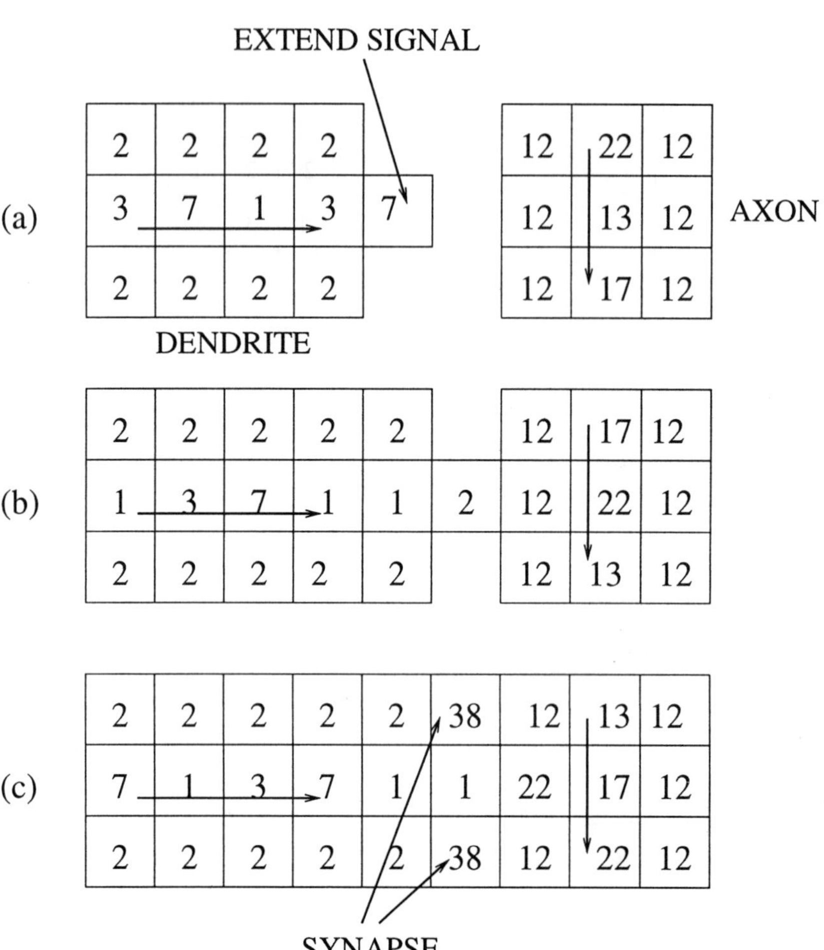

Figure 9.7: Dendrite to Axon Synapsing

has a state of 1, which we want to become a 5. Therefore the 2D state transition rule to turn the 1 into a 5 is 1.2.2.2.5–¿5. These signal or growth cells are used to generate the CA trails, by causing them to extend, turn left or right, split left or right, and Tsplit. When trails collide, they can form synapses. It is the sequence of these signal cells which determines the configuration of the CA trails, thus forming a CA network. It is these CA trails which later are used as neural network trails of axons and dendrites. Neural signals are sent down the middle of these CA trails. Thus there are two major phases in this process. Firstly, the CA trails are grown, using the sequence of signal cells. Secondly, the resulting CA trail network is used as a neural network, whose fitness at controlling some system can be measured and used to evolve the original growth sequence. To make this more explicit, it is the sequence of growth cells which is evolved. By modifying the sequence, one alters the CA network configuration, and hence the fitness of the configuration when it functions as a neural net in the second phase. From a genetic algorithm (GA) point of view, the format of the GA "chromosome" is the sequence of integers which code for the signaling or growth instructions. By mutating and crossing over these integers, one obtains new CA networks, and hence new neural networks. By performing this growth at electronic speeds in CAMs, and in parallel, with one CAM per GA chromosome, and attaching a conventional programmable microprocessor to each CAM to measure the user defined fitness of the CA based neural circuit, one has a means to evolve large numbers of neural modules very quickly. Using CAMs to evolve neural circuits, is an example of a type of machine that the author labels a "Darwin Machine," i.e. one which evolves its own structure or architecture. A related idea of the author concerns the concept of "Evolvable Hardware (EHW)" [6] where the software instructions used to configure programmable logic devices (PLDs) are treated as chromosomes in a Genetic Algorithm [4]. One then rewrites the circuit for each chromosome.

9.4 Further Details

This section provides further details on the implementation of the CA based neural networks. There were three kinds of CA trails in CAM-Brain, labeled dendrites, excitatory axons and inhibitory axons, each with their own states. Whenever an axon collided with a dendrite or vice versa, a synapse was formed. When a dendrite hit an excitatory/inhibitory axon or vice versa, an excitatory/inhibitory synapse was formed. An inhibitory synapse reversed the sign of the neural signal value passing through it. An excitatory synapse left the sign unchanged. Neural signal values ranged between -240 and +240 (or their equivalent CA states, ranging from 100 to 580). The value of a neural signal remained unchanged when it was in an axon, but as soon as it crossed a synapse into a dendrite, the signal value (i.e. signal strength) began to drop off linearly with the distance it had to travel to its receiving neuron. Hence the signal strength was proportional to the distance between the synapse and the receiving neuron. Thus the reduction in signal strength acted like a weighting of the signal by the time it reached the neuron. But, this distance is evolvable, hence indirectly, the weighting is evolvable. CAM-Brain is therefore equivalent to a conventional artificial neural network, with its weighted sums of neural signal strengths. However, in CAM-Brain there are time delays as signals flow through the network. When two or three dendrite signals collide, they sum their signal strengths (within saturated upper or lower bounds). It soon became noticeable that there were many many ways in which collisions between CA trails could occur. So many, that the author became increasingly discouraged. It looked as though it would take years of handcoding the CA state transition rules to get CAM-Brain to work. The intention was to have rules which would cover every possible collision possibility. Eventually a decision was made to impose constraints on the ways in which CA trails could grow. The first such constraint was to make the trails grow on a grid 6 cells or squares (cubes) on a side. This process (called "gridding") sharply reduced the number of collision types. It also had a number of positive side effects. One was that in the neural signaling phase, neural signals arrived synchronously at junction points. One no longer needed to have to handcode rules for phase delays in neural signaling summation. By further imposing that different growth cells advanced the length of the trails by the same number of squares, one could further reduce the number of collision types. With synchrony of growth, synchrony of signaling and gridding, it was possible to cover all possible types of collisions. Nevertheless, it still took over 11000 rules to achieve this goal, and this was only for the 2D version. The 3D version is expected to take about 150,000 rules, but due to the experience gained in working on the 2D version, and to the creation of certain software productivity tools, the 3D version should be completed by the end of 1995.

Considering the fact that the 2D version took 11,000 rules, it is impossible in this short chapter to discuss all the many tricks and strategies that were used to get CAM-Brain to work. That would require a book (something the author is thinking seriously about writing). However, some of the tricks will be mentioned here. One was the frequent use of "gating cells," i.e. cells which indicated the direction that dendrite signals should turn at junctions to head towards the receiving neuron. To give these gating cells a directionality, i.e. a "leftness" or a "rightness," special marker cells had to be circulated at the last minute, after the circuit had stabilized. Since some trails were longer than others, a sequence of delay cells were sent through the network after the growth cells and before the marker cells. Without the delay cells, it was possible that the marker cells would pass before synapses were formed.

Once the 2D simulation was completed (before the CAM8 was delivered) several brief evolutionary experiments using the 2D version were undertaken. The first, was to see if it would be possible to evolve the number of synapses. Figs. 9, 10, 11 show the results of an elite chromosome evolved to give a large number of synapses. Fig. 9 shows early growth. Fig. 10 shows completed growth, and Fig. 11 shows the neural signaling phase. In this experiment, the number of synapses increased steadily. It evolved successfully. The next experiment was to use the neural signaling to see if an output signal (tapped from the output of one of the neurons) could evolve to give a desired constant value. This evolved perfectly. Next, was to evolve an oscillator of a given arbitrary frequency and amplitude, which did evolve, but slowly (it took a full day). Finally, a simple retina was evolved which output the two component directional velocity of a moving "line" which passed (in various directions) over a grid of 16 "retinal neurons." This also evolved but even more slowly. The need for greater speed is obvious.

The above experiments are only the beginning. The author has already evolved (not using CAs) the weights of recurrent neural networks as controllers of an artificial nervous system for a simulated quadruped artificial creature. Neural modules called "GenNets" [7, 8, 9] were evolved to make the creature walk straight, turn left or right, peck at food, and mate. GenNets were also evolved to detect signal frequencies, to generate signal frequencies, to detect signal strengths, and signal strength differences. By using the output of the detector GenNets, it was possible to switch motion behaviors. Each behavior had its own separately evolved GenNet. By switching between a library of GenNets (i.e. their corresponding evolved weights) it was possible to get the artificial creature to behave in interesting ways. It could detect the presence and location of prey, predators and mates and take appropriate action, e.g. orientate, approach, and eat or mate, or turn away and flee. However, every time the author added another GenNet, the motion of the simulated creature slowed on the screen. The author's dream of being able to give a robot kitten some thousand different behaviors using GenNets, could not be realized on a standard monoprocessor workstation. Something more radical would be needed. Hence the motivation behind the CAM-Brain Project.

9.5 A Billion Neurons in a Trillion Cell CAM by 2001

Figure 9.8 shows some estimated evolution times for 10 chromosomes over 100 generations for a Sparc 10 workstation, a CAM8, and a CAM2001 (i.e. a CAM using the anticipated electronics of the year 2001) for a given application. In the current 2D version of CAM-Brain, implemented on a Sun Sparc 10 workstation, it takes approximately 3.4 minutes to grow a stable cellular automata network consisting of only four neurons. It takes an additional 3.2 minutes to perform the signaling on the grown network, i.e. a total growth-signaling time to measure the fitness of a chromosome of 6.6 minutes. This time scales linearly with the number of artificial neurons in the network. If one uses a population of 10 chromosomes, for 100 generations, the total evolution time (on a Sparc 10) is 100*10*6.6 minutes, i.e., 110 hours, or 4.6 days. This is obviously tediously slow, hence the need to use a CAM. MIT's CAM8 [2, 3] can update 25 million cellular automata cells per second, per hardware module. A CAM8 "box" (of personal computer size) contains eight such modules, and costs about $40,000. Such boxes can be connected blockwise indefinitely, with a linear increase in processing capacity. Assuming an eight module box, how quickly can the above evolution (i.e. 100 generations, with a population size of 10) be performed? With eight modules, 200 million cell updates per second is possible. If one assumes that the 2D CA space in which the evolution takes place is a square of 100 cells on a side, i.e., 10,000 cells, then all of these cells can be (sequentially) updated by the CAM8 box in 50 microseconds. Assuming 1000 CA clock cycles for the growth and signaling, it will take 50 milliseconds to grow and measure the fitness of one chromosome. With a population of 10, and 100 generations, total CAM8 evolution time for a four neuron network will be 50 seconds, i.e. about one minute, which is roughly 8000 times faster. Using the same CAM8 box, and a 3D space of a million cells, i.e. a cube of 100 cells on a side, one could place roughly 40 neurons. The evolution time will be 100 times as long with a single CAM8 box. With 10 boxes, each with a separate microprocessor attached, to measure the fitness of the evolved network, the evolution time would be about eight minutes. Thus for 1000 neurons, the evolution would take about 3.5 hours, quite an acceptable figure. For a million neurons, the evolution time would be nearly five months. This is still a workable figure. Note, of course, that these estimates are lower bounds. They do not include the necessary human thinking time, and the time needed for sequential, incremental evolution, etc. However, since the CAM-Brain research project will continue until the year 2001, we can anticipate an improvement in the speed and density of electronics over that period. Assuming a continuation of the historical doubling of electronic component density and speed every two years, then over the next eight years, there will be a 16-fold increase in speed and density. Thus the "CAM-2001" box will be able to update at a rate of 200*16*16 million cells per second. To evolve the million neurons above will take roughly 13.6 hours. Thus to evolve a billion neurons, will take about 19 months, again a workable figure. But, if a million neurons can be successfully evolved, it is likely that considerable interest will be focused upon the CAM-Brain approach, so that more and better machines will be devoted to the task, thus reducing the above 19-month figure. For example, with 100 machines, the figure would be about two months. The above estimates are summarized in Figure 9.8. These estimates raise some tantalizing questions. For example, if it is

Sparcc10	CAM8	CAM8	CAM8	CAM8	CAM2001	CAM2001
10000 CA cells	10000 CA cells	1 million CA cells	25 million CA cells	25 billion CA cells	25 billion CA cells	25 trillion CA cells
4 neurons	4 neurons	40 neurons	1000 neurons	1 million neurons	1 million neurons	1 billion neurons
1 Sparc10	1 CAM8	10 CAM8s	10 CAM8s	10 CAM8s	10 CAM2001s	100 CAM2001s
4.6 days	50 seconds	8 minutes	3.5 hours	5 months	13.6 hours	2 months

Figure 9.8: Evolution Times for Different Machines & CA Cell, Neuron & Machine Numbers

possible to evolve the connections between a billion artificial neurons in a CAM2001, then what would one want to do with such an artificial nervous system (or artificial brain)? Even evolving a thousand neurons raises the same question.

One of the aims of the CAM-Brain research project is to build an artificial brain which can control 1000 behaviors of a "robot kitten" (i.e. a robot of size and capacities comparable to a kitten) or to control a household "cleaner robot." Presumably it will not be practical to evolve all these behaviors at once. Most likely they will have to be evolved incrementally, i.e., starting off with a very basic behavioral repertoire and then adding (stepwise) new behaviors. In brain circuitry terms, this means that the new neural modules will have to connect up to already established neural circuits. In practice, one can imagine placing neural bodies (somas) external to the established nervous system and then evolving new axonal and dendral connections to it. The CAM-Brain Project hopes to create a new tool to enable serious investigation of the new field of "incremental evolution." This field is still rather virgin territory at the time of writing. This incremental evolution could benefit from using embryological ideas. For example, single seeder cells could be positioned in the 3D CA space under evolutionary control. Using handcrafted CA "developmental or embryological" rules, these seeder cells could grow into neurons ready to emit dendrites and axons [10]. The CAM-Brain Project, if successful, should also have a major impact on both the field of neural networks and the electronics industry. The traditional preoccupation of most research papers on neural networks is on analysis, but the complexities of CAM-Brain neural circuits, will make such analysis impractical. However, using Evolutionary Engineering, one can at least build/evolve functional systems. The electronics industry will be given a new paradigm, i.e. evolving/growing circuits, rather than designing them. The long term impact of this idea should be significant, both conceptually and financially.

9.6 The 3D Version

The 3D version is a conceptually (but not practically) simple extension of the 2D version. Instead of 4 neighbors, there are 6 (i.e. North, East, West, South, Top, Bottom). Instead of 6 growth instructions as in the 2D version (i.e. extend, turn left, turn right, split extend left, split extend right, split left right), there are 15 in the 3D version. A 3D CA trail cross section consists of a center cell and 4 neighbor cells, each of different state or color (e.g. red, green, blue, brown). Instead of a turn left instruction being used as in the 2D case, a "turn green" instruction is used in the 3D case. The 15 3D growth instructions are (extend, turn red, turn green, turn blue, turn brown, split extend red, split extend green, split extend blue, split extend brown, split red brown, split red blue, split red green, split brown blue, split brown green, split blue green). A 3D CA rule thus consists of 8 integers of the form CTSENWB–¿Cnew. The 3D version will enable dendrites and axons to grow past each other, and hence reach greater distances. The weakness with the 2D version is that collisions in a plane are inevitable, which causes a crowding effect, whereby an axon or dendrite cannot escape from its local environment. This is not the case with the 3D version, which is topologically quite different. A 3D version is essential if one wants to build artificial brains with many interconnected neural modules. The interconnectivity requires long axons/dendrites.

Fig. 12 shows some recent results in 3D simulation. A space of 3D CA cells (48*48*48 cubes) was used. A single short 3D CA trail was allowed to grow to saturate the space. One can already sense the potential complexity of the neural circuits that CAM-Brain will be able to build. In 3D, it is likely that each neuron will have hundreds, maybe thousands of synapses, thus making the circuits highly evolvable due to their smooth fitness landscapes (i.e. if you cut one synapse, the effect is minimal when there are hundreds of them per neuron).

9.7 Recent Work

At the time of writing (August 1995), the author is completing the simulation of the 3D version, working on the many thousands of rules necessary to specify the creation of synapses. So far, more than 100,000 3D rules have been implemented, and it is quite probable that the figure may go as high as 150,000. Since each rule is rotated 24 ways (6 ways to place a cube on a surface, then 4 ways to rotate that cube) to cater to all possible orientations of a 3D trail, the actual number of rules placed in the (hashed) rule base will be over 3 million. Specifying these rules takes time, and constitutes so far, the bulk of time spent doing CAM-Brain system. Software has been written to help automate this rule generation process, but it remains a very time consuming business. Hence the immediate future work will be to complete the simulation of the 3D version. Probably, this will be done by the end of 1995.

Early in 1995, the author put his first application on the CAM8 machine (which rests on his desk). MIT's CAM8 is basically a hardware version of a look up table, where the output is a 16 bit word which becomes the address in the look up table at the next clock cycle. This one clock cycle lookup is the reason for CAM8's speed. For CAM-Brain, a 16 bit look up table is too small. It is possible to give each CA cell in the CAM more than 16 bits, but tricks are necessary. The first CAM8 experiment the author undertook involved only 16 bits per CA cell. This chapter is too short to go into details as to how the CAM8 functions, so only a broad overview will be given here. The 16 bits can be divided into slices, one slice per neighbor cell. These slices can then be "shifted" (by adding a displacement pointer) by arbitrarily large amount (thus CAM8 CA cells are not restricted to having local neighbors). With only 16 bits, and 4 neighbors in the 2D case (Top, Right, Bottom, Left) and the center cell, that's only 3 bits per cell (i.e. 8 states, i.e. 8 colors on the display screen). It was not possible to implement CAM-Brain with only 3 bits per CA cell. It was the intention of the author to use the CAM8 to show the potential of the CAM8 to evolve neural circuits with a huge number of artificial neurons. The author chose an initial state in the form of a square trail with 4 extended edges. As the signals looped around the square, they duplicated at the corners. Thus the infinite looping of 3 kinds of growth signals supply an infinite number of growth signals to a growing CA network. There were 3 growth signals (extend, extend and split left, extend and split right). The structure needs exactly 8 states. The 8 state network grew into the 32 megacells of 16 bits each, which are available in the CAM8. At one pixel per cell, this 2D space took over 4 square meters of paper poster (hanging on the author's wall). A single artificial neuron can be put into the space of one's little finger nail, thus allowing 25,000 neurons to fit into the space. If 16 Mbit memory chips are used instead of 4 Mbit chips, then the area and the number of neurons quadruples to 100,000.

Placing the poster on the author's wall suddenly gave visitors a sense of what is to come. They could see that soon a methodology will be ready which will allow the growth and evolution of artificial brains, because soon it will be possible to evolve many thousands of neural modules and their interconnections. The visitors sense the excitement of CAM-Brain's potential.

Filling a space of 32 Mcells, with artificial neurons can be undertaken in at least two ways. One is to use a very large initialisation table with position vectors and states. Another, is to allow the neurons to "grow" within the space. The author chose to use this "neuro-embryonic" approach. A single "seeder" CA cell was placed in the space. This seeder cell launched a cell to its right and beneath it. These two launched cells then moved in their respective directions, cycling through a few dozen states. When the cycle is completed, they deposit a cell which grows into the original artificial neuron shape that the author uses in the 2D version of CAM-Brain. Meanwhile other cells are launched to continue the growth. Thus the 32Mcell space can be filled with artificial neurons ready to accept growth cell "chromosomes" to grow the neural circuitry. This neuro-embryogenetic program (called "CAM-Bryo") was implemented on a workstation by the author, and ported to the CAM8 by his research colleague Felix Gers. In order to achieve the porting, use was made of "subcells" in the CAM8, a trick which allows more than 16 bits per CA cell, but for N subcells of 16 bits, the total CAM8 memory space available for CA states is reduced by a factor of N. Gers used two subcells for CAM-Bryo, hence 16Mcells of 32 bits each. A second poster of roughly two square meters was made, which contained about 25,000 artificial neurons (see Fig. 13). Again, with 16Mbit memory chips, this figure would be 100,000. Gers expects to be able to port the 2D version of CAM-Brain to the CAM8 within a few weeks, in which case, a third poster will be made which will depict about 15,000 neurons (with a lower density, to provide enough space for the neural circuitry to grow) and a mass of complex neural circuits. Once this is accomplished, we expect that the world will sit up and take notice — more on this in the next section.

The author's boss at ATR's Evolutionary Systems department, has recently set up a similar group at his company NTT, called Evolutionary Technologies (ET) department. The idea is that once the ATR Brain Builder group's research principles are fairly solid, the author and the author's boss and I (whose careers are now closely linked) will be able to tap into the great research and development resources of one of the world's biggest companies, when the time comes to build large scale artificial brains. NTT has literally thousands of researchers.

The author would like to see Japan invest in a major national research project within the next 10 years to build "Japan's Artificial Brain," the so-called "J-Brain Project." This is the goal of the author, and then to see such a project develop into a major industry within 20 years. Every household would like to have a cleaner robot controlled by an artificial brain. The potential market is huge.

9.8 Future Work

A lot of work remains to be done. The author has a list of "to dos" attached to his computer screen. The first item on the list is of course, to finish the rules for the 3D version of CAM-Brain. This will take a few more months, and will probably need over 150,000 CA rules. Second, the experience gained in porting the 700 rules from "CAM-Bryo" from a workstation to the CAM8 will shortly enables Gers to complete the much tougher task of porting the 2D version of CAM-Brain to the CAM8. In theory, since there are 11,000 CA rules for the 2D version, and that each rule has 4 symmetry rotations, that makes about 45,000 rules in total to be ported. This fits into the 64K words addressable by 16 bits. The 3D version however, with its (estimated) 150,000 rules, and its 24 symmetry rotations, will require over 3 million rules in total. The 3D version may require a "Super CAM" to be designed and built (by NTT's "Evolutionary Technologies" Dept., with whom the author collaborates closely), which can handle a much larger number of bits that 16. The group at MIT who built CAM8 is thinking of building a CAM9 with 32 bits. This would be very interesting to the author. Whether NTT or MIT get there first, such a machine may be needed to put the 3D version into a CAM. However, with a state-of-the -art workstation (e.g. a DEC alpha, which the user has on its desk) and a lot of memory (e.g. 256 Mbyte), it will still be possible to perform some interesting evolutionary experiments in 3D CAM-Brain, but not with the speed of a CAM.

Another possibility for porting the 3D version to the CAM8, is to reimplement it using CA rules which are more similar to von Neumann's universal constructor/calculator, than Codd's. Von Neummann's 2D trails were only 1 cell wide, whereas Codd's 2D version were 3 cells wide, with the central message trail being surrounded by two sheath cells. The trick to using von Neumann's approach is incorporating the direction of motion of the cell as part of the state. The author's colleague Jacqueline Signorini advises that CAM-Brain could be implemented at far higher density (i.e. more filled CA cells in the CA space) and without the use of a lookup table. The control of the new states would be implemented far more simply she feels, by simple IF-THEN-ELSE type programming. "von Neumann-izing" the 3D version of CAM-Brain might be a good task for the author's next grad student.

With the benefit of hindsight, if the 3D version is reimplemented (and it is quite likely that my boss will have other members of our group do just that), then the author would advise the following. If possible (if you are implementing a Codd version) give the four sheath cells in a 3D CA trail cross section the same state. This would obviously simplify the combinatorial explosion of the number of collision cases during synapse formation. But, how then would the growth instructions be interpreted when they hit the end of a trail, and how would you define the symmetry rotations? If possible, it would also be advisable to use the minimum number of gating cell states at growth junctions for all growth instructions. Whether this is possible or not, remains to be seen. However, if these simplifications can be implemented (and of course the author thought of them originally, but was unable to find solutions easily), then it is possible that the number of 3D CA rules might be small enough to be portable to the CAM8, which would allow 3D neurals circuits to be evolved at 200 million CA cells per seconds (actually less because of the subcell phenomenon).

Once the 3D rules are ready, two immediate things need to be done. One is to ask ATR's graphics people to display these 3D neural circuits in an interesting way, perhaps with VR (virtual reality) 3D goggles with interactivity and zoom, so that viewers can explore regions of the circuits in all their 500 colors (states). This could be both fun and impressive. The second thing is of course to perform some experiments on the 3D version. As mentioned earlier, this will have to be done on a workstation, until the SuperCAM is built. Another possibility, is to redesign the 3D CA rules, to simplify them and reduce their number so that they can fit within the 64K 16bit confines of the CAM8 machine.

As soon as the 2D rules have been ported to the CAM8, experiments can begin at speed. Admittedly the 2D version is topologically different from 3D (in the sense that collisions in 2D are easier than in 3D), it will be interesting to try to build up a rather large neural system with a large number of evolved modules (e.g. of the order of a hundred, to start with). At this stage, a host of new questions arise. Look at Fig. 14, which is van Essen's famous diagram of the modular architecture of the monkey's visual and motor cortex, showing how the various geographical regions of the brain (which correspond to the rectangles in the figure, and to distinct functions) connect with each other. Physiological techniques now exist which enable neuro-anatomists to know which distinct cortical regions connect to others. Thus the geography (or statics) is increasingly known. What remains mysterious of course, is the dynamics. How does the brain function.

Van Essen's diagram is inspirational to the author. The author would like to produce something similar with CAM-Brain, i.e. by evolving neural modules (corresponding to the rectangles) and their interconnections. This raises other questions about sequencing and control, for example, does one evolve one module and freeze its circuits and then evolve another module, freeze its circuits, and finally evolve the connections between them, or does one evolve the two modules together, or what? Will it be necessary to place walls around each module, except for hand crafted I/O trails? The author has no clear answers or experience yet in these matters. The author's philosophy is "first build the tool, and then play with it. The answers will come with using the tool."

Another possibility for future work, is to try to simplify the whole process of rule making. Perhaps higher level rules can be made which are far fewer in number and allow the author's low level rules to be generated from them. If such a thing can be done, it would be nice, but the author believes there are still so many special cases in the specification of 3D CAM-Brain, that the number of high level rules may still be substantial. If these high level rules can be found, it just might be possible to use them and put them on the CAM8, so that 3D evolutionary experiments can be undertaken at CAM8 speeds.

Another idea is to use FPGAs (field programmable gate arrays) which code these high level rules and then to use them to grow 3D neural circuits. Each 3D CA cell could contain pointers to its 3D neighbors. In this way, it would be possible to map 3D neural circuits onto 2D FPGAs. This is longer term work. FPGAs are not cheap if many are needed. The author's RAM based solution has the advantage of being cheap, allowing a billion CA cell states to be stored reasonably cheaply.

It is not yet sure if it will be possible to port the 3D rules to the MIT CAM8 machine. The CAM8 is a 16 bit lookup table machine. 16 bits can only address 64K words. Since the 3D version expects to contain over 3 million rules (which includes all the symmetric rotations) a 64K memory is way too small. If putting the 3D version on the CAM8 is not possible, then the CAM8 will serve as a "tutorial" machine upon which to design a newer machine (a "SuperCAM") with CAM-Brain's requirements specifically in mind. One of the major tasks for the year 1996 will be the design of a superCAM. An alternative to a SuperCAM may be the use of existing "content addressable memory" technology, which may be able to update CA cells effectively. There is a "CAMemory" research group at NTT that ATR may collaborate with. If a small enough number of CAMemory Boolean function rules corresponding to CAM-Brain can be found (a big if), it is possible that NTT's CAMemory could be 50,000 times faster than the CAM8. Obviously, such a possibility is worth investigating.

The author feels that the nature of his research in 1996 will change from one of doing mostly software simulation (i.e. generating masses of

CA rules), to learning about the brain (i.e. reading about brain science to get ideas to put into CAM-Brain), and hardware design. These two activities will proceed in parallel. Of course, evolutionary experiments, on CAM8 for the 2D version of CAM-Brain, and on a 256 Mbyte RAM (DEC alpha) workstation for the 3D version, will also be undertaken in parallel.

Eventually, once CAM-Brain is ready, the brain builder research community will have a new tool to begin investigating these fascinating issues. The "SuperCAM" will be implemented in state-of-the-art VLSI (if the CAMemory option fails), in collaboration with NTT. However, further down the road, will be the attempt to design a "nanoCAM" or "CAM2001" based on nanoelectronics. The Brain Builder Group at ATR is collaborating with an NTT researcher who wants to build nano-scale cellular automata machines. With the experience of designing and building a "SuperCAM," a nanoscale CAM should be buildable which will have several orders of magnitude greater performance. Further research aims are to use CAs to make Hebbian synapses capable of learning. One can also imagine the generation of artificial "embryos" inside a CA machine, by having CA rules which allow an embryological "unfolding" of cell groups, with differentiation, transportation, death, etc. resulting in a form of neuro-morphogenesis similar to the way in which biological brains are built. The author's "CAM-Bryo" program is an early example of this kind of neuro-morphogenetic research.

9.9 Summary

The CAM-Brain Project at ATR, Kyoto, Japan, intends to build/grow/evolve an artificial brain of a billion artificial neurons at (nano-)electronic speeds inside Cellular Automata Machines (CAMs) by the year 2001. Quoting from a paper by Margolus and Toffoli of MIT's Information Mechanics group, "We estimate that, with integrated circuit technology, a machine consisting of a trillion cells and having an update cycle of 100 pico-second for the entire space will be technologically feasible within 10 years" (i.e. by 2000) [2, 3] In a trillion 3D CA cells (cubes), one can place a billion artificial neurons. Such an artificial nervous system will be too complex to be humanly designable, but it may be possible to evolve it, and incrementally, by adding neural modules to an already functional artificial nervous system. In the summer of 1994, a 2D simulation of CAM-Brain using over 11000 hand crafted CA state transition rules was completed, and initial tests showed the new system to be evolvable. By the end of 1995, a 3D simulation will be completed.

If the CAM-Brain Project is successful, it will revolutionize the field of neural networks and artificial life, because it will provide a powerful new tool to evolve artificial brains with billions of neurons, and at electronic speeds. The CAM-Brain Project will thus produce the first Darwin Machine, i.e., a machine which evolves its own architecture. The author is confident that in time a new specialty will be established, based partly on the ideas behind CAM-Brain. This specialty is called simply "Brain Building." At the time of writing, there are now 3 centers in the world doing work similar to CAM-Brain. The first is at ATR. The second is led by Todd Kaloudis at MIT (email tjk@mit.edu), and the third is in Switzerland at the EPFL under Eduardo Sanchez (email eduardo@lslsun.epfl.ch).

Finally, the author and his colleague Felix Gers is about to port the 2D version of CAM-Brain to the CAM8. Hence in 1995, it will be possible to evolve neural circuits with 25,000 neurons (or 100,000 neurons, with 16 Mbit memory chips) at 200 million CA cell updates a second. As mentioned earlier, the author expects that when this happens, the world will sit up and take notice. Twenty years from now, the author envisages the brain builder industry (i.e. intelligent robots, etc) as being one of the world's top industries, comparable with the oil, automobile, and construction industries. He sees an analogy between the very early rocket pioneers (e.g. the American Goddard, and the German (V2) von Braun) and the US NASA mission to the moon which followed. Today's 100,000-neuron artificial brain is just the beginning of what is to come. With adiabatic (heat generationless) reversible quantum computation, it will be possible to build 3D hardware circuits that do not melt. Hence size becomes no obstacle, which means that one could use planetoid size asteroids to build huge 3D brain like computers containing ten to power 40 components with one bit per atom. Hence late into the 21st century, the author predicts that human beings will be confronted with the "artilect" (artificial intellect) with a brain vastly superior to the human brain with its pitiful trillion neurons. The issue of "species dominance" will dominate global politics next century. The middle term prospects of brain building are exciting, but long term they are terrifying. The author has written an essay on this question [11] If you would like to be sent a copy, just email him at degaris@hip.atr.co.jp.

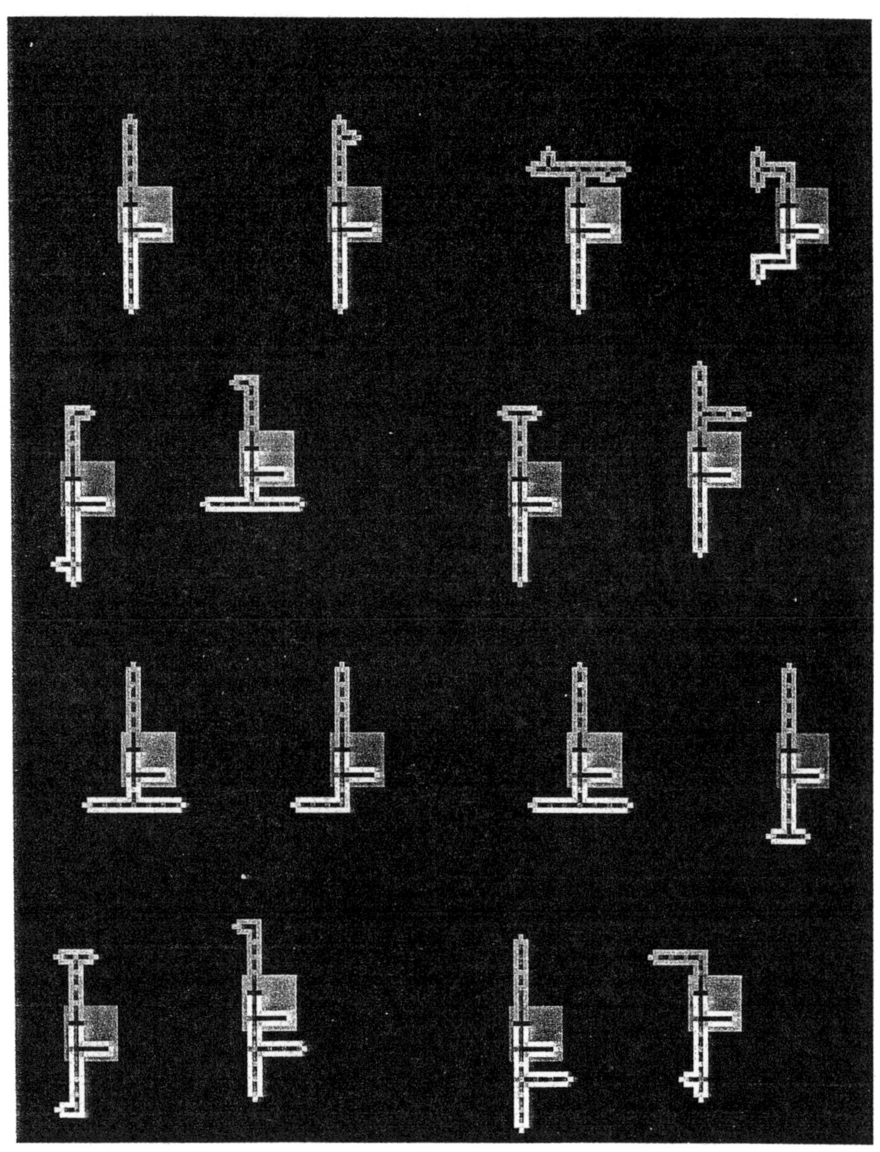

Figure 9.9: 2D CAM-Brain Early Growth

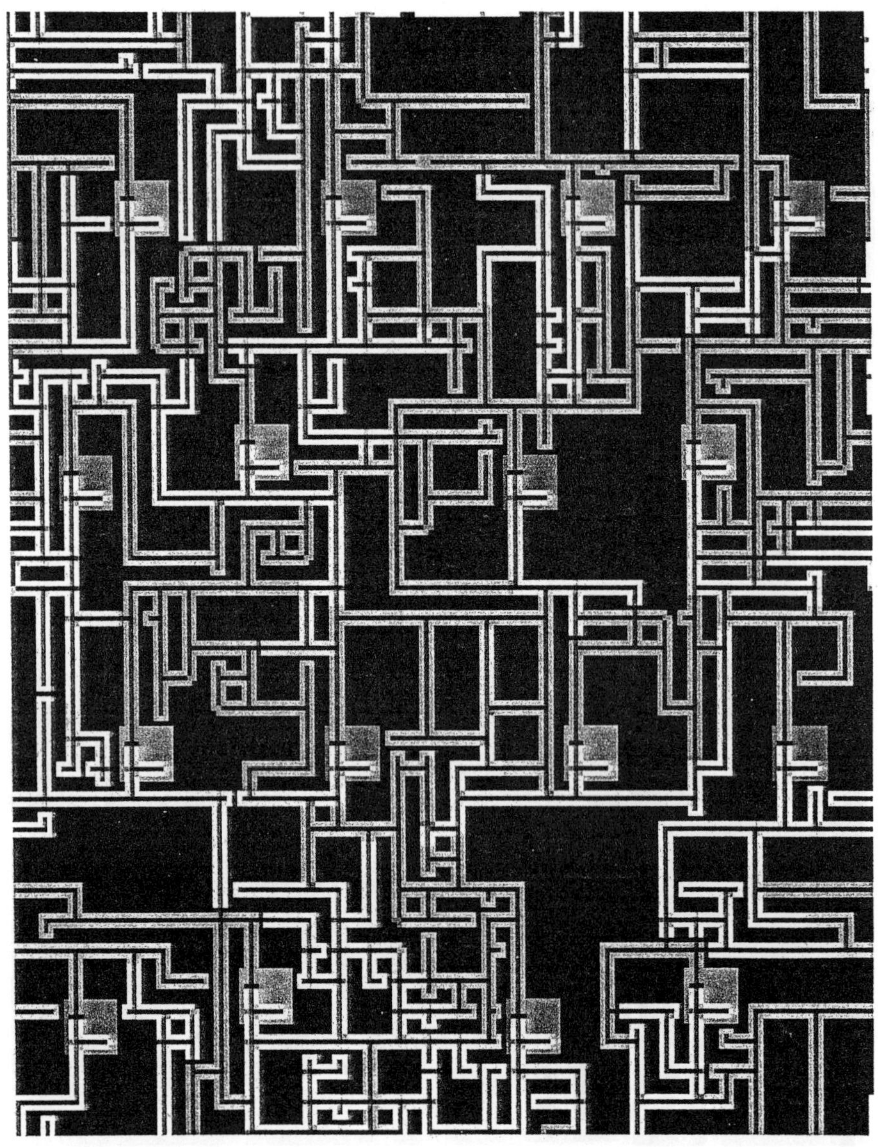

Figure 9.10: 2D CAM-Brain Completed Growth

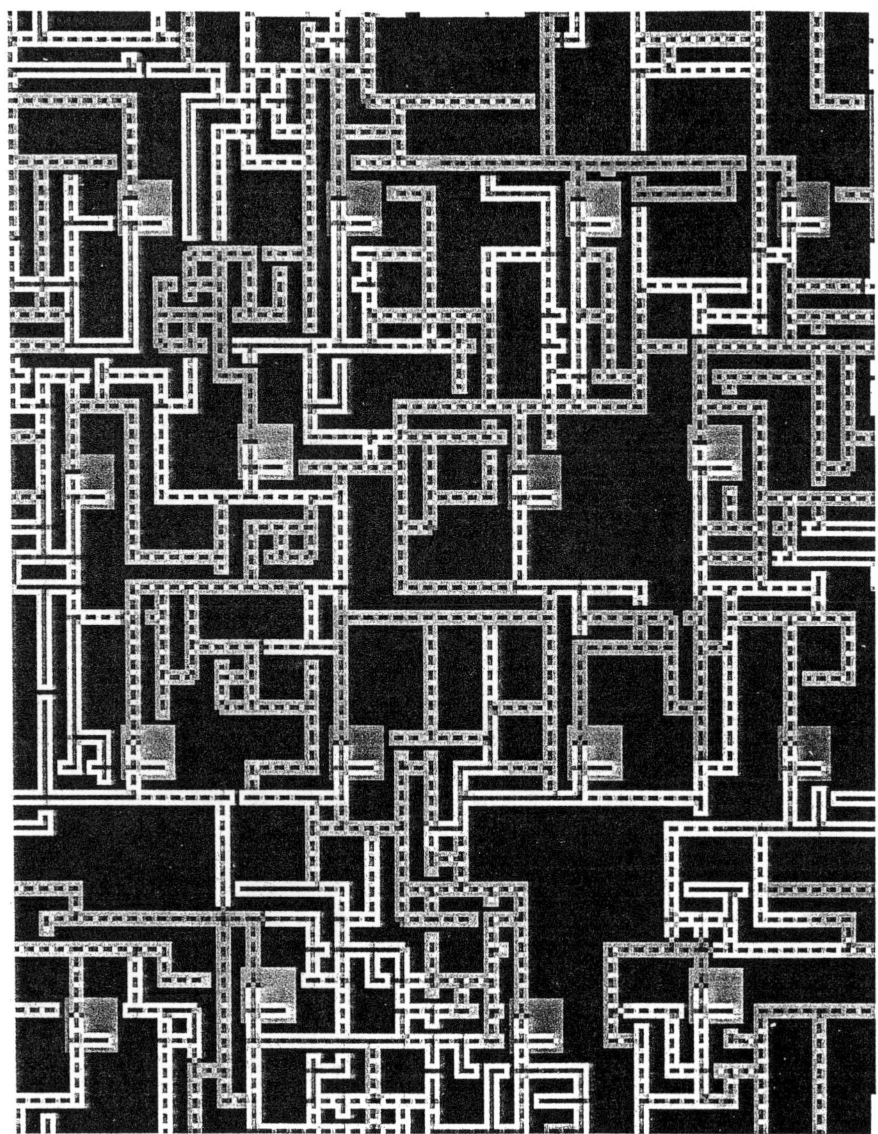

Figure 9.11: 2D CAM-Brain Neural Signaling

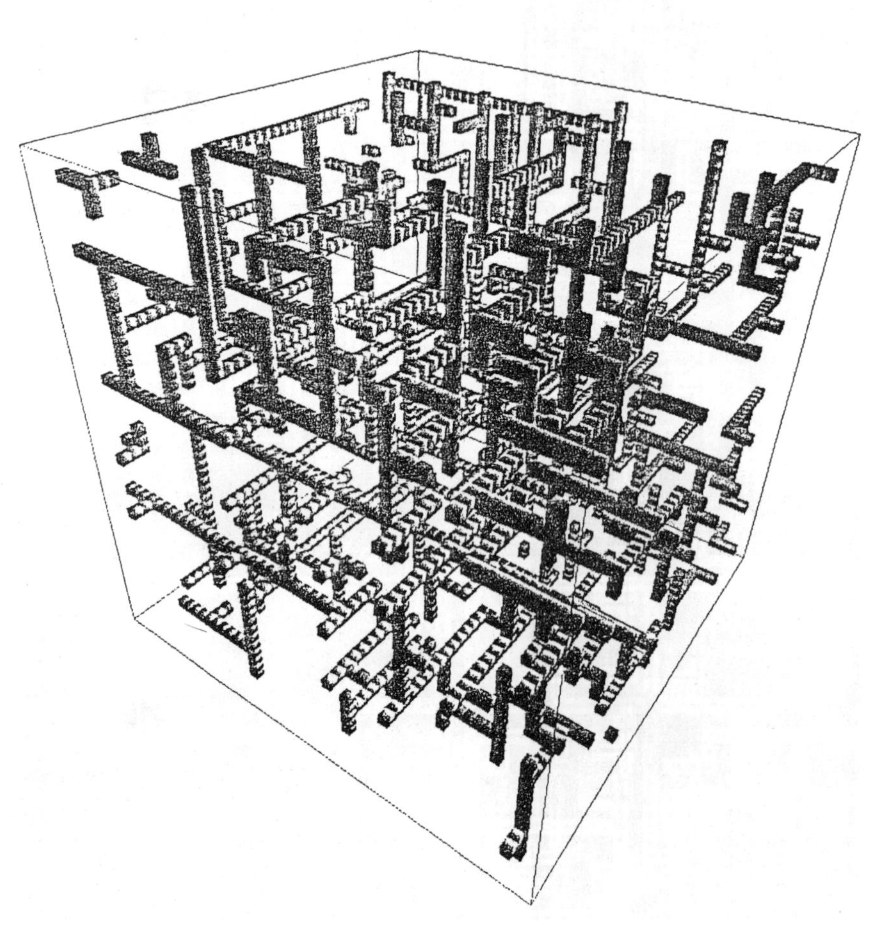

Figure 9.12: 3D CAM-Brain Non-Synaptic Growth

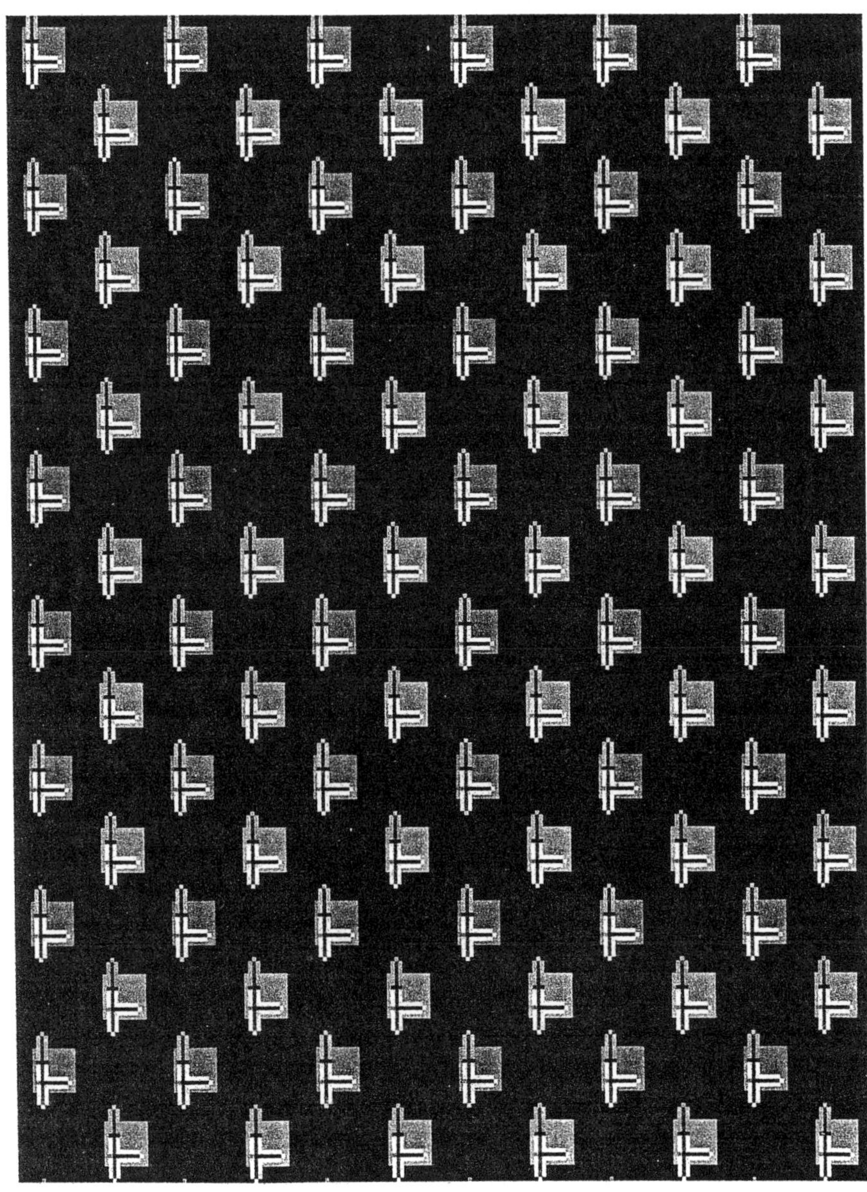

Figure 9.13: 2D CAM-Bryo

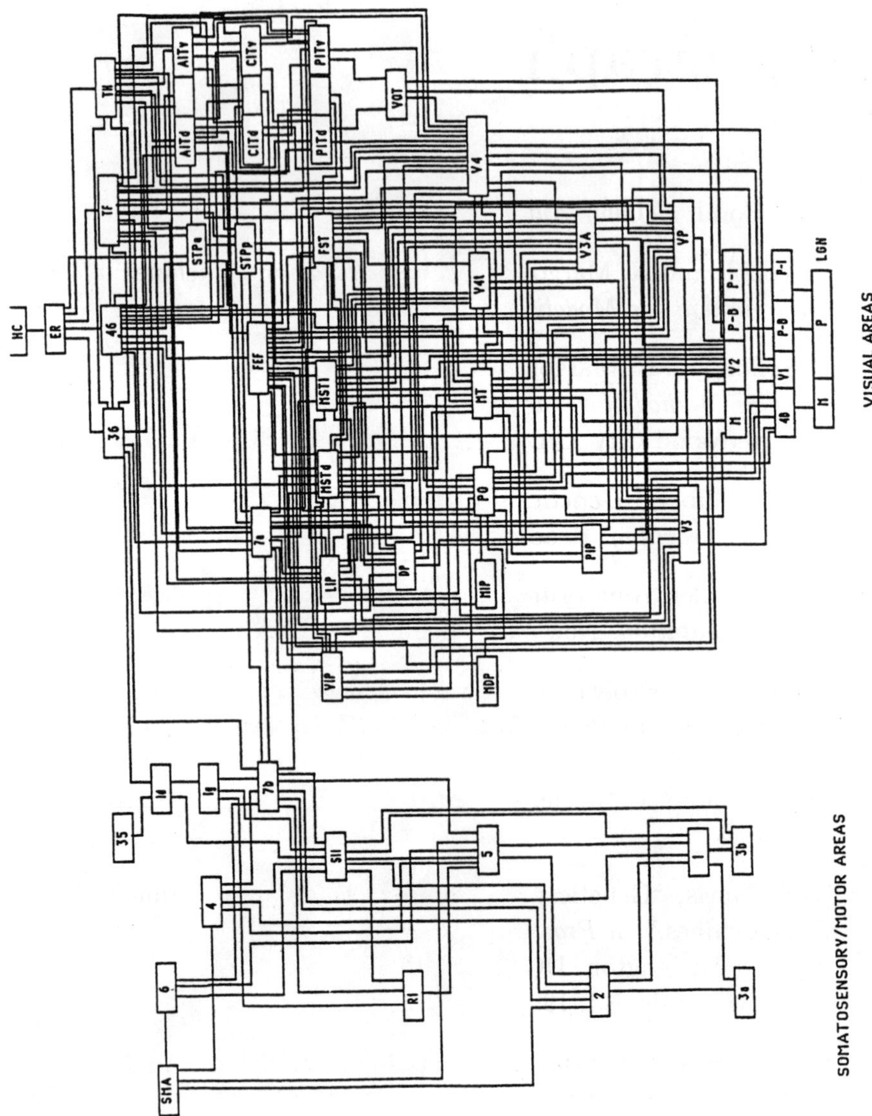

Figure 9.14: van Essen's Monkey Brain Architecture

Bibliography

[1] E. F. Codd, *Cellular Automata.* New York: Academic Press, 1968.

[2] T. Toffoli and N. Margolus, *Cellular Automata Machines: A New Environment for Modeling.* Cambridge, MA: MIT Press, 1987.

[3] T. Toffoli and N. Margolus, "Cellular automata machines," in *Lattice Gas Methods for Partial Differential Equations* (G. D. Doolen, ed.), Redwood City, CA: Addison-Wesley, 1990.

[4] D. E. Goldberg, *Genetic Algorithms in Search, Optimization, and Machine Learning.* Reading, MA: Addison-Wesley, 1989.

[5] K. E. Drexler, *Nanosystems: Molecular Machinery, Manufacturing and Computation.* New York: John Wiley & Sons, Inc., 1992.

[6] H. de Garis, "Evolvable hardware: Genetic programming of a darwin machine," in *Proc. of the Int. Conf. on Artificial Neural Nets and Genetic Algorithms, Innsbruck, Austria* (R. F. Albrecht, C. R. Reeves, and N. C. Steele, eds.), pp. 441–449, Springer-Verlag/Wien, 1993.

[7] H. de Garis, "Genetic programming: modular evolution for Darwin machines," in *Proc. of Int'l Joint Conf. on Neural Networks, Vol. I,* (Washington, DC), pp. 194–197, Lawrence Erlbaum Associates, Hillsdale, NJ, 1990.

[8] H. de Garis, "Genetic programming: Building artificial nervous systems with genetically programmed neural network module," in *Neural and Intelligent Systems Integration* (B. Souček, ed.), ch. 8, New York, NY: John Wiley & Sons, Inc., 1991.

[9] H. de Garis, "Circuits of production rule GenNets: the genetic programming of artificial nervous systems," in *Proc. of the Int. Conf. on Artificial Neural Nets and Genetic Algorithms, Innsbruck, Austria* (R. F. Albrecht, C. R. Reeves, and N. C. Steele, eds.), pp. 699–705, Springer-Verlag/Wien, 1993.

[10] H. de Garis, "Artificial embryology: the genetic programming of an artificial embryo," in *Dynamic, Genetic, and Chaotic Programming* (B. Souček and the IRIS Group, eds.), ch. 14, pp. 373–393, New York, NY: John Wiley & Sons, Inc., 1992.

[11] H. de Garis, "Cosmism : Nano electronics and 21st century global ideological warfare," in *a future nanotech book.* to appear.

Chapter 10

An Evolutionary Approach to the N-Player Iterated Prisoner's Dilemma Game

X. Yao and P. Darwen

The Iterated Prisoner's Dilemma game has been used extensively in the study of the evolution of cooperative behaviours in social and biological systems. There have been a lot of experimental studies on evolving strategies for 2-player Iterated Prisoner's Dilemma games (2IPD). However, there are many real world problems, especially many social and economic ones, which cannot be modelled by the 2IPD. The n-player Iterated Prisoner's Dilemma (NIPD) is a more realistic and general game which can model those problems. This chapter presents two sets of experiments on evolving strategies for the NIPD. The first set of experiments examine the impact of the number of players in the NIPD on the evolution of cooperation in the group. Our experiments show that cooperation is less likely to emerge in a large group than in a small group. The second set of experiments study the generalisation ability of evolved strategies from the point of view of machine learning. Our experiments reveal the effect of changing the evolutionary environment of evolution on the generalisation ability of evolved strategies.

10.1 Introduction

The 2-player Iterated Prisoner's Dilemma game (2IPD) is a 2×2 non-zerosum noncooperative game, where "non-zerosum" indicates that the benefits obtained by a player are not necessarily the same as the penalties received by another player and "noncooperative" indicates that no preplay communication is permitted between the players [1, 2]. It has been widely studied in such diverse fields as economics, mathematical game theory, political science, and artificial intelligence.

In the Prisoner's Dilemma, each player has a choice of two operations: either cooperate with the other player, or defect. Payoff to both players is calculated according to Figure 10.1. In the Iterated Prisoner's Dilemma (IPD), this step is repeated many times, and each player can remember previous steps.

	Cooperate	Defect
Cooperate	R R	T S
Defect	S T	P P

Figure 10.1: The payoff matrix for the 2-player prisoner's dilemma game. The values S, P, R, T must satisfy $T > R > P > S$ and $R > (S+T)/2$. In 2-player Iterated Prisoner's Dilemma (2IPD), the above interaction is repeated many times, and both players can remember previous outcomes.

While the 2IPD has been studied extensively for more than three decades, there are many real world problems, especially many social and economic ones, which cannot be modelled by the 2IPD. Hardin [3] described some examples of such problems. More examples can be found in Colman's book [1](pp.156–159). The n-player Iterated Prisoner's Dilemma (NIPD) is a more realistic and general game which can model those problems. In comparing the NIPD with the 2IPD, Davis *et al.* [4](pp.520) commented that

> The N-player case (NPD) has greater generality and applicability to real-life situations. In addition to the problems of energy conservation, ecology, and overpopulation, many other real-life problems can be represented by the NPD paradigm.

Colman [1](pp.142) and Glance and Huberman [5, 6] have also indicated that the NIPD is "qualitatively different" from the 2IPD and that "... certain strategies that work well for individuals in the Prisoner's Dilemma fail in large groups."

The n-player Prisoner's Dilemma game can be defined by the following three properties [1](pp.159):

1. each player faces two choices between cooperation (C) and defection (D);

2. the D option is dominant for each player, i.e., each is better off choosing D than C no matter how many of the other players choose C;

3. the dominant D strategies intersect in a deficient equilibrium. In particular, the outcome if all players choose their non-dominant C strategies is preferable from every player's point of view to the one in which everyone chooses D, but no one is motivated to deviate unilaterally from D.

Figure 10.2 shows the payoff matrix of the n-player game.

A large number of values satisfy the requirements of Figure 10.2. We choose values so that, if n_c is the number of cooperators in the n-player game, then the payoff for cooperation is $2n_c - 2$ and the payoff for defection is $2n_c + 1$. Figure 10.3 shows an example of the n-player game.

Number of cooperators among the remaining $n-1$ players

player A		0	1	2		$n-1$
	C	C_0	C_1	C_2	$\cdots$	C_{n-1}
	D	D_0	D_1	D_2	$\cdots$	D_{n-1}

Figure 10.2: The payoff matrix of the n-player Prisoner's Dilemma game, where the following conditions must be satisfied: (1) $D_i > C_i$ for $0 \leq i \leq n-1$; (2) $D_{i+1} > D_i$ and $C_{i+1} > C_i$ for $0 \leq i < n-1$; (3) $C_i > (D_i + C_{i-1})/2$ for $0 < i \leq n-1$. The payoff matrix is symmetric for each player.

Number of cooperators among the remaining $n-1$ players

player A		0	1	2		$n-1$
	C	0	2	4	$\cdots$	$2(n-1)$
	D	1	3	5	$\cdots$	$2(n-1)+1$

Figure 10.3: An example of the N-player game.

With this choice, simple algebra reveals that if N_c cooperative moves are made out of N moves of an n-player game, then the average per-round payoff a is given by:

$$a = 1 + \frac{N_c}{N}(2n - 3) \tag{10.1}$$

This lets us measure how common cooperation was just by looking at the average per-round payoff.

There has been a lot of research on the evolution of cooperation in the 2IPD using genetic algorithms and evolutionary programming in recent years [7, 8, 9, 10, 11, 12]. Axelrod [7] used genetic algorithms to evolve a population of strategies where each strategy plays the 2IPD with every other strategy in the population. In other words, the performance or fitness of a strategy is evaluated by playing the 2IPD with every other strategy in the population. The environment in which a strategy evolves consists of all the remaining strategies in the population. Since strategies in the population are constantly changing as a result of evolution, a strategy will be evaluated by a different environment in every generation. All the strategies in the population are co-evolving in their dynamic environments. Axelrod found that such dynamic environments produced strategies that performed very well against their population. Fogel [11] described similar experiments, but used finite state machines to represent strategies and evolutionary programming to evolve them.

However, very few experimental studies have been carried out on the NIPD in spite of its importance and its qualitative difference from the 2IPD. This chapter presents two sets of experiments carried out on the NIPD. We first describe our experiment setup in Section 10.2. Then we investigate the impact of the number of players in the Prisoner's Dilemma game on the evolution of cooperation in Section 10.3. We are mainly interested in two questions here: (1) whether cooperation can still emerge from a larger group, and (2) whether it is more difficult to evolve cooperation in a larger group. The evolution of strategies for the NIPD can be regarded as a form of machine learning using the evolutionary approach. An important issue in machine learning is generalisation. Section 10.4 of this chapter discusses the generalisation issue associated with co-evolutionary learning and presents some experiments with different evolutionary environments. Finally, Section 10.5 concludes with some remarks and future research directions.

10.2 Experiment Setup

10.2.1 Genotypical Representation of Strategies

We use genetic algorithms to evolve strategies for the NIPD. The most important issue here is the representation of strategies. We will use two different representations, both of which are look-up tables that give an action for every possible contingency.

One way of representing strategies for the NIPD is to generalise the representation scheme used by Axelrod [7]. In this scheme, each genotype is a lookup table that covers every possible history of the last few steps. A history in such a game is represented as a binary string of ln bits, where the first l bits represent the player's own previous l actions (most recent to the left, oldest to the right), and the other $n-1$ groups of l bits represent the previous actions of the other players. For example, during a game of 3IPD with a remembered history of 2 steps, $n = 3, l = 2$, one player might see this history:

$n = 3, l = 2$: Example history `11 00 01`

The first l bits, `11`, means this player has defected (a "1") for both of the previous $l = 2$ steps. The previous steps of the other players are then listed in order: the `00` means the first of the other players cooperated (a "0") on the previous l steps, and the last of the other players cooperated (0) on the most recent step, and defected (1) on the step before, as represented by `01`.

For the NIPD remembering l previous steps, there are 2^{ln} possible histories. The lookup table genotype therefore contains an action (cooperate "0" or defect "1") for each of these possible histories. So we need at least 2^{ln} bits to represent a strategy. At the beginning of each game, there are no previous l steps of play from which to look up the next action, so each genotype should also contain its own extra bits that define the presumed pre-game moves. The total genotype length is therefore $2^{ln} + ln$ bits. We will use this genotype for the first set of results below, Figure 10.5 through to Figure 10.8.

This Axelrod-style representation scheme, however, suffers from two disadvantages. First, it does not scale well as the number of players increases. Second, it provides more information than is necessary by telling which of the other players cooperated or defected, when the only information needed is how many of the other players cooperated or defected. Such redundant information had reduced the efficiency of the evolution greatly in our experiments with this representation scheme. To improve on this, we use a new representation scheme which is more compact and efficient.

In our new representation scheme, each individual is regarded as a set of rules stored in a look-up table that covers every possible history. As a game that runs for, say, 500 rounds would have an enormous number of possible histories, and as only the most recent steps will have significance for the next move, we only consider every possible history over the most recent l steps, where l is less than 4 steps. This means an individual can only remember the l most recent rounds. Such a history of l rounds is represented by:

1. l bits for the player's own previous l moves, where a "1" indicates defection, a "0" cooperation; and

2. another $l \log_2 n$ bits for the number of cooperators among the other $n - 1$ players, where n is the number of the players in the game. This requires that n is a power of 2.

For example, if we are looking at 8 players who can remember the 3 most recent rounds, then one of the players would see the history as:

History for 8 players, 3 steps: `001 111 110 101` (12 bits)

Here, the `001` indicates the player's own actions: the most recent action (on the left) was a "0", indicating cooperation, and the action 3 steps ago (on the right), was a "1", i.e., defection. The `111` gives the number of cooperators among the other 7 players in the most recent round, i.e., there were $111_2 = 7$ cooperators. The `101` gives the number of cooperators among the other 7 players 3 steps ago, i.e., there were $101_2 = 5$ cooperators. The most recent events are always on the left, previous events on the right.

In the above example, there are $2^{12} = 2048$ possible histories. So 2048 bits are needed to represent all possible strategies. In the general case of an n-player game with history length l, each history needs $l + l\log_2 n$ bits to represent and there are $2^{l+l\log_2 n}$ such histories. A strategy is represented by a binary string that gives an action for each of those possible histories. In the above example, the history `001 111 110 101` would cause the strategy to do whatever is listed in bit 1013, the decimal number for the binary 001111110101.

Since there are no previous l rounds at the beginning of a game, we have to specify them with another $l(1+\log_2 n)$ bits. Hence each strategy is finally represented by a binary string of length $2^{l+l\log_2 n}+l(1+\log_2 n)$.

10.2.2 Genetic Algorithm Parameters

For all the experiments presented in this chapter, the population size is 100, the mutation rate is 0.001, and the crossover rate is 0.6. Rank-based selection was used, with the worst performer assigned an average of 0.75 offspring, the best 1.25 offspring.

10.2.3 A Typical Run

A tyical run with four players with a history 1 ($n = 4, l = 1$) is shown in Figure 10.4. At each generation, 1000 games of the 4-player Iterated Prisoner's Dilemma are played, with each group of 4 players selected randomly with replacement. Each of these 1000 games lasts for 100 rounds. Starting from a random population, defection is usually the better strategy, and the average payoff plummets initially. As time passes, some cooperation becomes more profitable. We will examine more results in detail later.

10.3 Group Size of the NIPD

This section discusses the impact of group size, i.e., the number of players in the NIPD, on the evolution of cooperation and presents some experimental results. It is well-known that cooperation can be evolved from a population of random strategies for the 2IPD. Can cooperation still be evolved from a population of strategies for the NIPD where the

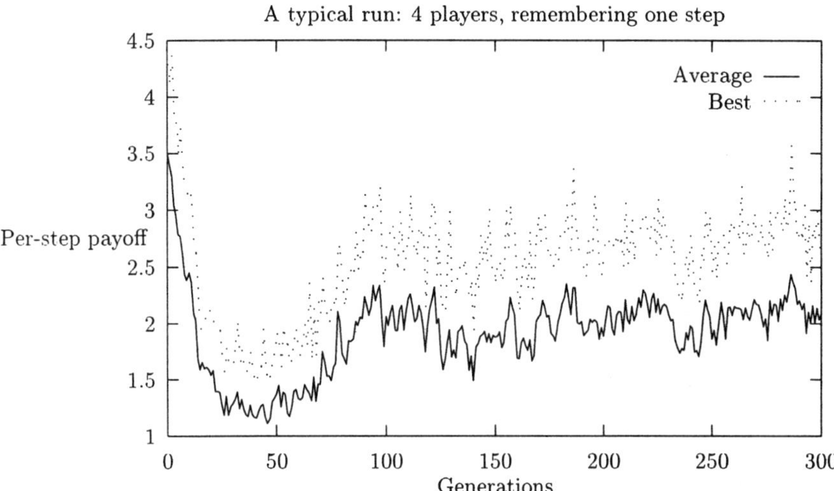

Figure 10.4: This shows the average and best payoff at each generation for a population of 100 individuals. Each individual is a strategy.

number of players is greater than 2? If the answer is yes, does the group size affect the evolution of cooperation in the NIPD?

Using the Axelrod-style genotype described above, we carried out a series of experiments with the 3IPD, 4IPD, 5IPD, and 6IPD games. In each of the following runs, the program stopped when more than 5 generations passed with the average payoff above the 95% cooperation level. Figure 10.5 shows the results of 20 runs of the 3IPD game with history length 2: out of 20 runs, there is only 1 which fails to reach 95% cooperation. Figure 10.6 shows the results of 20 runs of the 4IPD game with history length 2: 4 out of 20 runs fail to reach the 95% cooperation level, but only 1 of those fails to reach 80% cooperation. Figure 10.7 shows the results of 20 runs of the 5IPD game with history length 2: 6 out of 20 runs do not reach the 80% cooperation level. Figure 10.8 shows the results of 20 runs of the 6IPD game with history length 2: 9 out of 20 runs stay below the 80% cooperation level.

Figures 10.5 through 10.8 demonstrate that the evolution of cooperation becomes less likely as group size increases. Nonetheless, cooperation still emerges most of the time. As Axelrod's representation scheme used in those figures does not scale well with the group size, we use

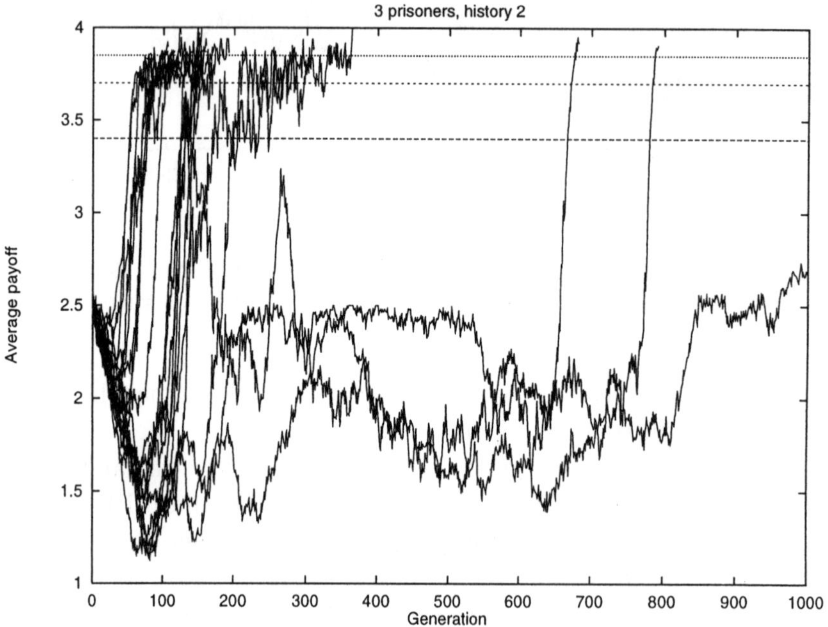

Figure 10.5: For the 3-player prisoner's dilemma with a history of 2, cooperation almost always emerges. Only 1 out of 20 runs fail to reach 95% cooperation using Axelrod's representation scheme.

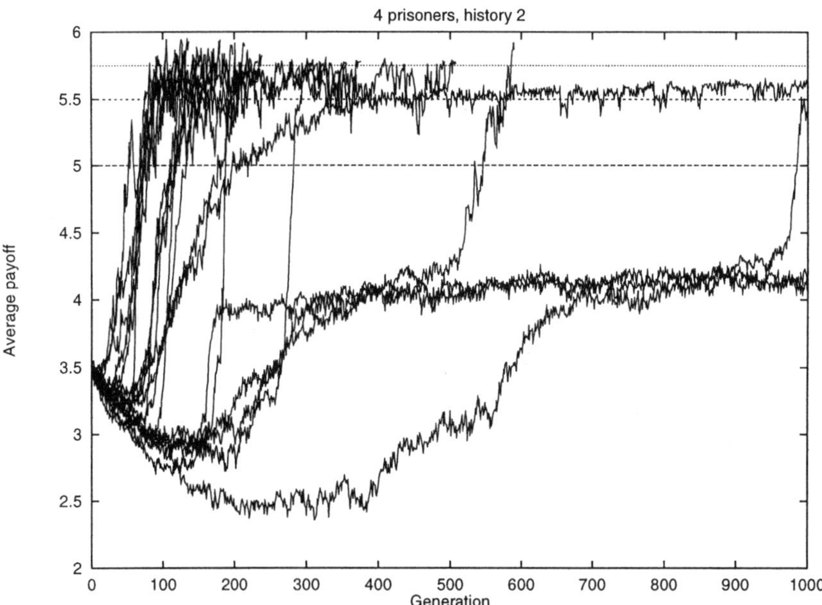

Figure 10.6: For the 4-player prisoner's dilemma with a history of 2, cooperation almost always emerges. Only 4 out of 20 runs fail to reach 95% cooperation using Axelrod's representation scheme.

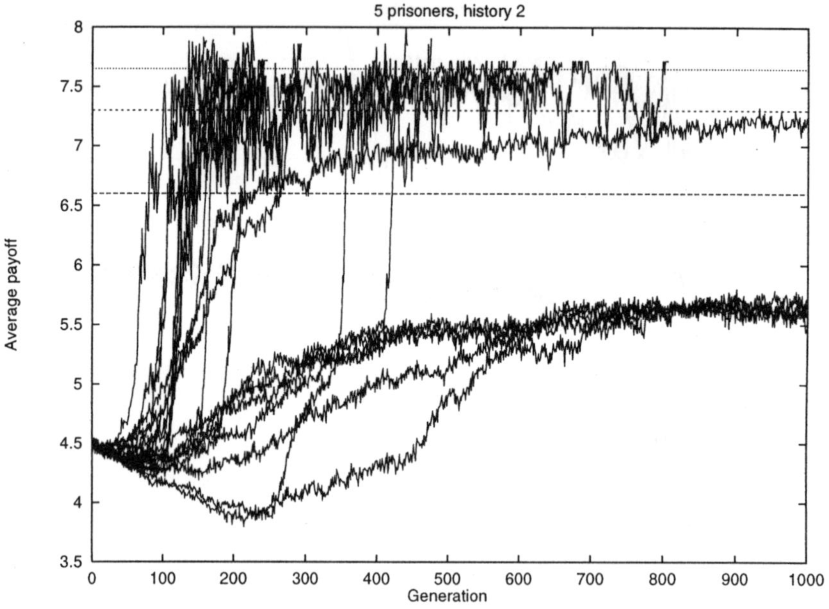

Figure 10.7: For the 5-player prisoner's dilemma with a history of 2, cooperation almost always emerges. 6 out of 20 runs fail to reach 80% cooperation using Axelrod's representation scheme.

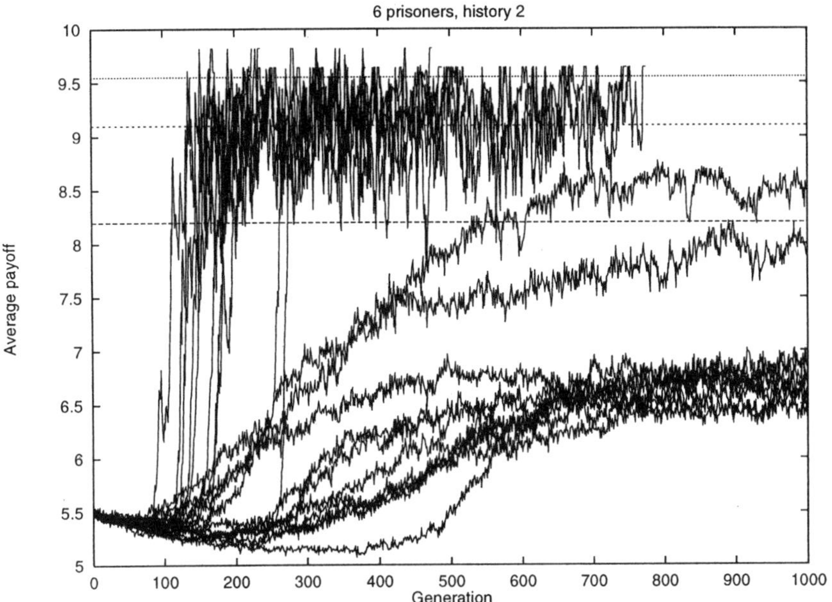

Figure 10.8: For the 6-player prisoner's dilemma with a history of 2, cooperation almost always emerges. 9 out of 20 runs fail to reach 80% cooperation using Axelrod's representation scheme.

the second representation scheme described in Section 10.2 to carry out experiments with larger groups.

We have carried out a series of experiments with the 2IPD, 4IPD, 8IPD, and 16IPD games. Figure 10.9 shows the results of 10 runs of the 2IPD game with history length 3. Out of 10 runs, there are only 3 which fail to reach 90% cooperation and only 1 which goes to almost all defection. Figure 10.10 shows the results of 10 runs of the 4IPD game with history length 3, where some of the runs reach cooperation but more than half of the 10 runs fail to evolve cooperation. Figure 10.11 shows the results of 10 runs of the 8IPD game with history length 2, where none of the runs reach cooperation. Figure 10.12 shows the population bias in the runs in Figure 10.11, to demonstrate that those populations have pretty much converged. Figure 10.13 shows 10 runs of the 16IPD game.

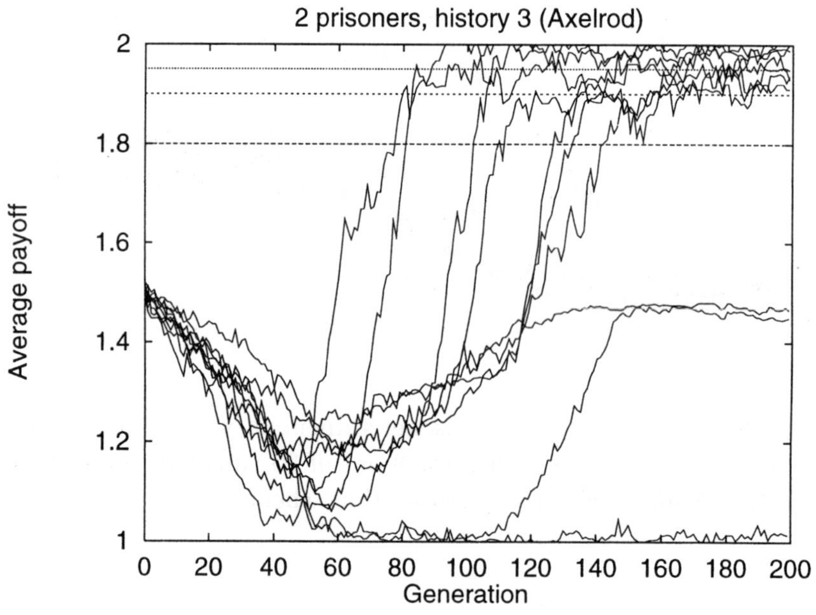

Figure 10.9: For 2-player prisoner's dilemma with a history of 3, cooperation emerges most of the time. Only 3 out of 10 runs fail to reach 90% cooperation, and only 1 run goes to almost all defection.

These results confirm that cooperation can still be evolved in larger

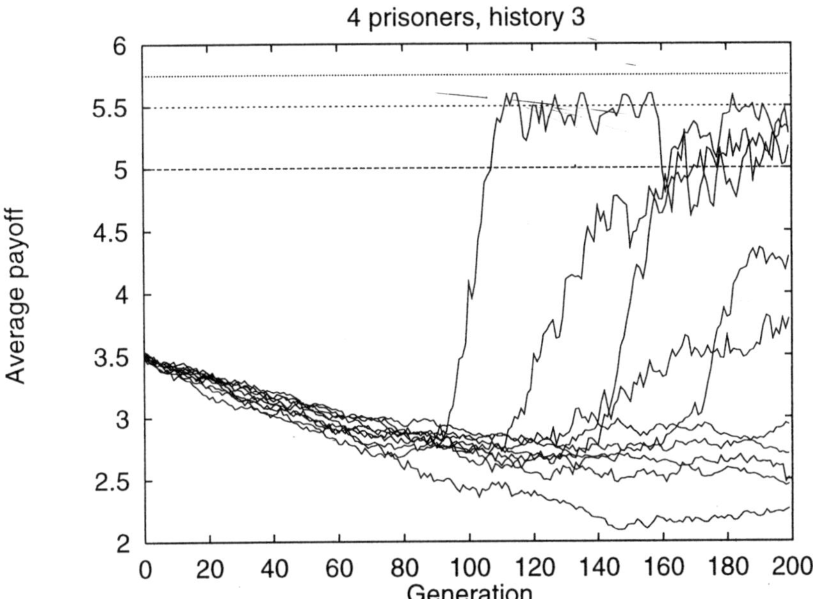

Figure 10.10: For 10 runs of 4-player prisoner's dilemma with a history of 3, cooperation breaks out some of the time.

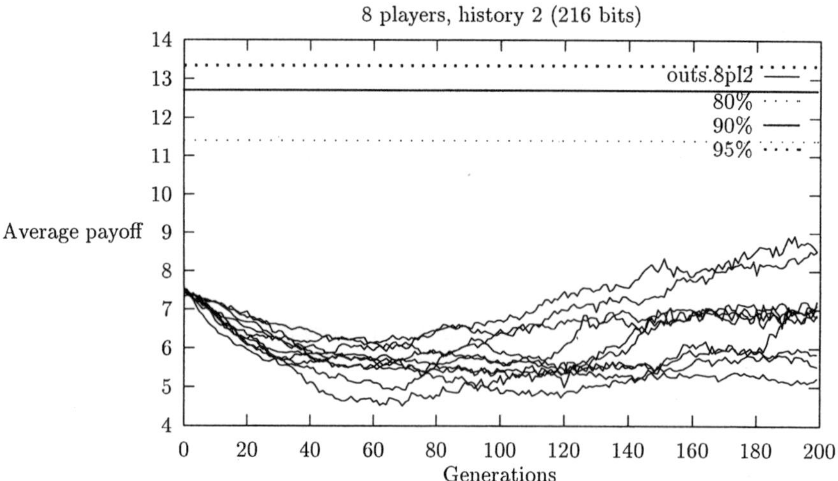

Figure 10.11: For 10 runs of 8-player prisoner's dilemma with a history of 2, cooperation never emerges. The horizontal lines at the top show the 95%, 90%, and 80% levels of cooperation. To demonstrate that these runs have converged, figure 10.12 shows the bias of the populations.

groups, but it is more difficult to evolve cooperation as the group size increases. Glance and Huberman [5, 6] have arrived at a similar conclusion using a model based on many particle systems. We first suspected that the failure to evolve cooperation in larger groups was caused by larger search spaces and insufficient running time since more players were involved in 8IPD and 16IPD games. This is, however, not the case. The search space of the 8IPD game with history length 2 is actually smaller than that of the 4IPD game with history length 3. To confirm that the failure to evolve cooperation is not caused by insufficient running time, we examined the convergence of the 8IPD game. Figure 10.12 shows that at generation 200 the population has mostly converged for all the 10 runs.

It is worth mentioning that the evolution of cooperation using simulations does depend on some implementation details, such as the genotypical representation of strategies and the values used in the payoff matrix. So cooperation may be evolved in the 8IPD game if a different representation scheme and different payoff values are used. Although we

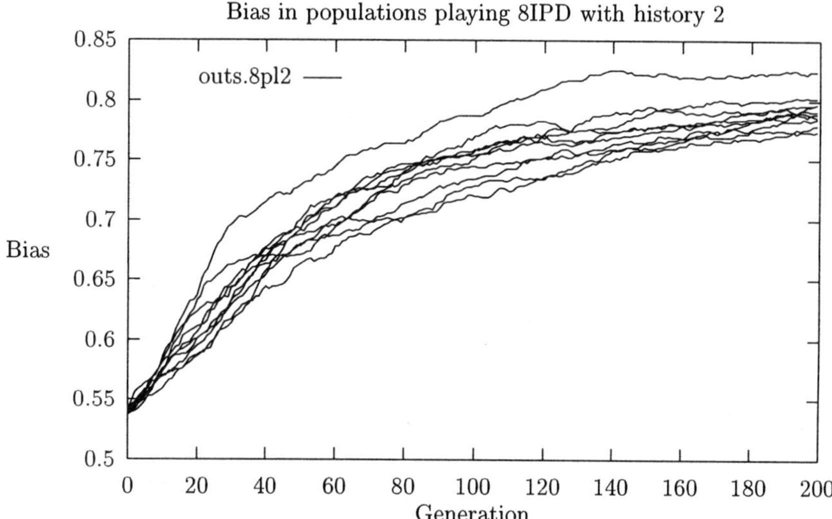

Figure 10.12: In 10 runs of 8-player prisoner's dilemma with a history of 2, where cooperation never emerges, the bias demonstrates that the populations have converged. Bias is the average proportion of the most prominent value in each position. A bias of 0.75 means that, on average, each bit position has converged to either 75% "0" or 75% "1".

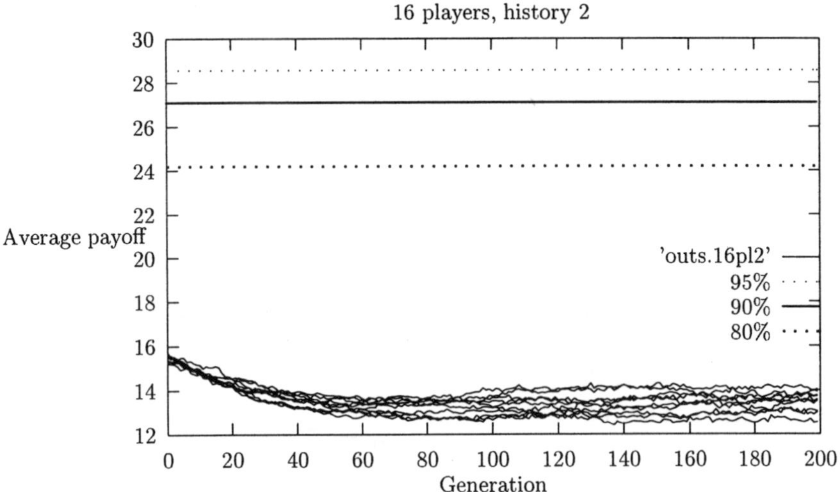

Figure 10.13: For 10 runs of 16-player prisoner's dilemma with a history of 2, cooperation never emerges. The horizontal lines at the top show the 95%, 90%, and 80% levels of cooperation.

cannot prove it vigorously, we think for any representation scheme and payoff values there would always be an upper limit on the group size over which cooperation cannot be evolved. Our experimental finding is rather similar to some phenomena in our human society, e.g., cooperation is usually easier to emerge in a small group of people than in a larger one.

10.4 Co-Evolutionary Learning and Generalisation

The idea of having a computer algorithm learn from its own experience and thus create expertise without being exposed to a human teacher has been around for a long time. For genetic algorithms, both Hillis [13] and Axelrod [7] have attempted co-evolution, where a GA population is evaluated by how well it performs against itself or another GA population, starting from a random population. Expertise is thus bootstrapped from nothing, without an expert teacher. This is certainly a promising idea, but does it work? So far, no-one has investigated if the results of co-evolutionary learning are robust, that is, whether they generalise well? If a strategy is produced by a co-evolving population, will that strategy perform well against opponents never seen by that population? In order to investigate this issue, we need to pick the best strategies produced by the co-evolutionary learning system and let them play against a set of test strategies which had not been seen by the co-evolutionary system. This section describes some experiments which test the generalisation ability of co-evolved strategies for the 8IPD game with history length 1.

10.4.1 Test Strategies

The unseen test strategies used in our study should be of reasonable standard and representative, that is, they are neither very poor (or else they will be exploited by their evolved opponents) nor very good (or else the will exploit their evolved opponent). We need unseen strategies that are adequate against a large range of opponents, but not *the* best.

To obtain such strategies, we did a limited enumerative search to find the strategies that performed best against a large number of random opponents. As most random opponents are very stupid, beating many random opponents provides a mediocre standard of play against a wide range of opponents. We limited this search to manageable proportions by fixing certain bits in a strategy's genotype that seemed to be sensible, such as always defecting after every other strategy defects. The top few strategies found from such a limited enumerative search are listed in Table 10.1.

10.4.2 Learning and Testing

We have compared three different methods for implementing the co-evolutionary learning system. The three methods differ in the way each individual is evaluated, i.e., which opponents are chosen to evaluate an individual's fitness. The three methods are

1. Choosing from among the individuals in the GA population, i.e., normal co-evolution of a single population like Axelrod's implementation [7];

Mean	Std Dev	Decimal	Binary genotype
8.100	0.083	1026040	1111 1010 0111 1111 1000
8.093	0.083	1022965	1111 1001 1011 1111 0101
8.091	0.083	1018871	1111 1000 1011 1111 0111
8.088	0.083	1032181	1111 1011 1111 1111 0101
8.088	0.083	1020921	1111 1001 0011 1111 1001
8.082	0.083	1028087	1111 1010 1111 1111 0111
8.077	0.083	1023990	1111 1001 1111 1111 0110
8.076	0.083	1037305	1111 1101 0011 1111 1001
8.076	0.083	1017846	1111 1000 0111 1111 0110

Table 10.1: Top few strategies from a partial enumerative search for strategies that play well against a large number of random opponents. This provides unseen test opponents to test the generalisation of strategies produced by co-evolution. The first 4 bits were fixed to "1", as were the eleventh through sixteenth bits. Virtually all of the best 50 strategies started by cooperating.

2. Choosing from a pool made of the evolving GA population and the best 25 strategies from the enumerative search, which remain fixed;

3. Choosing from a pool made of the evolving GA population and the best 25 strategies from the enumerative search, but the probability of choosing one of the 25 is four times higher.

For each of these, we obtained the best 25 strategies from the last generation of the GA, and tested it against a pool made up of both the seen and unseen enumerative search strategies, 50 in all.

10.4.3 Experimental Results

For each of the three evaluation methods, Tables 10.2 through 10.4 show the performance of the best strategies from the GA's last generation against opponents from (1) themselves, and (2) a pool made up of both the seen and unseen strategies from the enumerative search.

Normal co-evolution, no extra strategies in evaluation.
GA strategies play against themselves.

8pl1 (35% cooperative) against itself

		Mean	Stdv	Stdv of mean	Mean of opponents
0	11100001111011010011	7.240	3.978	0.126	6.296
1	11000001111011011011	7.285	3.985	0.126	6.392
2	11100000111111110011	7.335	3.052	0.097	8.434
3	01100010111111010011	7.258	3.202	0.101	7.889
4	11100101111111110011	7.180	4.160	0.132	5.883
5	01100000111111010011	7.000	3.090	0.098	8.111
6	11100101111111010011	7.171	4.125	0.130	6.127
7	01100001111111010011	7.241	4.027	0.127	6.286
8	00100000111111010110	7.165	3.122	0.099	8.341
9	01100100111111110110	7.706	3.523	0.111	7.949
10	10100000111111110001	7.274	3.083	0.097	8.395

GA strategies play against unseen strategies from enumerative search.

		Mean	Stdv	Stdv of mean	Mean of opponents
0	11100001111011010011	5.525	2.330	0.074	5.340
1	11000001111011011011	5.627	2.421	0.077	5.502
2	11100000111111110011	5.605	2.568	0.081	5.027
3	01100010111111010011	5.087	2.064	0.065	5.419
4	11100101111111110011	5.283	2.210	0.070	4.532
5	01100000111111010011	5.477	2.547	0.081	6.337
6	11100101111111010011	5.116	1.877	0.059	4.473
7	01100001111111010011	5.392	2.370	0.075	5.378
8	00100000111111010110	5.385	2.531	0.080	6.530
9	01100100111111110110	5.146	2.271	0.072	5.237
10	10100000111111110001	5.461	2.383	0.075	4.900

Table 10.2: Results of ordinary co-evolution, with no extra strategies during the GA evaluation. The GA strategies manage some cooperation among themselves, and hold their own against strategies they have not seen before.

Co-evolution, with addition of 25 fixed strategies from enumerative search.

GA strategies play against themselves.

		Mean	Stdv	Stdv of mean	Mean of opponents
0	1111100001111110100	11.678	1.715	0.054	11.965
1	1111100001111110100	11.706	1.553	0.049	11.994
2	1111100001111110110	11.440	1.603	0.051	11.922
3	1111100001111111110	11.721	1.581	0.050	12.027
4	1111100011111110100	13.264	2.521	0.080	10.636
5	1111100001111111110	11.714	1.584	0.050	12.025
6	1111100001111110110	11.420	1.669	0.053	11.895
7	1111100001111110100	11.678	1.705	0.054	11.985
8	1101100000111110100	11.618	1.781	0.056	11.958
9	1111100001111111111	11.670	1.688	0.053	11.974
10	1111100001111110100	11.649	1.697	0.054	11.973

GA strategies play against pool of 25 seen and 25 unseen strategies from enumerative search.

		Mean	Stdev	Stddev of mean	Mean of opponents
0	1111100001111110100	5.209	3.212	0.102	5.634
1	1111100001111110100	5.494	3.451	0.109	5.828
2	1111100001111110110	5.152	2.771	0.088	5.934
3	1111100001111111110	5.600	3.561	0.113	5.907
4	1111100011111110100	5.619	2.929	0.093	4.629
5	1111100001111111110	5.336	3.369	0.107	5.724
6	1111100001111110110	4.971	2.541	0.080	5.741
7	1111100001111110100	5.447	3.481	0.110	5.791
8	1101100000111110100	5.591	3.276	0.104	5.923
9	1111100001111111111	5.245	3.200	0.101	5.673
10	1111100001111110100	5.392	3.341	0.106	5.771

Table 10.3: Adding 25 fixed strategies to the evaluation procedure, along with the 100 co-evolving GA individuals, causes the GA to produce strategies that can cooperate more with each other, but are not exploited by the more non-cooperative strategies from the enumerative search.

Co-evolution, with the addition of 25 fixed strategies, which are 4 times as likely to be selected into the group of 8 players for 8IPD.

GA strategies play against themselves.

		Mean	Stdev	Stddev of mean	Mean of opponents
0	11111000011111110010	12.575	1.737	0.055	12.740
1	11111000011111110011	12.468	1.939	0.061	12.641
2	10111000011111010010	12.400	2.130	0.067	12.593
3	11111000011111111110	12.557	1.864	0.059	12.709
4	11111000011111110111	12.556	1.488	0.047	12.820
5	11111000011111010110	12.490	1.454	0.046	12.772
6	10111000011111110011	12.392	2.087	0.066	12.568
7	11111001011111111111	13.204	2.457	0.078	10.713
8	11111000011111111111	12.551	1.852	0.059	12.700
9	11111000011111110010	12.560	1.904	0.060	12.718
10	11111000011111110010	12.494	1.835	0.058	12.669

Best 25 strategies from GA search play against a pool of (1) 25 best from enumerative search, and (2) 25 unseen strategies from enumerative search. Note there is little diversity in the GA population.

GA strategies play against pool of 25 seen and 25 unseen strategies from enumerative search.

		Mean	Stdev	Stddev of mean	Mean of opponents
0	11111000011111110010	5.209	3.212	0.102	5.634
1	11111000011111110011	5.494	3.451	0.109	5.828
2	10111000011111010010	5.635	3.120	0.099	6.217
3	11111000011111111110	5.600	3.561	0.113	5.907
4	11111000011111110111	5.187	2.835	0.090	5.966
5	11111000011111010110	5.132	2.762	0.087	5.910
6	10111000011111110011	5.375	3.159	0.100	5.753
7	11111001011111111111	5.447	3.481	0.110	5.788
8	11111000011111111111	5.422	3.340	0.106	5.765
9	11111000011111110010	5.245	3.200	0.101	5.673
10	11111000011111110010	5.392	3.341	0.106	5.771

Table 10.4: Increasing the importance of the extra 25 fixed strategies causes the co-evolutionary GA to produce strategies that are even more cooperative among themselves, but are still not exploited by the unseen strategies of the enumerative search.

10.4.4 Discussion

Table 10.2 demonstrates that the co-evolution with the 8IPD produces strategies that are not very cooperative, as also demonstrated in Figure 10.11 earlier. Since the 8IPD is a game where it is easy to get exploited, co-evolution will first create strategies that can deal with non-cooperative strategies. The evolved strategies in Table 10.2 are cautious with each other and are not exploited by the unseen strategies from the enumerative search.

Adding fixed but not very cooperative strategies to the GA's evaluation procedure has a surprising effect. The evolved strategies in Tables 10.3 and 10.4 can cooperate well with other cooperators without being exploited by the strategies from the enumerative search, half of which it has never seen before. That is, normal co-evolution produces strategies which don't cooperate well with each other, and are not exploited by unseen non-cooperative strategies. Co-evolution with the addition of extra non-cooperative strategies gives more general strategies that do cooperate well with each other, but are still not exploited by unseen non-cooperative strategies. The experimental results also seem to indicate that the evolved strategies learn to cooperate with other cooperators better while maintaining their ability in dealing with non-cooperative strategies when the evolutionary environment contains a higher proportion of extra fixed strategies.

10.5 Conclusion

This chapter describes two sets of experiments on the NIPD. The first set of experiments on the group size of the NIPD demonstrate that cooperation can still be evolved in the n-player IPD game where $n > 2$. However, it is more difficult to evolve cooperation as the group size increases. There are two research issues here which are worth pursuing; one is the upper limit of the group size over which cooperation cannot be evolved, the other is the quantitative relation between the group size and the time used to evolve cooperation. Glance and Huberman [5, 6] have addressed these two issues, but did not give a complete answer.

The second set of experiments in this chapter deals with an important issue in co-evolutionary learning — the generalisation issue. Although the issue is the main theme in machine learning, very few people in the evolutionary computation community seem to be interested in it or address the issue explicitly and directly. We have presented some experimental results which show the importance of the environments in which each individual is evaluated, and their effects on generalisation ability.

Bibliography

[1] A. M. Colman, *Game Theory and Experimental Games*, Pergamon Press, Oxford, England, 1982.

[2] A. Rapoport, "Optimal policies for the prisoner's dilemma," Technical Report 50, The Psychometric Lab., Univ. of North Carolina, Chapel Hill, NC, USA, July 1966.

[3] G. Hardin, The tragedy of the commons, *Science*, 162:1243–1248, 1968.

[4] J. H. Davis, P. R. Laughlin, and S. S. Komorita, "The social psychology of small groups," *Annual Review of Psychology*, 27:501–542, 1976.

[5] N. S. Glance and B. A. Huberman, "The outbreak of cooperation," *Journal of Mathematical Sociology*, 17(4):281–302, 1993.

[6] N. S. Glance and B. A. Huberman, "The dynamics of social dilemmas," *Scientific American*, pages 58–63, March 1994.

[7] R. Axelrod, "The evolution of strategies in the iterated prisoner's dilemma," In L. Davis, editor, *Genetic Algorithms and Simulated Annealing*, chapter 3, pages 32–41. Morgan Kaufmann, San Mateo, CA, 1987.

[8] D. M. Chess, "Simulating the evolution of behaviors: the iterated prisoners' dilemma problem," *Complex Systems*, 2:663–670, 1988.

[9] K. Lindgren, "Evolutionary phenomena in simple dynamics," In C. G. Langton, C. Taylor, J. D. Farmer, and S. Rasmussen, editors,

Artificial Life II: SFI Studies in the Sciences of Complexity, Vol. X, pages 295–312, Reading, MA, 1991. Addison-Wesley.

[10] D. B. Fogel, "The evolution of intelligent decision making in gaming," *Cybernetics and Systems: An International Journal*, 22:223–236, 1991.

[11] D. B. Fogel, "Evolving behaviors in the iterated prisoner's dilemma," *Evolutionary Computation*, 1(1):77–97, 1993.

[12] P. J. Darwen and X. Yao, "On evolving robust strategies for iterated prisoner's dilemma," In X. Yao, editor, *Progress in Evolutionary Computation, Lecture Notes in Artificial Intelligence, Vol. 956*, pages 276–292, Heidelberg:Springer-Verlag, 1995

[13] W. Daniel Hillis, "Co-evolving parasites improve simulated evolution as an optimization procedure," In *Santa Fe Institute Studies in the Sciences of Complexity, Volume 10*, pages 313–323. Addison-Wesley, 1991.

Index